781.65
Y73B

D0204726

YOU JUST
FIGHT
FOR YOUR LIFE

Lester Young with Count Basie's Orchestra, circa 1938. Photo courtesy of the Institute of Jazz Studies, Rutgers University.

YOU JUST
F I G H T
FOR YOUR LIFE

The Story of Lester Young

FRANK BÜCHMANN-MØLLER

Foreword by Lewis Porter

PRAEGER

New York
Westport, Connecticut
London

Library of Congress Cataloging-in-Publication Data

Büchmann-Møller, Frank.
  You just fight for your life : the story of Lester Young / Frank
Büchmann-Møller ; foreword by Lewis Porter.
     p.   cm.
  Includes bibliographical references and index.
  ISBN 0-275-93265-6 (lib. bdg. : alk. paper)
  1. Young, Lester, 1909–1959.   2. Jazz musicians—United States—
Biography.   I. Title.
ML419.Y7B75   1990
788'.66'0924—dc19
[B]   89-3786

British Library Cataloguing in Publication Data is available.

Library of Congress Catalog Card Number: 89-3786
ISBN: 0-275-93265-6

First published in 1990

Praeger Publishers, One Madison Avenue, New York, NY 10010
A division of Greenwood Press, Inc.

Printed in the United States of America

The paper used in this book complies with the
Permanent Paper Standard issued by the National
Information Standards Organization (Z39.48-1984).

10 9 8 7 6 5 4 3 2 1

Copyright Acknowledgments

Grateful acknowledgment is given for permission to reprint the following items:

For the use of a variety of long and frequent quotations, *Down Beat* magazine, taken from issues from 1936 to 1966, by permission of the publisher.

Excerpts from "Lester Leaps In," published in the *Jazz Journal* (August 1958), are used by permission of the author, Dan Morgenstern.

Quotations from the interviews in the Jazz Oral History Report (funded by the National Endowment for the Arts) files at the Institute of Jazz Studies, Rutgers University, Newark, New Jersey, used by permission of the Institute.

Excerpts from *Hear Me Talkin' to Ya*, edited by Nat Shapiro and Nat Hentoff (New York: Rinehart, 1955) and *The Jazz Makers*, edited by Nat Shapiro and Nat Hentoff (New York: Rinehart, 1957), used by permission of the publisher, Henry Holt and Company, Inc.

Excerpts from *Good Morning Blues: The Autobiography of Count Basie*, by Count Basie as told to Albert Murray (New York, 1985), used by permission of the publisher, Random House, Inc.

Excerpts from "The House in the Heart" by Bobby Scott, in *Gene Lees Jazzletter*, vol. 3 no. 2 (1983):5–8, used by permission of the publisher, Gene Lees.

Excerpts from "Buddy and the President" by Brian Case, in *Melody Maker* (1979):37, 49, used by permission of the publisher.

Excerpts from *Unfinished Dream* by Red Callender and Elaine Cohen, (London, 1985), used by permission of the publisher, Quartet Books.

Excerpts from "Lester kann auch anders. . . ." by Pete Schmidt, in *Jazz Podium*, vol. 6 no. 7 (1957):11 and concert reviews appearing in various issues of *Jazz Podium*, used by permission of the publisher.

Contents

Contents

Abbreviations

as	alto saxophone
b	bass
bars	baritone saxophone
clt	clarinet
dir	director
dr	drums
g	guitar
JATP	Jazz At The Philharmonic
p	piano
rds	reeds
tb	trombone
TOBA	Theater Owners Booking Association
tp	trumpet
ts	tenor saxophone
vcl	vocalist

Foreword

Lester Young's life and music are the stuff of legend. There is not a jazz fan anywhere who does not know that Young was the "Pres." But maybe there is too much legend and not enough factual knowledge. It seems that very few of the younger fans and musicians have actually heard Young's music, or, even if they have, they do not understand how earth-shattering that music was in its day. And most people know that he died an alcoholic, but they do not know that he was one of the greatest wits ever.

The present biography and its companion "solography" by Frank Büchmann-Møller are desperately needed in order to set the record straight. The biography is by far the longest and most accurate account of Young's life ever done. It includes many new interviews with his friends and colleagues conducted by the author. It also clarifies the chronology of Young's career, presenting for the first time a complete description of his every movement from his birth in 1909 to his death in 1959. In order to do this, Büchmann-Møller has gone back to the old newspapers, oral history tapes, and other original sources and actually reconstructed Young's life story, filling in many previous gaps.

The companion volume is a complete guide to Young's recorded legacy, a solography (as author Jan Evensmo describes this type of work) which includes a description and critical review of Young's solos not only on every issued record, but on every scrap of private and unissued material. Here again, the author's research talents are evident. Building on the listing in my book, *Lester Young,* he adds recently discovered items never before mentioned anywhere, and for the known items he has filled in previously missing recording dates and personnels. This volume will also provide great enjoyment to those who can follow sheet music, because it includes notation of about eighty of Young's great solos and excerpts of as many more.

Büchmann-Møller is a professional librarian and a jazz saxophonist, and his dual qualifications as researcher and musician are reflected in these two meticulously prepared books. By combining a detailed biography with a full solography he has produced the most complete general introduction to Young's life and work.

Young's star continues to shine. There are fanatic "Presophiles" all over the world and even a Lester Young Society in Virginia. His most devoted fans are those who were lucky enough to have seen him in performance, but recent record reissues and the 1986 film *Round Midnight,* which was based largely on Young's life and dedicated to him and Bud Powell at the end of the credits, have certainly expanded that audience and created some younger fans. These two superb volumes will cause Young's star to shine even more brightly.

Lewis Porter
Rutgers University

Preface

Lester Young was unique, just as original and fascinating a musician as he was a human being. He created a style of playing which was the most important link between Louis Armstrong and Charlie Parker, but his greatest contribution to jazz was that he introduced a new way of playing, one which was revolutionary for its time and which added an extra dimension to the language of jazz.

When Lester Young came up through the ranks the tenor saxophone style was characterized by a big tone with a heavy vibrato and an expressive way of playing, dominated by dotted eighth notes and sixteenth notes phrasing, as introduced by Coleman Hawkins. Against this Lester Young presented a rhythmically relaxed way of playing and a light, almost nonvibrato sound; phrases were dominated by series of evenly placed eighth notes played legato, a style which influenced musicians of all instruments and which marked the beginning of modern jazz. Charlie Parker, one of the fathers of bebop, named Lester Young as one of his forming influences, as did John Coltrane, who in turn has inspired so many of today's tenor saxophone players. The cool jazz of the 1950s was directly based on Lester Young's light and relaxed style, and one of its originators, Miles Davis—who is still one of the key musicians of modern jazz—was highly influenced by Lester Young's very conscious accentuation, intonation, and weighing of the notes.

Despite the great importance Lester Young has thus had on the development of modern jazz, only a few works have been published with him as their sole subject. Shortly after this death two brief biographies came out in Germany and Italy, respectively. Werner Burckhardt and Joachim Gerth's *Lester Young*[1] and Vittorio Franchini's *Lester Young*[2] both maintain and strengthen the widespread misbelief that Lester Young's performances steadily declined after 1945. Not until twenty-five years after Young's death were books about him published in English. A new book published in France, *Lester Young: profession: président* by Luc Delannoy,[3] does not make much mention of his early career, but contains interesting interviews with some of the musicians who played with Young during his visit to France. Dave Gelly's *Lester Young*[4] gives a nice portrait of Lester Young, but the biography lacks basic research and contains several errors and misunderstandings. On the other hand, Gelly gives excellent and pedagogical explanations concerning changes in Young's sound.

The first major work on Lester Young is Lewis Porter's *Lester Young.*[5] It contains, among other things, a short biography and an unsurpassed and profound style analysis—the only one covering the whole of Young's career—followed by a catalog of works—not a real discography, but a list of issued and unissued music with Lester Young. In addition to these books, Jan Evensmo's *The Tenor Saxophone and Clarinet of Lester Young, 1936–1949*[6] ought to be mentioned. It gives the number of measures and a short critical appraisal of every Lester Young solo up to and including 1949.

Lester Young was very conscious of his roots and proud of being a black musician, as well as being aware of his influence on the younger generation of jazz musicians. Apart from this he was a musician of rare honesty. He was what he played, and his solos reflect the feelings he was experiencing at that particular moment. At his best his solos are universal and of a sincerity out of time and place, always able to convey something vital to the listener. Therefore a biography about Young that fails to deal with his music will only give half a picture of the man. The best entry into his music is to describe every one of his solos, either in words alone or supplemented by music. The reader, then, is advised to consult the companion volume to this work, *"You Got to Be Original, Man!": The Music of Lester Young,* which documents his music in this way. The author decided to compile a complete "solography" because it seemed to him impossible to pick out representative solos as examples of a special period. Young's soloistic qualities up to 1950 were so high and consistent as to make selection difficult, and his recordings after that time differ greatly in quality, compounding the selection problem.

I sincerely hope that these two books together will contribute to a better understanding of Lester Young, both as a musician and as a person. Should anyone feel inspired to sit down and listen to his solos once more as a result, then one of the main objects the books set out to achieve will have been accomplished.

Acknowledgments

During the six years I have worked on this project I have gotten help and encouragement from a lot of people. First of all, I am grateful to Karen and Arnvid Meyer at the Danish Jazz Center for their great hospitality and never-failing help and assistance of every kind; to Lars Christiansen at Holte Music Library for his great support and numerous valuable comments on the contents of the manuscript; and to Lewis Porter, who also proofread the manuscript and came up with several alterations. I am also indebted to Dan Morgenstern at the Institute of Jazz Studies, Rutgers University, who introduced me to the resources of the institute and who later solved several problems for me. I acknowledge my great debt to the following persons who agreed to be interviewed: Chris Albertson, Adolphus Alsbrook, Art Blakey, John Darville, Kenny Drew, Harry Edison, Roy Eldridge, John Gensel, Max Gordon, Freddie Green, Johnny Griffin, Roy Haynes, Dick Hyman, Hank Jones, Thad Jones, Willie Jones, Mel Lewis, Junior Mance, John Ore, Bill Potts, Buddy Rich, Idrees Sulieman, Bill Triglia, Ernie Wilkins, and Irma Young. Also, thank you to Arne Astrup, Leonard Feather, Norman Granz, Birger Jørgensen, John McDonough, François Postif, Don Schlitten, Claude Schlouch, Loren Schoenberg, Jørn Schøsler, Harry Schröder, Günther Schwartz, Bertel Skjoldborg, Thierry Trombert, Erik Wiedemann, Beverly Young, Mary Young, U.S. Reserve Personnel Center, St. Louis, Kansas State Historical Society, Musicians Union (New York), Musicians Union (Los Angeles), and Tuskegee Institute, for help and information of various kinds.

My visits to New York would not have been practicable without grants from the Funen Association of Jazz Musicians and the Danish Research

Council for the Humanities, who also made the translation into English possible. A special thank you to John Irons, who did a great translating job, and to the management and the staff at Odense University Library for their support and interest in the project.

Finally, I would like to express my heartfelt thanks to my wife, Emmy, for her unlimited encouragement, understanding, and patience.

YOU JUST
FIGHT
FOR YOUR LIFE

1

Childhood and Adolescence (1909–1928)

To many people interested in jazz, the name New Orleans sounds romantic, immediately conjuring up nostalgic associations with the birth of jazz, but New Orleans at the turn of the century was a town of stark contrasts. Although it.could be extremely attractive, with its incredibly lively world of music and entertainment, it could be just as repulsive in terms of its physical conditions and level of hygiene, which were among the worst in the United States. The road system was badly maintained, only a few of the streets were graveled, and only the most important, such as Canal Street, were paved.

Located at the mouth of the Mississippi delta, with its moist, unhealthy climate, and surrounded by large expanses of marshland, New Orleans in summer was infested with mosquitoes. Another plague from the insect world was provided by large, red cockroaches, which thrived in the innumerable latrines. Since the groundwater was so close to the surface, it was not possible to start laying out underground installations as early as in other large towns, and a sewage system was not begun until 1892. There was also a refuse dump in the middle of town, whose odor in summer spread over a large area, spiced with the added whiff of the gutter. Drinking water was taken directly from the Mississippi. This lack of hygiene resulted in New Orleans repeatedly being visited by epidemics, the most frequent of which were yellow fever and cholera. These epidemics struck hardest at the black population, and in 1900 their mortality rate was as high as 4 percent. At the same time that the sewage system was installed, the battle against the mosquitoes and for pure drinking water began; because of these efforts there has not been a fever epidemic there since 1905.

In 1904 the population of the city passed the 300,000 mark. Blacks accounted for about one-third of the population, giving New Orleans a higher proportion of black people than any other U.S. city. Of this group, one third were of mixed origins, the so-called Creoles. The original meaning of the term *Creole* was a person descended from the first white French-speaking settlers, who kept French as their mother tongue and upheld French culture in general.[1] The black Creoles have a more dramatic origin, descending from a large influx of women of mixed race who had fled to New Orleans in 1809, chiefly because of a revolution by slaves on the French Caribbean islands. These women, devoid of education and possessions, were forced to support themselves as best they could, usually by prostitution. Frequently, young upper-class whites had one of these beautiful, French-speaking girls as their mistress. This did not prevent them from later marrying a white girl from their own class; however, it was customary for them to provide for the mistress and for any children that had resulted from their relationship. In this way, the ethnically mixed population of black Creoles originated with a strain of French culture imported from the Caribbean islands.

These black Creoles felt themselves to be socially superior to the rest of the black population in New Orleans, but the passing of a race law in 1894 which laid down that anyone with the slightest drop of black blood should be considered black led to their being exposed to the same discrimination as other black people. Even though New Orleans was less strict than other southern towns in this respect, blacks could not live wherever they chose, and were restricted to ghettos, among other places in the town center.

Another aspect of discrimination against blacks in Louisiana was the poor quality of education available to them. In 1910 black schools had twice as many pupils per class as white schools, and black teachers earned less than half that of their white counterparts. Most classes for blacks took place in small or substandard premises such as hired houses, churches, and even condemned buildings. Even though the blacks knew perfectly well that the only way to improve their condition was by means of education, schools in Louisiana were among the worst attended in the United States. In 1920 only 61 percent of black children between the ages of seven and thirteen attended school, compared with 93–96 percent in the northern states, and most of these children went to school very irregularly, since elder brothers and sisters often had to take care of the home while their mother worked. Playing truant from school in the southern states was more the rule than the exception and was never complained of by the teachers.[2]

The century had scarcely begun when a newly married couple moved to the Algiers quarter in the eastern part of New Orleans on the south bank of the Mississippi, from where you can look across the river to the old French quarter. Algiers was an area where there were few blacks—under 10 percent—and the couple, Lizetta and Willis Handy Young, doubtless chose it for a reason: Willis—called Billy—had ambitions about leaving his lower-middle-class origins and climbing the social ladder.

Billy grew up close to the little town of Thibodaux in Lafourche Parish, about fifty miles southwest of New Orleans. Here blacks almost equaled whites in number, and Thibodaux was the center of an agricultural area, with large areas devoted to sugarcane, cotton, maize, and vegetables, the harvesting of which was dependent on black labor. Billy's father, Jacob, was born a slave in Virginia and came to the Thibodaux area as a young man. In 1862, when Lafourche was occupied by Union troops, Jacob's master fled, taking all his slaves with him to Texas, where Jacob's two eldest sons were born. After the civil war and the abolition of slavery Jacob returned with his family to Louisiana, where he settled about a mile outside Thibodaux and worked as a smith and a cooper. Here the family gained two more sons, William Handy and Willis Handy, the latter being born in 1872.[3]

In the years between the end of the Civil War and the turn of the century, several race laws were passed in Louisiana which gave the state the reputation of discriminating more harshly than the other southern states. The Ku Klux Klan began to flourish, and the Young family were no exception in being exposed to some rough racist experiences. Just as the sugarcane was about to be harvested in 1887, a strike broke out among the black workers around Thibodaux. Since the strike began to take on the character of an armed insurrection, the army was brought in, resulting in the death of thirty black workers. This violent event certainly left its mark on the minds of Billy and his brothers. Only William Handy chose to settle on the land as a worker when he grew up; the other sons all became musicians, a job the descendents of plantation slaves always found especially attractive because a musician's life had an independence diametrically opposed to that of workers who were bound to the soil.

William Handy settled as a farmer in the small town of Natalbany, Louisiana, in Tangipahoa Parish, about five miles north of Hammond and sixty-five miles north of New Orleans. His family was accompanied by his parents, who spent their declining years in the small town as owners of a store. Billy visited them with his family around 1922, a date based on the fact that his son, Lee, can remember that he was about five years old at the time: "All I can remember, it sounds like to me, it was called Natalbany where they just had a store. You know how in the small towns where they just have a commissary or whatever they call them. That's all they had, was just the one store where you bought everything, you know, all of your supplies for whatever. But my auntie and my uncle and my grandmother and grandfather lived there."[4]

Billy became a musician by a devious route. He first decided to learn his father's trade as a smith but afterwards was seized by the desire to educate himself more, inspired by the black teacher and reform pioneer Booker T. Washington's thoughts and ideas.

After the Civil War there was much debate among the black population about how one could gain the same civil rights as the whites. Washington felt that the best way for Negroes to improve their social position was to get a practical education. On July 4, 1881, he opened a school in Tuskegee, Alabama (about forty miles east of the capital, Montgomery), with himself as the sole teacher for nearly fifty pupils. Tuskegee Normal and Industrial Institute, as the school was initially called, soon grew to be one of the world's leading centers for black education. To begin with, the school mainly emphasized practical subjects but gradually broadened its range to include agriculture, nursing, housecraft and needlework, technical sciences, economics, natural science, the humanities, music, and the various art forms. About 1890 Billy was admitted to the school, where he studied history and music.[5] In order to be able to pay for his education he returned home during the vacation to work as a smith.

At Tuskegee Billy got to know all the instruments in the orchestra. He had a good ear, which, combined with his innate musicality, enabled him to learn how to play practically all types of instruments, from brass and woodwind to stringed instruments, piano, and drums. His favorite instrument was the cornet. After completing his education Billy returned to his parents in Thibodaux. He is in all probability the cornet player called Willie Young who played in the Youka Brass Band, which was active only during the year 1904.[6]

It is not known whether Billy taught while in Thibodaux, but it is certain that he was employed as a history and music teacher a couple of years later at New Orleans University.[7] The school was situated on St. Charles Street and Leotine in the town center and was founded in 1873 as a Methodist institution for the higher education of blacks, there also being a junior school.

When Billy first moved into town he rented a room from a black Creole couple named Johnson who had a beautiful, light-skinned daughter named Lizetta. She was about ten years younger than he. Lizetta had Billy as her teacher at New Orleans University, and they gradually became fond of each other, since they also had a common interest in music. Lizetta was an excellent pianist. When she had completed her teacher education, with needlework as one of her subjects, they decided to get married, after which they moved to the Algiers area of the town.[8] Not long after this Lizetta's parents moved from New Orleans to the small town of Woodville in Wilkinson County in the southwest corner of Mississippi. The town lies close to the Louisiana border and is a terminus for the railroad line down to Baton Rouge. In 1909 Woodville had only about 2,500 inhabitants, about one-sixth of the entire population of Wilkinson County. In this area the blacks made up about 80 percent of the population, most of them living in the country districts, where they worked in the cotton fields.[9]

The New Orleans of that period was saturated with music all year round and, thanks to the mildness of the climate, most music-making took place outdoors. There were several symphony orchestras and innumerable march and dance orchestras, as well as a tradition of playing music on every conceivable occasion, be it festive or sad. Dancing played an important part in social life, and public balls were held every weekend along the banks of Lake Pontchartrain. Here many different places of entertainment were open to whites and blacks where one could relax from the constrictions of everyday life and fish, swim, eat and drink, dance, or just listen to the many orchestras. In New Orleans itself there were also opportunities for enjoying oneself in Lincoln Park and the adjacent Johnson Park; here too different orchestras played concerts or dance music. For the poorly educated black population this profusion of music was an essential—if not the only—cultural element in their lives. Literature was denied them, since they were not able to read or could do so only with difficulty, and such art forms as ballet, opera, or painting were reserved exclusively for the white population.

In his spare time Billy also played music; this hobby gradually began to turn into a professional occupation. He gave music lessons in his own home and started a band, with Lizetta as piano player. He was apparently a good band leader, having his finger on the pulse of the public and being well capable of advertising himself; this can be seen from the fact that he gradually increased his repertoire, having several different bands at one and the same time to be used in parades or for dances and entertainment. The trumpet player Henry "Red" Allen, who grew up in Algiers at the same time as Lester, can remember his father playing trumpet in one of Billy's bands. Billy's musical flexibility also helped him, in that any musician unable to play on a job would be replaced by Billy himself, who otherwise stuck to conducting. The best known of his music pupils was the piano player and composer Clarence Williams, who paid twenty-five cents in 1911 for each of the ten or so lessons he had at Billy's house.

In 1909 Lizetta became pregnant for the first time. As the birth became imminent, she traveled to her parents' home in Woodville. The child was born on August 27, a fine healthy son who was baptized Lester Willis Young. Shortly after his birth mother and son returned to New Orleans. Her decision to go home to her mother to give birth is certainly connected with the high infant mortality in New Orleans at that time, coupled with the fact that midwives were a rarity among black people. Lester has also supplied an explanation: "My mother was scared, you know, that type, so she wanted to go back home to the family, in case something happened, that type. So after I was straight, and she made it, and everything was cool, then she takes me to New Orleans and we lived in Algiers.''[10]

Under Lizetta's care Lester grew up to be a happy, loving child with an independent and sensitive mind. Both Billy and Lizetta had become Baptists and took Lester with them to church as often as possible. He began to contribute to the family economy at the tender age of five or six, polishing shoes, selling newspapers, or distributing handbills for the many activities that took place in New Orleans all year round. Together with his friends he eagerly followed the many parades which passed through the town, and above all he loved the drummers.

"I loved this music so well," he recalls. "See, in New Orleans they had these trucks that go around and advertise for a dance this night, and it excited me, so I'd be the handbill boy. They'd give me some handbills, and I'd be running 'round giving out handbills. And I just loved that music so much that I'd be running until my tongue was hanging out like this. Still I didn't know my father was a musician, you dig? And I'd know the stops, they'd certain stops on corners and things like that."[11]

It might sound strange that Lester did not know at this point that his father was a musician. The explanation, however, is that Billy no longer lived in New Orleans at the time. Around 1915 he became the principal of a high school in Bogalusa, Louisiana, about sixty miles north of New Orleans on the Pearl River,[12] a rare promotion for a black to achieve at that time. Lizetta chose, on the other hand, to remain in Algiers with Lester and his younger sister, Irma, who was born on July 18, 1912. This time Lizetta had traveled down to Billy's parents in Thibodaux when the birth was due. Another son came into the world, this time in New Orleans, on March 7, 1917, and was given the pompous-sounding name Leonidas Raymond, shortened to Lee for everyday use. The name Leonidas was the result of Billy's enthusiasm for one of the Greek heroes who, in 480 B.C., held the pass at Thermopylæ with a force of 300 Spartans against a superior force of 6,000 Persian warriors.

Billy naturally visited his family as often as possible, but there was probably not much time to devote to music during those years, since much of his leisure time in New Orleans was spent trying to raise money. Lack of money was a constant problem for black schools at the time, but Billy found a solution for this by going to the black brothel area and collecting money from the pimps and brothel keepers, many of whom were willing to contribute something for the education of young blacks.[13]

His job as principal, together with the accompanying administrative burdens and the constant begging for money, became too much for Billy in the end. In 1919, when he got the chance to become leader of a circus band, he decided to change direction completely and to devote himself to music. His marriage to Lizetta was also deteriorating by this time, without doubt partly because he was home less and less of the time, and also since he had found a new woman, Sarah, whom he wanted to marry. In 1919 Lizetta and Billy agreed to go their separate ways, and Billy was given custody of the three children. He left Bogalusa—probably at the start of the summer vacation—to fetch the children in New Orleans and to get his band organized, for it had to have a repertoire ready for the carnival season, which began in the fall. At the same time Sarah joined the family and, in the course of the summer, she and Billy were married in the small town of Tippeydill, Louisiana. Unlike Lizetta, Sarah had no musical background, but even so she was gradually drawn into the musical environment and learned to play several instruments, including banjo and saxophone. The children were also included in the music lessons as they became old enough to play. Lester began by playing the violin and the trumpet, but eventually chose his old love from the New Orleans parades—the drums. By the age of ten he was proficient enough to become a member of his father's band. His individualistic nature can be sensed even at this early age, for he developed his own technique. A drummer normally holds the left drumstick with all five fingers and the right between the thumb and index finger. Lester held the right drumstick between his index and second finger and was evidently so good at it that Billy didn't feel it was necessary to correct him.

Billy had made an arrangement with the Hagenbeck and Wallace Circus to lead a band that played in its sideshow (probably a minstrel show). When the carnival season began, he left New Orleans with the circus, his children, and his band, never to return. His marriage to Sarah was a success, and she became a good stepmother for the children, who adored her from the day she became part of the family. Lizetta stayed for a while in New Orleans, where she married, taking the surname Grey. Later she chose to move to Woodville to be near her parents, and it is known that Lester visited her there in the early 1930s. Finally she moved to Los Angeles in 1944.

As was customary for circuses at the time, Hagenbeck and Wallace traveled from one town to the next by railroad. They lived in Pullman cars and loaded the show's tents and stands onto open wagons. Meals were taken in a special restaurant car. Billy's band was built around his family; apart from Lester on drums, his two nephews with their wives also played, together with Irma, who had started to play saxophone. The nephews' names were Isiah "Sport" Young and Austin "Boots" Young; both were good musicians who could play more than one instrument. They could both play saxophone, like their wives, and Boots was also a splendid trombone and bass player. They were brothers and traveled together with Billy's band for several seasons, until they grew tired of touring and left for Hammond, Louisiana, around 1923.[14]

Circus shows followed a predetermined route through the southern states to certain towns each year. Each show had its own route, so that they never got in each other's way or competed with each other. The minstrel show had its own big top. Before the performance began, an audience had to be gathered, and this was achieved by everyone in the show going out onto the platform in front of the big top to advertise the show. The trumpet player Leonard Phillips played in Billy's band for several years from 1924 on and has described what used to happen: "All the show would come out on the bally, all the people, all the show would come out in the front, the band too. They've got a big platform, you'd come out there and the band would play. We used to play marches on the bally and we played something like 'Runnin' Wild.' "

"The people would be standing around on the ground looking," he continues, "and they've got a spieler who would tell them about the show. He would be calling: 'Hey! Hey! Come over here, this is where it is! Come on in, it's a good show!' Some people call him a spieler and some call him a barker. We played a couple of numbers while the people were coming in. Then we got in there, and before the show we'd play a couple of tunes. We played something like 'Wang, Wang Blues,' 'How Come You Do Me Like You Do, Do, Do' and 'Yes Sir, That's My Baby.' "[15]

Out on the "bally" Billy would try to catch people's special attention by holding his saxophone in an eccentric way. The piano player Jimmy Rowles, who used to play with Lester in the early 1940s, is sure that Lester's way of holding the saxophone diagonally out to the right could be an imitation of his father, since Billy used to hold his saxophone upside down when he played.[16]

The minstrel tradition was originally a white form of entertainment, where the performers blackened their faces and parodied the Negroes' songs, music, dance, and way of telling stories. After the Civil War, blacks also began to participate in minstrel shows, especially in the southern states, and even these performers added extra black with the aid of burnt cork. This was the case at Hagenbeck and Wallace's, where all employees were white except for those who took part in the minstrel show, who were all black. The show itself had its own stereotyped form. The first act consisted of several jokes between a type of spokesman, who stood in the middle, and two or more men sitting in a semicircle. Between jokes the spokesman, or one of the others, sang a ballad or two. The second act was more varied and could consist of all types of features, such as monologues, songs and dance numbers, instrumentals, a little vaudeville show, parodies of well-known operas, and so on. Finally, all the participants came on stage for a hoedown.

By the time they were five or six years old, Irma and Lee began to perform in the second act of the minstrel shows, singing and dancing at first, but being given other roles as soon as they were ready for them. Lester was about twice as old when he began to perform, and he was only used for dance and the occasional song. He gradually came to hate most of the "Uncle Tomming" that went on, and his talents as a showman were also limited. Irma and Lee had more natural talent in that direction, and they used to sing together such numbers as "Does Your Mother Know You're out, Cecilia?" Irma also appeared as the lady who is sawn in half, and Lee had his own section, where he was a blackface comic doing banana-skin comedy. He wore a huge bow tie almost larger than himself, a sailor's hat, and a little black jacket.

The audience used to throw money up to the children when they performed. Lee developed a special technique he called "milking the audience," which consisted of making the music stop each time someone threw a dime up to him by shouting "Hold it!" He then danced or tap-danced a little before picking the coin up and allowing the music to continue.[17]

Of the show itself Leonard Phillips can remember that "Lester, Lee and Irma had an act together. Lester could dance like hell, and Lee, and all of them could dance and sing. The chorus girls used to dance to 'Way Down Yonder in New Orleans' and 'I Wanna Marry a Girl Like My . . .' and Irma danced in the chorus. Their mother didn't do nothing in the chorus, she'd look after the money. We called her Mrs. Young and she didn't play in the show. We also played 'Margie' and 'Last Night on the Back Porch,' 'Baby, Won't You Please Come Home,' 'If You Don't Want Me, Tell Me So' and 'Bugle Blues' which was the one that Lee would feature with the saxophone."[18]

Even though blacks and whites mixed during the carnival show, there was no discrimination among the employees. But as a black man in the southern states, Lester experienced many episodes that made a deep impression on him and helped to shape his attitude toward whites. Once Sport got into a fix and, for some unknown reason, was pursued by a crowd of lynch-happy whites. Lester came to his aid and helped him to get away to safety, probably saving his life on that occasion.

A further striking episode occurred when Lester was twelve or thirteen years old and went to a church service in a small southern town, together with Billy and Irma. The only Baptist church in the area was built for whites, but, together with some other Negroes, they were allowed to sit on the back bench. The preacher raged about "black sin" and "as black as hell." His entire sermon was marked by such strong racial prejudice that, backed by the authority vested in them by the church, the words branded themselves on Lester's mind. The preacher finally insisted that the only path to salvation was to receive the forgiveness of sins, but it turned out that only whites were allowed to go up to the altar! This episode made Lester feel guilty because of his color, a feeling he got rid of only during the last years of his life.

The carnival show was on tour from April to November, after which Billy's band was linked to the Theater Owners Booking Association (TOBA), which arranged engagements for the band during the winter with vaudeville or minstrel shows in theaters in cities or large towns. During that time Billy and his family would live in such towns for the winter months. For example, they spent one of the first winters after leaving New Orleans in Memphis, the winter of 1923–24 was spent in Warren, Arkansas; and several winters were spent in Minneapolis.

These winter stays meant much-needed schooling for Lester, Irma, and Lee. Billy normally taught them when they were on tour, but this teaching was never for more than a couple of hours at a stretch, and Lee was the only child to receive any form of proper education. Neither Lester nor Irma got beyond third or fourth grade level, and Lester achieved only a modest competency in reading and writing. His signature as an adult looked like that of a child who had just started school. This lack of proficiency gave Lester an inferiority complex, which later prevented him from reading or signing contracts if it in any way could be avoided.

Billy's decision to leave New Orleans and move north can be seen in the context of the great migration from the South to the North whose upsurge was in the 1915–19 period, when between 300,000 and 400,000 blacks moved, mainly to such large industrial cities as Chicago, Detroit, New York, and Philadelphia. The reasons for this were many. World War I virtually put a stop to migration from Europe, and many immigrants returned to Europe to defend the country of their birth. At the same time, the American war industry began to boom, and this placed a new demand on labor. Many factories started advertising campaigns, including advertisements in the largest national newspaper for blacks, the *Chicago Defender*. These offers of work in the North for much higher wages than black workers in the South were used to were almost irresistible, especially since the cotton harvests in both 1915 and 1916 were savaged in the states of Louisiana, Mississippi, Alabama, Georgia, and Florida by a boll weevil invasion, which ruined the yield. Several large floods in 1915 in the same states made the situation even worse, with many thousands of farm workers suddenly made unemployed or only able to obtain employment for a wage far below subsistence level. By moving from the southern states the workers saw a chance of gaining greater equality, without the humiliating discrimination they were constantly exposed to, and with better educational opportunities for their children. During the first couple of years mainly male workers set off, but families subsequently began to join them, together with people working in the health and service sectors, such as doctors, dentists, lawyers, artists, musicians, and preachers.

When Lester and his family reached Minneapolis, it was a town slightly larger than New Orleans, with roughly 380,000 inhabitants, of which only 3,900 or so were blacks. The town is situated close to huge wheat-producing areas and was the center for one of the world's largest primary wheat markets. Its milling and timber industries were also among the largest in the United States. Minnesota was one of the twelve northern states that forbade segregation in schools, and this meant that Lester, Lee, and Irma not only took part in mixed classes but were also taught by white teachers. This was something of an upheaval for Lester, since his sporadic schooling up to that point in no way corresponded with the teaching he received in Minneapolis. Schooling here meant that he had to be in classes with children several years younger than himself, something which can scarcely have been stimulating or inspiring for him. Playing truant was also not tolerated in the northern states, where pupils were expected to attend classes all year round, so that Lester was not so easily able to travel with Billy's band when it suited their plans.

Moving to the North nearly always lived up to the expectations of the blacks as regards living standards and educational opportunity, though many had not reckoned with the higher costs of living. They were, however, often disappointed by how they were treated by the whites, for a growing dislike sprang up as the number of blacks increased. In the South the blacks knew how they would be treated; here they felt unsure and insecure. In Hagenbeck and Wallace's Lester had felt himself to be an equal, despite episodes of discrimination, but in Minneapolis all sorts of things could happen. As he was extremely sensitive and thin-skinned, he contrived to protect himself by not talking about anything personal.[19]

Lester played drums in Billy's band for more than three years, but around 1922 he changed instruments. At this point he was about thirteen, on the verge of puberty. His cumbersome drum-kit came to interfere with his interest in the opposite sex. This is how he describes his decision to change instruments: "Every time I'd be in a nice little place and meet a nice little bitch, you dig? her mother'd say: 'Hey Mary, come on, let's go!' And I'd try to pack my kit so fast, and I watched this little bitch, you dig? and her mother called her once, twice and I was trying to get this shit straight, so I said 'Fuck it! I'm through with drums!' All the other guys got their clarinet cases, trombone cases, trumpet cases and here I am wiggling around with all this shit. Fuck these motherfuckers! And I really played them, I could play my ass off. I played them for three years."[20] Another reason was his laziness: "Bein' lazy, y'know. Carryin' all them drums got to be a real grind. I decided I'd better get me a lighter instrument. That's all there was to it, man."[21]

As his next instrument Lester chose alto saxophone, which was to be his main instrument for the next six years. Like the other children in the family, he had a fantastically good ear and could quickly learn to play anything he heard. Billy and Sarah encouraged their children to be individuals and never hindered them from trying out new instruments. Lee in particular changed instruments frequently. At the time he was less interested in music than in playing baseball or basketball. But it was impossible not to learn how to play if you were part of Billy's family. He was ambitious on his children's behalf and wanted them to be something. The quickest way to reach that goal at the time was inside the worlds of professional sport and entertainment. Billy used to say: "My sons will never be a porter, my daughter will never be a maid. You're going to have to learn to play music." This meant that he was very pleased to observe how quickly Lester and Irma learned.

The two elder cousins, who both played saxophone, were natural models for Lester and, as he improved, he was eager to test his mettle against them, especially against Boots, who was pretty proficient. His opportunity came when Boots got a job playing at an evening dance in a small town they had come to on their tour. Lester followed him with his saxophone under his arm but was refused admittance because he was wearing short pants, so he cannot have been more than about fourteen or fifteen years old. He managed to creep in the back way, however. Arriving unchallenged on the stage, he calmly unpacked his saxophone and literally blew Boots off the stage. Boots was so mad at Lester for interfering and stealing everybody's attention that he was about to start a fight, when Sarah, who was fortunately in the hall, came to the victor's rescue and took him home, still drunk with the joys of victory.[22] This joy in playing and desire to test his skill against others never left Lester.

Just how quickly Lester was to learn can be seen from the following memory of Leonard Phillips of his time with the Young family. Phillips was a couple of years older than Lester and grew up in Warren, Arkansas, and he provides us with interesting information about what sort of music was played in Billy's band and about the sort of music Lester was inspired by:

In 1921 there was a guy who brought a band together, a schoolband, his name was professor Parson. He started us up, so I first started playing E-flat clarinet in Myrtle Street School. He got a band together and we started rehearsing. My mother played organ in the church. My mother taught us, so I already read music when I first started playing. I didn't have too hard a time learning to play, because I had a pretty good start. Then in 1924 Lester Young's father came to my hometown. He had a show there. We called him "Billy" Young in showbusiness. The show closed in my hometown, and he stayed there and put on a show, say, twice a week, maybe the first of the week and on Friday. They had a big apartment in Warren they rented for the winter. They stayed there until around March 1924. They left with one of these shows.

I got talking with Mr. Young, and he told me to come up. He wanted to talk with me and he said: "I think you've got some promise of making a musician!" So I said: "OK." That knocked me out, I wanted to advance myself. So Otto "Pete" Jones on trombone and my brother Clarence and several other guys out there, we got ten pieces together and he started rehearsing us.

We would go up to his place, he would talk to us, you know, and tell us about music. He was teaching me how to play different tunes, "Wang, Wang Blues" and "You've Been a Good Old Wagon," and he was teaching about the horn too, taught the scales and everything, chords and things like that. He didn't teach Prez that. He would play it natural, his ears could tell. When he played a solo he would play the chords anyway, his ears could tell him what to do.

Prez was playing his ass off then. He was that far ahead of us. He was already playing like he had been playing for years. He could play anything he wanted to play, you know, he had a good ear. He was a guy that didn't practice much. He was about fourteen or fifteen years old when we got the band together. We were practicing music, but he was practicing tunes. He would be playing some tunes that he hears, tunes like "Baby, Won't You Please Come Home" and "Jada." He was playing these tunes. Out of just listening to them I couldn't play them, you know. I could play the marches that we've been playing in the band with professor Parson. But Billy Young said: "I'll show you how to play jazz." He could play it too, you know, he played nice trumpet. He was in it too, but Prez played ungodly jazz. It was all right, we liked it, but he was far ahead of his time, he was way ahead of time.

We used to look up to him, we were all kids together. We didn't call him Prez, we called him "Bub." His father called him "Bub" and Lee called him "Bubba" and Irma called him Lester.

The 15th of April 1924 Billy sent for four of us, Pete Jones, myself, my brother Clarence and another cat called "Hamp," Jesse Hamilton. My brother played basshorn, tuba, and Pete Jones played trombone and I played trumpet at that time. Jesse Hamilton played E-flat peckhorn and was a good comedian and he could dance. He was a better comedian than he was a musician.

I quit playing clarinet when I heard Louis Armstrong play "St. Louis Blues" with Bessie Smith around 1923 or something like that. That's when I wanted to change. I've played E-flat clarinet in the band, but then I started to play cornet. My mother bought them records with King Oliver playing with a team called "Butterbeans and Susie," a vaudeville team. He made some records with them, King Oliver. That's when Louis did "St. Louis Blues" with Fred Longshaw playing piano. Louis got a mute in it. That was the prettiest song I think I've ever heard in my life, it made me crazy to hear that. I used to just sit and listen to it, I used to play it all the time.

I played cornet when I went with Mr. Young, and I've been playing it for about a year. I heard that record before I knew Willis Young, and I wanted to play the cornet real good. He told me how to do so and he said: "If you go with me I'll get you a nice, pretty trumpet!" Trumpets were just coming out then. When I got with him only few people had trumpets. He had one, he had every kind of instruments. He had high class instruments, goldplated and silver. He used a silver trumpet when he played in the carnivals and used the gold playing for the vaudeville.

We all had big Pullman cars, where the show stayed, the show travelled on them. All them people stayed in the Pullman cars, the show furnished them. The guy who had that show was named Billy Clark. This was a carnival show, and we went from town to town to play on this. We played fairs, we played towns. See, in that time people didn't see nothing, there was no radio, no TV, so they wanted to see the show wherever it came up.

At that time there was not too much to listen to, you know. We would listen to the Original Dixieland Jazz Band. Then after that we got together, Lester, Pete and myself and played Bix and Frankie Trumbauer. But in 1924 we would listen to what you'd hear. We ran into a lot of bands playing, like Paul Whiteman. When he played fairs he were playing outside, everybody would come and hear. In down South white people would sit over there and black people would sit there, but they were listening to the same music. We heard Paul Whiteman in 1924–5 and Vincent Lopez and Ted Lewis. All them bands were playing what you'd call ragtime jazz. We used to go out and hear these bands and another band too, Coon-Sanders. A lot of time we didn't have to be segregated, because we'd be up in the Northern states like Nebraska, Kansas and Minnesota.

On the first carnival tour the furthest north we went was Indianapolis, and we played Sandgap, Kentucky, Lexington, Kentucky, Bowling Green, Kentucky, Knoxville, Tennessee, Chattanooga, Tennessee, Tiptonville, Tennessee, Roanoke, Virginia and Flomaton, Alabama. I'll never forget Harlem, Kentucky. That was on our first tour in 1924, I'll never forget that. They would call us all kind of names and all that stuff, you know. We had six-seven girls on the show, on the bally."[23]

Phillips also remembers that when they played "Yes Sir, That's My Baby" in the show, Lester did the slaptonguing and that "anything he played he would improvise, he would put something to it."

He would dress it up, marches and everything. He played tenor on the carnival show, but when he played in the band he played alto. He never did play the tenor with his father's vaudeville band.

Billy Young taught the children, you know. Every day they had to go to class, just his three kids, Lester, Lee and Irma. He would say: "Oh, come over here, it's schooltime!" One day he told me, I'll never forget this, he taught me this, he called me "Deek": "Look, Deek. When you're on the bandstand playing you see women out there, and they will come out there for every band that comes to town. The nice girls won't stand by, watch the girl that stands by. The girl that comes up, she knows every band that comes to town!" And he was right. Once we played in Denver, Colorado, and Andy Kirk had been there, and this girl told us and said: "Can we come to your room? We know all in Andy Kirk's band, and we give all of them some!" So, you see, he was right, and we called them band rats, that's what he called them, band rats. The girl that stands back and look at you and wait for you to pick up, that's a nice girl.

Once Lester cut Louis Jordan. Louis Jordan's father used to have a band on the minstrel show called the "Rabbit Foot," and Louis was in that band playing clarinet. He was a pretty good clarinet player. At that time he was young, he was in his short pants too, and his father was a hell of a musician too. Then Louis put the clarinet down and started playing the soprano sax, and it was on that he was battling with Lester. Lester was playing alto and Louis was playing the soprano. That was in 1924 when I first went with the Young band, it was on the first tour, in April.

We met up with them in Greenville, Mississippi. Louis was playing with a local band, a danceband, and he and Lester got battling at each other. They played "Runnin' Wild," blues and so on. We used to play the blues in E-flat and B-flat, that's the blues keys. E-flat is the best key for blues, it gives you that good blues feeling. They also played "Yes Sir, That's My Baby," yeah, it was these two tunes they played. Lester blew so much horn, so when he was getting Louis, Louis started slaptonguing. But Lester could play the same thing slap-tongue that he'd play on melody. I've never heard anybody do it but he, so that's when everybody turned round and said: "Oh, that man's got him!" Louis got over his horn like he could at that time, but Lester ran away from him on his horn. Louis played all right, but he couldn't play the horn like that.

Even when Lester was in short pants he was playing better than anybody we've ever heard. Pete said: "You know one thing, Phil?" I said: "What, man?" He said: "We have never heard somebody play like "Bub" on the saxophone." All the cats we saw were moanin', they never ran over their horn, and we went a lot of places. Up in Devil's Lake, North Dakota, there was a little band up there, six or seven pieces, and they heard Prez play. They heard him with his father's show on the carnival. We started out on the bally playing, and Prez was playing that horn, he was going over it. The musicians had a fair where they had a platform where they had ten cents dances. You'd pay a dime and go in and dance. Most of the fairs had a band on five-six pieces, sometimes they had a bigband. But the man that had this band he begged Mr. Young and told him he would give Prez five-six dollars a week, which was a lot of money then, but he told him: "No, he's too young." Lester was only about sixteen. The man said: "How did he learn to play all that stuff?" "Oh, man," I said, "he learned it from his daddy. He knows how to play them all!"

The carnival show closed around Thanksgiving Day in Palatka, Florida, and we stayed there for a while. Then we got together a band and rehearsed the vaudeville show for about a week. The vaudeville show was different from the carnival show, and Mr. Young got that show together and then we went on the TOBA circuit.

Our first vaudeville date was at "81 Theatre" in Atlanta, Georgia, in November 1924. Our next date was Greenville, South Carolina, and our next date was Pensacola, Florida, and our next date was in Columbus, Georgia. All places we played a week and we traveled by train. The Pullman cars were for the carnival show, on the vaudeville we had tickets. We were about fifteen people on the show including the band and everything, we were seven in the band. In the carnival show we had six chorus girls, Lee Young, Lester Young, Irma Young, Mrs. Young, Mr. Young, me, Pete Jones, Clarence and James Clark, he played clarinet. It was the same band and chorus girls on the vaudeville show, but some of the comedians from the carnival show they didn't take. They didn't take a guy called "Shadow" and they didn't take "Dirty Red," a blues singer and dancer, he told jokes and things. Mr. Young fired him in Tampa, Florida, in the carnival show. Something was wrong with his bladder, and he had a place to stay for himself, so we left him in Tampa, Florida. Then we had another act on the carnival show called "Shorty" and David. They acted as "David and Goliath" in the vaudeville show too. We had a singer, her name was Grace Carter. She got sick on the show in Atlanta and she had to go home. She only played the "81 Theatre" on the vaudeville. She was in the carnival show singing and dancing too.

Soon after that we left Tampa, Florida, and went to Lakeland, Florida, and stayed there. There was a guy down there in Florida who had a big tent and a minstrel talk show. This was early 1925. Mr. Young got this show together, and that's the town where we went back to the minstrel show. It didn't do much good. We tried it out in De Land, Florida, and then we went to Sarasota and then we went to Flomaton, Alabama and it folded up in Mobile, Alabama. There were two C-melody saxophones in the Young group, but nobody played them until the vaudeville. Mr. Young was the only one who played the C-melody, Lee played alto and Irma played alto and Mrs. Young played baritone in the vaudeville.

In Flomaton we would leave Mr. Young. Sidney De Paris's father had the same kind of show that we had. David from "David and Goliath" had been on the De Paris show and he told us and said: "We don't get no money with Mr. Young. Business has got bad." He'd give us fifty cents maybe a dollar for each performance, so we got tired of that. De Paris sold us some tickets to come over and hear his show in Mobile, Alabama, so we left. I left, Pete Jones left and James Clark.

We played the same kind of music on both the carnival show and the vaudeville show. We didn't play marches on the vaudeville, but we did on the minstrel show when we did the parades.

Mr. Young didn't have the qualifications for the minstrel show. He was supposed to have a big marching band of twelve-fifteen people for the show, but he had only six-seven pieces, and he had Lee playing drums. Lee was about ten-eleven years old and he couldn't play drums for that. We had two trombones and three trumpets and a clarinet and a basshorn in that marching band.

My brother had left the vaudeville show in Pensacola, Florida. We had about seven-eight pieces in the band, but Mr. Young wouldn't put up the kind of money to enlarge it. The minstrel show used to have fifty-sixty people, he had only fifteen, so it didn't go. It folded up in Mobile, Alabama, and then he got Cootie Williams on trumpet and his brother on trombone and another guy named Ralph on trumpet. I've forgotten his name.[24]

Cootie grew up in Mobile, Alabama, and had gone with his father to see the show and was so enthusiastic that he insisted he wanted to play in Billy's band. So his father went back to have a word with Billy about it and they agreed that Cootie should be given a chance. "They took me," Cootie remembers. "I was only fourteen and my brother had to go too, my father said. I got fifty cents a day and ate with the family. It lasted a summer and was great."[25]

Meanwhile Leonard Phillips had gone off with the De Paris show, but it came to a halt in Charlotte, North Carolina, in November 1925. That did not mean the end of his ties with Billy and Lester, however, for in 1926 he was once more engaged to play in the Young Family Band. This is how Phillips tells the story:

Then we, Pete, James and I, went home back to Warren, Arkansas. We stayed there and I got a little band together with six pieces, and we went all over Arkansas in the winter. When the spring came again we'd all go with another show called the "Great White Way Show," and they didn't make no money. The guy who had the show was Jim Thomas, and Clarence played alto saxophone. Mr. Young had teached him saxophone all the time when we were in his show. He quit playing the basshorn when he went with us. The two others were Frankie Badour on drums and P. D. Herbert played piano. We didn't make no money, and in Memphis, Tennessee, in 1926 we quit.

Then Billy Young sent for us again. He sent for all of us to come back on the show. He had a little show in Illinois somewhere, so he sent us tickets. Frankie didn't go, he went back home, and Herbert and Mr. Young got into some disagreements, so he quit and left. But anyway, we went up to this little show up in Illinois which we called a gilley show, a small show that didn't travel with Pullman cars but with wagons like the circus. That's what Mr. Young did, but Mrs. Young was on another show. He had two separate shows, Lee and Irma were with her and Lester was with him. But this show didn't make no money. He said: "Deek, you and Pete, I want to take you with me. See, I'm going with Mrs. Young. I will turn this show here over to Kitchen." That was the man who was the spieler, the barker, so he turned it over to him. Mrs. Young had this big show with "Lackman and Carson," and Lester had already gone over there before we got there. From Carbondale, Illinois, Mr. Young took Pete and I with him and we went over to the show with Mrs. Young and we stayed on that show until it closed in El Reno, Oklahoma, in late October 1926.

Mr. Young rehearsed a danceband when we stayed on that show and we got three-four more guys in the danceband. We had trombone, two saxophones and trumpet. We would rehearse that on the show while we were traveling. He got the band together and booked it to a dance in Minneapolis.[26]

The time spent with the Lackman and Carson show was enjoyable for the children. Lee can remember that there were many different types of entertainment to be had, including roundabouts, ferris wheels, stalls with various types of prizes, and lotteries, as well as a Wild West show, which was very popular. Billy's band performed in a minstrel show, and during the breaks the children used to run off to ride on the mules, or to earn some pocket money running small errands.

The atmosphere of the circus was good, and all the employees felt themselves to be members of one large family. They all stuck together, and if there was any vandalism or a fight in the offing on the part of the public, they would shout "Hey, Rube!" and all would come rushing over and help to restore law and order. According to Leonard Phillips, "With 'Lackman and Carson' we played the same kind of music as we did in the vaudeville and carnival shows, 'I Love My Baby,' 'Baby, Won't You Please Come Home,' 'Five Foot Two, Eyes of Blue,' and 'I Never Knew I Could Love Anybody.' "[27] Shortly before they were due to leave the Lackman and Carson show an awkward episode occurred, as Leonard Phillips distinctly remembers:

There was a girl on the carnival show named Clara, she was crazy about Lester. It was in El Reno in October around the time we used to go to Minneapolis. His father didn't want him to go with this girl, he said she wasn't the type of woman for him. She was older than Lester, she was in her twenties and Lester was sixteen-seventeen years old, and he got mad, you know, and the "old man" did something to him that hurt him all his life, he slapped Lester, and Lester cried and left. Mr. Young said one thing about Lester after he left, he said: "He never slashed me in his life, he never talked bad to me and nothing, and I hit him. That thing hurts me."

We were looking for Lester to come and play on the show. His horns were there, but nobody did see him, he didn't show up. But this chick knew where he was, and we went and found him, and we told him to come on back. He was in town. Some guy had a little band and he was playing in it in El Reno. We said to him: "Come on back, man. This is no place for you, an old horse town like this, come on!" He said, he called his father "Pop," he said: "Yeah, but Pop, he did me wrong. I never slashed, and I was just talking, and he ran over and slapped me. I couldn't take it, I left."

The show was there for a week, and this must have happened around Tuesday, and we were gonna leave Sunday, going to Minneapolis, and naturally we didn't want to go without him, because he was the star. We found him and brought him back and convinced him that the "old man" was sorry of what he did, that his temper got bad. He always respected his parents, the "old man" was a respectable man, but sometimes he would be hardheaded. But we got him, so everything was all right when the show closed. He came back the same day the show would close at night, and he came back and got up and blew that horn crazy, you know. Everybody was glad to see him. That was on Saturday, and Sunday the whole group that would go to Minneapolis went to Minneapolis.[28]

This was not the first time Lester had disappeared—it was something he often did if it looked like Billy was going to indulge in some corporal punishment. Unlike Sarah, Billy was pretty strict in bringing up the children. If he got angry he sometimes used to punish them with his razor strop, which came to be called "greasy Jim," as Lee often found out to his cost. Lester, on the other hand, used to run away whenever he could see that Billy was on the warpath; he ran off about a dozen times between the ages of eleven and eighteen. Billy never really learned to understand Lester, but he respected him tremendously for his musical talent. You could get a long way with Lester by talking quietly and sensibly with him, whereas an authoritarian stance with the threat of a beating never helped. When Lester ran off, it wasn't just a question of a night or two—he often did so for a couple of weeks or so. Even so, he always kept an eye on where the band was playing, so that he could come back home when he felt the time was ripe. Lee can remember one incident when Lester was sixteen years old and had been away for an unusually long time: "I remember one time in the South, he ran off to some place in Oklahoma, and we were getting ready to go back to Minneapolis, and I don't think they'd seen him for seven or eight weeks, and my dad had just gone up to the window to buy tickets for us to go back to Minneapolis, you know? And my mother was just crying because she was gonna leave Lester there—and hadn't seen him in ages, and my dad went up to the window and says, you know, 'Give me two halves and two wholes'—those were tickets, you know—you'd buy them in half fare, you know? And so my mother said to my daddy to look round, and Lester was standing over by the door, and he said, 'Make that 3 halves.' "[29]

Billy and Sarah never talked to Lester about where he'd been after he had come back. He just quietly took up his seat in the band once more, as if he had never been away. Nobody ever found out where he'd been or how he'd been able to get along.

On another occasion there was an embarrassing and humiliating episode that Lester never forgot, because he was thrown out of the band for being too bad at reading music. Billy used to teach his children how to read music on a large blackboard, on which he used to write different types of exercises. Both Irma and Lee were quick to pick it up, but Lester learned his voices and exercises by heart, thanks to his good musical ear, so he did not think it was necessary to learn how to read music. One day, however, he was shown up. Lee recalls that this was about 1925, a date which seems right, since Leonard Phillips can also remember what happened on that occasion. Here is Lee's account: "Once we were rehearsing when we were kids, and my father told Lester he was making mistakes. Now he was really playing right, but my father was trying to catch him out, because he wasn't reading his part, only playing by ear. So he took his instrument and got up and played maybe one note wrong on purpose, telling Lester that was what he should have played. So Lester just sat there and played it in exactly the same way, mistake and all, and my father realized he'd been fooled and got so mad he hit him with his yardstick!"[30]

Lester has said more on the subject: "When I was coming up playing in the band I wasn't reading music, I was bullshitting, but I was in the band. And my sister, you see, she was playing, and I'd get close to her and pick up on the parts, you know, training marches and all that shit like that. And finally my father said one day: 'Kansas, play your part!'

And he knew goddamn well I'd lose my ass, he knew I wasn't reading. 'Play your part, Kansas,' he said "Lester, play your part!' And I couldn't read a motherfucking note, not a goddam note. He said: 'Get up and get your fucking ass and work on some scales. Get up!' "

Lester goes on: "Now, you know, my heart was broke, you dig, and I went in crying my little teardrops and I was thinking, I'll come back and catch them, if that's the way they want it. So I went away and I learned to read the music still by myself and I came back in the band and played this music and shit. All the time I was copying from the records also with the music, so I could fuck these motherfuckers completely up. And I read the music and shit and everything was great. But all the motherfuckers who laughed when they put me out when I couldn't read came up to me and said: 'Won't you show me how to go? How to play that?' And I showed them. I showed them shit!"[31]

It says quite a lot for Lester's musicality that it took more than three years for the others to discover that he could not read music and that they found out only by chance. Leonard Phillips and the other musicians hadn't suspected anything up to that point, as his own commentary on the affair shows: "I thought he was reading the way he played it to me. He was fakin' it, but it sounded good to us."[32]

After Billy, his family, and his band had said goodbye to the Lackman and Carson show in El Reno, they traveled north to Minneapolis to spend the winter there, a time recalled by Leonard Phillips:

See, his father had already booked a dance up there, and the first day of November, I'll never forget it, when we went to play for the dance we never saw the ground, there was snow up there. So we went in and played the dance, and everything was packed and everything was nice.

He had a nice place, he already had this big house rented up there in Minneapolis for all of the musicians and everything. Some people who'd been on the show before, he knew them, they were takin' care of the house. All of us stayed in one room, Lester, Pete and I, so we had a good time playing, good food to eat, rehearse. There was a big room where we'd rehearse practically every day.

We didn't have a job right after that one. We made ten dollars, which was a lot of money then, for that night. At that time I didn't do nothing but eat. I didn't smoke, I didn't drink, I didn't do nothing, it was a straight life.

We stayed in Minneapolis all that winter until next spring. We made our headquarter there. While we stayed there we got this big band together, eleven pieces, that he would take into Radison Hotel. We played there, and he would book jobs like mad for that band, the "New Orleans Strutters."

We made it good. He started booking things, and then we started working in Minneapolis. We got work all the time. Every week we would play in a place called the South Side Ballroom, we used to play there all the time, and Radison Hotel and St. Paul Hotel. We had a good band and good entertainment, we used to sing together, we used to sing "Ain't She Sweet."

We was a big name in Minneapolis, you know, because we got most of the good work. At that time in Minneapolis there was no big band, I mean no big white band. Minneapolis wasn't segregated, both black and white people would come and listen. The pianoplayer, his wife, was white and the drummer's wife. Nobody shared the bill with the Young group. He had the whole show by himself, and the show would last about an hour and a half.

With Mr. Young's dance band we played waltzes. You'd have to play waltzes if you played a dance. A lot of people liked to waltz, it was a popular thing. Then we played tunes like the "Charleston," and we played "I Want a Little Girl," "If I Could Be One Hour with You Tonight," "Bye, Bye, Blackbird," "Five Foot Two, Eyes of Blue," "My Blue Heaven," "My Melancholy Baby," "I'm Coming, Virginia," "The Stampede" and "Tiger Rag." When Mr. Young said: "Let's get in the blue book" he meant, we'd play a number by ear. We had a whole lot of numbers without music, head arrangements, like "Tiger Rag," "Sand," all kinds of blues and "How Come You Do Me Like You Do."

Lester played all the solos and he loved the blues. We had three saxophones, Lester Young on alto and tenor, Clyde Turrentine—he's got a son, a bad saxophone player, Stan—was playing tenor and Ben Wilkerson. I think his name was Ray Jones, he played banjo, and another Ben Wilkerson was playing drums. Even it was the same name there was no relation. Pete Jones played trombone, we had two trombones, and Mr. Young was playing tuba. Durbis Oliver played piano, and myself and Arthur Williams played trumpet. That was a real big band in those days, ten-eleven pieces. We started playing with this band in December 1926, and I played with that band until we quit and went with Art Bronson in January 1928.

In Minneapolis Lester and I went to school. It was a small grammar school, and Lee and Irma went there too. They would go to school in the winter.

His father had a big influence in Minneapolis. He could go anywhere and get what he wanted. I played all Conn trumpets, he bought me Conn's and asked me how I liked them, King's, Buescher's. He gave me a Buescher trumpet for Christmas, a pretty one too. Most of everybody in there had Buescher's, but the C-melody saxophones were Conn's.

Louis Armstrong was hot then with his Hot Five, and we listened to Fletcher Henderson and Ben Bernie. Everybody in the band listened to them and to the Casa Loma Orchestra and Gene Goldkette. We had plenty of records with them and Red Nichols, Frankie Trumbauer and Bix Beiderbecke and Benny Goodman. We had "Davenport Blues" with Bix, and after Bix got with Paul Whiteman we used to listen to him a lot.

When we got to a town we'd go to the record store and listen to records. They'd give you a bunch of records to play and tell you the newest they had, like "The Five Pennies" by Red Nichols, and Jack Teagarden played a hell of a solo on that. Jack Teagarden changed the trombone around. Before he came around they played a slide horn, but he wouldn't slide, and everybody then would copy him, like our trombone player.

You didn't hear them much live in them days. People would come around every now and then, and we always would go when a band came to Minneapolis, like when Ben Bernie came in, Gene Goldkette, Coon-Sanders, Vincent Lopez and Paul Whiteman. Those bands would come to theaters.

Most people were moanin' on saxophone then. The only cats to play solo on sax was on the alto. Tenor players didn't, well, Bud Freeman did, but Lester didn't care about Bud. Lester liked Frankie Trumbauer. Hawkins played too much with the Henderson band. Frankie made records with a small group where you could really dig him. We listened to a lot of Stump Evans and Prince Robinson too.

See, that kind of people made records with five pieces, six pieces so you could dig a cat's solo more than in a band where he played maybe eight bars, sixteen bars, maybe one chorus, never over a chorus with a bigband. Hawkins never played that much for himself, he played with Fletcher. He made a record called the "Stampede," and we used to play that. We had a stock arrangement on that, and Lester had a solo on that where he played alto. Lester was crazy about Bix, crazy about Frankie Trumbauer and crazy about Benny Goodman. We heard the Ben Pollack records with Goodman. Lester was playing "Singin' the Blues" by Frankie Trumbauer and Bix Beiderbecke around in the house, and I was listening to it too and said: "Man, who is that guy playin' the trumpet?" and he said: "His name is Bix." At that time you had to know who it was, because they didn't put the names on the records. There were a few records that had all who were playing on it, like individual players, you know, like Louis. His name was on the Bessie Smith record when she sang "St. Louis Blues."

Bix made some records too under his name, "In a Mist." We played that too, and Lester listened to that too, it was a piano piece. We liked that and we played it together. We picked up the lead on it, and Lester played the lead and gave us the harmonies. He had that kind of ear, natural. He'd tell you, he said: "I don't know what note it is for you. It's my note, you hit this note!" He's got the sound, at that time he didn't know the chord progressions. He said: "Play this note, Phil. Pete, you play this note and let us hit it together." It came to him like that, pretty.

Lester listened to a lot of Louis too and learned his solos. All he'd do was to listen to him, he had that kind of ear. We used to go to a record store, and maybe a month later he said: "Deek, you remember this?" He was playing, I've forgotten what it was, but it was from some place where we had listened to records, and he played it. I'd say: "Yeah, man!" He said: "We're gonna learn that!" So we got together, you know. I was easy to pick up, and Pete was easy to pick up what he gave us. See, he was just born a genius, he was a born musician. I mean, he didn't know what note, he wouldn't say: "You play D-flat," he just said: "You play this on your horn, and you play this note!" And we played it and we got it down.

Red Nichols was out there way before Bix and he was more popular than Bix, Red Nichols and his Five Pennies. Lester liked him too. Most of the records we played we all liked them, I mean the ones that we'd fool with. Most of the records had the new sound, we always would get some. "Man, I like this, that's pretty! Here, let's get that, man!" So we'd get it, get together and learn it. Sometimes I'd learn some Bix solos myself. I learned "Singin' the Blues" and "Clementine." Lester would learn that too because Frankie had a solo on it. That was when he was in the Gene Goldkette band. Lester learned the ones with Frankie playing on them, and I learned the ones with Bix playing on them, and Pete learned the ones with Tommy Dorsey. "Louisiana" with Paul Whiteman we played too. Both Bix and Frankie had solos on that, so Lester and I learned that too. "Mississippi Mud" we learned too. That was with a small group from Paul Whiteman's band, the Rhythm Boys. We also learned "I Love My Baby." I think it was Bix's Combo, Rollini played the bass sax.[33]

In an interview Lester has explained why Trumbauer was his absolute favorite saxophonist: "Frankie Trumbauer and Jimmy Dorsey were battling for honors in those days, and I finally found out that I liked Frankie Trumbauer. Trumbauer was my idol. When I started to play, I used to buy all his records. I imagine I can still play all those solos off the record. He played a C-melody saxophone. I tried to get the sound of a C-melody on a tenor. That's why I don't sound like other people. Trumbauer always told a little story. And I liked the way he slurred his notes. He'd play the melody first and then after that, he'd play around the melody."[34]

On another occasion Lester said: "I had to make a decision between Frankie Trumbauer and Jimmy Dorsey, you dig? I wasn't sure which way to go, you dig? I had these motherfucking records, and I'd play one of Jimmy's and I'd play one of Trumbauer's and all that shit. I didn't know nothing about Hawk then, you dig? Finally Trumbauer was my man. Did you hear him play 'Singin' the Blues'? That tricked me."[35] He so liked "Singing the Blues" with Trumbauer and the cornet player Bix Beiderbecke that he always had it with him in his trunk.

Trumbauer often played together with Bix Beiderbecke, and these two musicians were Lester's greatest source of inspiration and the foundation of his particular style of playing. Trumbauer had a light, almost vibrato-free tone and played with a smooth, technically elegant style with melodic phrasing; Beiderbecke had a lyrical style of playing with beautiful melodic lines in the improvisations, which appealed to Lester and had a more lasting influence on him than Trumbauer. He once said about Beiderbecke that he sounded "just like a colored boy sometimes. He was fine."[36] In another interview he said: "I have great big eyes for Bix. I used to be confused between him and Red Nichols, but finally I had to put Bix on top."[37]

Lee Young has shed light on how Lester developed his master technique. In an interview on WKCR August 27, 1988, he told how at that time they had several records with, among others, the classical virtuoso Rudy Wiedoft, and that Lester used to listen to these, practicing six to seven hours a day. This helped him to articulate precisely while playing intricate lines at fast tempos.

In Minneapolis the Young family lived close to another musical family, the Pettifords. The father, Harry "Doc" Pettiford, had formed a family band with himself, his wife, and the oldest of their eleven children. Lester used to meet one of the elder brothers as much as was possible, taking tours into consideration. One of the youngest children was called Oscar, later a well-known bass player, whom Lester played with for a short period in 1943.

Billy and his band were linked to the Orpheum Circuit, the largest booking agency in Minneapolis, which secured the best and most highly paid engagements for him. In order to make Billy's band less expensive, the agency asked him to reduce it from eleven to nine players. "They wanted to cut two men out of the band," Lee remembers, "and he was a high-principled man and he would not, and so they continued to do those little one-nighters up in Bismarck, North Dakota, you know, Devil's Lake, they used to play all over the Dakotas."[38]

Toward the end of 1927 the band arrived in Bismarck, North Dakota, and it was here that Lester met a saxophonist of his own age with whom he later came to play a lot. The man's name was Eddie Barefield, and at the time he was piano player in Clarence Johnson's band. "It was 55 below zero weather there that winter," Barefield recalls. "This hotel we played in, the Spencer, was right on the corner. They had an annex where we stayed, and we didn't have to go outdoors to go to work. We only played two hours a day, that was from 6.00 to 8.00 for the dinner hour. And that's all we had to do, and the job paid $30.00 a week."

He continues: "In this annex where we lived lived Lester Young's father and his family band. Lester Young and his little brother Lee, he wasn't big enough to play then. But they'd dress him in a tuxedo and he would conduct the band. Irma, his sister, was on saxophone, his mother played the piano and his father played tenor sax. Lester was playing alto. One day I heard a knock on the door. I hadn't met him then, but I heard a knock on the door and he opened the door. 'I'm Lester Young. Who is that playing saxophone?' I said: 'Frankie Trumbauer.' He said: 'Do you mind if I listen?' So he came in and we met. He started to borrow these records. We became good friends there and he used to come over every time he had a chance, when they weren't out."[39] In order to obtain precisely the records he wanted, Lester also used a postal order firm, which sent the records he had ordered in advance to the next address on their tour route.

Leonard Phillips remembers the following about Lester's playing at this point:

At that time Lester played alto, so he learned the solos on alto. He played the C-melody sometimes, but he didn't bother it too much. He played tenor, alto and soprano. He played the solos on alto, but he could play them on tenor the same way, but he was just playing alto. Lester never practiced. He warmed up, he just played what came to his mind. I never heard him around blowing his horn practicing. He just started playing tenor when he got with the Blue Devils, but he quit playing tenor and went back to alto, because when he left Bronson and went back to Minneapolis he was playing alto. He went back to his father and was playing tenor then, but when he went back to Bronson in 1930 he was playing alto.

He did an act on "Tiger Rag" too. He turned the mouthpiece around and played the horn upside down with the bell pointing straight to the floor. When he played that he took breaks. He would also put his left hand behind the back and the fingers at the bottom of his saxophone, and his right hand would be in front of him fingering the top end. He did that with all the bands at that time. He said that he couldn't put on a floor show, so he would just play an act.

The tricks with the saxophone he started with Mr. Young's danceband in Minneapolis. He saw a cat somewhere playing the horn behind him like I said, and then he thought about that when he played "Tiger Rag" which featured him. It was his number, "Tiger Rag," and we played it way up in tempo too. He played the horn upside down when he made all the breaks, and then after when we got to the trio part and got back to the chorus again he put it behind him. He'd break the house up, I mean the house would break down when he did that, because you would not see it done the way like that. He used that trick with anybody he played with at that time, King Oliver and the Blue Devils.[40]

It was also during this period that Lester learned the particular jargon he later became famous for, a way of speaking prevalent in TOBA circles. "It's not like hip-slang, it's entirely different," Lee has explained. "If you listened real good you might be able to tell, but when we were young, Lester and I used to stand around for an hour and talk and no-one would know what we were saying."[41] Lester used part of this way of speaking in his daily speech for the rest of his life. He also threw in a good batch of words and expressions of his own invention for good measure.

Despite occasional friction between Billy and Lester, Lester's relationship with his father was warm and grateful. "I really appreciated what my father did for me," he said later. "He knew so much. He tried to teach me everything."[42] Lee has expanded on this: "They were very close. He bought Lester everything you could think of. He would buy Lester four and five suits at a time. I didn't get any new clothes until Lester left home. I think my dad knew the guy was a genius when he was a kid."[43]

Leonard Phillips also made the following comment about Billy: "Willis Young didn't play as good as Lester, he didn't play better than me, that's why he liked me so well. He said: 'You play like Joe Oliver or Louis Armstrong. You got a lot of power! In New Orleans on them parades they would like you, because you play loud and strong!' I said: 'Thank you!' He would always take me away to go with him. The last time I saw him was in 1930 when we were with Art Bronson's band up in Montana somewhere. He died in 1943 in Los Angeles."

"He should have had a lot of money when he died," Phillips added. "I don't know if he did, but he made a million dollars on Lester and them as kids. They drew, because you didn't see kids as tough as they were. Lee could sing and dance, Irma could sing and dance, and Lester could sing and dance. On the carnival he had a dance called the 'Skate,' where he'd skate all over, he was a good dancer too. He didn't want to sing, because his voice was too high, but they were all gifted."[44]

Shortly after New Year's Day 1928 Lester found out that the plans for the rest of the winter tour were to travel via Dodge City through Texas and back to Phoenix, Arizona. Lester had gradually grown sick and tired of the southern states, with their humiliating experiences and their degrading attitude toward all people who didn't happen to be white, so he tried to persuade Billy to look for engagements in some of the northern states where there was less discrimination, such as Iowa, Nebraska, or Kansas. Billy refused, and Lester, accepting the consequences of his attitude, said farewell to the Young Family Band.

2

On His Own Two Feet (1928–1933)

Considering the fact that Lester, now eighteen, had been playing professionally for a number of years, together with his social and racial status, it is amazing that he stayed with his family for so long. The explanation for this must lie in the strength of the bond he felt toward his family, in the secure nature of his existence, and in his friendship with Leonard Phillips and Pete Jones. In addition to this, Pete married Irma in 1927 and so became Lester's brother-in-law. The marriage, however, was short-lived; Leonard and Pete later left Billy's band, while Irma decided to stay on.

Lester had now outgrown his father, in more than one sense. He was 5 feet 11 inches tall and weighed about 160 pounds,[1] but he did not give the appearance of being big. Most striking were the relatively light color of his skin, inherited from his mother, his red hair, a pair of penetrating green eyes, and comparatively small feet. His voice was high and boyish, and he had a friendly, obliging, and unassuming way about him, which made it easy for him to come into contact with other people.

Leonard Phillips remembers leaving the family band thus: "In January 1928 Mr. Young was going on in Texas, and we decided we won't go on in Texas, so Lester quit in Salina, Kansas. We, Pete and I, stayed with Billy Young until we quit in Wichita, Kansas. Money was short, so I pawned one of my suits and got enough money for me and Pete to go back to where Lester was. So when we came back there he said: 'What are you all doing, man! I'm so glad to see you all!' We were all three of us tight together, you know, and he said: 'There's a guy got a band. He want to enlarge his band rather to a ten piece band, so he's got about six pieces now, do you hear?'"[2]

The man Lester was talking about was the piano player Art Bronson, who had a band called the Bostonians, for some unknown reason, since not a single member of the band came from Boston. Bronson had heard Lester at the Wiggly Café in Salina, where Lester had been fortunate enough to join a small band shortly after he had started out on his own. Phillips has the following to say about the transition to Bronson's band:

When we came in town Bronson was glad to get us, and we all three joined his band at the same time in Salina, Kansas. When Lester left, his father took everything he had. He took all his horns, he had a clarinet, a baritone, an alto and a soprano, that was his instruments. He took his clothes too, everything except what he had on him. He had a clarinet with keys too, it had no holes. His father gave him hell and said: "You don't want that? You want a clarinet with some holes in it? So you play this clarinet like a saxophone!" That's the first I've ever seen like that, but he didn't really start playing clarinet until he went with Basie.

There was another guy that had a band around there, Ted Williams. He got jealous at Art Bronson. He would do anything to do things hard for him, but he couldn't do it, because we were blowing so much, that everybody quit listening to him.

We had an alto player from Jamaica, he played first alto with the Bronson band, but he left and was now playing alto in Mr. Young's band. Then he left and went to hometown, and then we got to thinking about him as a first alto player for Bronson's band, because he could read like mad. His name was Albert Walters. Bronson sent for him and got him to play first alto, and then we did have a reed section. We had another guy, Buford Boswell, playing third alto. Lester was playing tenor then, he never played alto with Bronson. Boswell was already in the band playing alto, so Lester said: "Give me a tenor!" so Bronson went down in the store and got him a Pan-American tenor. I'll never forget it, it was a cheap horn! Buford was a good reader and played pretty good solos too.

Art Bronson's band was Albert Walters, Buford Boswell and Lester Young on saxophones, Ted Williams and myself on trumpets, Pete Jones on trombone, George Hudson on bass, Herb Hanners on banjo, Percy Walker played drums and Bronson played piano.[3]

Perhaps Phillips remembers the circumstances surrounding Lester's change to tenor saxophone somewhat incorrectly: Lester, at any rate, has given a different version, claiming that he began by playing alto sax—which may very well be correct, since Albert Walters joined the band just a little later. This is Lester's version:

I was playing alto, and we had this evil assed motherfucker. He had a nice, beautiful background, you know, mother and father and a whole lot of bread and all the shit like that. So, every time we'd get a job—this was in Salina, Kansas—so, every time we'd go to see this motherfucker. We'd all be ready, we'd be waiting for ninety years to get us to work, you know. And he said: "Wait for me until I get my shirt on, and get my tie on,'' and all that shit, and everybody'll be waiting, disgusted.

So I told the bossman, his name was Art Bronson, I said: "Listen, why shall we go through this shit?" I say: "You buy me a tenor saxophone and I play this motherfucker and we'll be straight then." And he went to the music store, got me a tenor sax and we split. As soon as I got my mouth 'round it I knew it was for me. That alto was a little too high for me.[4]

On another occasion he made the following comment: "When I saw the beat-up tenor he bought, though, I almost changed my mind. It was an old Pan-American job. But I played it and liked it, what's more."[5]

The reason Lester liked the old secondhand Pan-American could well be linked to the difference in construction, as compared with other tenor saxophones. This make was a little shorter and had a narrower bell, which gave it a lighter sound, something in the region of a C-melody saxophone—and this harmonized well with the sort of ideal sound Lester was striving for at that period. The saxophone was Lester's own property—the first he had ever owned.

In the Midwest and the Southwest, the established bands—the so-called territory bands, to which the Bostonians belonged—had divided up the various areas among themselves, so as not to steal one another's jobs. Each band covered a certain area, outside of which it was not well known. If a band was asked to play inside another band's territory, it always checked first to make sure the rival band had no objection before accepting the engagement.

The Bostonians played in many of the same places Lester had visited previously with his father's band, especially the Dakotas, Nebraska, Colorado, and Kansas. Leonard Phillips also remembers that "with Art Bronson we also played the Indian reservations in South Dakota. We played in Rapid City, South Dakota. Bronson got a booking up there, and it was when Lester was in the band in 1928. We played there for about three days, and 2,000–3,000 people showed up each night. Everybody liked the music, you know. We played some blues, blues was pretty famous in those days. The Indians were into the blues, they were into everything. Right there they knew what was going on."[6] Lester stayed with Art Bronson for a year, until January 1929, when he returned to the Young Family Band. The band had been on tour with a tent show but had become stranded in Albuquerque, New Mexico, where Lester joined it.

The piano player John Lewis grew up in Albuquerque and later came to play in Lester's own band; but he can remember Lester as far back as this period: "When I was still very young in Albuquerque, I remember hearing about the Young family settling there. They had a band and had come in with a tent show and been stranded. There was a very good local jazz band, called St. Cecilia's, that Lester played in. He also competed with an excellent Spanish tenor player and housepainter named Cherry. I barely remember Lester's playing. He had a fine, thin tone."[7]

At the same period a piano player by the name of Ben Webster was working at a local cinema in Amarillo, Texas. Apart from playing to silent movies, he was a member of a band which called itself Dutch Campbell's Band. In this band two brothers also played, the trombone player Keg Johnson and the saxophone player Budd Johnson. Webster was impressed by Budd's saxophone playing and wanted to change to this instrument—and his chance came when he met Billy Young.

"Lester Young's father," Webster recalled, "who was a teacher and bandleader, came to Amarillo along with Lee Young to pick up a piano player. I took the opportunity to ask Lester's father if he needed a sax player. He said he did, and I told him I didn't have an instrument. He laughed and said he'd find an instrument for me. Then I told him I couldn't read. He finally fell out laughing then, but he told me, he'd teach me. So I went to Albuquerque with the Youngs, and for three months, Lester's father taught me how to read. He was a very good musician. I remember Prez used to sit and practice with me every day, and he'd try to help me as much as he could.[8] Lester's father mostly played trumpet," he added, "but he could play anything and, what's more, he was a master teacher."[9]

That summer was dramatic and emotional for Lester in several ways. In Albuquerque he met a girl by the name of Beatrice, whom he went out with, and Ben Webster saved him from drowning. In their spare time the younger members of the band used to amuse themselves by going down to the Rio Grande for a swim. On one occasion Lester was caught by the current and tossed around in the water. Webster was a very strong swimmer and, together with the guitar player Ted Brinson, managed to get Lester safely to shore. On another occasion Lee fell into a sand-hole out in the river; here too Webster came to the rescue. "I was drowning and I'd gone under for the last time!" Lee once said in an interview. "I was only a little boy, about ten or eleven, and he just picked me up under one arm and carried me home. He was a big guy then, you should have seen what a physique he had![10] Lee dived right in again," Webster recalls, "but Lester didn't want to think about swimming for a long time after that."[11]

In the fall of 1929 Billy took the Young Family Band on tour once again. In the course of his stay in Albuquerque he had reorganized the band and increased its size, and Lee had now become the drummer. The tour took them westward, and the band played for a week or more in each town. In Phoenix, Arizona, the stay was a longer one, since Billy was fortunate enough to get an engagement playing a couple of times a week in a public park, apart from the jobs as a dance band. Billy's original plan was to travel across Arizona to California, but Lester didn't want to go along with him. At the end of the year he once more said goodbye to his family, staying behind when the band traveled via Yuma and Tempe to Los Angeles. Here Billy settled as a music teacher and later found work in the black musicians' trade union, Local 767.

Lester, on the other hand, returned to Minneapolis, which served as a sort of home base for him during the following few years. His great ability, coupled with his good humor and sociability, made it easy for him to find work, even in the ensuing years, when the Depression struck hard at the entertainment business. Contrary to what had been assumed earlier, Lester did not at this time play in Eli Rice's Cotton Pickers, a band based in Minneapolis.[12]

In Minneapolis Lester also met up with Eddie Barefield once more, and the two of them made an unusual duo for a short time. "Lester Young had left his father's band and came to Minneapolis playing tenor," Barefield recalls. "That's when he and I used to get together, just the two of us, and play school dances just with the sax alto and tenor and no rhythm or anything. Just played the two of us."[13]

Barefield claims that Lester and he formed a duo in the spring of 1928, but this must be incorrect, since Lester was with Art Bronson at that point. The spring of 1930 was probably correct. They had not had long together, however, before the Blue Devils arrived in Minneapolis and took Lester with them on their travels. The band was led by Walter Page, who played both baritone saxophone and tuba. He heard Lester play and was so enthusiastic that he persuaded Lester to come along with the band. The saxophone player Buster Smith, who played in the Blue Devils, remembers Lester's arrival: "He was playing tenor and baritone then; in fact he played so much baritone, that Walter Page lay *his* baritone down and said he wasn't going to play it anymore. Lester joined us then and Walter left just a little later and Ernest Williams and I took over."[14]

The Blue Devils were based in Oklahoma City and had been founded by Walter Page around 1927. In the years up to 1930 the band met with considerable success and became one of the best territory bands. It was a feared rival in band contests, since it nearly always emerged from the fray as the winner, but these triumphs were also to prove the cause of the band's eventual dissolution. Rival bands enticed the Blue Devils to join them instead by offering higher wages.

Like most of the other territory bands, the Blue Devils were run extremely democratically. All takings were split equally, and should anyone have any special problems, this would be taken into account. Musicians were hired and fired by majority vote; this system was also used for choosing jobs and deciding on payments. The band always played throughout the winters in the Ritz Ballroom in Oklahoma City, and in the Dreamland Ballroom in Little Rock, Arkansas, during the summer months. During spring and fall the band went on tour in Texas, Oklahoma, Missouri, Iowa, Nebraska, and Kansas. Kansas City was an especially popular town to play in, since the club owners there never interfered in the band's choice of music.[15]

The exact lineup of the band in the 1930–31 period is difficult to determine, but the following musicians were in the band in the spring of 1930, when Lester replaced Reuben Rodney as tenor sax player: James Simpson and Harry Smith (tp), Druie "Chap" Bess (tb), Theodore "Doc" Ross and Buster Smith (as/clt), Charles Washington (p), Reuben Lynch (g), Walter Page (b), and Alvin "Mouse" Burroughs (dr).[16]

A fine portrait of Lester and the influence he already could have on his slightly younger colleagues is given by the writer Ralph Ellison. Ellison came from Oklahoma City and grew up with the guitar player Charlie Christian, originally intending to become a professional trumpet player. In a commemorative article on Christian, Ellison said that "perhaps the most stimulating influence on Christian, and one with whom he was later to be identified, was that of a tall, intense young musician who arrived in Oklahoma City sometime in 1929 and who, with his heavy white sweater, blue stocking cap, and up-and-out-thrust silver saxophone, left absolutely no reed player and few young players of any instrument unstirred by the wild, excitingly original flights of his imagination. Who else but Lester Young, who with his battered horn upset the entire Negro section of the town. One of our friends gave up his valved instrument for the tenor saxophone and ran away from home to carry the new message to Baltimore, while a good part of the efforts of the rest was spent trying to absorb and transform the Youngian style."[17]

Lester did not stay long with the Blue Devils, moving back to the Bostonians after only a couple of months. "Lester came back to Bronson in 1930," Leonard Phillips recalls. "It must have been in the latter part of May or first part of June. He left Bronson in Scottsbluff, Nebraska in November 1930 and went back to Minneapolis. I stayed with Bronson up till 1932, when King Oliver took the band over in March 1932."[18]

Phillips doesn't mention the lineup of Bronson's band at this point, but in a number of *Down Beat* from 1947 there is a photo that shows Lester with two other members of the Bostonians, the alto sax player Odie Cromwell and the tenor sax player Sam Allen.[19]

During a tour with the band Lester came at one point to Denver, Colorado, where his sister Irma visited him from Los Angeles. The tenor sax player Paul Quinichette grew up in Denver, and he met both of them on this occasion. He puts the year at 1933, but this must be a mistake. Quinichette heard Irma play saxophone at a jam session and was deeply impressed: "She could scare you to death on that alto," he recalls. "I've sat up and played with her. Lester was working with a band named Art Bronson in Denver, Colorado, and she came in to see him and she was sittin' there jammin'. They had a place they called the Hole, downstairs. We jammed till maybe noon the next day, and Irma was down there playing like mad. She was fabulous. Great musician. She could play chorus after chorus. Fantastic ideas in her mind, all the time."[20]

Quinichette also remembers that the two Youngs sounded almost identical on their instruments, despite the fact that Irma was playing alto and Lester tenor sax. Without a doubt jazz lost a great sax player when Irma shortly afterwards laid her sax aside to devote herself to song and dance.

Back in Minneapolis Lester was hired by Eddie Barefield once more. Barefield had a six-man band at the Nest Club, consisting of the leader himself (as/clt), Lester (ts), Leroy "Snake" White (tp), Frank Hines (p), Charles Oden (b), and Mose Strange (dr).[21] In Minneapolis Lester had met a white, Jewish girl named Bess Cooper, and they got married in 1930. On July 27, 1931, they had a daughter, christened Beverly, but shortly after the family was struck by a great tragedy. Bess had to go into the hospital for an operation, after which she bled to death. Lester was so grief-stricken that he never mentioned her to anyone afterwards. Because of his work he was unable to keep Beverly with him, so she was brought up by foster parents in Minneapolis. Lester visited her regularly whenever he was in town. As if Bess's death had not been a hard enough blow, he received another shock when Beverly, scarcely a year old, was struck by a serious illness, which she fortunately managed to survive.[22]

The job at the Nest Club lasted until June 1931, when Barefield dissolved the band to go to Chicago. Lester joined Eugene Schuck's Cotton Club Orchestra instead, which he toured with throughout Minnesota during the summer. When the fall came, Lester left the band and, until the spring of 1932, played partly with the piano player Frank Hines and a drummer at the Nest Club and partly with the piano player Paul Cepha's band in the South Side Club in Minneapolis. During that period he also visited Mississippi and Louisiana for six weeks to see his grandparents in Woodville and to play in Natchez and in Baton Rouge. It has been reported that around this time Lester briefly joined Gene Coy and His Happy Black Aces, an impressive territory band that also included Isiah Young. Lester could have been engaged after his stay in Baton Rouge and may have toured with the band back to Minneapolis.

By this time Lester was beginning to make a good name for himself. He had not as yet finally decided on the tenor sax—just as often he played alto, and he certainly also must have had a clarinet. In the larger bands the sax player was required not only to be able to double up on several saxophones, but also to be proficient on the clarinet, since arrangements from the period often inserted a several-part clarinet piece.

The singer Jimmy Rushing and the alto sax player Benny Carter both heard Lester for the first time around this period. Rushing recalls: "I met Prez when he was playing alto, as a matter of fact he was playing downstairs in a cabaret in Minneapolis, Minnesota. All the guys spoke then what a great musician he was. What made him so great was when everyone ran a chord, he'd run it the other way. Everybody'd be baffled about it, but he'd run it right. He was a great cat."[23] Benny Carter recalls: "It's too bad more people couldn't have heard Lester play alto sax. When I was on the road with McKinney's Cotton Pickers in 1932 we hit Minneapolis and somebody told us about a wonderful alto player in a local club. I went to hear Prez and was enraptured. It was the greatest thing I'd ever heard. He had a definition and a mastery that I don't think he ever felt necessary to display on the tenor."[24] Lester made such an impression on the musicians in the Cotton Pickers that he was offered a job as alto sax player, but he declined, since he didn't want to give up the tenor sax.[25]

Not long after, the Original Blue Devils came to Minneapolis, and they succeeded—by use of cunning, admittedly—in enticing Lester to join them. Since Lester had last played with the Blue Devils, Walter Page had left the band and Ernest Williams had taken over the leadership. Several other players had been replaced. The trumpet player Leroy "Snake" White, whom Lester had played with in Eddie Barefield's band, had come along, and when he heard that Lester was at the Nest Club, he took the rest of the band there to hear him. They were all so enthusiastic that they immediately wanted to have him in the band, but Lester was reticent and unwilling to be persuaded. In the film *The Last of the Blue Devils* (1979), Ernest Williams and Buster Smith explained how they nevertheless managed to hire Lester. "The first time we was there, he wouldn't go. We couldn't move him. So we went back to Sioux City and bought a new Ford. We showed him: 'Have you seen the new Ford?' And the next hour during the day he came with his suitcase!"

The date for Lester's entry into the Thirteen Original Blue Devils must have been early spring, since, on April 9, 1932, the *Chicago Defender* lists the lineup of the band at an engagement in the Ritz Ballroom in Oklahoma City as follows: Leonard Chadwick, James Simpson, Leroy "Snake" White (tp), Druie Bess, Jowper Jones (tb), Theodore "Doc" Ross, Buster Smith (as/clt), Lester Young (ts), Charles Washington (p), Reuben Lynch (g), Abe Bolar (b), Raymond Howell (dr), and Ernest Williams (vcl/dir).[26]

Williams and Smith have a couple more amusing memories of Lester. He always used to travel with chewing gum in his trunk, as well as pork and beans. Women also found him appealing. In Sioux City the girls trooped up outside the house where Lester and the other two were staying but were too shy to make contact. They stood outside the door of his room and whispered to Williams and Smith: "What's Lester now doing? What's the matter with him? I wanna talk to him!" The band was teetotal, and Lester, who did not touch liquor at this stage, had his own favorite drink, which didn't coincide with the others'. "Why don't you drink some cocoa?" Williams asked him once, and received the reply: "Give me some orange soda, man!"[27]

With Lester's arrival the band now had the best reed section in the whole of the Southwest. Buster Smith, in an interview, talked about the band's battles with other bands and about the sort of things that could happen:

Whenever we'd meet a band in some town we'd arrange a battle of music. Of course, a lot of the time there'd be two bands and sometimes more playing the same places and we'd always have a battle then. We'd usually just have one bandstand and one band would play thirty minutes, and then the other would play thirty minutes. One band would try to cut the other one with their arrangements and their attack and so forth, and the soloists in the bands would have personal contests. The Blue Devils was a great band for a battle of music. Every time we'd find another band, we'd grab them and give them a hard time. In our band we had three reeds that would help ourselves a little extra. It was me and Lester Young and Theodore Ross. Ross and I played alto and would put tenor reeds on our horns, and Lester would put a baritone reed on his tenor and then that brass couldn't drown us out. We played as loud as the brass did. People thought it was real great, the reeds being as loud as the brass section. Of course they didn't know the real story. . . .

We usually called our music barrelhouse or gutbucket. It was considered sort of rough music. We didn't use the word jazz very often. But about the sweet bands, we saw them occasionally, but they usually had their territory and we had ours. Most of the time they had Illinois and Wisconsin and Minnesota and around there sewed up pretty well. The two big bands we heard most were Lombardo and Garber. Of course most of us played that sweet stuff once in a while. It was all according to the kind of audience you had. You couldn't play our kind of music in some of the big places, the "high collar" dances. No, they wanted that hotel music. We found out our stuff was too rough. The first time we learned about that was in 1932 when we went to Iowa and got booked around Sioux City and later in Illinois and Minnesota. Now, like I told you, Lombardo and Garber had that territory all to themselves. When we went up there with the repertory we had, we couldn't play it at all; we had to lay it down and go to playing that sweet music. We didn't mind too much though because the sweet stuff was easier to play; there was nothing to it. We played hotels where they wanted to have dinner with their music. A lot of them, of course, were sitting within eight feet of the bandstand, and they didn't want a noise in their ear. They didn't pay much attention to what we were playing anyway.[28]

It was during these years that Lester got to know the guitar player Charlie Christian better. Christian was seven years younger than Lester, and when the Thirteen Original Blue Devils played at the Ritz Ballroom in Oklahoma City there was often the chance of a jam session. This did not take place at the Ritz, however, which was reserved for whites, so the black people used to go en masse to Slaughter's Hall on East 2nd Street, also called "Deep Second." Here Christian had his musical debut, and Lester certainly played there too. He can remember this about Christian: "We used to go out in the alley and jam." [29]

During the first few years of the 1930s Lester developed enormously, musically speaking—something which was obvious even for a man like Leonard Phillips. The two of them met again in 1932, when Phillips came to Oklahoma City with Art Bronson's previous band, which continued under the leadership of the singer Tiny Taylor for a couple of months after Art Bronson had disbanded it and before King Oliver took over. "When we were on tour with Tiny Taylor," Phillips recalls,

the Blue Devils were playing in Oklahoma City on the place called the Ritz Ballroom. That's where the band played all the winter, so we met them there and had a little session, the members of the Blue Devils and Clifford McTier, our guitar player, and me. We went around Lester's house where he and Leroy White lived together, and Lester's wife and Leroy's wife and Leroy's kid, Roy, he was a baby then. So we had a session there, just one guitar and horns, but McTier played a good guitar. Lester played the same style like he did when he was fourteen, he didn't change that much, maybe he played faster, because he always was fast.

He could play a hundred choruses and play them all different. We knew that, he would tell us that. Way back he used to say: "I can play a hundred choruses and play different for every chorus!" I heard him say that up in Minneapolis. He jammed there so much and played there for himself with just piano and drums. That was in 1930 and 1931 when he played with Frank Hines. He said: "When you play by yourself you can do that, because different ideas come to you."

When he came to the Blue Devils he had changed. He played a whole lot of horn when I met him in Oklahoma City at the jam session at his apartment. He said that he'd been stretched out on his horn when he'd been playing by himself, and he said that he practiced on gigs like that. [30]

The economic depression after 1929 led to the closing of many halls and theaters throughout the United States. People had less money in their pockets, and fewer were prepared to spend it on going out and having a good time. Especially in the country, where the Thirteen Original Blue Devils were often on tour, times were hard. In the spring of 1933 the band was traveling around in Kentucky and West Virginia, where they were not very well known in advance. This caused an economic catastrophe, and that in turn led to the band being dissolved: "Those were tough times," Lester recalls. "The band was getting bruised, I mean really bruised, playing to audiences of three people."[31]

Buster Smith recalls:

We were on tour and landed in Newport News, Virginia. I guess it was the wrong time of the year or something, and we were in a little speakeasy joint, and we couldn't do any good in a place like that. The band was still on a commonwealth basis and we couldn't go anywhere or accept a job unless we had a vote on it. And nearly always, seven of the boys would pull one way and five or six would pull the other way, and we would end up doing nothing and staying where we were. We missed our best opportunity around that time when Fats Waller wanted us to work for him. We were in Cincinnati and Waller wanted us to play for him on WLW in Cincinnati. He offered us 800 dollars to play for him on an hour and a half show and some of the guys thought it wasn't enough. So we didn't get the job, but went on back to Newport News and started to play around there to get enough money to come back West. We were playing in a town called Martinsville where a guy named Dr. Baldwin had a combination store there with a dance hall. He hired us and we stayed there a few weeks. We didn't like it, but we were broke and couldn't leave. Then a guy from Beckley, West Virginia came over and told us he had a steady job over there at a white night club. We went on over and played about three nights and found out he had us working on a percentage. He had quoted us a straight price for the job and then turned around and took a big cut out of our salary for himself. We were pretty mad but we couldn't do anything about it, because the guy wasn't twenty-one.

Now we had a couple of taxi-drivers to carry us over to the joint every night and they were waiting till the end of the week to collect their money—about seventy dollars. Well, about that time Zack White came down from Cincinnati and tried to steal some of our boys, but we told him he'd had to take *all* of us, or nobody would go. The taxi-drivers found out that two or three boys were going to sneak off anyway, so the drivers went up to the police and had our instruments attached, so we wouldn't get away without paying all that cab fare.

So we had to stay there. The hotel man at our hotel heard about it too and *he* put us out of the hotel—so there we were. We stayed on three or four nights and the law would come down where we were playing and bring us our instruments. We would play and then put them back in their cases and the police carried them right on back and put them in jail. We had about thirteen or fourteen pieces in the band.[32]

* * *

Finally, one of the trombone players got smart, hid his horn outside the window and gave the sheriff the empty case.

Pretty soon we were all doing that. We never did make any money and when we got thrown out of our hotel, everybody got disgusted. One of the fellows wrote home for train fare, and the rest of us left by freight.[33]

* * *

So we decided to hobo away from there, go somewhere and rent some instruments till we could get enough money to send back and get our instruments and pay off the money which amounted to about two hundred dollars by then. Well, we hoboed all the way to St. Louis and stayed around there two or three days and saw nothing was happening.[34]

"There we were, sitting around with these hoboes, and they showed us how to grab a train," Lester remembers. "We made it—with bruises. We got to Cincinnati, no loot, no horns, all ragged and dirty, and we were trying to make it to St. Louis or Kansas City. I found a man who had an alto and loaned it out for gigs, so I managed to play a couple of dates. Finally we all had a meeting—and we decided it was 'every tub'— every man for himself. Well, I got to Kansas City, got hold of a tenor, borrowed some clothes from Herschel Evans—he was playing with Bennie Moten."[35]

Buster Smith maintains that it was in the fall of 1933 that the Thirteen Original Blue Devils were dissolved and that he, together with Lester and others, joined Bennie Moten's band. The date for joining the band is right, but it must have been in the spring of that year that he and Lester and the others arrived in Kansas City, since Leonard Phillips remembers that Lester at that point was hired to play in King Oliver's band. Phillips also has a more plausible suggestion as to whom Lester borrowed clothes from, since Lester and Herschel Evans definitely did not know each other at that time:

When I'd been with King Oliver for about a year, Lester came in the band about in May 1933 or something like that. In King Oliver's band was at that time Leslie "Jack" Holt—he was a good alto player and played a lot of solos—Sam Allen and Francis Whitby on saxophones, Arthur Williams and me on trumpets, Pete Jones on trombone, Edward "Eddie" Anderson on bass, DeWitt "Debo" Mills on drums and Charlie Toran piano and Clifford McTier on guitar, he was a good arranger too.

This tenor player, Francis Whitby, quit in Joplin, Missouri, because the King wouldn't pay for his new horn. He told him he could go to hell: "I paid for my horn, you pay for your horn!" So Francis got mad and left.

Pete was the manager of the King Oliver band, so he and King went to Kansas City to look for a tenorplayer, and Louis Armstrong was up there too, they ran into Louis's band.

When the Blue Devils band broke up in Virginia, they all hoboed back to Kansas City, and when they came to Kansas City we were looking for a tenorplayer. So Lester saw Pete and said: "Hey man! I'm in bad shape, I'm broke, I ain't got no money, ain't got no clothes, ain't got nothing! If you got a job for me, I'm gonna take one. I ain't working, I just came back. I hoboed all the way back from Virginia!"

When Pete went to Kansas City and came back with Prez he said: "Hey man! What're you doin'!" and I said: "Man, we got a tenorplayer now!"

Another guy in the band, Sam Allen, lent him some of his suits to wear. He told us what rough time he'd had, so we tried to let him look good like we would. Lester stayed in the band until November 1933. That's when he went with Basie to Little Rock, Arkansas and then Fletcher Henderson sent for him. The other tenor player, Francis Whitby, he wasn't bad, he was a nice tenor player.

King Oliver said that Lester was a good man. He said that he knew that horn, and he gave him much solo space. When we played "Tiger Rag" he gave him about ten choruses. What King used to like hear him play was "Good Night, Sweetheart," it was our going-home-tune.

King Oliver never played cornet at that time, he played trumpet. The Buescher people gave him a goldplated trumpet, a special trumpet that they built for him.

The teeth were bothering him. He had pyorrhoea, and he already had false teeth at that time. Once he had a bridge, but the pyorrhoea made the bridge come out, and he couldn't play for a while in 1933, for a month or six weeks or something until he got his teeth made. He would have bother with his stomach too, because he would eat so much. When he sat down for breakfast he'd have some eggs, a pound of bacon, a pound of grits, a pound of coffee and two sticks of butter. Once we played in West Virginia in a small town in a barbecue place called the "Barbecue," a lady fixed breakfast for us in the morning. She had hot biscuits, fried rabbit, fried chicken and homefried potatoes. He ate a whole pan of biscuits and then gave the lady a dollar in order to fix some to take with him.

When he got trouble with his stomach it would hurt him and he started drifting. He couldn't play enough, and a lot of the time he wouldn't be on the band. Tiny Taylor would lead the band then.

He was about 6 feet tall and weighed about 250, something in that neighborhood. He didn't hang out with nobody. He always stayed to himself. We'd go out, but he didn't drink. He'd smoke pot and he used to give us some. What he liked was plenty of food.[36]

The saxophone player Buddy Tate, who later became Lester's colleague in the Count Basie orchestra, had first met Lester when the Young Family Band came through Sherman, Texas, where Tate grew up. Their second meeting took place in Tulsa, Oklahoma, while Lester was playing with Oliver. By chance they had both booked in to the same hotel, and Tate recalls:

I was with Victoria Spivey's Revue. She'd just made the first black picture, "Hallelujah" for King Vidor. We were in a hotel in Tulsa, Oklahoma, best hotel in the world at that time for blacks, I believe. Owner was an oil magnate, and he had a Steinway in the lobby and everybody'd go in there and jam.

We were down there one morning, jamming, high, having a good time, when somebody said to me there was a tenor player upstairs, Red Young. I went up. He was lying in his room, three or four corn pads on his toes. I woke him up. I says, "We're having a session downstairs, why don't you come along and play because I haven't heard you play tenor?"

I'll never forget that sound—light, very light, but aah! Everybody put their horns down on the floor and left. He scared everybody to death! He played like that on the alto, too, but I'd thought the tenor would slow him down some, but it didn't. Lester said, "Look—I didn't come down here to do a concert." That was in the early Thirties.[37]

Many guesses have been made up till now concerning when and for how long Lester stayed with Oliver. Phillips's claim is borne out by Francis Whitby, who remembers that he left Oliver about May 1933, because Oliver refused to buy him a new gold-plated Conn tenor saxophone.[38] The bass player Adolphus Alsbrook says that he was with Oliver for six weeks, from June 30 to August 13, 1933, and that Lester was in the band throughout that period together with, among others, Sam Allen, Leslie "Jack" Holt, and DeWitt Mills. He also recalls that Lester had moved back in with Beatrice.[39] John Hammond recalls that he heard Lester with Oliver in 1933, which should remove any remaining doubt on the matter.[40] Lester himself was unable to date his stay, but he does recall the following: "He had a very nice band and I worked regularly with him for one or two years around Kansas and Missouri mostly. He had three brass, three reeds and four rhythms. He was playing well. He was old then and didn't play all night, but his tone was full when he played. He was the star of the show and played one or two songs each set. The blues. He could play some nice blues. He was a very nice fellow, a gay old fellow. He was crazy about all the boys, and it wasn't a drag playing for him at all."[41]

The reason Lester left Oliver was, once again, his unwillingness to travel to the southern states. The Frederick Brothers had booked the band from Kansas City for a tour to the South to the Ridgeway Inn in Nashville, Tennessee, where the band was to play during the winter season 1933–34; but Lester quit before the tour started.

3

The Kansas City Years (1933–1936)

At the time Lester took his leave of King Oliver's band, Kansas City, Missouri, had the highest concentration of clubs, bars, and hotels in the whole United States, the number of bars well exceeding 200, with jazz being played in at least 50 of them. The city was a nodal point for the transport system and a center for the corn and cattle trade, and with this volume of business came a need for entertainment, a need more than met by the liberal policies of Thomas Joseph "Tom" Pendergast once he had been elected to the city council in 1911 at the age of thirty-nine. Pendergast established a close working relationship with the gangsters in the city and, from 1925 onward, controlled the entire city's administration. Gradually his power also came to extend to the police force and the judges of the city. No effects of the federal Volstead Act, which was passed in 1919, instituting Prohibition, were felt in Kansas City. Pendergast's friend, the gangster Johnny Lazia, controlled the entire production, distribution, and sale of beer and spirits. When Prohibition was finally abolished in 1933, the only difference was that customary procedure became legal.[1]

Neither did the economic depression that followed the Wall Street crash of 1929 make much impact on Kansas City. No theaters, clubs, or dance restaurants were forced to close there; on the contrary, after 1930 the city attracted many musicians from throughout the southwestern United States. This was also economically convenient for the club owners who, in many instances, could make do with hiring a couple of proficient rhythm players, thus automatically attracting soloists to the club who were eager to play. In 1930 Kansas City had more than 400,000 inhabitants, of which slightly more than one-fifth were black. The blacks lived around the business areas south of the Kansas River, where the most famous clubs were also located—between 12th and 18th Streets. The Missouri River forms the boundary between Kansas and Missouri, and even though this boundary is between the North and the South, there was an even stronger form of discrimination in Kansas City, Missouri, than one might first have suspected. "The schools in Kansas City, Kansas were integrated," bass player Gene Ramey explains. "All the rest of the schools in Missouri and Kansas were integrated, you know, and very peaceful living there. But you couldn't even sit with the white people in a club over on the Missouri side unless the boss really just went on and bent over backwards and said, 'Come over here and talk,' you know. Like the Reno Club, they would go get Basie or Jo Jones, or somebody, and come on, bring them over to the table and sit with them and talk."[2] 12th Street lay in an area which appealed to both white and black audiences, and this meant that many of the clubs there, such as the Reno Club, were cut in two by a demarcation line down the middle of the room to the stage, with a bar, seats, and dance floor for each group.

An important part of the city's musical life consisted of the innumerable jam sessions that took place after the musicians' normal working hours. Some of the most popular places for musicians were the Subway on 18th Street, the Reno Club and the Sunset Club, both on 12th Street, and Yellow Front Saloon. The Sunset Club was run by Piney Brown and, as Gene Ramey recalls, "was really something. About ten feet, maybe twelve feet, wide and maybe sixty feet long. You know, it was just like goin' down a hallway. I think they hired a piano player and a drummer, but sometimes there would be maybe ten musicians up on the stand. This was where I first met Prez and Ben Webster. They took a liking to me, so they had me coming over there every night. They would fight it out 'til daylight, sometimes ten o'clock in the morning. In those days nobody bothered if you saw a musician, or if you heard music at eleven o'clock the next morning, you know."[3]

The Subway was especially popular among out-of-town musicians, because all participating musicians here were given all they could eat and drink. This club was also run by Piney Brown, and his unusually helpful attitude toward the musicians made him something of an institution. He was a great jazz fan and, thanks to his political connections, he could manage such things as getting a musician out of jail. The Reno Club was run by a gangster by the name of Sol Epstein. His connection with Johnny Lazia meant that the police never interfered with what went on in the club, which always had a good show and a good band.

On average the musicians were badly paid, since the gangsters ignored all union rates and there were plenty of musicians around. In 1934 the musicians at the Reno Club earned only one and a half dollars a night for playing from 10 P.M. to 5 A.M. Two years later their wages had risen to two and a half dollars, but their playing time had been increased by one hour. To increase the amount of money they could take home, each nightclub, excepting the most elegant, had installed a metal box, called a "kitty," which the audience could put money in; the money would then be equally divided among the musicians when the night was over.

It was during the many jam sessions that the special Kansas City jazz style evolved. One of its characteristics was an extensive use of riffs by the band. A riff is a short, rhythmically marked phrase of two or four bars, inspired by the popular boogie-woogie style of the piano players. Boogie-woogie is characterized by a strong, rhythmic style of playing, which employs a single figure repeated in a certain rhythm in the left hand, and having its counterpart in the righthand figure, often one or two bars in a blues number, which is repeated throughout a chorus, after which the piano player moves on to another figure in the next chorus.

From this style of piano-playing there gradually developed a band style based on riffs where the brass section's contribution is answered by, for example, the reed section. This style of playing was first cultivated by Count Basie's band, which often finished a number by playing three different riffs off against each other, using the trumpet, trombone, and saxophone sections.

Riffs had been known for many years and were nothing new in jazz at that time, but "the difference in the Kansas City riff and riffs other places out through the world," Eddie Durham explains, "was, the Kansas City riff always carried a melody that you could write a song from. All those riffs can be a song, like Lester Young with 'Symphony Sid.' That was a riff, but it made a melody. And some of the riffs that I heard up East, they didn't make good melodies."[4]

A riff was usually used to back up soloists during jam sessions, especially during a blues number, where it was repeated again and again while gradually adapting to changes in the chord sequence. This stimulates the soloist to give his very best, and at the same time gives the rhythm more drive and swing. Certain ear-catching riffs can form the basis of themes or arrangements, for example in Count Basie's "One O'Clock Jump" and "Swinging the Blues." Many of Lester's later compositions are also built up out of riffs, for example "Jumpin' with Symphony Sid," "Lester Leaps In," "Neenah," and "Lester's Mop Mop Blues."

The most important innovation, however, had to do with the basic rhythm. Until then jazz had had two stressed beats to a bar, normally the second and fourth beats, but gradually musicians began to give all four beats equal stress. This tendency can already be heard on records by Benny Moten's band in 1932, where Walter Page plays a walking bass. In Count Basie's band this flowing rhythm reached its highest point, thanks to the subtle playing that took place between Walter Page, Freddie Green, and Jo Jones. The rhythm section now came to function as a single unit, and this gave a sense of calm and control to the music, no matter what the tempo was. This in its turn gave maximum support to the various sections within the band and to the soloists. One of the consequences of the rhythm section playing in this way was that the soloist now could hang a tiny bit behind the beat, which gave the impression of relaxed playing, rather than almost having to pull the rhythm section along behind him by being ahead of the beat, as had been the practice up to that point.

Lester was one of the first musicians to use this relaxed style of playing. Another stylistic characteristic was that, by around 1933, he "had a very spacey sound," Ramey recalls. "In fact, I still kinda' try to play like that now. He would play a phrase and maybe lay out three beats before he'd come in with another phrase. You know, 'stead of a more continuous staying on style, like Bird would play, you know. He had kinda' loosened up."[5]

The first engagement Lester had in Kansas City was with the tenor player Clarence Love, who played in El Torreon Ballroom, one of the best dancing places for blacks in the city, on 31st Street. Love's band was both popular and highly regarded among other musicians because of its refined style of playing; even so, members had to be able to read music well, something Count Basie once found to his cost, for he was fired in 1932 for not being able to read music fast enough.

Around December 1, 1933, Clarence Love's band left Kansas City to go on tour down in Texas, but Lester stayed on and joined a new band which Benny Moten was forming, together with George E. Lee as co-leader. Bennie Moten had led one of the most popular bands in Kansas City for several years, but 1933 was a critical year for him too; while Lester was with Clarence Love, Moten had been forced to dissolve his band, because it had gotten stranded while on tour. Moten hoped that George E. Lee, who was a marvelous entertainer, would help him to regain his former popularity. The band got work at Club Harlem, in the same building as Paseo Hall on 15th Street, the largest dancing place in the city, with room for more than 3,000 guests.

In this band Lester was in the company of some of the best jazz musicians in Kansas City. This was the lineup: Joe Keyes, Oran "Hot Lips" Page and Dee Stewart (tp), Dan Minor (tb), Eddie Durham (tb/g), Tommy Douglas and Jack Washington (clt/as/bars), Lester (ts), Leroy Berry (g), Walter Page (b), Jo Jones (dr), and Jimmy Rushing (vcl).

During the first week of December Fletcher Henderson arrived in Kansas City with his famous band. Lester did not want to miss the opportunity of hearing Henderson's greatest soloist, the tenor player Coleman Hawkins, who had been a tremendous source of inspiration to many tenor saxophone players, Herschel Evans among them. "That was the time I first heard Coleman Hawkins," Lester recalls. "I'd always heard so much about Hawk—he was from St. Joseph, Missouri—and while I was working at the Paseo Club, Fletcher Henderson was in town. I ran over to dig him between sets; I hadn't any loot so I stayed outside listening. Herschel was out there, too."[6]

During his engagement Hawkins slipped home to St. Joseph one day to visit his family. "So when he went over there," Leonard Phillips relates,

Fletcher Henderson asked for a tenorplayer to play for him that night. Lester asked Herschel Evans: "Why don't you go and make it, Herschel?" "No, I can't make it, Red." Herschel couldn't read so good. In Kansas City they called Lester "Red." His mother was lightskinned and he was red. "Marine Red" that was what we called him, and after that we called him "Kentucky Red."

Lester said: "You scared to go, man?" "Yeah man, I'm scared to go!" Fletcher Henderson was a name in those days. Prez said: "I ain't scared, man!" and then he went and played that night.[7]

This description matches Lester's own pretty well:

I ran a million miles to hear Coleman Hawkins play and he wasn't there. So Fletcher Henderson ran out saying: "Don't you have no tenor players here in Kansas City? Can any of you motherfuckers play?" You know, that type of shit like that. Herschel was out there, you dig, but he couldn't read. So them motherfuckers just said: "Red"—they called me "Red" then, say: "Red, go and blow this goddam saxophone!" And I'm coming to see Coleman Hawkins, they told me how great he was, I ain't seeing the fuck how great he is, you know? That type of shit. So they showed me on in and I get up and grabbed his saxophone and played the motherfucker and read the music and read his clarinet parts and everything. Now I got to run back to my job where there's thirteen people in it. Run ten blocks back to get to them.[8]

Fletcher Henderson was deeply impressed by Lester's performance. It takes some doing to sit in with a strange band and sight-read the music, especially since Henderson wrote most of his own arrangements, many of them in difficult keys. Henderson's band then left Kansas City to travel all the way to Chicago, after which it moved south to play in Nashville, Tennessee, on December 13.[9] On its way north the band visited Kansas City once again (Jo Jones puts the date at December 18),[10] and on that occasion Coleman Hawkins and Lester met in a jam session that has gone into jazz history as the greatest of all time.

There are several reasons for this jam session having become so famous. First, it lasted a long time, until almost midday the following day, and that was unusual, even for Kansas City. Second, Hawkins met his match on the tenor saxophone for the first time. Third, it was a duel between two contrasting styles, where Lester's elegant, light, and relaxed way of playing won the day. Hawkins's style of playing was diametrically opposed to Lester's. He was only five years older than Lester but had been recording since 1921 and thus came to be immensely important for the role of the tenor saxophone in jazz, since he was the first man to free it from its role as a sort of circus instrument. In the decade from the mid-1920s to the mid-1930s his style was almost supreme, until Lester appeared on the scene. Among his most important pupils were Leon "Chu" Berry, Herschel Evans, Dick Wilson, and Joe Thomas.

Hawkins used fairly hard reeds and special mouthpieces with large openings, which enabled him to produce a large, round tone which was a match for the most penetrating of brass instruments. He used plenty of vibrato and, at the beginning of his career, a lot of staccato, which later gave way to a smoother style of playing. Even so, this later style was somewhat jagged because of his frequent use of dotted eighth notes. His pauses were few and short, almost nothing more than for taking breath, and this made his playing sound a bit breathless in faster numbers. Emotionally speaking, his solos could be called extrovert, almost to the point of sounding aggressive. They were made up of short phrases of two or four bars and always kept within the bar lines and the structure of the melody. He was one of the first men to improvise on the harmony scheme of the melody instead of on the theme itself; often he even used the harmonies with passing notes. He linked arpeggios in a refined way and used as many embellishments as possible when so doing. He was also taken up with different timbres and often played with a growl or overblowing the tenor sax to reach the harmonics, which lie outside the normal range of the instrument.

Opposed to this was Lester's new style of playing, a style which sounded revolutionary at first. His ideal sound was a light, thin tone, almost completely devoid of vibrato or intruding sounds and, compared with Hawkins, his tone was somewhat weak, partly because he used softer reeds, but also because he didn't blow all that hard or use growl or overtones. Another difference was that, as opposed to Hawkins, he carefully sought out tones from the harmonic foundation of the music for his considerably simpler melodic solos. Lester was also interested in timbre, but he made use of a whole series of alternative fingerings of his own invention to this end, fingerings later adopted by a host of other saxophone players. He used this technique frequently when repeating notes, changing the fingering for each repetition, thus keeping the same note but constantly changing the timbre. To take an example: A is normally played with the first and second finger of the left hand. By also closing the keys for the right hand's second, third, and fourth fingers you can also produce an A, but it has a more closed sound.

In the fall of 1933 Hawkins was at the height of his fame and influence, respected and admired, whereas Lester was just beginning to make a name for himself among musicians as a soloist with an inexhaustible range of ideas and formidable technical skill. Up to this point he had done no recordings, but had worked the entire Midwest and played with countless musicians in a whole host of after-hours sessions.

After the concert with Henderson on December 18, Hawkins went over to the Cherry Blossom. "Some people seem to think the Cherry Blossom was a ballroom," Gene Ramey relates, "but it was the old Eblon Theater turned into a huge nightclub. It was on Vine Street, between 18th and 19th, directly across the street from the Booker T. Washington Hotel, which had become the most popular one for musicians."[11] The furnishings were in Japanese style, with a large Buddha on the stage and waitresses dressed as Japanese. The piano player Mary Lou Williams used to play with Andy Kirk's Clouds of Joy at Pla-Mor Ballroom at that time, together with the tenor players Ben Webster and Dick Wilson, and she can clearly remember how Hawkins fared:

The word went round that Hawkins was in the Cherry Blossom, and within about half an hour there were Lester Young, Ben Webster, Herschel Evans, Herman Walder, and one or two unknown tenors piling in the club to blow.

Bean didn't know the Kaycee tenor men were so terrific, and he couldn't get himself together though he played all the morning. I happened to be nodding that night, and around four a.m., I awoke to hear someone pecking on my screen.

I opened the window on Ben Webster. He was saying, "Get up, pussycat, we're jammin' and all the pianists are tired out now. Hawkins has got his shirt off and is still blowing. You got to come down."

Sure enough, when we got there, Hawkins was in his singlet, taking turns with the Kaycee men. It seems he had run into something he didn't expect.

Lester's style was light, and, as I said, it took him maybe five choruses to warm up. But then he would really blow; then you couldn't handle him on a cutting session. That was how Hawkins got hung up. The Henderson band was playing in St. Louis that evening, and Bean knew he ought to be on the way. But he kept trying to blow something to beat Ben and Herschel and Lester. When at last he gave up, he got straight in his car and drove to St. Louis. I heard he'd just bought a new Cadillac and that he burnt it out trying to make the job on time. Yes, Hawkins was king until he met those crazy Kansas City tenor men.[12]

Gene Ramey was also present on that occasion and recalls: "I slipped away from school that night, and about four of us went over there. We'd heard about the sessions coming in, you know, so we got there. There was Ben, Herschel, Dick Wilson, and about three or four of the local tenors, and Hawk. And man, Hawk was cuttin' everybody out. But Prez got him. He tore Hawk up so bad, Hawk missed a date in St. Louis. Hawk was still trying to get him at 12 o'clock the next day. Seemed like the longer Prez played, the longer they had that head-cuttin' session, the better Prez got. He played more creative things.''[13] The news of Lester's victory over Hawkins traveled like wildfire and was the topic of conversation among musicians throughout the United States; it also paved the way for Lester's future engagement with Fletcher Henderson's band.

At the beginning of 1934 Lester and Herschel Evans exchanged jobs, Lester joining Count Basie and his Cherry Blossom Orchestra and Herschel going over to Bennie Moten and George E. Lee. Around March 1, 1934, Count Basie traveled down to Little Rock, Arkansas, to play at Sam Baker's Terrace Gardens for a couple of months. The lineup at that time was the following: Joe Keyes, Oran "Hot Lips" Page, and Dee Stewart (tp), Dan Minor (tb), Lester, Buster Smith, and Jack Washington (reeds), Basie (p), Cliff McTire (g), Walter Page (b), Jo Jones (dr), and Jimmy Rushing (vcl).[14]

During this engagement Lester took an unusual step to get into Fletcher Henderson's band. He knew perfectly well—just as many other musicians did—that Hawkins was going to leave Henderson, having been offered a job in England. Since he was full of self-confidence and eager to join a leading band, he now made use of his friendship with the trumpet player George Dixon.

The two had gotten to know each other during a jam session at the Subway in Kansas City a year previously, when Dixon came to town with the piano player Earl Hines's band. This band had its regular job at the Grand Terrace in Chicago, but in the early spring of 1934 it was touring the eastern states, and during the week of March 12–18 it was playing at the Lafayette Theater in New York. Dixon got the opportunity of helping Lester out in the course of that week, since he got to chatting with Fletcher Henderson at the Savoy Ballroom in the early hours one morning. Dixon asked Henderson: "How's everything?"

> "Terrible," he said.
> "What's wrong?"
> "You know Coleman Hawkins is leaving the band," he said.
> "Leaving?" I said. "Well, where's he going?"
> "To join the Jack Hylton Orchestra in London," Fletcher said. "In London, England."
> "I've got just the man for you," I said. "Read this letter."
> I had just received an airmail special delivery letter that day from Lester Young telling me that if I could find anything for him he would be willing to leave Kansas City, Missouri. We went right to the phone and I got Lester on the line to talk to Fletcher. Fletcher made arrangements for Lester to meet him in Detroit at the Greystone Hotel the following Saturday, March 31, 1934.[15]

Dixon's account sheds new light on this story, since Lester himself has kept quiet about his own part in the affair and has said only the following: "I went to Little Rock with Count Basie, and I got this telegram from Henderson saying: 'Come with me.' I was all excited, you know, about this big time shit. And I showed them the telegram. I said: 'What do you think I shall do, Count, about it?' He said: 'Ain't nothing I can do,' and I split and went to Detroit.''[16]

Dixon's account is definitely correct. Lester had enjoyed playing with Basie's band, but at the same time he was ambitious and eager to get to New York and be part of a nationally famous band, thus becoming better known himself and able to gain the recognition he deserved, for he was certainly in no doubt as to what he was worth. His mode of action here can be seen from two points of view: partly as a form of security and a receipt for what was his due, partly as an offer he could show Basie and his musical colleagues. It enabled him to quit without hurting their feelings, and this was definitely the most important thing for Lester at this point. Also, it made it possible to return without any loss of face if he failed. It cannot, however, have been easy for Lester to take the final decision. Buddy Tate, Jo Jones, and Dan Minor all remember how unsure Lester was about whether he was doing the right thing. Tate played with Nat Towles's band and had also arrived in Little Rock during these momentous days. He tells the following story:

He'd just received a telegram from Fletcher to join him in Detroit, but he was afraid to take the deal. We stayed up all night, drinking whiskey out of a fruit jar.

I talked to him, I said, "Pres—take it." He said, "I think I could make it, but I understand the band is full of cliques and I just don't know how they'll treat me." They'd just lost Coleman Hawkins, see, and they wanted a huge sound. I'd have been a better replacement, really.

Anyway, I said go ahead and take it because if you don't like it, you can always come back. He said, "Yes, but the part that hurts is to go and be a failure and come back and face your friends."

He left, and I took his chair with Basie's first band.[17]

Jo Jones recalls: "I had to put a pistol on Lester Young before he would go to join Fletcher's band, because he didn't want to go—no way! Imagine, we were in Little Rock and here he gets an offer for 75 dollars a week, plus a uniform. . . . If Basie had said, 'No, you can't go,' Lester would have stayed, I know that."[18] "I had to literally drag him onto that New York bus," Minor narrates. "There was no way he wanted to go, even though he was going to get 75 dollars a week and we were drawing 14 dollars."[19]

After Lester had finally decided to join Henderson, he didn't wait until March 31, but left Basie a week earlier, so that he could practice with the band in New York before the start of the tour. In all probability this was Henderson's idea, since the band had to audition for the management of the Cotton Club on Lenox Avenue in New York that very week. This was a prestige job which the band's booking agency, Mill's Artists Bureau, had been working for for a long time.

Lester didn't know anyone in New York he could stay with, so Henderson allowed him to move in with him on 139th Street in Harlem to start off. The trumpet player Jack Wilson replaced Bobby Stark in Henderson's band in February–March 1934 and recalls that he and Lester lived on the same floor and used to go out together in the evenings to various jam sessions.[20]

A couple of days after Lester arrived, the audition at the Cotton Club was to take place. It went badly, for the band in general and for Lester in particular, since his welcome from the members of the band was highly critical.[21] The other saxophone players had wanted to have Leon "Chu" Berry replace Hawkins, since his tone and style of playing were very close to Hawkins's own—so Lester's worst fears were justified. That wasn't all. To try to help Lester and get things going smoothly, Fletcher Henderson's wife, Leora, wanted to teach him to imitate Hawkins! "This bitch to Fletcher Henderson's wife would take me down to the basement to the old windup phonograph and ask me, 'Lester, can't you play like this?'—Coleman Hawkins things. Every morning that bitch would wake me up at nine o'clock to try to teach me to play like Coleman Hawkins. And she played trumpet herself—circus trumpet!"[22]

On the surface Lester was polite enough, but deep down he was really hurt by Leora's attitude and the saxophone players' rejection of him. Nobody could find fault with his musical genius, his skill as a soloist, or his ability to read music, but he just couldn't take anyone telling him how he ought to play. "I had in mind what I wanted to play," he has explained, "and I was going to play that way. That's the only time that ever happened, someone telling me to play differently from the way I wanted to."[23]

Those first days in New York also came to affect Lester in the longer term, both personally and musically. During a jam session he met the singer Billie Holiday, then scarcely nineteen years old, and she was to become one of his closest friends. They also swung together musically extremely well; Lester's feelings for her are beautifully expressed in his last interview: "When I first came to New York in '34 I used to live there for a long time. She was teaching me about the city, which way to go, you know, and everything. Yeah, she's still my Lady Day."[24]

Billie has told about their first meeting and about how indispensable they became to each other: "It was at one of these sessions I first met Lester Young. From then on Lester knew how I used to love to have him come around and blow pretty solos behind me. So whenever he could, he'd come by the joints where I was singing, to hear me or sit in."[25]

Despite Leora's and the saxophone players' treatment of him, Lester decided to stay with the band. He had the optimism of youth that things would turn out right in the end, coupled with a stubborn determination to prove to them all that he could make out. In the band he met the musicians Russell Smith, Joe Thomas (who replaced Jack Wilson), and Henry "Red" Allen (tp), Claude Jones and Keg Johnson (tb), Buster Bailey, Hilton Jefferson, and Russell Procope (reeds), Horace Henderson (p), Bernard Addison (g), Elmer James (b), and Walter Johnson (dr).

The band set off on March 31 on a six-week tour of one-nighters, which took it to Detroit, Columbus, Toledo, Chicago, Davenport, Des Moines, Omaha, St. Joseph, Kansas City, St. Louis, Evansville, Lexington, Huntington, West Virginia, Bluefield, West Virginia, Charlestown, Indiana, and Wheeling. During the tour Lester got some words of praise in a couple of newspaper articles in the *Chicago Defender* and the *New York Amsterdam News*: "Two new men have joined the Henderson band, Elmer James, bass player, and Lester Young of Kansas City, one of the most celebrated Negro tenor saxophone players in the music world."[26] After the tour the *Chicago Defender* carried the statement that "critics feel that both Fletcher Henderson and Coleman Hawkins have suffered because of their split. And that Lester Young, Hawkins' successor, is rated by many to be the equal of the old master."[27] John Hammond writes in *Melody Maker* that "Lester Young, Hawkins' successor, is a sensation, I am told. I haven't yet heard this redheaded star. Reports about him vary; no less than ten swell Harlemites have told me that he swings more than Hawkins, and has actually 'cut' the master on occasions. Mebbe so, although I find it hard to believe. There are others who find his 'tonation' not quite as satisfying. But about one thing there seems to be no disagreement: he is next to Hawkins as the best tenor man."[28]

As the band was so famous, its engagements were looked forward to by both critics and audiences during the tour. In Chicago Henderson played at the Savoy Ballroom on April 8, where the band also got involved in a battle of bands with Mill's Blue Rhythm Band. A report of the evening states the following: "While both Fletcher and Mill's Blue Rhythms lived up to expectations, 'twas the work of Millinder that kept the house packed from early evening until well past midnight. Then at the same time it was the playing of Fletcher Henderson's band that kept a number of musicians standing around the bandstands until almost morning. The musicians, and there were many from local bands who attended, seemed to prefer Fletcher's band, but the dancing public went hook, line and sinker for Millinder's antics and the Harlem strains of the band he led."[29]

In Kansas City Henderson played at the University of Kansas for a dancing public at the Union Ball Room. The student newspaper covered the event: "There was something in the jungle beat of Fletcher Henderson's rhythm that did things to our supposedly civilized university students at the Senior Cakewalk Friday evening. When Henderson offered the 'Call of the Wild,' only a restraining thread of Puritan decorum prevented many of the young men from dragging their partners out by the hair in the good, old cave-man fashion.''

''Although every number was roundly applauded,'' the review continued, ''the playing of 'I Got Rhythm' and the 'Carioca' won the warmest reception from the dancers. Probably the greatest compliment paid the orchestra was the way many of the Hill's musicians hung around the visiting organization with the wide-eyed admiration of the small boy meeting the President.''[30]

Henderson's musicians could manage less than a week's break in New York before they were off on tour again to, among other venues, Philadelphia. After this the band returned to New York, where they played at the Apollo Theater in Harlem in the week of June 1–7. The guitar player Bernard Addison left the band at that point and had been replaced by Lawrence Lucie. There is also a review from the Apollo engagement: ''Fletcher Henderson and his boys play hot jazz with a refined quality about it and the maestro himself, modest and unassuming, is so friendly and gentlemanly that you want to like what he has to offer. Not playing for Harlem shows all the time they were a trifle behind pace in occasional numbers. Charles Holland has a sweet crooning voice and the audience liked the entire setup.''[31]

At this point the band planned to take up its engagement at the Cotton Club, but the management got cold feet at the last moment, since it did not feel sure that the band played in the right kind of nightclub style for its white audience, and withdrew its contract. Lester was thus forced to tour with the band once more, until the end of June, when the musicians returned to New York for a rest before a job planned for the Lafayette Theater starting on July 7. Nothing came of this engagement either and, as Henderson had been so imprudent as to terminate his contract with Mill's Artists Bureau, no immediate jobs were forthcoming.

Lester had felt pretty lonesome in the band all this time. Henderson was the only man who respected his style of playing and could see his potential; the others complained about the size of his tone and said that he was almost swallowed up by the rest of the reed section. Since he also had to put up with jibes and sarcastic remarks about his playing, it finally became too much for him. The drummer Jo Jones was one of those who got to know Lester best, and he says that Lester ''was too tender, he was too tender. He just didn't like to see nobody, not one human being mistreat another human being. He was very sensitive.''[32]

This trait in Lester always led him to avoid cliques, and since this was a case of being excluded from such cliques, he made use of the band's unfortunate plight at this point as a godgiven excuse to quit. ''I wasn't happy with all the motherfuckers whispering on me every time I was playing," he once said. "I wanted to split, so I went to Fletcher and I said, 'Will you give me a nice recommendation? I go back to Kansas City.' And he says, 'Oh, yeah!' right quick. 'Thank you' and I went to Andy Kirk's band and had a nice time."[33]

Lester certainly did not know about the details surrounding his departure. He himself seemed a bit surprised at the speed Henderson accepted his suggestion, but Henderson was in fact on the point of firing him. Shortly before he had been talking to Andy Kirk over the phone and had complained about how badly Lester fitted in with the band. Even though he liked Lester personally, he too preferred a large, round tenor tone, which would have allowed the band to settle down. Henderson and Andy Kirk agreed on an exchange—Kirk got Lester and Henderson got Ben Webster.[34]

Lester's departure can be fixed at mid-July 1934, thanks to a couple of articles by John Hammond, the first dated New York, July 13, 1934: "Fletcher has brought back his marvelous new second trumpet, Irving 'Mouse' Randolph, and during the latter part of the week there'll be a new tenor man."[35] A month later he writes: "Fletcher now has a new tenor saxophonist, Lester Young having returned to the Andy Kirk band in Kansas City. This new saxophonist is Ben Webster, and I hold him in very high esteem. Beautiful tone and good musicianship. There is still only one Hawkins, however."[36]

Before releasing Lester, Henderson called together all the members of the band and told them this: "It looks like I'm going to have to let this boy go because he'll never have any peace staying here with you. But before I do, I want to tell you this. He can outplay you, you, and you. And you're going to hear about him."[37]

Lester's stay with Henderson was so badly timed that he missed a recording session on March 6, 1934. Apart from this, a group of Henderson musicians under the name of Henry "Red" Allen made a series of records on May 1 and July 28, 1934, but by the latter date Lester had certainly left New York. Even so, Lester might have made his first recordings about this time. This is evident from Tom Lord's book on the piano player Clarence Williams, where he suggests Lester as one of the two unknown alto players who took part in a session on June 28, 1934, recording "Tell the Truth" and "Sashay, Oh Boy!" This date ties in with the week Henderson's band was back in New York and was waiting for its engagement at the Lafayette Theater. Williams himself said in 1950 that he made use of Lester for a single recording, but unfortunately nothing can be proved, because the only saxophone sole—on "Sashay, Oh Boy!"—is by Cecil Scott.[38]

Shortly afterwards Lester traveled to Kansas City to join the most popular band in the Southwest. Andy Kirk's Clouds of Joy was based in

Kansas City, so Lester came back to musicians he already knew. The piano player in the band was Mary Lou Williams, who was also a gifted composer and arranger. She remembers this about Lester's stay: "When Ben Webster left Andy Kirk, Lester Young joined us in Kansas City, but he didn't stay with us very long. We missed Ben Webster on account of sound but Lester was more free and whatnot in solos to play a hundred solos and never repeat. Ben Webster was the type of guy that could put so much in one bar. If you played with him he could do so much with one bar than any other man could do. Lester would play twelve or fifteen choruses and each of them would sound different."[39]

Precisely the same thing happened with Kirk that had happened with Henderson—Lester's sound didn't fit in with the band's, so he was fired after a short time, toward the end of the summer. Curiously, enough, Buddy Tate, who had replaced Lester in Count Basie's Cherry Blossoms, also replaced Lester in the Clouds of Joy, since Basie's band had been dissolved in the meantime.

Lester now decided to leave Kansas City after all the personal and professional setbacks he had been up against; he left for Minneapolis, where he hoped to make a fresh start. Here he joined the trumpet player Rook Ganz's band in October; in November he got work at the Cotton Club in the saxophone player Boyd Atkins's band, where Ganz also played trumpet. He stayed in Minneapolis for almost six months, after which he returned to Kansas City once more, where he kept body and soul together by playing when possible at the Sunset Club and the Subway. There was keen competition between musicians, with only a few loose jobs going; Lester could play just about enough to make ends meet. "Life in K.C. in them days was hard, man," he recalls. "We were all scufflin' like mad. Saturday and Sunday we'd get a gig or two, but Monday, Tuesday, Wednesday, Thursday, Friday there was nothing' much to be had."[40]

Even though he had no permanent job, he went out playing as often as possible so as to improve even further, especially to the Subway, where he arrived early in the evening and could reckon on getting a free meal. Leonard Phillips recalls that "he also stretched out at the Subway in Kansas City when nobody played but him down there until the cats came in. Everybody would come in after their job, but he would have been there since about 9 o'clock, and they started coming in at 1 or 2. He said that that's why he learned how to play a whole lot of different solos."[41]

In April 1935 he got a steady job, since he joined a band at the Yellow Front Saloon which included Jo Jones on drums, Eddie Durham on guitar, and George Hunt on trombone. The same spring the sax player Budd Johnson was also working in Kansas City, and he can distinctly remember Lester and himself going round the town to the various jam sessions:

"Pres used to come and get me, wake me out of a deep sleep, pour whiskey down my throat, and say, 'Get up! So-and-so just came into town, and he's over there blowing. Let's go get him!' One guy in particular I remember—Georgie Auld. Pres said, 'Let's put him in the middle. You get on one side, and I'm going to be on the other, and we're going to blow him out of the joint!' That was Kansas City for you."[42]

Leonard Phillips passed through Kansas City at this time and he recalls: "I heard Budd Johnson jam with Prez when he came to Kansas City. In some kind Budd was a better musician than Prez, musically. I don't mean playing, because he could arrange and all that. Prez was a more technical player, he was playing changes by ear. He didn't know what the hell it was until later when he got with Basie. He'd know what they were, but he didn't know the names of them."

"At that time you didn't see no chord changes on the music," he explains, "With Basie he would learn the names of them and all that. Buck Clayton would play them and tell him what he was playing, and the Count was learning him too. Lester told me later on how he learned the names of the chord changes. He said: 'I've been playing this stuff all the time, but I didn't know the names. I've been playin' it all the times.'"[43]

In May Earl Hines's band came to Kansas City to play at the Main Street Theater. Shortly before, their tenor player, Cecil Irwin, had been killed in a traffic accident, so Lester was called for an audition to see whether he fitted in with the band. Among other numbers they played "Tiger Rag," and Charlie Carpenter, who later became Lester's manager, was there. He recalls that Lester must have made a great impression on the musicians, since they listened to him intensely while he improvised one chorus after another. Afterwards Lester and Earl Hines went off on their own and talked for fifteen to twenty minutes.[44] Unfortunately, Lester didn't get the job; Budd Johnson did. Shortly afterwards, when the job at the Yellow Front Saloon expired, Lester moved once more to Minneapolis.

4
With Count Basie
(1936–1940)

In all probability Lester's prime reason for returning to Minneapolis was the chance of getting a steady job; even so, a positive factor must certainly have been that he returned to well-known, secure surroundings after a period of disappointments and setbacks. He was reemployed at the Cotton Club in Rook Ganz's band, which had Jo Jones as drummer and Adolphus Alsbrook on bass.

When he had finished work he used to listen to the radio; one evening he picked up a broadcast from the Reno Club in Kansas City that made him prick up his ears. It was a program with Count Basie and His Barons of Rhythm, and it sounded so good that Lester felt like joining the band. The band consisted of the trumpet players Joe Keyes and Carl "Tatti" Smith, Buster Smith—called "Prof"—on alto sax and clarinet, Slim Freeman on tenor sax and Jack Washington on alto and baritone sax, Clifford McTier on guitar, Walter Page on bass, Basie on piano, and Jesse Price on drums. Lester didn't care for Freeman's style and sent a telegram to Basie, suggesting that Basie hire him as a first tenor sax. Basie was somewhat surprised to begin with, but he accepted, since he already knew Lester, though he too had needed time to get used to Lester's style of playing. "I'll always remember when I first heard Lester," Basic recalls. "I'd never heard anyone like him before. He was a stylist with a different sound. A sound I'd never heard before or since. To be honest with you I didn't like it much at first."[1]

"So I joined Basie," Lester explains. "It was very nice. Just like I thought it was going to be."[2] Adolphus Alsbrook recalls that Lester left Minneapolis on February 2 or 3, 1936, to go to Kansas City,[3] and Basie soon became pleased with him, since he fitted into the band well. "When

Lester came in there on tenor," he recalls, "I figured I had just about
what I needed for what we were doing in the Reno. We didn't have very
much room on that bandstand anyway. But what I also mean is that I
had a hell of a reed section. With Lester in there with Prof and Jack
Washington we were cooking with gas, lots of gas. We all liked to hear
Lester play. As for his tone, truthfully, I never did really think about it.
I mean, I didn't think there was anything odd about it or anything like
that. I knew it was special, but everything he did was special. I just liked
the sound he got on his horn. It sounded right for what I wanted in
there. It just sounded natural to me."[4]

The hours at the Reno Club were long. The band played every day
from 9 P.M. to 5 A.M., an hour's floor show at 9 P.M., 12 midnight, 2
A.M., and 4 A.M., as well as dance numbers in the in-between periods.
The bandstand in the Reno was not very large, since it had originally
been designed for six players, so Basie had to move down to the floor if
the Barons of Rhythm wanted to play, while Walter Page had to have a
hole made in the huge mussel-shell which went across the stage, so as
to have room for his bass at the very back of the bandstand, with the
fingerboard sticking up through it.

On Sunday nights the musicians got together for the so-called spook-
breakfast, which was a popular part of the Kansas City musicians' social
life. "Anybody who'd stay up all night we called spooks or ghosts,"
Gene Ramey explains.[5] At these spook-breakfasts a hard week's work
was rounded off by a pleasant get-together, where a meal was naturally
enough followed up by another jam session.

Without including spook-breakfasts, a week's work was well over sixty
hours; for this Basie was paid $21 and the other musicians $18—not
much, if you consider that Lester was getting $75 with Henderson, and
that was a black band, which would get only about half as much as a
white band of corresponding quality would earn.

In Lester the Barons of Rhythm gained a powerful soloist; at about
the same time Oran "Hot Lips" Page also appeared for a short time as
specially featured trumpet player and singer. Jo Jones didn't come down
to Minneapolis to be the band's drummer until during the summer, and
McTier left the band some time during the spring to join another big
band.

In this band Lester found his proper niche for the first time in his
career. His style fitted in well and his sound blended perfectly with Buster
Smith's alto sax, since he too preferred a light tone. The band played
with direct enthusiasm, spontaneity, and a relaxed group feeling, which
resulted from their having known each other from previous bands, such
as the Original Blue Devils or the Bennie Moten band. For the most part
the repertoire consisted of head arrangements, which often came into

being in the course of a single evening, or of arrangements by Buster Smith.

The band quickly gained a fine reputation, not only among the inhabitants of Kansas City, but also farther afield, since there was a radio transmission every evening from the Reno Club. Buster Smith has his own explanation as to why the band had such good public appeal: "The thing that knocked everybody out about the band was that we played things different every night. They would hear us play a tune one night and the next night we might play the same tune entirely different."[6]

That spring something important happened for the band: John Hammond heard them by chance on the radio. He was a great Benny Goodman fan and had followed the band to Chicago. During a break he had gone out to his car to listen to the radio. He happened to pick up Kansas City, and over his speaker came the sounds of Count Basie's band. He became pretty enthusiastic about the sound and fetched Goodman out to listen to it. He wrote that Basie

can adapt himself to any style, sounding alternately like Basie, Wilson, Waller, Hines, and swinging all the time. Benny Goodman, it may interest Basie to know, thinks that he has the most powerful drive of any band in the country, judging from his nightly performances over W9XBY (Kansas City, 1550 kilocycles). . . .

I almost forgot to say that Lester Young's tenor playing in Basie's orchestra is so good that it seems impossible that it was the same guy who took Hawkins's place in Fletcher's band two years ago and failed to distinguish himself.[7]

* * *

I soon found out that the band was on the air every night from 1 to 1.30, and managed to leave Goodman a bit early so that I could tune in my car radio and be ravished by the Basie sounds. Lester's solos had a cohesion and architecture that were unique in my musical experience, and I realized that much of his inspiration came not only from the rhythm section but from the background riffs which always sounded fresh and improvised. Unlike the New York experience, Lester was speaking a language common to everyone else in the band, and this was the secret of his authority and invention.[8]

* * *

I was overwhelmed. This band was so different from all the others which could be heard in the U.S.A.! It had everything: magnificently relaxed rhythm, exciting scores—all head arrangements, since funds didn't run to written ones; and what a collection of soloists! The climax was on Saturdays. The band played from eight in the evening till eight in the morning, backing three shows which included Jimmy Rushing and Hattie Noel, a marvelous singer and comedian; above all, it played for dancing, with the highspot being the "spook dance."[9]

Basie's band had changed lineup slightly at this point, as can be seen from an article in *Down Beat* in July 1936: Joe Keyes, Dee Stewart, Carl

"Tatti" Smith (tp), Buster Smith, Lester, Slim Freeman and Jack Washington (reeds), George Hunt (tb), Walter Page (b), Cliff McTier (g), Mack Washington (dr), Basie (p), and Alice Dickson and Jimmy Rushing (vcl).[10]

Hammond listened as often as he could to Basie's band over the radio and wrote enthusiastic reviews, such as this one in *Down Beat:*

I want to say categorically and without fear of ridicule that Count Bill Basie has by far and away the finest dance orchestra in the country. And when I say this, I am fully aware of Benny Goodman, Fletcher Henderson, and Chick Webb.

Basie is the only one who can compare with the original Fletcher Henderson orchestra. He has excellent soloists, although not quite comparable to Hawkins, and Red Allen at his best, and a driving rhythm section more exciting than any in American orchestral history. Like Fletcher, Basie excels in writing rhythmic figures which send the soloists to new heights every night. The arrangements are sometimes complicated, but the band always plays with that supreme freedom that one associates with Kansas City.[11]

At the same time he began to persuade Willard Alexander from Benny Goodman's booking company, Music Corporation of America (MCA), to sign a contract with Basie, so that the band could travel east; also, without Basie's knowledge, he was engaged in negotiations with the American Record Company for a favorable contract for Basie. Meanwhile, his rave reviews of the band had made others begin to get similar ideas, and when he eventually managed to get down to Kansas City in July 1936 with a contract in his hand, it was only to discover that Dave Kapp from Decca had gotten there first and secured a contract with Basie. Hammond was furious, not only that Kapp had gotten there first, but also because the contract was distinctly harsh. Basie had committed himself over a three-year period to record twenty-four sides for a single $750 payment, without getting so much as a cent for royalties or a percentage of sales—and without any hope of breaking his contract. Hammond did manage to get the conditions watered down, however, for he later went to the musicians' federation in New York and complained about the way Decca had treated Basie, since $750 was less than half that normally paid for a contract of the type Basie had agreed to; Decca agreed to pay the federation's minimum amount. There was no shaking the conditions concerning royalties and percentage of sales, however, something Basie must have come to rue many times later on, since the band's hit numbers—such as "One O'clock Jump" and "Swinging the Blues"—brought in nothing at all for him or his musicians.

Basie fell for Kapp's contract first and foremost because the offer of recordings also included free transport to Chicago, where the nearest studio was situated. "I never will forget what Lester said when I took him aside and told him about that," Basie relates.

I think I must have passed the word on to the other fellows before Lester got to the Reno that night. So when he came in, I called him over, got us a couple of nips, and we went and stood outside the doorway to the back alley, where we usually went when we wanted to have a little private sip and a little personal chat.

"Well," I said, "I got some great news. I think we'll take a Pullman into Chicago and do some recording for Decca."

And all he did was just sort of stand there looking into space like he hadn't heard what I said because he was listening to something else or thinking about something else. Then he looked at me again.

"What did I hear you say? Did I hear you?"

"Yes," I said. "We're going to Chicago to make some records for Decca."

And he just stood there and looked at me and looked away and then looked at me again. Then he went into his sweet-talking thing.

"Listen, Lady B, you all right?"

"Oh yes," I said. "Everything's okay. I got me this contract with Decca."

And he just stood there nodding his head, thinking about it, and then the next thing he said was like he was talking to himself.

"Well, okay. So now we'll find out what happens."

Then he finished his shot and looked at me and mumbled and went back into his sweet-jive thing again.

"Hey, look. I tell you what, Lady B. Let's go back in there and get us another little taste, and maybe you'll tell me that again." [12]

Hammond's first visit to Kansas City did not turn out as he had planned, but musically speaking it was an overwhelming experience for him, one where Lester impressed him even more "live" than he had done over the radio. "The second evening," Hammond narrates,

I ended up in a joint on 18th Street where another boogie woogie pianist was playing, Clarence Johnson. I must have been about eight in the morning and Lester Young was there, in marvelous form, piling chorus upon chorus.

One of his most characteristic traits was his passion for playing. Music seemed to be his only stimulus, his sole reason for living. If he wasn't playing, he enjoyed listening to his fellow musicians, as if to enrich himself with their discoveries. But outside music Lester lapsed into indifference, as if the vital spark had left his body to seek refuge in a dream which left him untouched by the trivia of this world. . . . But when he played all this was forgotten. He would launch himself headlong into improvisations which with each new chorus renewed themselves as if by magic; it was as though his energy and originality knew no bounds. Lester could improvise on the same theme for an hour at a stretch, without once giving the impression that he might be running short of ideas. And there was not the slightest touch of exhibitionism about it. His features evinced not the slightest emotion and his whole being was concentrated in the music. [13]

When Hammond was in Kansas City, Slim Freeman had left the band, so that there were only ten men, something which surprised him.

Hearing Count Basie's band is an experience I will never forget. The stage was all set for a complete disillusionment, for I had been plugging the band only from its radio work, sight unseen. I was almost scared to go near it, lest I might have to retract some of the raves I have been scattering about. But after spending only one night in the place I came away convinced that the band has the makings of the finest the country has ever known (it isn't so far from that state right now).

The first thing that flabbergasted me was the realization that all the music I had been hearing over W9XBY every night was from a mere ten piece group: three rhythm, three saxes, four brass. The voicing of the arrangements is so deft that the band had sounded at least like a five brass four reed combination. . . .

Outstanding in the reeds, of course, is Lester Young, who would be an asset to any band in the country on tenor. He is the kind of guy who just likes to make music, with the result that he is always to be found in some unlikely joint.[14]

It is incredibly difficult to start by playing for eight hours and then go on to play in jam sessions for a further five or six hours. One way of overcoming the fatigue involved is to smoke marijuana, something which practically all the Kansas City musicians did—as did many musicians in general. Lester had learned to smoke from Budd Johnson and used it daily for the rest of his life.

One of the conditions of Decca's contract was that Basie expand his band to fifteen players. In the summer of 1936 the first important pair of musicians arrived: the trumpet player Buck Clayton and the tenor sax player Herschel Evans, who had played together in Buck's band in Los Angeles, but who were now on their way to New York to become members of Willie Bryant's band. Clayton's original idea was to stay in Kansas City for just a few days to visit his mother, but on Hot Lips Page's recommendation he was hired by Basie.[15]

When Buck was engaged to play in Basie's band, he already knew something about them: "When we were in California, Herschel used to call up the band. He used to call up Reno long distance and tell whoever answered the 'phone, whoever he'd be talking to and it might have been a girl, but anyway, he could hear the band playing, and he'd say, Buck come here. And I'd listen. I'd listen on the 'phone, to these guys and I'd say, damn, boy those guys are sure swinging, which they were."

"And then Herschel had worked with them before," he adds, "and he'd tell me all about them, he'd worked with them when Basie was playing with Bennie Moten at different times. And he told me all about Lester. He told me all about Jo Jones. All about Page, Lips, Basie."[16]

Basie knew Herschel and wanted to have him in the band, because he liked tenor players who could play solos and Herschel was one of the Hawkins-influenced sax players who was most personal in his playing. Before inviting Herschel, however, Basie asked Lester if he minded his joining the band. When Lester said he didn't, this began Basie's tradition of having two tenor soloists in the band.

About August Basie decided to take the band out of the Reno Club on tour, so it really could learn to play together. The tour was arranged by Maceo Birch, the most proficient booking agent in Kansas City, and the band mainly toured Oklahoma, Kansas, and Nebraska. After the tour the band had no fixed job during the months of September and October, but had a deal with the local musicians' federation to play during the breaks, or eventually as first band, when outside bands came to Kansas City.

Unluckily for Basie, Buster Smith left the band shortly after Hot Lips Page had left for New York. Smith did not really believe in all the talk about moving east, so he accepted an offer to play with Claude Hopkins. It was difficult to find a proper replacement for him, but Buck Clayton had played with an alto sax player by the name of Caughey Roberts, whom he could recommend and who now lived in Los Angeles.

About this time, the beginning of September 1936, Lester received the news that his father had had a heart attack and was lying at home seriously ill in Los Angeles. He asked for a few days' leave, and Basie was generous enough to lend him his car—a Buick—which Maceo Birch drove, as Lester didn't have a driver's license. The idea was that Lester could take Caughey Roberts back with him from Los Angeles. On his way to California he passed through Albuquerque, where John Lewis met him and heard him play. "We had a lot of brass beds in that part of the country," he recalls, "and Lester used to hang his tenor saxophone on the foot of his bed so that he could reach it during the night if an idea came to him that he wanted to sound out."[17]

In Los Angeles Lester saw his family for the first time since 1929. He arrived in town in the middle of the night and drove straight to his parents' house. Lee remembers:

I was asleep upstairs, and my mother brought him upstairs, and she said to me, you know, Lester had a very high voice, you know, and my mother said, she touched me and woke me up and said, "Lee, do you know who this is?" And I looked up, and I said, "No, who is it?" And she said, "This is Lester!" And Lester looked at me and he said, "Oh, look at how big he is!" I said, "Listen to his voice. He sounds like a girl!" That's what I woke up saying.

He stayed about ten days I think, and he brought a dog with him, I think—you know, he loved dogs. He always had a dog, but he always gave them the darndest names. This dog he had, it was a Belgian police dog, all black, and his name was Tonics, you know, because he used to have a musical saying, "Get your tonics together," so he named this dog Tonics.

He left the dog here with me, and when he was here, that's when I was saying our voices were so similar, even though I was trying to make fun of him. I didn't realize that my voice has the same timbre as his. The dog would think I was Lester a lot of times, so he left the dog with me, and this dog tore up three suits and shirts, and I took the dog out, which is Watts now, but there was nothing out there years and years ago; there was nothing out there but trees and all that, and I took the dog out there and let him loose, even though I loved dogs, I let him out of the car, and we never did see Tonics since.[18]

Fortunately, his father recovered and was soon able to give music lessons again, as well as going to work at the Musicians Union. Lester didn't miss the opportunity of dipping into Los Angeles's musical life, and his participation in several jam sessions made such a deep impression that he was mentioned in the local press.

When he came back to Kansas City with Caughey Roberts, Basie slipped off to Chicago. During his trip, Basie made a deal with a pair of musicians. The violin and guitar player Claude Williams was to join the band when it reached Chicago, and the trombone player Dan Minor, who played in St. Louis with Jeter-Pillars, was to come to Kansas City as quickly as possible.

Basie's replacement in the band while he was in Chicago was Margaret Johnson, who was only seventeen years old. She played with a powerful style, reminiscent of a mixture between Earl Hines and Basie, and she and Lester soon became inseparable. "He was crazy about her," Gene Ramey recalls,[19] and "she fell in love with Lester from the first note he played before her."[20] Their relationship lasted only for a short time, however, since Basie's contract with the Grand Terrace was settled. This meant that Willard Alexander could book in the band's tour from November 1, 1936, a tour which was to take them all the way to New York around Christmas time.

At some point in the fall, Lester was once more in New York for a short while. This can be seen from Louie Metcalf's reminiscences, for he recalls: "In the fall of 1936 I was back again in New York City at my Renaissance Casino headquarters. I put together a show and a band and I opened my own operation at the Bedford Ballroom in Brooklyn, New York. Billie Holiday and Orlando Robeson were my vocalists. 'Snakes Hip' Tucker was the dancer. The band were Hot Lips Page, trumpet; Lester Young, Rudy Powell, Happy Caldwell, reeds; Jonas Walker, trombone; Billy Taylor, bass; Clarence Holiday, guitar; Alfred Taylor, drums and Louie Metcalf, trumpet and leader."[21]

According to the *New York Amsterdam News,* Metcalf was at the Renaissance Casino, 138th Street and 7th Avenue, on October 4, and on Sunday, November 1, his band played together with Kenny Watts and His Kilowatts at "the grand opening of the Bedford Ballroom, 1153 Atlantic Avenue, Brooklyn, N.Y.," as well as playing dance music there on the following Sundays.[22] According to the advertisement, Billie Holiday was featured, along with Valda Hatten, Orlando Robeson, and Ethel Fray. Lester was able to play with Metcalf only during the month of October at the Renaissance Casino, since he had to be back in Kansas City at the end of the month. The insecure working conditions the Basie band had prior to leaving for Chicago were his reasons for coming to New York, and he was doubtless recommended to Metcalf by Hop Lips Page, who certainly didn't omit to tell Lester that Billie was working there at the time. Without knowing it, she acted as bait for Lester, who had a tremendously high opinion of her after getting to know her in 1934.

Halloween Night—Saturday, October 31—was Basie's last night in Kansas City, and this was celebrated by a large ball in the Paseo Hall itself.[23] In fact, it was the last evening but one, since the band was used as a warm-up for Duke Ellington's famous band on the following Monday. This should not be seen as a battle of bands in any way, for as soon as Basie and his musicians had finished their act, they packed their instruments and left by bus, so as to reach Chicago as quickly as possible.[24]

Just as they were about to leave, there was near-panic, for Walter Page's wife wanted her husband to stay home. Jo Jones recalls: "We begged his wife, 'Let him come for a month and we'll send him back.' We wasn't leaving Kansas City without Walter Page."[25] Fortunately, Page finally went with them, and it was in part thanks to him that the Basie band's rhythm section was later considered one of the best in the history of jazz.

At the time of their departure, Basie and his Fourteen Barons of Rhythm had the following lineup: Joe Keyes, Buck Clayton and Carl "Tatti" Smith (tp), Dan Minor and George Hunt (tb), Caughey Roberts, Lester, Herschel Evans, and Jack Washington (reeds), Walter Page (b), Basie (p), Jo Jones (dr), and Jimmy Rushing (vcl). They were replaced at the Reno Club, by the way, by Margaret Johnson, who had filled in so convincingly for Basie that the management chose her to play there with her own band.

The engagement at the Grand Terrace was due to start on November 6, and the band arrived in Chicago three days early to begin rehearsals. Most of what they played at such engagements, where there was both entertainment and dancing, was not jazz at all. During the show, when the band was to accompany soloists and many other types of artists, they could be called upon to play anything from tangos, waltzes, and extracts from classical music to popular melodies of the time. Only after the show was over and the dancing began was the band able to get into its stride and show off its own repertoire.

The Grand Terrace, on 3955 South Parkway, had a very beautiful locale. At the back was the bar, and the walls were all clad with mirrors, punctuated with small blue lamps. In the evening, when the lights were

on, the room looked rather like a star-studded night sky. As at the Reno
Club, the band was to perform daily, with three shows every evening
from 9.30 P.M. to 3.30 A.M., and four on Saturdays, from 10 P.M. to 5
A.M.

Basie's band had replaced the illustrious Fletcher Henderson's, which
had been playing there since May 16, and it was not mature enough to
cope with such an engagement, as the first afternoon rehearsal revealed.
"They had us playing 'The Poet and Peasant Overture' as our big show
number," Basie recalls. "The band just didn't make it, and there was
nothing in the show that gave us a real chance to display ourselves properly." [26]

One of the reasons for the fiasco was that several of the musicians
could not read music well enough. Ed Fox, owner of the Grand Terrace,
first wanted to fire the band. Most of the musicians also wanted to quit
the job, but the chorus girls were mad about the rhythm section and
managed on the same day to convince Fox to keep the band, while Alexander tried to convince the musicians to change their minds. Henderson
also helped by generously offering to leave behind some of his repertoire
of popular melodies for Basie to use, since the band had been refused
permission to play its own numbers on the radio broadcast "Coast to
Coast." The reason for this was that the band's repertoire consisted
almost exclusively of its own compositions, which were almost completely unknown to the public outside Kansas City.

After intensive rehearsing, Basie managed to carry out the month-long
engagement, but it was scarcely an unqualified success, since the audience didn't really relish the band's style. "That was the worst engagement I think that we ever had," says Buck Clayton. "We could play
dance music, but when it came to reading parts, that's when we found
out we had these guys in the band that couldn't read." [27]

Moreover, the music made it necessary to concentrate too much on
reading notes; this interfered with the band's relaxed style of play and
resulted in unequal performances. John Hammond visited the Grand
Terrace and wrote "that the band had its ups and downs. On one Saturday night, when Red Norvo, Mildred Bailey and I arrived, the band
played music the likes of which I have never before heard. Unbelievably
subtle and soft, the band had more power than any I've come across,
and that includes the old Fletcher Henderson group. The solos from Lester
Young, Buck Clayton, Basie, and the work of the rhythm section as a
whole had an indescribable effect on me—and I was cold sober. The
next night, however, the band was ragged and loud; I suspect that there
must have been the same variations in quality throughout the engagement." [28]

Other reasons for the band's lackluster performance were the poor
quality of many of the musicians' instruments and the fact that basic

blowing technique and instruction had been neglected in many cases. The leading trumpet player, Joe Keyes, was a typical example of this. "He was a very good musician," Buck Clayton recalls. "Very good trumpet player. But he always played a bad horn. He never did have a good trumpet. He always played a little bit out of tune. But they weren't concentrating on being in tune, they were concentrating on swinging. And Joe Keyes was a good swinging first trumpet player except for that. If he had a good horn it might have been a different thing. But he had a horn that had rubbers all around it."[29]

A review of the band that appeared in *Metronome* should be read in the light of the above description of the band's instruments. George T. Simon wrote the following harsh—but doubtless true—words about Basie's band in Chicago: "True, the band does swing, and it's only been caught on the air where 'tis said, copyright restrictions don't allow [it] to play some of its best tunes. But that sax section is so invariably out of tune. And if you think that sax section sounds out of tune, catch the brass! And if you think the brass by itself is out of tune, catch the intonation of the band as a whole!! Swing is swing, but music is music, too. Here's hoping the outfit sounds better in person."[30] Basie was very mad about this review at first, but later on he used to quote it with a self-ironic smile on his lips. It led indirectly to a series of sensible changes whereby the band gradually came to consist of competent musicians throughout.

While Hammond was in Chicago, he made use of the opportunity to get a small group of Basie's musicians on record before the band came to New York to begin its recordings for Decca. On the raw autumn morning of November 9, 1936,[31] Count Basie, Walter Page, Jo Jones, Jimmy Rushing, Lester, and Carl "Tatti" Smith met with Hammond at the Café DeLisa to plan the recording in detail. The original idea was to have Buck Clayton as trumpet player, but their tough program, with long rehearsals in the afternoons and performances in the evenings, had temporarily ruined his lips. For reasons of contract, Basie's name was not allowed to appear on the records, so the group called itself "Jones-Smith Incorporated," since these two had the commonest surnames.

"The group was so pleased with the first playback that there was never a breakdown," Hammond recalls. "I made two or three versions of each of the four tunes we could record in our three-hour period, although each was cut without interruption, each a flawless performance. By one o'clock the date was over, and the band on its way to bed. It was an intimate, exhilarating experience for us all, leaving that studio bushed—as we used to say—yet knowing we had four little jazz masterpieces."[32]

There is a freshness and timelessness about these recordings that makes them just as exciting to listen to today as the day they were first recorded. This is due not only to the way in which the rhythm section functions, but to a great extent to Lester's playing. Here he reveals himself as a full-blown, mature musician devoid of any signs of nervousness or reserve. "Lady Be Good," "Shoe Shine Boy," "Boogie Woogie," and "Evenin' " have all become classics, and if you leave out the recordings with Clarence Williams, where Lester is buried in the saxophone section, then you have to agree with Jan Evensmo that "this recording debut is probably the best ever made by any jazz musician."[33]

In Chicago Lester reestablished links with the trumpet player Roy Eldridge, whom he had first met in Baltimore in 1934 when he came to town with Fletcher Henderson. At that time Eldridge played with McKinney's Cotton Pickers, but he now had his own band at Sam Beer's Three Deuces on North State Street.[34] Eldridge was just as hooked on playing as Lester was and, after working hours were over, he drove over to the Grand Terrace. "He loved to jam," Eldridge remembers about Lester. "When the Basie band would play the Grand Terrace in Chicago in the late thirties, I'd pick up Lester and Jo Jones every night after work and we'd play until way into the daytime. We'd go to DeLisa or to Martin's Chicken Sack or to Martin's on the west side."

"At those sessions Lester was always building," he continues. "Those weren't cutting sessions and they never left you hung up and they never tried to tire you out. There was no animosity at all in those sessions. We just went out to play and had a ball."[35]

At the beginning of December the job at the Grand Terrace expired, and the band continued its tour eastwards. As was his wont, Lester made use of every opportunity that presented itself to play as much as possible apart from his work with the band. On one occasion in Detroit he was so inspired that he played seventy-six choruses on "Sweet Sue," a solo that lasted an hour and a quarter!

His inspiration did not come only from outside the band, however. He had in Herschel Evans a companion and counterpart who, with his emotional playing, was a constant reminder to Lester that there was another tenor sax player of stature within the band. On the evening they arrived in New London, Connecticut, a fearful storm was raging. Hammond had once more traveled from New York to hear the band, and he remembers that there was some special fire and fervor at work between the two giants that evening. "Storm or not," he relates, "that night in New London was one to remember. Lester and Herschel, two completely opposite kinds of jazz players, became involved in a battle of saxes. Herschel had the big 'Texas sound.' Lester's sound was unusually light for the instrument—something like the Frankie Trumbauer, C-melody sax sound. But his inspiration never flagged. He could play sixty choruses, each different from the last, each building from the preceding one. Actually no one could win a contest against Lester; he could cut anyone in the world. But their contrasting sounds, their alternating choruses, inspired them to play better than either would have without the other. They were totally different personalities, too. Herschel was the banker of the band. He saved his money, and when he made loans to the other players, he charged interest. Lester lived in a world of his own, communicating very little with anybody, speaking his own language. He chose to be different and he was.[36]

Despite their differences, Lester and Herschel were very fond of each other, admiring each other's skill on the instrument and able to tease each other in a friendly way. Once Herschel asked: "Why don't you play alto, man. You got an alto tone!" Lester tapped his head and answered: "There's things going on up there, man. Some of you guys are all belly."[37]

Shortly before Christmas, Basie's band at last arrived in New York, a city most of the musicians had never been in before and which they therefore expected a great deal of. On Christmas Eve they had their premiere at the Roseland Ballroom, one of the best-known dancing spots at the time. On that occasion George Simon noticed that some progress had been made:

Though the men still suffer from an inability to sustain notes on the same even pitch, a fault that crops up mostly in slow tunes—they do sound in tune when it comes to biting off notes or even playing some smartly written figures on faster numbers.

Right now it's those written figures that make the band stand out and show promise of really amounting to something in the future. There's some brilliantly conceived stuff there; figures that not only swing in their own right, but which also fit into some cleverly worked out swing patterns. The men are beginning to feel them more than they did at first; they're relaxing more, and consequently, deriving greater benefits from them. One part of the band that has been consistently fine from the very beginning is that rhythm section. The four men really do swing out in no mean fashion; they give in every sense of the word. . . .

The two melody sections, as mentioned before, are responsible for holding back the band. Intonation and blend are not yet good. In colored sax sections that's sometimes overlooked, but it can't be in brass units. There are as compensation a few outstanding soloists. In the brass the only new man, Buck Clayton, sends you with interesting stuff obviously played with much feeling. Lester Young and Herschel Evans both carry off their share of hot tenor passages adequately enough.[38]

Hammond also wrote a review of the band on this occasion, and his judgment diverges only slightly from Simon's: "Count Basie broke no records at Roseland," he wrote, "but sounded on occasions quite magnificent, at least to these ears. During his last week there, occupying Woody Herman's bandstand, the orchestra really outdid itself, but I may well warn the readers, that mine is still a minority opinion about the band. The great drawback is its inconsistency: the ability to sound magnificent and clean and in tune when a handful of people are in the place and quite the opposite when there is a large and critical crowd. In fairness to the band, however, I think it only fair to say that this stage is definitely passing."[39]

New York was just the place for Lester, and the month he spent in the city was important both for the band as a whole, because it came into contact with some musicians who later were to join, and for Lester in particular, since he met a young nurse of Italian extraction there called Mary. He moved in with her in the course of 1937. Apart from that, he also reestablished contact with Billy Holiday. Hammond is of the opinion that they met each other again at the first recording they made together, on January 25, 1937. On the face of it, it sounds unlikely that more than a month should elapse before they ran into each other, for at this time she was singing at Clark Monroe's Uptown House in Harlem, a cellar jazz house on the corner of 7th Avenue and 134th Street, where there were frequent jam sessions in which Lester was certain to have participated. Both musically and privately, they hit it off from the word go, since they had a lot in common; among other things, they both liked to smoke a joint in pleasant surroundings, and both had a favorite drink called "fifty-fifty," or "top and bottom," which consisted of half port and half gin.

But it was within the sphere of music that their partnership blossomed in the most beautiful way, from their very first recordings. Here Lester shows an almost supernatural ability to feel in advance how Billie wants to sing, for he is able to create, in a four-bar introduction, an atmosphere that suits her perfectly. This is linked to the fact that it was important for Lester to get to know the texts of the melodies and songs he played.

All their records are now classics, and it is somewhat difficult to understand that they did not sell more at the time than they did—the sales figure is at the same level throughout the whole of 1937 and 1938. Billie's records were on Brunswick, aimed primarily at the urban black population. These were workers who, for the most part, had moved to the cities during the great migration at the turn of the century. They had gradually come to have the same dreams as the white working class, and this meant that the songs Billie was to sing had the same banal texts as pop songs designed for a white audience. If it hadn't been for Billie's natural talent and the quality of her musicians, most of her recordings would have been long since consigned to oblivion.

For Lester these recordings meant that he was seriously able to show his romantic and lyrical side for once, since he was mostly featured in Basie's quicker numbers, while Evans was used for the slower ones. His solos and obbligato playing on Billy's records are also superbly adapted to her singing, making up part of one beautiful unity. He never dominates in any way during his accompaniment, complementing her singing so perfectly and sensitively that you could speak of a duet, where the parts are equally divided. You can also notice from the recordings how close they became; gradually a familiarity and intimacy becomes apparent between them, almost vibrating from the grooves.

Their friendship was, however, purely Platonic, since Billie preferred her men to be more of the tough-guy type—Lester's diametric opposite. "At the time of my first meeting with Billie she also met up with Lester Young," related Buck Clayton, who was also on many of Lester and Billie's joint recordings, including their first, "and there was one of the greatest companionships that I've ever seen, and that is all it was, and ever would be. They were so close that many believed them to be in love, but that was never the case. If you've ever seen two guys become great pals, then you can see the companionship of Billie and Lester. I know this, because I was one of the 'Unholy Three,' as we used to call ourselves when we were together in some pad in Harlem. Lester had his girl friends, and Billie had her boy friends, and there was never any confusion. However, I do believe that if they had to, they would have given up all the girl friends and all the boy friends, and still they would have remained no more than great friends."[40]

The trumpet player Harry Edison supplements Buck Clayton's statement with these words: "Billie Holiday left Count Basie right after I joined the band, and went with Artie Shaw. I made many records with her, and we became just very close friends, very dear friends, but Lester and her were closer than anybody. They were never girl friend and boy friend. People associated them with going together for years, but they were just absolutely good buddies. Prez had a good lady friend, and Billie had a fantastic devoted man friend, and they were all friends."[41]

When Basie's band came to New York many of the musicians, Lester among them, moved into the Theresa Hotel in Harlem. Lester did not live there throughout his stay, however; after an unpleasant experience, when a rat had popped up among his shirts, he moved in with Billie and her mother.

Billie took care of Lester, showed him round the city and was always a welcome guest at the jam sessions he took part in. At one he met Leon "Chu" Berry, who was considered to be the greatest tenor saxophone player next to Coleman Hawkins. Berry did not have his saxophone with him, but when a duel between him and Lester was in the offing Benny Carter went and fetched it. Berry suggested that they start with "I Got Rhythm," which was grist to Lester's mill. "He blew at least fifteen choruses, none of them the same, and each one prettier than the last," Billie recalls. "When the fifteenth one was down, Chu Berry was finished."

"Chu's gang were die-hards, and they were sick," she concludes. "All they could say was that Chu had a bigger tone. What the hell that meant, I'll never know. What the difference how big a tone is or small, so long as Lester's line was moving in that wonderful way, with those chords, changes and those notes that would positively flip you with surprise?"[42]

Benny Carter can also remember the episode, but corrects a little his own attitude to the combatants. "Of course I admired Lester," he says. "But I thought very highly also of Chu, who was in my band for a time and a close friend. I doubt that I'd want to set them against each other or to humiliate anyone—least of all Chu."[43]

Many of these jam sessions were arranged by the Dane Timme Rosenkrantz—the jazz baron—and by John Hammond, who has related the following about one of the first battles Lester took part in after arriving in New York: "A few days after the Roseland opening I arranged an after hours session at the Greenwich Village dive called the Black Cat, so that Benny Goodman could have a chance to hear the Basie rhythm section plus Lester Young and Buck Clayton. After Lester had played a few choruses, Benny turned to me and said that it was the first time he had ever heard a completely natural sound on the tenor sax."[44]

On another occasion, Hammond wrote these flattering words about Lester: "The other night Benny Goodman, Basie, Lester Young, Joe [*sic*] Jones, Buck Clayton and Harry James got together in a small Harlem joint and jammed from two-fifteen to six in the morning. The music was something tremendous, for every one distinguished himself. But one conclusion was inescapable: that Lester Young was not only the star of the evening but without doubt the greatest tenor player in the country. In fact I'll stick my neck out even further: he is the most original and inventive saxophonist I have ever heard."[45]

The regular band at the Black Cat was a quintet which consisted of the trumpet player Bobby Moore, the tenor sax player Lonnie Simmons, the guitar player Freddie Green, the bass player Frank Clarke and his brother, Kenny, on drums. Bobby Moore, Freddie Green, and Kenny Clarke were the most impressive members of the group; when Claude Williams and Carl "Tatti" Smith left Basie's band shortly after the engagement at the Roseland Ballroom, Basie hired both Freddie Green and Bobby Moore.

Another outstanding person Hammond opened Basie's eyes to was Billie Holiday. Basie already knew about her from her reputation, for, long before the band reached New York, Lester had raved about the impression she had made on him when he heard her in 1934. "This girl can sing!" he had told, among others, Jo Jones. "She has a distinctive style."[46] Hammond persuaded Basie one evening to go with him to Monroe's Uptown House to hear her, and Basie was so convinced of her talent that he hired her for the band as soon as her engagement at Monroe's expired. Billie's first job with Basie was on March 13, 1937,

Lester Young, circa 1937. Photo from the Timme Rosencrantz Collection, courtesy The Danish Jazz Center.

in Scranton, 125 miles from New York. Hammond traveled once more to hear the band and had a guest with him as well on that occasion—the English critic Stanley Dance, who later wrote:

The floor was jammed with dancers and its balcony encouragingly jammed with listeners. New York opinion had been decidedly against the band. When it appeared at Roseland it was evidently somewhat rough and unreliable. Since then there had been changes made and never in my life have I heard a full-sized orchestra swing so much as Basie's did that night. It played a swarm of miraculous arrangements, mostly I gather, by Basie himself, and not one more than three pops all evening. . . .

The rhythm section is undoubtedly the finest there is, for there's not a weak spot in it. Jo Jones, the drummer, produces an easy natural and ideally suitable swing, and is much more than ably supported by Freddie Green and Walter Paige [sic], guitar and bass respectively.

The reed section is remarkable too, in that it boasts two excellent tenors—Lester Young and Hersal [sic] Evans. Both are swell musicians playing the right kind of jazz and although their styles are by no means similar I'd not care to say that I found one more enjoyable than the other. The section tone is of that specialized kind which ease of description will soon necessitate our using a tag like "Kansas City Style" or something. But the two tenors are its chief feature, and it is a wonderful thing to have two musicians like that, in one orchestra, spurring each other on to greater endeavors. . . .

As if all this instrumental talent were not enough, Basie has two of the best vocalists extant in this year of grace, for Billie Holiday joined him on that memorable night at Scranton and he already had James Rushing. Basie is extremely fortunate, for good vocalists of either sex are damnably scarce.[47]

This review clearly shows what progress the band was making. The rhythm section was now perfect, whereas the brass section still lacked a couple of powerful soloists to relieve the pressure on Buck Clayton and George Hunt. They came in the course of the next fifteen months, however, in the form of the trumpet player Harry "Sweets" Edison and the trombone players Benny Morton and Dicky Wells.

During the spring Lester came across his old friend Leonard Phillips once more. Phillips, who had settled in Washington, D.C., recalls:

In 1937 in something like March, Basie was booked at the Howard Theater, Washington D.C. They had a layover for a couple of days, so Lester was looking for me. He went up to a place where there was a jam and Booker Coleman was playing piano. He asked Booker and said: "Are there some musicians here named Otto Jones and Leonard Phillips?" Booker said: "Yeah, you talk about Pete and Phil?" "Yeah!" he said, "sure I know him. He's my good friend. Can you tell me how to get in contact with him?" Booker said: "Yeah, I'll tell you. Come on, let's get in the car and I'll take you over to where Phil is playing!"

So he brought him over to the "Hangover Club" on 14th Street, but we had closed, we closed at two and we had just left. But Booker came over to my house, he knew where I lived, and they got me and Julius Pogue, a tenor player. We were working on a job together with Dennis Briscoe, we called him "Tex," a bass player. He and Booker had the band at the "Hangover." Lester said to me: "Why don't you come on, man? We've got a place to take you!" Booker was playing piano too up at this jam session place, so he said: "Yeah, let's all go up there. This is the cat I've been wanting to hear, 'cause Phil and all them have been talkin' about you. You're all good friends, aren't you?" Prez said: "Yeah, we're like brothers. Pete is my brother-in-law." Then we got in the car and went up to Freddie Woods at "7 and T" on the corner of 7th and T Street, and they had a regular piano player, Toby Miles, oh, he could play some piano! Walter Page came up there and brought his bass, and Chester Brown came with his guitar. They didn't have no drums.

When Lester came up to the bar, Paul Jones, the tenor player, said: "I'm ready for him!" But Red Elkins, a trumpet player, said: "He's ready for you! He's ready for all cats like you! So he was ready for you when you first started playing. When he first started blowing his horn he was ready for you!" Paul said: "I'll find out tonight!"

Paul was supposed to be the greatest tenor player around Washington and he started blowing. Then soon Walter Page came up and started playing his bass. Paul started playing "I Got Rhythm" and he played seven-eight choruses. Toby played a solo, and then Page took a solo, and Chester took some choruses. He played like Charlie Christian on his acoustic guitar. Then later on Chester got an amplifier. When they had all played and Chester ended his solo, Prez fell in and he tored "I Got Rhythm" all up in pieces. He went through everything in it. Paul Jones was trying to do that on this "I Got Rhythm." He said: "Shit man, he played 'I Got Rhythm' and every time he'd come in with a different feeling!" The drummer we had playing with us at the "Hangover Club," Elmer Toyer, he said after the audience hauled after Prez's solo: "Man, what is he doing? Listen, Paul!" Paul said: "Oh, no man! He's good!"

When Prez came in he started swinging, and then he started to tell the cats to give him some four breaks, and then he played two to three choruses making breaks. That should have been recorded! That was one of the sessions that every time a cat would see me and know me would say: "Man, I'll never forget that night when you brought Prez up there, man!" I said: "Yeah, man!" It didn't excite me, because I've been with one of the best all my life.[48]

That spring the band had a couple of successful engagements in New York, at the Apollo Theater on 125th Street and at the Savoy Ballroom on 140th Street and Lenox Avenue. The black audience here in Harlem was much better able to appreciate the band's special style of playing than the white audience at the Roseland Ballroom, who preferred standard dances like waltzes and tangos.

The musicians had now moved from the Theresa Hotel to the Woodside Hotel, which was subsequently to be their favorite address whenever they were in New York. The hotel was situated at 2424 7th Avenue and 142nd Street in Harlem and was run by three brothers. It had practical facilities, including a large communal kitchen, and had small apartments with their own kitchen for those musicians who had their wives with them. There was also a large room in the cellar which the band was allowed to use for rehearsals. Lester lived there too, of course, though Mary still lived in the city during the first years of their relationship.[49]

Since Willard Alexander was not able to get a permanent job for the band at a hotel, dance restaurant, or club, as was the case for Earl Hines, for example, or for most of the white bands, Basie's band was obliged to spend most of the year on tour, with the hope of resting up from one-nighters when they got engagements that lasted for a week or two.

Being on tour in the 1930s could offer both exciting and amusing experiences, but it probably had more drawbacks than advantages. It was exhausting to have to travel all the time and, since it was both uncomfortable and expensive to take a plane or a train, the band had to hire a bus—and buses did not have the comfort or facilities of buses today. The roads were bad, and accidents and breakdowns were frequent, especially in mountainous areas and in winter. The distances to be covered were often long, up to 500 miles, so that when the musicians finally arrived, tired out, at their destination for the evening, there was often only time to change clothes in some grimy changing room—or in the washroom if nothing else was available—before the band went on stage. Often there was not enough time to have a meal before the musicians boarded the bus once more to get to their next port of call in time.

Since the musicians had to meet the cost of board and lodging out of their own wages, it was very difficult for those who had a wife and perhaps children to provide for to save money. "When we weren't on a steady job, our salary was twenty-four dollars a night," Buck Clayton recalls. "But we never worked over three or four nights a week. We weren't known enough to work as much as Basie works now. So we'd work two nights a week and make forty-eight dollars or three nights a week make another twenty-four. We never made seven times twenty-four."[50]

When the band was still relatively unknown, it used to hire a bus from Mr. Lerf. "This bus used to go down the highway sideways," Jo Jones relates, "and Mr. Lerf, to make us look like a big act, used to send over a good bus from Newark and from the Woodside. He put all our stuff in there and then, just as we come out of the tunnel where you got that airport, then we'd exchange buses and get this crooked bus. So when we come back into New York off our little tour, then we'd have the crooked bus they'd take the good bus and we looked like a big act."[51]

To reduce expenses even more, the musicians sometimes hired a house instead of spending the night at a hotel, and all ate together at the same time. Both Billie and her replacement, Helen Humes, were good cooks, and everyone was content with the meals they prepared. On one of their first tours the band traveled to the deep South, which was not without its problems. Freddie Green relates that "the busdriver was white, because it was a white company we chartered the bus from. We went to some houses and some hotels—black hotels, you know, because it was in the south. We went to black restaurants in the neighborhood."[52]

The alto sax player Earle Warren joined the band in April 1937 as a replacement for Caughey Roberts, and he recalls that their driver came from America Orchestra Service in New Jersey and that his name was Jimmy LeMarr. He was a pleasant guy, liked by everybody. If something happened to the coach en route, he took care of it on the spot, while the others made use of a well-earned rest and, among other things, stretched their legs and played baseball at the roadside. Warren also recalls that Freddie Green once left one of the coach windows open while they were playing at a theater in Memphis. A thief made use of this opportunity and stole Green's new overcoat and Lester's long black coat. Luckily Green had a little black spring coat and a trench coat, so that Lester, when it was cold, could borrow the trench coat, and Green had to make do with his spring coat. They must have looked quite a pair, for the rest of the band christened them the Dootsie twins.[53]

Billie has also described the conditions prevalent on such tours. Among other things, she describes how difficult it was to earn enough money to take care of her hair and clothes, and how frustrating it was never to have the chance to sleep in a proper bed, and the band almost always had to move directly from one job to the next.

They often spent much of their travel time playing dice. Once, on a return journey from West Virginia to New York, Billie joined in for the first time, and it turned out that she had beginner's luck. "Billie was left-handed and she never shot dice in her life," Jo Jones recalls.

Lester Young had one dollar and he said, "Come on, Billie, shoot this dollar for me." She's in the back of the bus. It was around the Christmas week. Incidentally she broke up everybody. She just took everybody's money because they told her wrong and she shot dice wrong and broke the whole band. You know, if you shoot 12 you win, if you shoot 2, if you shoot 7—whatever they told her, whatever, she won. This was a very cute thing. This was an inside thing. It's important—you know, you're telling somebody wrong and she doesn't know what she is doing, but she's winning. She broke everybody.

Jack Washington said, "Get 'em, baby" and I was sitting up in the front and laughing. We got some neck bones and rice and beans and she put the pot on and she told everybody goodnight. You know, she put the money down her bosom, she wouldn't give Jimmy Rushing no money, she wouldn't speak to Basie. She didn't speak to the bus driver or nobody; she went around the corner and said, "I'm putting the pot on." Poor Lester Young always wanted a Packard car and he never did win one. He never made no money the whole time he stayed with Basie's band; he got broke shooting dice. He never could win.[54]

Shooting dice was a passion with Lester. Earle Warren agrees with Jo Jones that he was constantly unlucky. After a job he used to take a rest on the back seat of the coach and have a drink, after which he got hold of the dice and went up the aisle, shaking them in the others' ears, repeating the words "Sweet music, sweet music!" If anyone felt like playing, he was the first to lose, Warren recalls.[55]

Lester had leisure interests other than gambling, however. He was interested in sport and played both baseball and golf. Sometimes the bands had their own baseball team, and competitions were held when two bands met. Basie's team often played against Harry James's band, and they also played several times against Benny Goodman's band in New York's Central Park. Benny Goodman had a pretty hot team that won all its matches in 1938. Earle Warren can remember some of the members of Basie's team: "Prez was the pitcher. He threw a backspinning ball which made the guy hit the ball on the ground. I played short stop, Herschel was first base, Jack Washington was second, and I forget who was on third. We used to practice on the roadside in the spring when we were down south, and all through Texas."[56]

Apart from these sporting contests, Basie's band was also involved in a series of musical trials of strength against other bands; one that took place on January 16, 1938, at the Savoy Ballroom against Chick Webb's band has found a place in jazz history. It was an eventful evening all round, since it started with Benny Goodman's famous Carnegie Hall concert, which included a jam session to which he had invited Lester, Buck Clayton, and Basie's rhythm section, minus Jo Jones. The jam session section was not a great success, however; the *New York Times* wrote that "last night's 'jam session' seemed to last a good ten minutes, and though soloist after soloist of the band tried in turn to contribute something original to the ensemble, little or nothing of the sort materialized."[57]

Simon didn't disagree, and he wrote in *Metronome* that "though there were some good passages from Lester Young, Buck Clayton, Count Basie, Harry Carney, Walter Page, and Benny, the twenty-minute version of 'Honeysuckle Rose' was uninspired, uninspiring, and lagged pretty sadly until Harry James bit into a few choice figures towards its close. Even then, the listeners, including the most thoroughbred cats, were quite obviously restless and didn't tend the jammers any smaller ovation than they deserved. The setting was just unfortunate, that was all."[58]

After this Lester and the other Basie musicians went over to the Savoy Ballroom to try their strength against Chick Webb and his musicians, who were really on their home ground, since this band was the favorite of the Savoy Ballroom audience. "I'll never forget the night we played the battle of music against Chick Webb at the Savoy," Jimmy Rushing recalls. "The place was packed so tight you couldn't move.

They had all the lights off and a spot centered on Chick and his drums. I said to myself, this is it. He had one of the best bands around then and had never been beaten at the Savoy, which was their home. We were kind of nervous for the first couple of sets, but after a while we started jumping and knocked the crowd out and won the battle. All the papers had stories about that night, and it helped the band a lot."[59]

Rushing is correct in stating that the evening was a good advertisement for the Basie band, but he is incorrect in claiming that the band beat Chick Webb. Even so, Simon also was convinced that Basie had won. He wrote enthusiastically:

Count Basie did it! For years nobody was able to lick Chick Webb and Chicks within the walls of his home Savoy Ballroom, but on January 16, right after Benny Goodman's concert further downtown in Carnegie Hall, a milling throng that included such notables as Duke Ellington, Red Norvo, Mildred Bailey, Eddie Duchin, Gene Krupa, Lionel Hampton and the Benny Goodman family jammed into Harlem's Hottest Hot House to hear and see the Count gain a newspapermen's decision over the famed Chick.

Basie had everything that night! Seldom has any band, anyplace, cut loose with such unmitigated swing the way the Count's Cohorts did that memorable eve. . . .

To put it briefly, the battle was one of solid swing versus sensational swing, both brilliantly swung, but with the sincerity of the former triumphing over the showmanship of the latter. Basie's a bluesplaying (with variations) band if ever there was one, devoted its attack to the body, to the heart, with a steady hammering of truly sending rhythm figures behind the truly sensational solos of trumpeter Buck Clayton, tenor saxophonists Herschel Evans and Lester Young, and its piano-playing leader, and with an ensemble and steady rhythmic attack (led by drummer Jo Jones) that was truly devastating.[60]

The daily press had a clearer picture of the result. The *New York Amsterdam News,* for example, wrote:

While thousands of frenzied fans jammed the dance floor and musical contempories took their places on the sidelines to note the landing of each telling arrangement punch, Chick Webb, king of the drums, and William (Count) Basie, royalist of the keyboard, fought a wide-open battle of swing at the Savoy Ballroom Sunday night.

And while the principals in the major contest rested during the gentler interludes, Ella Fitzgerald, queen of the swing songbirds, defended her throne against the onslaught of Billie Holiday, who herself throws a mean left mike. Both Chick and the Count had been gunning for the big night, and the percussionists, Webb at his drums and Basie at the piano, used every trick in their repertoire to step in and land the winning blast. Throughout the fight, which never let down in its intensity during the whole fray, Chick took the aggressive, with the Count playing along easily and on the whole more musically scientifically. Undismayed by

Chick's forceful drum-beating, which sent the audience into shouts of encouragement and appreciation and caused beads of perspiration to drop from Chick's brow onto brass cymbals, the Count maintained an attitude of poise and self-assurance. He constantly parred the Chick's thundering haymakers with tantalizing runs and arpeggios which teased more and more force from his adversary. . . .

Chick Webb and Ella Fitzgerald were declared winners by popular vote of the "battle of swing" Sunday night after the ballots were counted. Chick led Count Basie two to one, and Ella polled three times as many voices as Billie Holiday.[61]

Down Beat's description of the course of events is in line with this assessment:

The affair drew a record attendance and hundreds were turned away at the box office with the crowd tying up traffic for several blocks in that vicinity. Applause for both bands was tremendous and it was difficult to determine which band was the more popular.

Nevertheless, the ballot taken showed Chick Webb's band well in the lead over Basie's and Ella Fitzgerald well out in front over Billie Holliday [*sic*] and James Rushing. . . .

Feeling ran very high between the supporters of the two bands, and it was a fight to the finish. Both bands played magnificently, with Basie having a particular appeal for the dancers, and Webb consistently stealing the show on the drums. Ella caused a sensation with her rendition of "Loch Lomond," and Billie Holiday thrilled her fans with "My Man." When Ella sang she had the whole crowd rocking with her. James Rushing had everybody shouting the blues right along with him. Handkerchiefs were waving, people were shouting and stomping, the excitement was intense. . . .

General consensus of opinion agreed that both bands played magnificently making the decision a very close one.[62]

This evening helped to stabilize the band's fine reputation, and the engagement in the week around March 1 at the Apollo Theater was also a musical high-water mark. It was, unfortunately, the last job Billie Holiday was to have with the band; immediately afterwards she was fired by Willard Alexander. There were several reasons for this. Billie was tired of touring, for one thing, and she refused to sing more blueslike material—which Alexander had asked her to do—remarking that Rushing already took care of that extremely well. There were rumors that Hammond was involved in her being fired, but Alexander strongly denied that this was the case and said that "the reason for her dismissal was strictly one of deportment, which was unsatisfactory, and a distinctly wrong attitude towards her work." He added, "Billie sang fine when she felt like it . . . but . . . we just couldn't count on her for consistent performance."[63]

Billie had been popular with most of the members of the band, since she had been on an equal footing with them, and they could not help admiring her interpretations of song-texts and her fine musicianship generally. It was a blow for Lester, of course, not having her around any more; judging from the recordings, they were closer at that time than they had ever been before.

For a few months Rushing was the only vocal soloist—until Helen Humes was engaged in July 1938, at about the same time as trombone player Dicky Wells. She too has spoken about her touring with the band, which was tough but endurable, thanks to the unique camaraderie among the musicians. "Sometimes I'd have to get off the bus," she recalls,

and I'd be scared to get off cause they'd all look out the window. Oh, shucks. And they'd say, "Billie didn't pay us no mind." I said, "Well, she's used to you. I got to get used to you." But they treated me like I was a little sister. They were just as sweet as they could be.

And I treated all of them like they was my children. I was sewing on buttons, you know, and doing up the cooking all the time because, you know, it's kind of hard trying to get food in a lot of places down there. And I'd be fixing lunches. But they were all so nice. Just the nicest bunch. I don't know, of course, Sweets, he was something else. He was really funny. And Lester Young and Vic Dickenson, they used to just keep us going all the time. Because we'd be on the bus and we'd be sleeping and we'd hear the dice clicking. They'd say, "Wake up, come on here and let's get this stuff on the road here." They'd say, "This is our lucky day," and they'd be the first ones broke. So we'd go all the way to the next place as long as somebody had money.

When we'd get down South we'd have to go over some rickety bridges and Basie would say "Stop the bus." He'd get off and walk across the bridge. He was scared the bus was too big for them little old bridges, you know. Sometimes a whole lot of them would get out and walk across.

I remember one time we got on the train and Earle Warren, he's just as white as you can get them. So Earle was sitting there in the coach with us and the conductor came and he said, "Look here you, you got to get out of here." Earle said, "I don't know why." And he said, "We don't have no mixed." Earle said, "Well, I'm not white." He said, "You ain't fooling us, you go on up there in the next car." And then when Earle got ready to get off he said, "See there you had me up in that car and I'm going." We had Earle go into different places and get us food, you know, when we were down South. That was just the way it was.[64]

Helen Humes fitted in with Basie's musicians just as well as Billie had done, and she took an active part in their leisure-time activities. "She used to gamble with the guys," Buck Clayton recalls, "like we'd shoot craps on the bus for four hundred miles sometimes. And she would be right back in the back of the bus shooting craps with all the rest of us or playing poker or whatever it was. She liked to do it. Everybody liked Helen."[65]

Basie's real breakthrough came in the summer of 1938, when the band played at the Famous Door, quite a small club at 66 West 52nd Street in New York. Willard Alexander has explained how this engagement was worked out:

By the summer of 1938 there seemed no place for Basie to go. Then I got the idea of putting him on 52nd Street. It was crazy. The clubs couldn't accommodate a big band on their stands, and they were so small, fourteen men would blow the walls out. But being desperate, I went to the two guys who ran the Door—Al Feshin, big and tough, and Jerry Brooks, little and tough. It was the beginning of the summer, and they had no air conditioning and no business. They were desperate enough, so I managed to get them over to Steinway Hall on 57th St. to hear the band. Once they heard Basie at the Nola Studios, they were talking like it couldn't be done but they sure wanted to do it.

The hangup, of course, was the club's lack of air conditioning. With difficulty, they could seat sixty people. But can you imagine what it would have been like without air conditioning in New York's summer heat and humidity? When I was convinced that Feshin and Brooks really wanted Basie, I stuck my neck out and offered to get the money to install a cooling unit.

. . . there was no band that played with the coordination and precision of Basie's. Those guys didn't just play together. They used to breath together. That's what gave the band its fantastic punch, no matter how softly they played.[66]

On one occasion the jazz critic Charles Edward Smith was down there to hear the band, and he would never forget "Count Basie's fourteen men playing 'King Porter Stomp' with such steam that the leader's hands dropped off the piano and he sat listening to them with a slight, incredulous smile that reminded me of Fletcher Henderson's in the same kind of situation."[67]

Ahmet Ertegun, who was one of the founders of Atlantic Records, can also remember the evenings at the Famous Door: "Man, we lived in those days! It was unbelievable to us to see and hear those guys in person!"[68]

What made the band something exceptional as compared with the other bands of that period was not simply the rhythm section and the soloists, but the rare phenomenon of all members of the band having the same sense of rhythm and an understanding of how everything should fit together. "I tell you each one knew the other's move," Benny Morton explains.

Basie could sit down at rehearsal and just start playing the piano and a couple of fellows would join in and in half an hour's time they had a new number. No title. It's just another number. And the contribution was done by the members of the band. If you struck an idea first another guy joined you, and supplied the harmony. If the saxophones got it we didn't interfere with them; the trombones got a difficult figure which was an answer to that and this is something no one can teach. This is something for which you have to have good ears among all the players, and that band had the greatest rhythm sense of any that I have ever played in.

It was a conversation. You could have three different movements going, plus the rhythm section. I want to compliment the players of that band as well as the rhythm section, because if the players other than the rhythm section are a little poor in rhythm, it makes it tougher for the rhythm section to do what it's doing. Well, they had no interferences that way. That's one reason why I say that it was one of the greatest rhythm bands, because from the bottom to the top that rhythm was there.[69]

The engagement made Basie's name famous in a big way throughout the United States, not least because of the three weekly CBS broadcasts. The success was so big that, instead of the original six weeks, the band played from July 11 to the middle of November. The band's records also sold well, and many musicians began to become aware of the qualities of both the band in general and of Lester in particular, and they came in droves whenever the celebrities came to visit their hometowns. Thad Jones and his brothers Hank and Elvin grew up close to Detroit, and Thad has provided us with a fine picture of how Lester would seem to a bunch of responsive young musicians. "The first time I saw him was in Detroit, Michigan, and it was my first opportunity to hear the Basie band," he recalls.

My friends and I bought every record that Basie made in those days, you know. You could buy a 78-record for 75 cents, so we managed to scrape together enough bread to buy these records and we had stacks of 78-records, and that was when I first came in contact with the sound of Lester Young. All of us who heard him were totally in awe with this sound. It was so different and beautiful and so vital, and it was like magic, like a magic tapestry that was continuing to be woven right before your very eyes and ears.

So when Count Basie made one of his rare trips to Detroit—we knew about those things way ahead of time—we immediately began to scrape the money together to get down there, because we had to go three to four miles to Detroit. We got there and all of us—who all were young musicians by the way—worked our way through the totally packed ballroom and it took us ten to fifteen minutes to come near the bandstand, and all of us wound up standing right in front of Lester Young, naturally.

He was playing a saxophone that looked as though it should really have been in the shop. Around the keys it was turning green in spots and there was a rubber band or two around some of the keys, and we said, "How can he do this?" And then we looked at his attitude towards the music. It was like the horn only became an instrument through which the soul of Lester Young was expressed, it was like a transmitter, you know. When he'd still be up to play I would look around, and people would slow down their dancing just so that they could listen, because everybody realized then, even the people who didn't really pay that close attention to details as far as the music was concerned, everybody seemed to sense that they were witnessing one of the greatest musicians of all time.

It was like he was the minister and we were his congregation out there. He was speaking words of wisdom to us, and very prophetic, because his style, what he was doing then, changed the whole concept of tenorplaying. He was the one who did it. He showed another way to go. It was like listening to a saxophone with a sound of a flute with that clear just mellow, rich, round sound. It wasn't associated with what we came to recognize as the sound of a tenor saxophone. Lester Young had a tenor saxophone sound that was different, and it was more like a bell-flute sound. Perhaps that was the main thing that attracted everyone to it.[70]

In December 1938 Basie took up an engagement at the Strand on Broadway in New York, and at the same time Shad Collins became a member of the trumpet section. He and Lester became close friends; a couple of years later, when Lester formed his first band, Shad was to be trumpet player in the group. Harry Edison can remember the following incident from the band's time at the Strand: "Basie wanted a production number and Jimmy Mundy did an arrangement on 'I Struck a Match in the Dark,' which Earle Warren was to sing. When the lights went out and Earle started, we were all supposed to strike a match and light up the stage. Well, when Earle made his introduction, Prez struck a match, held his part up, and set fire to it! That was the end of that. He didn't like Earle Warren's singing, and he always imitated singers and made a comedy out of it."[71]

It was typical of Lester to play that sort of joke. Freddie Green recalls the following about his gags and practical jokes: "He made so many of them on the spot. Most of the things he came up with was original, you know, things you've never heard before. He was a very original man."[72]

Another facet of Lester's humor was his renaming of his associates, a custom his father also had and one which was common in the black population. Lester's way of doing it was unique, however, since he was so perceptive in his characterization that many of his pet names stuck. There was nothing malicious in it at all, "and the way he did it," Freddie Green explains, "it was like a—not a humorous thing—but like a loving thing."[73]

One of his most famous nicknames was the one he gave Billie Holiday. Jo Jones can remember how it came about. "It started in Baltimore," he says. "We were leaving the Royal Theater and you know how we used to go in the back to get the food, in the house. So we were sitting in the bus to get the food and Freddie Green was sitting with Lady Day. Some guys were having fun. They had been on Pennsylvania Avenue and they come in and they was using all kind of language. I said, 'Wait a minute. You guys can't do that. There's a lady present.' So Lester Young and Buck Clayton always sat at the back of the bus, so Lester busts out laughing and says, 'What do you mean, lady?' I said, 'There's a lady in here. You guys can't do that.' So right away he says, 'Lady Day.' "[74]

On the other hand, it was Billie who started calling Lester "President," because she felt that he was the best tenor player in the country, a title that was later shortened to "Pres" or "Prez."

The nicknames Lester gave his colleagues had partly to do with their external appearance, but could also have to do with their skills or oddities, or simply be a word-play on their real names. "Prez was inventive in everything, both in his playing and his talking," Harry Edison relates. "He gave me the name 'Sweets,' and I don't know why, but it stuck all those years. He named Basie 'The Holy Man' because he carried all the money and was the band leader."[75] Freddie Green was "Pepper" or just "Pep," and Buddy Tate "Moon." Benny Morton was called "Morton Gable," because he looked like Clark Gable, but was also called "Mr. Bones." Buck Clayton was "Cat Eye," Snooky Young "Rabbit," and the first trumpet player Ed Lewis was called "Big D." Dicky Wells had stomach problems for a while, so it was almost inevitable that Lester began to call him "Gas Belly"! Walter Page was called "Big 'Un" or "Horse," and Jo Jones was called "Sampson." Herschel Evans came from Texas and therefore got the name "Tex." Since Earle Warren always looked like he was smiling when he played, he was naturally enough christened "Smiley." Jimmy Rushing had several nicknames, because he was short and squat, the best-known being "Mr. Five by Five," but he was also known as "Honey Bunny Boo" and "Little Jim." George Matthews was shortened to "Truce," and Muggsy Spanier had to put up with being called "Muddy Spaniels." Neither Roy Eldridge nor Illinois Jacquet was all that tall, but they were nimble on their instruments, so Lester referred to them as "The Two Midgets." Jack Washington was called "Weasel," Eli Robinson "Mr. Eli," and Emmett Berry "Rev." Jimmy Powell came to be called "Neat," Helen Humes "Homey," and Mr. Snodgrass, who was Basie's manager for a time, was renamed "Lady Snar." The piano player Bobby Scott, whom Lester got to know in the mid-1950s, wasn't very old at that time, so Lester called him "Bobby Socks."

On December 23, 1938, John Hammond had arranged a concert in Carnegie Hall in New York with the title "From Spirituals to Swing," which Lester took part in on three occasions. In the first part of the concert he played in two small swing groups called the Kansas City Five, and the Kansas City Six. With the Kansas City Five, consisting of Buck Clayton, Freddie Green, Jo Jones, and Walter Page, he accompanied Jimmy Rushing and Helen Humes, after which the same group plus

Leonard Ware on electric guitar played an instrumental set. After the interval, Lester was reunited with the Basie band, who had Hot Lips Page with them as guest soloist for one number, and he played a stunning solo in "Blues for Lips," one of the high moments of the concert.

After this, the band went on tour again, but it was hit by a tragedy on January 21. Herschel Evans had a heart attack while on stage in Hartford, Connecticut, at the Crystal Ballroom and collapsed. "A friend came up and got him and carried him, brought him on back to New York," Buddy Tate recalls, "and Prez came back to New York. They had about three or four days off. They all stayed at the Woodside and Prez said he used to go knock on his door because he wouldn't go right to the hospital. He waited about three days before he'd go. He was waiting to see his girl friend, said he wasn't going until she showed, you know. So Prez said he's go see him, knock on the door, said sometime it would take him so long to open the door and one day, he peeked through the hole and he was on his knees, saying his prayers. Of course, when he went to the hospital, he didn't make it." [76]

Evans died on February 9 at Wadsworth Hospital on 185th Street, but the burial took place in Los Angeles, where his girlfriend lived. "The night Herschel's body was being taken on the train to California we played the Savoy Ballroom," Jo Jones remembers, "and people were out on the street to tell us that the train was passing. There were nearly 5,000 people in that ballroom and someone called us from the 63rd Street station to say that the train was on its way. And we stopped the dance until the train passed through about ten or twelve blocks away, then we continued." [77]

Herschel's death was a painful loss for Lester, and he found it hard to feel at home in the band for a while. "It was the hardest thing in the world to keep Lester Young on the bandstand," Jo Jones recalls. "He kept Herschel's chair vacant next to him with his hat and coat on it and every night Jack Washington would have to hold him, because he'd get up and try to leave." [78] Herschel and Lester had been close friends right since their first meeting in the beginning of the 1930s in Kansas City, and they were mutually respectful of each other's playing. On the other hand, Billie Holiday and Herschel were not the best of friends, which must be the reason for her claiming in her book that Lester and Herschel's relationship was marked by rivalry and tension; in fact, there was no malice between them at all. The tension that could be noticed on stage was a natural result of their both being ambitious soloists, and nothing was more evident that the professional jealousy which is always present between two soloists on the same instrument. Buck Clayton also recalls that Lester and Herschel never said an unkind word to each other and that there existed a mutual respect between them. [79]

"Herschel Evans was a natural," Jo Jones adds. "He had a sound on the tenor that perhaps you will never hear on a horn again. As for the so-called friction between him and Lester, there was no real friction. What there was was almost like an incident you would say could exist between two brothers. No matter what, there was always a mutual feeling there."[80]

"They used to get hold of a group of tenor players," Jo Jones remarks, "and make them each drink three quarts of whiskey in an hour. I've never seen so many people get so drunk in my life. And if those guys could cut it after that they were in. And when Lester and Herschel would get to play and exchange choruses it was like a tennis match. People's heads'd be going from side to side. And the band would be out of time and raggedy, but the people would still come flocking, because we were doing something different and exciting. And people would say, 'Listen to that, they're mad at each other,' but they didn't know, they didn't know how close they were."[81]

Confirmation of Jo Jones's assessment of their relationship comes from what Lester himself has said about Herschel. "We were nice friends," he told François Postif, "but there wasn't no bullshit or nothing. We got up on the bandstand and played, like a duel, you know. And then other nights we'd get along nice, you know what I mean? What I mean is coming through one's instrument, you dig? He was a nice person. I was the last to see him die. In fact I paid the doctor his bill and everything. So, he loved his instrument and I loved mine too. So fuck you, fuck me!"[82]

Throughout his life Lester kept this warmth of feeling for his friend. In 1976 Phil Schaap talked to the bass player John Ore, who had played with Lester in the 1950s. "He told me," Schaap recalls, "that Young didn't talk much, but that when he did speak about the old days he would mention Evans fondly and remark how much he missed him. The feelings were clear."[83]

It was difficult to find a suitable replacement for Herschel Evans. Jack Washington, who was also an excellent soloist, but who—unintentionally, to be sure—was overshadowed by the two tenor giants, was asked if he would like to change over to tenor saxophone, but he declined. Count Basie then thought of Buddy Tate, who had taken Lester's place during an engagement in Little Rock in 1934, when Lester traveled to New York to be with Henderson. Tate, however, was with Nat Towles's band in Texas at the time, so a temporary replacement was found in Elbert "Skippy" Williams for the saxophone section. Tate recalls:

I got a telegram from Basie to meet the band in Kansas City, and they had another boy with the band, Skippy Williams, who I did like, a very nice person. And they brought him from New York.
So actually, I was on trial. We were all on trial and so I meet the band in

Kansas City and you know who meets me in the lobby? Prez. Everybody's in bed because I get there about 8:00 in the morning, 8:30. So Prez meet me in the lobby of the Booker T. Washington Hotel. He says, "Gee, Tate, it's so nice to see you." I said, "It's nice to see you too. Oh, I listen to everything you do." So he says, "Yeah, well, look like we making it." I says, "You're making it all right." So he says, "I tell you, let's go have breakfast." I says, "Okay." So he says, "You got to excuse the fellas because they were out late last night and we played a dance and this is homecoming. I just can't sleep." So we go to a place where he used to go in Kansas City. You know, he loved red beans and rice, so he ordered red beans and rice for himself. He said, "Give him the same thing." He ordered me some. He was very sensitive, so I says, "Okay." I ate red beans and rice, too. So then he says to me, "Have you been listening? Have you been keeping up on your instrument?" So I says, "Well, I've been trying. I've been listening, oh, yeah, I listen all the time." "Well," he says, "if you playing anyway like you were the last time I heard you, it will be your engagement. There's a lot of ladies want the engagement, Lady Berry, Lady Webster. They're good players, but they don't fit. And if you're playing like you did the last time I heard you, it'll be your engagement." [84]

Buddy Tate got the job and fitted into the band very well, since he had a style of playing not very different from Herschel Evans's.

The Basie band did not return to New York until the beginning of July 1939, where they played once more at the Famous Door. Tate, who had not been in that vast city before, can clearly remember the nature of his arrival:

When we got to New York, I had a pocketful of money and I'm standing at Grand Central Station. And I know I looked terrible. I know you could see country all over me. And these guys, they'd been out from New York for a long, long time. Everybody would run and grab cabs. Nobody said nothing to me. I didn't know what the Woodside was. I didn't know anything. That's where everybody stayed then, you know, at the Woodside Hotel. And I didn't know where to go. I looked around and there was nobody there, and Prez was standing in the corner. He called me on over, you know, he says, "You have to forgive the ladies. They haven't seen their madam queens and everybody's lonely. So that's why they leave you. They mean well." So he carried me on up to the Woodside.

He would call me Lady because he always just say, "You're so refined and you're so nice. I got to give you a Lady name because I don't ever see you mad at anybody or anything. You're just so nice and you deserve that elegant name, Lady." So that stuck. That's why he called me Lady Tate. [85]

The drummer Willie Jones used to play with Lester during his last three years. He got to know Lester well and has a further explanation as to why Lester called his colleagues "Lady": "His reason for saying 'Lady' was, because, you know, his playing was with finesse, was so beautiful that he would be addressing your soul. To him a woman represented sophistication, dignity, delicateness, beauty, you know, so this is a quality that should exist in all human beings, so that's the reason why he would address you in that manner."[86]

Buddy Tate moved into the Woodside Hotel next to Mary and Lester, who lived in a common-law marriage which was not without its problems, not least on account of their different ethnic backgrounds. Lester was faithful by nature, even though his charm as regards women might lead one to believe the opposite. "He was a beautiful cat and he had a lot of class," Tate recalls. "When he was on the road, he'd have a ball, but when he was in New York he'd stick with his old lady, just as though he was a one-woman man."[87]

Lester liked to be surrounded by women, and Tate's last remark should be understood as meaning that Lester sometimes used to have parties after the show in female company, without that meaning anything more than it does at face value. "Prez always kept his private life to himself," Harry Edison relates. "He was a one-woman's man, he wasn't promiscuous. His private life was his own, and he didn't have his girl friends all around the band all the time like some other guys who had girls in every place, you know, girls all around. So I didn't see too much of his wives, even I've met them all. His first Mary was white, and she was beautiful, she was fine. She's still living in Los Angeles."[88]

In the summer of 1939 Coleman Hawkins returned to the United States after five successful years in Europe. One of the first things he did on arriving was to visit Lester to hear the details concerning Herschel's death, which had also had a strong effect on him. Lester and Hawkins met several times afterwards at jam sessions, with Billie as a constant, faithful listener. One early morning she fetched Lester at the Famous Door and they went down to Puss Johnson's Tavern on St. Nicholas Avenue in Harlem, where a jam session had been arranged. Both Lester and Hawkins played for all they were worth; they gave it all they had. Reviewing this session later, *Down Beat* referred to some members of Fats Waller's band who thought that Hawkins had gotten the better of Lester, who said he had had enough after the first hour. Billie was in Chicago when she read the article and, faithful to Lester as always, she went straight up to the editorial office and had a notice put in contradicting what she had just read. "Young really cut the Hawk," she wrote, "and most everyone there who saw them tangle agreed on that."[89]

The small clubs on 52nd Street were favorite spots for jam sessions. Ralph Watkins from Kelly's Stable has explained how he used to arrange them: "We had some of the most amazing jam sessions. We'd have like ten great sax players at one time—Lester Young, Sam Donahue, Babe Russin, Chu Berry, Coleman Hawkins, Georgie Auld and others. One of the things that always amazed me. You know how great

Lester Young was? Well, he'd go great until the Bean walked in. Then he'd freeze. I never saw anything like it. But the Bean was tough to top."[90]

The engagement at the Famous Door expired that September, and after one more engagement at the Roseland Ballroom, MCA booked the band on a tour to its first visit to California. The first engagement on the West Coast should have been at the Palomar Ballroom in Los Angeles on October 4, but the famous dance hall went up in flames a couple of days before the premiere, while Charlie Barnet's band was playing to a full house. Fortunately, everybody managed to get out unscathed, but many of the band's instruments and arrangements were lost when the building was completely gutted. The rumor was that the fire had been started deliberately to prevent Basie from playing in a place previously reserved for white bands. Instead, Basie's band was sent further north to the Sweets Ballroom in Oakland, after which it was engaged to play at the Paramount Theater in Los Angeles.

At this period Lester was already an inspiration for young saxophone players, one of his most important pupils being Dexter Gordon, who grew up in Los Angeles. "I got a chance to hear Lester with the Basie band in Los Angeles," Gordon has said. "They came out there in 1939. All the cats cut school that day—the opening day at the Paramount Theater. Herschel had just died, so I didn't get a chance to hear him. Lester was really in his thing then—very exciting, very dynamic."[91]

"They opened with 'Clap Hands Here Comes Charlie,' " Gordon continues, "and Lester came out soloing—and he was just fantastic. I really loved the man. He was melodic, rhythmic, had that bittersweet approach. And, of course, in his pre-Army days he had such a zest for living. It felt so good to hear him play."[92]

After this, the band moved northward again, this time to play at the San Francisco World Exhibition for two weeks. "We enjoyed that," Buck Clayton remembers. "We were playing outdoors, on a special stand. It was really great. We all had sharp uniforms and everybody was crazy about the band."[93]

Basie's band returned to New York in December and had a few well-earned rest-days before taking part in Hammond's second "From Spirituals to Swing" concert on Christmas Eve. Apart from playing with Basie in a short program, Lester also took part in the jam session section and in a small swing group, called the Kansas City Six once more, with Buck Clayton and Basie's rhythm section, with Basie being replaced by the guitar player Charlie Christian from Benny Goodman's band. The group opened the concert with three numbers which have all been issued on record. Christian was one of Lester's earliest disciples, and they had the same feeling for melody and rhythm, something which clearly had a

Lester Young soloing at the World's Fair, Treasure Island, Calif., October 1939 with the Count Basie Orchestra. Photo courtesy of the Institute of Jazz Studies, Rutgers University.

stimulating effect on Lester on this occasion, as he had been very much on his own up to that point as regards how jazz ought to be played.

The jam session section was last on the program. As was the case with the Goodman concert in Carnegie Hall the previous year, it was something of a washout, this time because the session had to be broken off half-way, since the concert hall had to shut not later than midnight. "Joe Sullivan, Pete Johnson and Count alternated on the piano," a reviewer wrote, "but Hampton missed the train, and his turn at the drums. Harry Edison expressed himself and Lester Young testified. But the jam session was rushed—as Mr. Hammond had explained and apologized to the audience—through necessity. The result could not help being confused and short."[94]

In January 1940 Shad Collins was asked to leave the band for some unknown reason. He was replaced by Al Killian, a proficient first trumpet player with notes in the high register of the instrument as his specialty. Lester felt that the firing of Collins had been unjust. The two had become close friends, and the loss of Herschel Evans had probably led Lester to become even more attached to Collins.

The year 1940 was very successful, musically speaking. It was a year when the band rose to great artistic heights, but also one which was to prove dramatic for both Basie and Lester. Willard Alexander had left MCA at the beginning of that year and joined the William Morris Agency. Basie, who had worked well with Alexander, then tried to break his contract with MCA so that he could follow Alexander. MCA, however, was unwilling to lose a goldmine like Basie. The band had now reached the top and was probably playing better than it ever had done or was to subsequently. To punish the band, it was sent on a tough tour across the United States during the hottest months of the summer, July and August. The band played for three weeks in Hollywood and, after a month of one-nighters, returned to New York and played at the Apollo Theater in the third week of October.

Basie had become so fed up with MCA by this time that he felt like dissolving the band. Benny Goodman was also somewhat despondent, for Lionel Hampton had quit. The two of them put their heads together and began to plan the formation of an all-star unit, consisting of Basie and his rhythm section, Buck Clayton, Lester, Charlie Christian, and Goodman. The group went to the studio to do some test recordings— the equivalent of present-day demonstration tapes—and, judging from the fine, swinging music these informal records offer, it really could have been a fantastic band.

Unfortunately, the plans got no further than this, since Basie managed to get a settlement with MCA, allowing him to break with them on the payment of a fine of $10,000, and to start with Morris after the new year.

There were only sporadic engagements available for the band during November, and Lester spend most of his enforced vacation at a newly opened place in Harlem, in the Hotel Cecil on West 118th Street, called Minton's Playhouse. Basie played at the Savoy Ballroom once more from November 30 to December 12; this was to be Lester's last engagement with Basie for the time being. Immediately afterwards he quit. There were many reasons, but none of them had anything to do with superstition. "That story about leaving me because he didn't want to record on Friday 13th was ridiculous," Basie himself has explained. "I don't know where these stories come from. Prez was never into things like that. He wanted to go out on his own, to get a little group of his own going. I hated to see him go, but at least he went honestly and I couldn't blame him for his ambitions. I enjoyed him every night he played."[95]

"When Prez first came to me at the Reno Club in Kansas City," Basie continues, "it was like nothing we'd ever heard. And it was consistent. In all the years he was with our band he never had a bad night. No matter what happened to him personally, he never showed it in his playing. I can only remember him as being beautiful."[96] Convincing proof that Basie is not exaggerating in his last claim can be found in the records produced by the band and in the live recordings that were broadcast. Lester was on all the recordings of that period and demonstrates such consistently high quality in his solos that it would be impossible to pick out any of them as being better than the others.

The source of the misunderstanding about Friday the 13th is, in fact, none other than Lester himself. One of *Down Beat*'s reporters asked both him and Basie why Lester had left the band, but neither of them wanted to talk about it. The reporter was stubborn, however, and said that Lester could at least tell him why he wasn't going to be on the recording to be made on December 13. To get rid of him, Lester gave the following answer: "Go 'way and lemme sleep—a man's got no business makin' music on Friday the 13th."[97]

By making such a remark, Lester was able to avoid talking about the real reasons for the break with Basie and to keep his inner ambitions to himself. As *Down Beat* got nothing tangible out of the interview, they had to guess, and in an article about Basie's transition from MCA to the William Morris Agency they even wrote that "Don Byas will probably inherit Lester Young's tenor chair. Basie has been using several subs since Young was fired."[98]

Lester was ambitious and high-spirited and did not want the idea that he had been fired to stick to him. The situation is not unlike that when he left Henderson's band and asked for a written statement to prove he hadn't been fired, for a short while later the following reader's letter could be found in *Down Beat,* signed by Mrs. Lester (Mary) Young:

May I correct Mr. Ed Flynn, who wrote, in the Jan. 15 Down Beat, that Lester Young (formerly of Count Basie's orchestra) was fired.

My husband was not fired. He quit for reasons of his own. I will appreciate your making this clear.[99]

We can be sure that it was Mary and not Lester who sent the letter, since Lester always sought to avoid trouble if he possibly could, though he certainly must have complained and grumbled so much about Flynn's claim that Mary wrote the letter to get some peace and quiet at home.

Lester decided to leave Basie for several reasons. First and foremost, he was tired of playing in big bands. "Basie was like school," he once said. "I used to fall asleep in school because I had my lesson, and there was nothing else to do. The teacher would be teaching those who hadn't studied at home, but I had, so I'd go to sleep. Then the teacher would go home and tell my mother. So I put that down."

"In Basie's band there always would be someone who didn't know his part," he continued. "Seems to me that if a musician can't read, he should say so, and then you help him. Or you give him his part before. But Basie wouldn't. I used to talk to him about it, but he had no eyes for it. You had to sit there and play it over and over and over again. Just sit in that chair. . . . You don't get a chance to play. You walk to the mike for your eight bars or sixteen bars and then you sit down. You're just sitting there and reading music. There are no kicks for me that way."[100]

Lester was first and foremost a soloist, not a sideman. Another thing he found unreasonable and unjust was that Basie was lauded to the skies by managers, advisors, and radio people, while the rest of the band members were treated almost as if they were extras. Moreover, Lester frequently came up with a musical idea for an arrangement or a theme, but on the recordings it was Basie's name that appeared, and he collected all the royalties. It was pretty normal, though, for bandleaders made some extra income that way; even so, Lester wanted recognition for that which was his. To get something out of it, he asked for a raise, which was refused—and this was certainly one of the main reasons for the break. "It seems that Prez wanted 125 dollars, and he [Hammond] told Basie that he wasn't worth it, or something like that," Gene Ramey recalls. "The way Prez used to tell me—as I said before, as close as Prez and I were, and I was the best man at his wedding and like the father of his children there for a long time, he used to tell me these things."[101]

Whatever happened, Lester was really hurt at Hammond interfering, since he had always thought him to be a friend who had helped to put him, Basie, and Billie Holiday on the map. He must have felt it was a stab in the back, for he avoided Hammond as much as possible after that and didn't rate him as a friend any more. "Prez never got over it, never got over it," Ramey explains. "And when that man would come down to Birdland, he'd sit down there with a smile on his face. And Prez, rather than using curse words, he called everybody Tommy Tucker. And he said to Jo and I, he said, 'Lady Ramey and Lady Jones, Tommy Tucker's in the house!' "[102]

A final reason should be sought in Lester's peace-loving temperament. As previously mentioned, he hated any kind of trouble and therefore always tried to make up any differences that arose. "The most greatest thing that he ever did was with Scotty, who was the saxophone player," Jo Jones recalls. "They were coming out of Clark Monroe's Uptown House at 10 o'clock in the morning, across the street from the church, and trying to be quiet and Scotty and Monroe got into a fight. Lester Young got in the middle of the fight and he was the one that got socked in the eye. Scotty and Monroe quit fighting and went to the market to get a steak to put on his eye to take the swelling out. He said, 'Oh, you caught the Sunday on me.' So he took the steak off his eye and said, 'Let's cook this fellow.' Oh, he was a beautiful person."[103]

If he could see that it was impossible to help stop some unpleasant scene, however, then he went off on his own. The situation of the Basie band, with its long row with MCA and accusations flying back and forth and probably with arguments within the band resulting from the uncertainty, must certainly have influenced the timing of Lester's departure, for it was only two to three weeks after Lester's break that Basie reached a settlement with MCA.

Lester must also have had a dream of a small band, where there would be much greater opportunities for displaying talent than was the case in a big band. Lester had seen how successful Coleman Hawkins had become after returning from Europe and saw no reason he himself couldn't become an equally successful bandleader, since they were both soloists of the same stature. Lester's tragedy was simply that certain organizing and mental qualities are required for anyone who wants to lead a band—qualities he did not possess.

5

The War Years (1941-1944)

After leaving the narrow confines of the Basie band on December 12, 1940, Lester must at first have experienced a sense of release—something similar to what he must have felt once before, when he had said goodbye to the Young Family Band. The parallel is striking, for, just as he had returned to his father's band for a brief period after a couple of years on his own, so he was to return to Basie after his first experiences as a bandleader.

During the first weeks he only had a couple of jobs taking part in radio broadcasts or concerts which really were jam sessions, from the Village Vanguard in New York. The Village Vanguard was only two years old, and the owner, Max Gordon, remembers that Lester only visited the place on Mondays.[1] On the other days of the week he took part in jam sessions at, among other places, Minton's Playhouse, Jimmy Ryan's, and Monroe's Uptown House. It only took him until shortly after New Year's Day, 1941, to form a small group. Blowing with him was his old friend from the Count Basie band, the trumpet player Shad Collins, and the rhythm section consisted of younger, innovative musicians, such as the piano player Clyde Hart, the guitar player John Collins (not related to Shad), the bass player Nick Fenton, and the drummer Harold "Doc" West. Already Lester showed a tendency to surround himself with younger musicians, one he retained throughout his life, in that the entire rhythm section consisted of players who, in some way or other, were connected with the new type of jazz, bop, which was then in the developmental stage. Fenton and West he found at Minton's Playhouse, where they had been playing with the piano player Thelonious Monk and the tenor sax player Kermit Scott, and Clyde Hart was one of the pioneers of bop, just as John Collins was one of the first guitar players to adopt Charlie Christian's style of playing and develop it further in the bop direction.

The sextet practiced every day in the cellar of the Woodside Hotel, but there was not much work to be had. A recording of a radio broadcast from the beginning of 1941 does exist, however; Clyde Hart was unfortunately unable to take part in it, but even so it is possible to get an impression of how the music was organized. They dispensed with any initial presentation of the theme. Both the numbers we have start with solos, and not until the end do a couple of choruses follow, based on unison riffs from the wind instruments and the guitar. This unusually loose form can of course be seen as a reaction on Lester's part against the arrangements of the Basie band, where less and less room was given to the soloists as time went on. Maybe it was the form he knew from his very first period with Basie at the Reno Club that was being developed.

Every Monday Lester took the group with him down to the Village Vanguard, where the trumpet player and composer Johnny Carisi heard them on several occasions. He recalls: "Lester was one of the guys, that to this day, I could stand to play twelve choruses of something. You know no matter who they are. He was one guy that could always, just when you think he had done it, he would, like, back off a little bit, he would goof and then descend on you again, only more so than before, get everybody crazy, man. That time everybody put their horns down, and Lester would just play—seriously, ten, twelve, fourteen choruses. And nobody else did that. They took their two or three, and that was it."[2]

Lester's group finally got an engagement at Kelly's Stable on 52nd Street, starting on February 27, where they were to come on after Coleman Hawkins's band. The engagement was terminated early, on March 17, however; John Collins can remember how it came about. "Well, it wasn't long before we had trouble," he relates. "There was a walkway from the kitchen that ran right next to the bandstand. At one point Lester came off and I think one of the waiters bumped into him. Next thing you know they got into an argument—and Lester walked right out. Bang! After we'd rehearsed for weeks—just because he felt he wasn't being treated with appropriate respect."[3]

Lester wasn't just queening it when he quit Kelly's Stable; that wasn't part of his nature. There was a white singer named Una Mae Carlisle who was fill-in piano player. She got on well with Lester and the group—who were all black—and the reason for Lester's reaction must certainly have something to do with this fact. The waiter may have grossly insulted Lester with some distasteful remarks which contained racial undertones. "It was a good band," Lester later remarked, "the boss was a crow; he didn't like mixing."[4] Carlisle liked Lester's group so much that she chose it to accompany her on four sides for Victor, the only records Lester got the opportunity of making with his sextet.

After the job at Kelly's Lester's group got no more engagements. He himself managed to earn a little on recordings made for Billie Holiday and Sammy Price, but, apart from that, he was forced to earn his daily bread by going round to the various jam sessions, where the odd coin or two occasionally came the musicians' way. The house piano player at Monroe's Uptown House during those years was Herbie Nichols. He recalls that "the President [Lester Young] never coasted in those days. He was an eager beaver."[5] Many of the musicians whom Lester played with in those jam sessions were young people who had him as their idol and considered him to be their spiritual father. When he stood on the stand he was often the oldest one there, even though he was only thirty-one years old at the time. When he played, young musicians such as Charlie Parker, Dizzy Gillespie, Thelonious Monk, Kenny Clarke, Charlie Christian, and Joe Guy listened to him with respect.

Hurt, bitter, and confused at the way things had developed, Lester was finally forced to dissolve his band in May 1941, since there were apparently no further engagements to be had. John Collins remembers that John Hammond came with the offer that Lester should be a member of a fixed band for Billie Holiday. "Prez wouldn't consent to that," Collins said. "As much as he loved her—and he did—he was on his own. He didn't need her or anyone else to front his band. If he wanted that he could have stayed with Basie."[6]

Lester's problem was that he had no idea about how he should conduct himself to secure jobs. He had no manager and no recording contract to stick to. He was not the type for self-advertisement, and he in fact did not want to have anything to do with the economic and practical matters a bandleader's job entails. Once, when asked if he would consider organizing a big band, he answered: "Would I care to form a big band? Oooh, I would love to, but I wouldn't go for the okeydoke—them headaches, them evil spirits. I can barely make it with five. Like the old lady told me, there's always a bastard in the bunch, and you never know who it is."[7]

Lester finally had no other option than to contact his brother Lee in California to find out whether he could help. He could; the result was that Lester and Mary left Woodside Hotel and New York for Los Angeles, where Lester was to be a member of Lee Young's Esquires of Rhythm. This band was based at Billy Berg's Club Capri, which was situated on La Cienga and Pico Boulevards in Hollywood. When Lester arrived in May 1941, it had the following lineup: Guydner Paul Campell (tp), Hubert Maxwell "Bumps" Myers (ts), Arthur Twine (p), Red Callender (b), Louis Gonzales (g), and the bandleader himself (dr/vcl). Despite the fact that the band already had a tenor player, Lee was adamant about not firing Myers. "Everybody imagined, because Lester was my brother, when he came out, he was gonna join the band, that I was gonna get rid of Bumps Myers," Lee relates. "Well now, Bumps was really, you know—everybody in L.A. loved Bumps, you know, big smile, infectious smile—and he was a big guy, but really, just like a little, chubby bear or something. But a nice man. But I had no intention of axing Bumps. What I ended up doing was having two tenors, one trumpet and a guitar, you know, which is really a big sound that people didn't believe."

"But we had a lot of arrangements made for them," he continues, "and we used to rehearse six days a week, I think it was, and we would learn one arrangement per day, you know."[8]

To begin with, Lester was prevented by strict trade union rules from playing as a full member of the band, so for the first six months he appeared as a guest artist. "They wouldn't allow Lester to play with the band when he first arrived," Lee also mentions, "and they told him he had to appear as a guest; he could play three sets a night—but he had to play on the floor, he couldn't play on the bandstand with the band. We would play a set—we would play three sets a night—and then we would introduce Lester Young, and he'd come out and stand in the middle of the floor and play three tunes. He couldn't play but three, and then he would play nine songs a night."[9]

Even though it was a fixed job, it must have been sheer torture for Lester, who was so eager to play, not to be made more use of in the course of an evening. He did manage to find some outlet for his energy, however; he took part in various sessions at the many jazz places in town, such as those on Central Avenue, with its Jack's Basket Room, Last Word, Club Alabam, the Turban Room, and the Brown Bomber. Here he met a number of talented young musicians, such as the piano player Joe Albany, who was only seventeen years old, and the twenty-year-old drummer Chico Hamilton. "I remember Pres telling me the chords to 'Sweet Lorraine'—the bridge," Albany recalls. "I didn't know it at the time. I was going mostly by ear, but it felt good."[10]

While Lester was waiting to go on to play with the Esquires of Rhythm, he used to sit at the back of the stage on a milk-crate with a bottle of liquor, passing the time playing a card game called tonk, together with the other musicians. Club Capri was a popular place for many musicians who were in Los Angeles from time to time, and there were always some of them who used to come in for a talk with Lester and to hear him play.

In November 1941 he got his union card and could play as a full member of the band. Lee suggested at that juncture that they call themselves Lee and Lester Young's Band. At the time, Duke Ellington's band was also in Los Angeles. His co-arranger, Billy "Sweet Pea" Strayhorn, did some arrangements for the Young brothers' band before they became part of Ellington's standard repertoire, including such numbers as "Take the A-Train," "Flamingo," and "My Little Brown Book." The band was also lucky to have numbers arranged by such talented arrangers as Gerald Wilson and Dudley Brooks.

"When Lester joined the band as a full member," Red Callender recalls, "we really started to swing at full throttle. We loved playing Sweet Pea's tunes . . . in fact, playing in that band was like being involved in an intense love affair. Naturally we played many Basie hits, like 'Lester Leaps In' and 'Tickle Toe.' We were a crowd-pleasing band, playing tunes like 'Stairway to the Stars' as well. Lee had a fine voice: the audience loved his vocals. Our theme song was a tune I wrote down called 'On Again, Off Again' and Lester played my tune 'Pastel' as a solo."[11]

The opening night for Lee and Lester Young's Band at the Club Capri was December 1, 1941, the same night the Ellington band had its premiere at the Trianon Ballroom on Firestone Boulevard in Hollywood. Duke's drummer, Sonny Greer, had fallen ill, and so Lee was asked by Ben Webster and Jimmy Blanton if he would consider being Greer's substitute that evening. Lee got all het up about this, since he had always wanted to play with a big band. Even though it was the evening of his premiere, the Ellington band exerted a greater pull on him than his own band. "But Billy Berg, you know, he was very fond of me," Lee relates. "He had to be, because he says, 'You've got to be the craziest man in the world. How can you be the leader of a band and you're not gonna make your opening?' And I said, 'There's no need talking about it; I'm going to play with Duke tonight.' And I left him, and I played the Trianon with Duke and them that night. Luckily, when I came back the next night, I still had a job, but you know, it was only because the man liked me."[12] Lee cannot remember who replaced him that night, but is certain that Lester and the others were able to find a solution.

Every Tuesday and Saturday evening the radio station KHJ broadcast directly from Club Capri. A couple of numbers from the evening after the premiere have been issued, and they give an impression of the large sound the band had, since the tenor saxophone is used as a trombone voice with some deep held notes.

In Bumps Myers and Lester the band had two sax players who, stylistically speaking, were diametric opposites, a situation like that in the Basie band. Myers was a couple of years younger than Lester and played with a large, round tone in a style influenced by Coleman Hawkins. He was an excellent player and tested Lester to the full, so it was naturally these two the audience and reviewers paid most attention to. Dave Dexter, *Down Beat*'s New York editor, who was on a round trip in Los Angeles and Hollywood in the summer of 1941 to get his finger on the pulse of jazz there, was not greatly impressed. He wrote that "Lee Young has a fair black outfit at the Capri Club on Pico Boulevard with Lee's brother, Lester Young, on tenor, but at best it's a crew which rates well below countless others in Chicago, Kansas City and New York. 'Bumps' Myers, also a tenor saxist, shares hot choruses with Les Young. A majority of the band's followers told Down Beat they preferred his work to that of the ex-Basie star.'' [13]

Dexter's review dates from the period when Lester was only guest soloist, but even after Lester had become a full member of the band, the audience's favorite was Myers. "The consensus of the crowd last night at the Club Capri (Hollywood)," *Down Beat* wrote at the beginning of 1942, "was that Myers was playing more interesting tenor than his boss." [14] *Metronome*'s reviewer was also impressed by Myers and wrote that Lester "was getting one helluva run for his money, though, from a tooter named Bumps (I think that's what they called him) Myers." [15]

It is of course natural for an audience to prefer the local man to an outsider, especially in Lester's case, since he played in a style which for most people was still something very new. Lee can also remember that the audience had to get used to Lester's style of playing before they could appreciate it: "Everyone felt as though Bumps Myers, the people here in town, which was the tenor player, would really blow Lester away, because they always had their favorites, but it took them about a couple of sessions to understand what he—Lester—was about." [16] He also relates that "when he played with us, the most requests that Lester got was playing ballads, you know, such as 'These Foolish Things' and 'I Can't Get Started.' The lay person would always know what he was playing, and I really think that's why he was so well known among the lay people, because I think they related to what he did, because they could understand; he didn't play over their heads. Like in later years, when bebop first came in, the people didn't know what the musicians were playing, you know, that was really just for musicians, you know, and even some of the musicians didn't understand it at the time. But I really think the guy really did play melodic, and he played beautifully." [17]

Musically speaking, things were going fine for Lester, and it was definitely a relief to him that he was able to concentrate on the music once more without having to concern himself with the functions of a bandleader. This was Lee's province, since he had a natural talent for leadership. "Lee Young and Lester Young were like night and day," Callender recalls. "Probably the only thing they shared in common except their musical family background was their love of sport, particularly baseball. Lee was, and is, a leader, an extrovert, a consummate businessman, dependable, organized, health-conscious, a terrific golfer, a great drummer—a 'drum college all by himself' as Sir Charles Thompson puts it. Lee's only vice was ice cream and malts. Other guys would be sitting around sipping booze while Lee would be sipping a milkshake. Though Lee never censured anyone for what they did, if they were smoking pot or whatever, Lee was cool. He's a very clean-cut person with a broad spectrum of interests."[18]

If things were going well for Lester at the professional level, at the personal level problems were beginning to arise, since his relationship with Mary was getting worse. In terms of race, California was like a southern state. This meant that whenever they were in town they were constantly being exposed to various types of unpleasantness, since Mary was white. She hadn't enjoyed Lester's complete love from the start, but the racial discrimination he was exposed to now was more than he could bear. He finally moved out of the house they were living in on West 38th Street in the black part of Los Angeles to a hired room in a three-storey house his father owned.

The room was sparsely furnished, with a bed, a chest of drawers, and his indispensable portable gramophone, which he had with him wherever he went. When he was in his room the record-player was always on, for music was a necessity for Lester—he liked all sorts of music, as long as it was beautiful. He seldom played jazz; most of all he played popular music with a male singer, and later on Frank Sinatra was his favorite. "Favorite records?" he once said. "I like variety. I don't like to get hung up with one thing. Anything they play over the radio that I like, I'll get it. Just all music, all day and all night music. Just any kind of music you play for me, I melt with all of it."[19]

A changed version of Lee and Lester Young's Band had its premiere at the Club Capri on February 24, 1942. The trumpet player was now "Red" Mack Morris, who played in a style reminiscent of Buck Clayton and was a proficient singer as well. The only white man in the group was the piano player Jimmy Rowles, who had previously played with the guitar player Slim Gaillard and the bass player Slam Stewart. Rowles had joined the group as a replacement for Arthur Twine, who had died suddenly of a heart attack in the fall of 1941. Slim and Slam then continued as a popular duo; they had their premiere at the Club Capri on the same night as the Young brothers' band. "Slim and Slam—Lee and Lester Young and Their Orchestra plus three side-men (a seven-piece band with four leaders) debuted at the Capri," *Down Beat* wrote in its review. "Your reporter hasn't had a chance to catch but reliable sources have it they sound plenty good."[20] Things apparently went well, for a little while later you could read that the "hot spot of the town is now quite definitely the Capri, where hold forth the new Slim and Slam and Lee and Lester Young band, the Spirits of Rhythm and unannounced attractions from time to time."[21]

Jimmy Rowles can remember that time at the Club Capri and that the members of the band used to call Lester Uncle Bubba. He remembers

Lester as being quiet and always extremely polite. If he got upset once in a while, he used to take a small whisk broom out of his top jacket pocket and give his left shoulder a brush. Rowles also noticed that Lester was always well-dressed in a suit, with a leaning toward double-breasted pinstripes, and that he wore tab collars, small trouser cuffs, pointed shoes, and Cuban heels. Rowles also recalls that the older musicians didn't really appreciate Lester and, even as late as 1941, didn't really feel he was an equal.[22]

Rowles also had difficulty in understanding what Lester said; it took him quite a while to break into his language. Red Callender also recalls that

everything Lester said was almost in code; he had his own private language. "Where's your pound cake?" meant where's your wife or girlfriend. To Lester, pound cake was so rich, you couldn't get any better than that. Wearing a hat meant having sex. If he saw a fat lady go by on the street, he'd say la de da de . . . which meant all ass and no body. If he liked what he saw he'd say "peaches and cream." He'd comment on everyone, though he never poked fun at people in a cruel manner. Lester was an extremely sensitive human being who bruised easily. His gestures and manners were so exact, they became classic. He also had a distinct little whistle. When the band members heard it, we knew it was time to play.

I loved Lester dearly, enjoyed hanging out with him. He was a soft-spoken man who couldn't hurt a fly. We mostly rapped about music and his experiences on the road."[23]

Billy Berg was not allowed to keep the Club Capri, which, for some inexplicable reason, closed down in April 1942. "Then one night," Rowles recalls,

we had only been there about six months, when we came to work there was a juke box in the middle of the floor, and something had happened and they'd taken the entertainment license away, so we were all out of work. But Billy Berg turned around. About a week later or two weeks later my phone rings and he says, "Well, are you working?" and I say, "No," and he says, "Well, you are now!" So I say, "Where am I working?" and he says, "I'd bought a new club. Be at the corner of so-and-so and Beverly Fairfax tomorrow afternoon at three o'clock and I'll explain the whole thing to everybody."

So we went all over there, the whole bunch of Lee and Lester and a trumpet player from St. Louis named Paul Campbell.

When Billy Berg bought his new place he called it the Trouville Club and all the motion picture people used to come there, in fact they used to come to the

Capri too. I worked with Lee and Lester Young then, Slim and Slam played together and alone and Joe Turner sang with the Spirits of Rhythm with Teddy Bunn, Leo Watson and they had Eddie Beal playing piano with them, and everything was switched around.[24]

Shortly after the Trouville Club opened Billie Holiday came out to California to sing with Lee and Lester Young's Band for two whole months—from May onwards—which made Lester very happy. They took up their customary trips around town after working hours, just as they had previously done in New York. Billie liked the band too, though she was at first a little reserved as far as Jimmy Rowles was concerned, on account of the color of his skin. She complained to Lester that she didn't like him, whereupon Lester replied, "I don't know—this cat can blow." Rowles and Billie eventually became very good friends, however, and he accompanied her later on several occasions.

That Billie had a fine, enjoyable time in Hollywood is confirmed by the following extract from her memoirs: "It was a crazy group Lester assembled at Billy's place. I can hear them now even though I can't remember all their proper names. We used to rock that joint. Bette Davis came in one night and danced herself crazy. Lana Turner used to come in every Tuesday and Thursday. That girl can really dance, and she did at Billy's. She always asked me for 'Strange Fruit' and 'Gloomy Sunday.' She used to like to dance with young Mel Tormé, who used to win all of Billy's lindy contests. Maybe he couldn't cut the cats at the Savoy in Harlem, but he sure could dance."[25]

From Billie's time at the Trouville Club several radio recordings exist of Lee and Lester Young's Band, both with and without Billie as soloist. They reveal that the band had a hefty swing and that the arrangements were sometimes quite complicated, with spicy harmonies and some often elegant and unexpected turns of phrase.

One of the guests who often came to listen was a young man named Norman Granz, who at the time was employed by MGM as a film editor. He often used to talk with the musicians, and he got the idea of arranging jam sessions where the public would pay to come in. These could be held at the Trouville Club on Sunday afternoons, the only day in the week when there wasn't any music. Billy Berg agreed to the idea, and the first arrangement was launched on a Sunday in mid-June 1942 and lasted from 4 P.M. to 7 P.M. Lester, who was one of Granz's favorite musicians, was the main attraction, and all who took part were paid a fixed rate of $9 for three hours of music. The other musicians involved were "Red" Mack Morris and Taft Jordan (tp), Joe Ewing (tb), Eddie Barefield (cl), Nate Cole (p), Oscar Moore (g), Wesley Price (b), and Lee Young (dr).

The afternoon was a success and whet Granz's appetite. More Sunday afternoon sessions followed, and on June 28 Lester was on stage with two other giants of the tenor sax, Ben Webster and Joe Thomas. The pressure must have been great on that occasion; *Down Beat* reported that they were "literally carving each other into strips."[26]

Lee Young recalls that Lester loved these jam sessions and was especially fond of the challenge of playing tunes he didn't know beforehand. "If he didn't know the tune, he'd say, 'Don't call the chords to me. Just play the chords and I'll play.' And I'd seen him do it many a time, you know; they just started playing, and he didn't know it, but he would play it—but he would say it confines you too much if you know it's a D flat 7, you know, you start thinking of the only notes that will go in that chord, and he would say that's not what he would hear. He wanted to play other things and make it fit. And he did."[27]

In July Billie returned to New York. Her place at the Trouville Club was taken by Marie Bryant, who was good at both dancing and singing. Bumps Myers also left the band then for a short time to play with Jimmie Lunceford. John Hammond had heard Lee and Lester Young's Band on the radio and liked it so much that he contacted Barney Josephson, owner of the two Café Society clubs, to try to get them to come to New York. Josephson agreed to take the band for a month and contacted Los Angeles to hear how the musicians felt. Only Lester had played in New York previously, so everybody was excited at the offer. They agreed to open at the Café Society Downtown, 2 Sheridan Square in Greenwich Village, on September 1, 1942.

While in California, Lester had received various tempting offers from time to time to go back to Count Basie's band, but he didn't want to, since he felt happy and at ease with Lee, who took good care of the business side of things. Apart from this Lester was given as much free space as he needed: "It was supposed to be a good band," Lee recalls, "and we thought it was, because we were in Hollywood and went to Café Society. We went for four weeks and stayed six months!"

"You know, if Lester had any business difficulties at this time," he continues, "he'd call me on the phone and get me to talk to them. He didn't want to have any dealings with business. 'I only want to play my horn,' he used to say. He thought business would interfere with his playing. I don't have to explain to anyone how close Lester and I were, because you really shouldn't have to explain about family ties."[28]

At the Café Society Downtown Lee and Lester Young's Band took over from the Teddy Wilson group. For the premiere both Bumps Myers and the trumpet player Paul Campbell, whom Lester had given the nickname "Ripty Gipty" on account of his tiny stature, returned to the band. Apart from this the only alteration was that Jimmy Rowles, who had not been able to resist an offer from Benny Goodman, was replaced by Charles Thompson, called "Sir" by Lester; and Thompson was replaced by Clyde

Hart in January 1943. The band was a success from the start, and their engagement was extended time after time. The musicians enjoyed playing at the Café Society, since Josephson always made sure that details such as the loudspeaker system, the tuning of the piano, the lights— things that so irritate musicians if they are not in perfect working order—were taken care of. It was always a good show, and in the months the Young brothers played there, many artists performed, such as the Reviewers with Adolph Green, Judy Holliday and Betty Comdon, the boogie-woogie piano players Albert Ammons and Pete Johnson, as well as the classical pianist Sam Reichman Lewis. In short, all possible tastes were catered to.

With so many people performing on the same evening, there were long breaks between the spots when Lee and Lester Young's Band were on stage. This made the evenings very long. "It was quite an experience to be there, just bad on the health," Red Callender recalls.

The only drag about the Café Society Downtown was the hours. In L.A. we worked from 10 p.m. to 2 a.m. In New York, we're making more bucks, but the hours were from 8 p.m. to 4 a.m., which is too long a stretch to be involved in music; the money should have been twice as much and it wasn't. By the time you get off, you're exhausted. During our breaks we'd go out the back door to the alley, stand around drinking, smoking weed, chewing bennies—anything to keep going because the gig was so long. Lester turned us on to his version of a boilermaker. The bottom layer was 151-proof rum, topped off with Rainier Ale. We'd drink these down and it was a bomp. . . . All the musicians who were in New York at that time came by to dig Prez. Everybody would try to cut him, but Lester blew them all down. Ben Webster would try to keep up with Lester both on the bandstand and out in the alley drinking booze. Unfortunately Ben couldn't hold his liquor the way Prez could and he ended up frustrated, drunk and beaten down by Lester's horn. Even Coleman Hawkins would come by the Café Society to hear Lester because his sound was so unique.[29]

Sir Charles Thompson also remembers that period of his career as something special and can also add something about Lester's way of leading a band.

Café Society was the most high class jazz night club in the world as has ever been. It was really an exciting place, a wonderful and a very beautiful night club, and they had the top entertainment in the world.

Our band played and the band played for shows, you know. Actually it was Lee and Lester's band, and in the band was featured Red Callender. Beautiful human being. Very, very wonderful musician, friend of mine. He was playing the bass, and there was another guitarist.

And there was a trumpet player by the name of Paul Campbell who came from St. Louis. He had played with some of the midwestern bands in St. Louis. And there was another tenor player named Bumps Myers. He was a good tenor player.

It was a good band. Bumps really had a style of his own, in a way. Bumps was—I don't know how to describe his style but I think he had his own little personality, you know, and he was a nice person too, and it was quite interesting to see the way that Lester accepted having another tenor player in his small band.

Lester led the band with his eyes. He hardly said anything except hey baby, or you know, everything that Lester had to say usually was complimentary, you know. And he had nothing to say hardly at all except through his horn, but you could look at his eyes and tell what he was thinking if you were with him.

Now, I would say actually most of the you might say the discipline or any words which were spoken, which were very few, perhaps, were done by his brother Lee, who was very business orientated. He was more of a businessman, you know. And Lester strictly was a jazz player, but—now by no means am I saying that Lester did not lead the band, because he did lead the band. But you see in a good band like that, you really don't necessarily need a leader because all the men understand what's happening. You call the number, you name the tune or you call it by number—or before you get on the bandstand, well we're going to play such and such and such a thing. So when you get on the bandstand you know what's happening and everybody's just waiting for the beat to start.

I think Lee actually probably counted off a lot of the tunes, and then some was done by Lester. But there is no doubt that it was Lester's band, you know, really. Lester was the leader, there's no question about it. I mean, like every band, some bands who have leaders, sometimes they have somebody else in the band who maybe starts off certain pieces or does a few things like that. But, you know, as a man or as a professional performer, everyone recognizes who the leader is, and there was no question about it that Lester was the leader of the band because he was the great jazz player, and he was the man people really came to hear as the leader. But he wasn't the type of person that was interested in being known as the leader, because he was a jazz player who played his horn for the love of it and he just played. And he never acted as a leader, he just played.[30]

The band's success came to an abrupt end when Lee and Lester received the news that their father had died after a protracted illness on February 6, 1943. Lee traveled to Los Angeles immediately to arrange the funeral and to help Sarah, who had become an invalid several years previously, when one of her legs had to be amputated. Willis Handy's death came as such a blow to Sarah, however, that she died only two weeks later.

Lee stayed on in Los Angeles, and several of the members of the band also traveled back to California. Lester, however, chose to return to New York after the funerals. Even though he wasn't exactly a family man, the loss of both his father and his stepmother within so short a time was a hard blow for him; his relationship to his father especially had been a warm and a strong one.

When Lee and Lester Young's Band unfortunately split up in this way, Lester was obliged to return to his former pattern of playing wherever a jam session was getting going. This unstable form of existence continued almost until April 1943, when he became a member of the tenor saxophonist Al Sears's big band. Sears had started up his big band in October 1942 on account of a long engagement at the Renaissance Casino in New York that ended at the beginning of April, a couple of weeks after Lester had joined.

Sears then went with his band to Camp Polk near Alexandria, Louisiana, his first stop on a long tour of military bases throughout the United States. This tour had been arranged by the United Services Organizations (USO), a nonprofit concern started in 1941 to cater for all types of entertainment for the troops. The tour started on April 13, and Lester found himself in the company of a host of good musicians: Al Sears, Budd Johnson, Edgar Sampson, and Fats Green (rds), Howard Callender, Alexander Carion, and Allen Brown (tp), Ted Donelly and George Williams (tb), Wellman Braud (b), Marlowe Morris (p), Christopher Columbus (dr), and Kenneth Preston (vcl). Their weekly wage was $84.50 apiece, with Sears as leader receiving $115.

The band's saxophone section in particular was impressive, and Lester was to have some splendid tenor sax duels with Budd Johnson. Budd recalls that the great Arthur Rubinstein was also on this tour. It made a great impression on him that Lester drank continuously, from the time he got up until he went to bed at night. When he went to a liquor store he didn't buy just one bottle, but five or six at a time.

"How can you drink so much like that?" Johnson once asked him.

"Well, I never want to lose this feeling," he said. "This is the feeling I had when I made it with the horn, all the records with Basie and everything."[31]

Al Fisher, who was a fan of Lester's, had been called up at that point, and he recalls that the band's visit was an unforgettable experience for him. "As neither a musician or a critic," he wrote to *Jazz Review,* "it is difficult for me to describe the effect that Lester's music had on me. I can only say that his arrival with a USO troupe at an Air Force base in Sheppard Field, Texas, while I was there was probably the high of the war for me, and that contemplates both armistices. Lester was working with a fine group of Negro musicians, including Al Sears . . . and when he stepped out in front with his pork-pie hat and dark glasses (no USO monkey suit for him), he blew the crackers, the hayseeds, and even we studiedly casual easterners right out of our seat. It was only one of many memorable nights that Lester gave me, but it is one I remember best."[32]

The tour lasted until October 1, 1943, when Al Sears was forced to disband, since the USO had no more funds. Home again in New York, Lester accepted an invitation to replace Don Byas in Count Basie's band for the week of October 8–14, since Byas had fallen ill. The young alto saxophone player Preston Love, who was a substitute for Earle Warren when the latter was on leave, can clearly remember this job, which took place at the Apollo Theater: "We opened with an up-tempo version of Swingin' the Blues, and at the first notes of his famous recorded solo the whole house went wild!"[33]

After this job Lester was once more without fixed employment for a couple of weeks, until he was engaged in November to play in the first bop group, led by the trumpet player Dizzy Gillespie and the bass player Oscar Pettiford. The drummer was Harold "Doc" West, later replaced by Max Roach, and the piano player was George Wallington, sometimes replaced by Thelonious Monk. Typical of the group's style was its unison thematic choruses, an idea first conceived by Pettiford, since he felt that the usual pattern of melody on trumpet accompanied by sustained low notes on the tenor sax sounded too corny. Wallington has told of those historic days, but has reversed the order of Don Byas and Lester in his narrative (Byas joined the band around December 1, 1943, after Lester had left).

"Dizzy used to take me to his house and we'd play and he showed me his songs," Wallington recalls. "Then he and Oscar started the band at the Onyx. Charlie Parker was supposed to join us but they say he couldn't get a cabaret card. I really don't know. Anyway, we had Don Byas, then Lester Young. Billie Holiday used to sing with us sometimes and Sarah Vaughan used to come in too. All the bandleaders used to come in to hear what we were playing—Jimmy Dorsey, Benny Goodman, Charlie Barnet, plus musicians in those and other bands, also Coleman Hawkins, Roy Eldridge and other great jazzmen."

"I don't know if we thought of what we were doing at the Onyx as something historic," he adds, "but we did know we were doing something new and that no-one else could play it and that everyone was coming to listen."[34]

Billie Holiday was at the Onyx Club about then with Al Casey's Trio, which alternated with the Gillespie-Pettiford group; so it was more than natural that she sang the occasional number where she worked together with Lester once more.

About the same time—from November 5 on—Count Basie began an eight-week engagement at the Lincoln Hotel in New York, which was owned by Mrs. Maria Kramer. She liked swing music in general, and the rhythm section in the Count Basie band in particular. It was something of an experiment for her to book the band at the Lincoln Hotel, since no black band had played there before. The engagement proved to be a great success, however, and during the ensuing years she booked the band at regular intervals to play in the Blue Room at the Lincoln Hotel on 8th Avenue, not far from 44th Street.

At this time Don Byas, who played in Basie's saxophone section, had serious drinking problems. When he drew a gun during one of the breaks of an engagement at the Lincoln Hotel in his drunkenness, Basie fired him on the spot and asked Jo Jones to try to get Lester to come back to the band as his replacement.

"I went round to the White Rose and got Lester," Jo Jones recalls, "and Lester didn't know what I was doing. I bought him a beer and told him, 'You're due at work tomorrow night at 7 o'clock. You come to the Lincoln Hotel, etcetera.' And there he was! Nobody said nothing; he just sat down and just started playing, and nobody thought about nothing. They didn't say, 'Hello, Lester, where have you been?'' or nothing. He came back in the band just like he'd just left fifteen minutes ago."[35]

Even so, it was a surprise for everyone—not least among them Basie himself—that Lester, having turned down various offers, turned up at the Lincoln Hotel. The exact date is not known, but it must have been shortly before December 1, 1943.[36] What changed Lester's mind about playing in a big band can only remain a source of conjecture, but it may well have been the instability of his life about that time and his desire to get a fixed job with a regular income.

Every evening Mrs. Kramer used to sit at a table close to the bandstand and listen to the music. On such occasions she wanted to hear the rhythm section in action, and this gave the reed and brass sections a chance to take a well-earned break relaxing in the bar. It was quite difficult for black bands to get anything but short engagements in the larger New York hotels, so Basie's musicians made the very most of it. Mrs. Kramer also paid them pretty well, which in itself was somewhat unusual, since such jobs were normally paid at a lower rate than one-night stands.

Shortly after New Year's Day, 1944 Basie's band began an eight-week tour, which took it to such places as Adams, Newark, Pittsburgh, Detroit, Milwaukee, Cincinnati, and Philadelphia. By the last week in February they were back at the Apollo in New York once more, and from April 6 through May they played at the Lincoln Hotel.

The trombone player, Dicky Wells, can remember a custom that Lester started whenever one of the musicians played something wrong. "It was at the Lincoln that Prez got his little bell," he recalls. "If somebody missed a note, or you were a new guy and goofed, you'd hear this bell going—ding-dong! If Prez was blowing and goofed, somebody would reach over and ring his bell on him. 'Why, you . . .' he'd say when he'd finished."

"Jo Jones had another way of saying the same thing," he continues. "Bing-bing-bing he'd go on his cymbal rod. When you first joined, you would take it kind of rough, but later you'd be in stitches with the rest, and take it as a joke. They'd ring a bell on Basie, too. And if Prez saw someone getting angry, he'd blow the first bar of Runnin' Wild."[37] Lester had taken the idea with him from the Reno Club in Kansas City, where a large bell hung on one side of the bandstand and was used by both Lester and Jo Jones if anyone in the band played a wrong note.

Apart from his Basie band obligations, Lester still took an active part in the various jam sessions on 52nd Street and in Harlem whenever an opportunity presented itself. The tenor sax player Dexter Gordon came to the Big Apple from Los Angeles in the spring of 1944 with the singer Billy Eckstine's band. This big band consisted of a whole range of promising young musicians who were later to become the most prominent exponents of bop—Charlie Parker, Dizzy Gillespie, Clyde Hart, Oscar Pettiford, and Sarah Vaughan. "Prior to this time, I didn't come out to play too much," Gordon recalls. "I mean to jam. I was just struggling to play those parts in the band. I didn't feel I *should* come out and play. But in 1944, I went down to Minton's one night and got on the stand and sat in between Lester and Ben, so that was a hell of an experience for me. It was a gas. I say 'sat' because at that time everybody was sitting down playing. There was no standing up."[38]

After the engagement at the Lincoln Hotel, Basie's band set off on June 1 on a long tour, which took it right across the United States to the West Coast. It was to be more than two years before Lester came back to New York. One of the first stops on the way to California was a two-week engagement in Chicago at the Regal Theater, at 4719 South Parkway. Dicky Wells and Lester were both afflicted by minor health problems at this point. "I had my tonsils removed," Wells recalls, "because they kept swelling, and I also had stomach disorders. That was because I was drinking quite a bit, trying to stay together. I guess anyone but Basie would have fired me long before. He didn't want to have you on the bandstand if you felt bad, and I'd lay off a week or two, and he'd tell Lady Snodgrass to bring me my money! After I'd had my tonsils out, Lester's burst on him. That was in Chicago. They got the house doctor in the hotel, and Prez said afterwards, 'Where the hell did you get that cat from? He must have been a horse doctor, cutting away at all the wrong places in my throat!'"[39]

Lester soon recovered, but his confidence in doctors was shattered. From that time on, he was dead scared of anyone in a white coat and avoided seeking help, even if it was necessary. He never went to a dentist, and this led to his being subject to toothaches during his later years, which he preferred to relieve by means of liquor rather than by dental treatment.

The band traveled on from Chicago to Columbus and Cleveland, playing one-night stands. There were intermissions of up to a week in Youngstown and Kansas City, where the band played at the Tower. Kansas City was no longer the open, lively town Basie had left in 1936. In the intervening years the Pendergast era had been curtailed. Many of the nightclubs where live music had been played had either been closed down or transformed into ordinary bars. The night-life of the town was in a state of decline, but there were still clubs Lester and other similarly inclined could go to play after their working hours at the Tower were over.

On August 1, Basie's band began a two-month stay on the West Coast, including two weeks at the Orpheum in Los Angeles. From here they traveled north to play for a further two weeks in San Francisco and Oakland before returning to Hollywood for a month's stay at the Plantation Club, starting on September 7.

In Los Angeles Lester was to make his film debut, in the short *Jammin' the Blues* by the photographer Gjon Mili. The film is a masterpiece both musically and in terms of shooting technique. It lasts for less than a quarter of an hour, but once seen it is never forgotten. It was not a problem-free film to make, as can be seen from the review in *Down Beat* after the premiere:

Now that we have seen Jammin' the Blues we can unreservedly rate it, despite obvious faults, as the most notable jazz treatment to come out of Hollywood to date. The credit goes not to Warner Brothers but to Norman Granz, who is largely responsible for what went into it in the way of music; and to Gjon Mili (who had never directed a picture before) for the original photographic treatment. They had to battle Mr. Studio to accomplish every notable advance over trite studio formula methods.

What they accomplished can be judged from some of the difficulties encountered. One of the main problems in a picture of this kind is mechanical. Musical sound-track is recorded before a picture is photographed, the musician or singer pretends to play or sing exactly the same notes recorded, meantime guided by a playback of the sound track.

Anyone who is familiar with jazz will understand why it is difficult to synchronize a good jazz performance, the essence of which is an improvised, spontaneously created solo. In this case the musicians were attempting to synchronize to improvised solos recorded a full month previously. Granz had phonograph recordings made of the solos so that the boys could take them home and memorize them. The idea worked very well except in the case of Illinois Jacquet and Lester Young. Lester, it's our opinion, didn't try very hard.

Drum solos are especially difficult to synchronize. Good results were obtained by Granz by recording some of the more complicated passages, such as "rolls," on the set during shooting and dubbing these sections into the track. However, we have a suspicion that some of the drumming that Sid appears to do was recorded by Jo and vice versa.

Mr. Studio objected to the appearance of a white musician with Negroes. Of course, he didn't object personally, but it just wouldn't go with Southern audiences. Granz was asked to eliminate Barney Kessel or to get a Negro guitarist to "fake" his playing in the picture. Granz refused but had to be satisfied with photography that hides the fact that Kessel is white from all but the most discerning eyes.

Lester Young during the recording of the sound track to ''Jammin' the Blues,'' August 1944, with John Simmons (b), Jo Jones (dr), and Marlowe Morris (p). From the collection of Don Schlitten.

Mr. Studio wanted "hundreds of jitterbug dancers in a gigantic spectacle of rhythm." Mili and Granz managed to get it down to the Archie Savage-Marie Bryant routine, a formalized thing that smacks of the Katherine Dunham influence and adds nothing but doesn't detract too much. Marie Bryant's vocal on Sunny Side of the Street isn't hard to take.

The music in Jammin' the Blues is not notable considering the calibre of the musicians. It is not their best, but it is still the best of its kind ever heard in a picture.

The names of the boys are given on the main title (that we should live to see this day!), but here they are again: Lester Young, Illinois Jacquet, Harry Edison, Jo Jones, Sidney Catlett, Red Callender, John Simmons, Marlowe Morris, Barney Kessel.[40]

Harry Edison doesn't agree with the article's criticism of Lester's lack of effort in learning his solos. "We had a hard time remembering what we played," he narrates. "Some of us had to write it out and put the music on the floor, you know, and look down now and then. Prez didn't have to do that. He had a good memory; he could remember his solos. He didn't have any problems remembering his solos because his solos weren't hard, but they were with so much feeling, with so much soul. He didn't put a whole lot of notes in a solo. He put the right note in the right place at the right time, just like Count Basie. His timing was perfect."[41]

An interesting detail is that the actor Humphrey Bogart, a keen jazz enthusiast, saw to it that the musicians were paid more than originally promised. One day he met Illinois Jacquet outside the studio and, in the course of their conversation, he heard about the rates of pay they had agreed to. Norman Granz recorded more than twice the amount of music eventually used in the film, and since the recordings took place on several different occasions, not all the musicians were present at all the takes.

The film is composed of three numbers: the slow-tempo "Midnight Symphony," the medium-tempo number "On the Sunny Side of the Street," and the final up-tempo "Jammin' the Blues." The start of the film especially is unforgettable. Lester is sitting in a forward-leaning position so that his porkpie hat is almost vertical. Then he slowly raises his head. While the smoke from his cigarette wafts upward, he puts the tenor sax to his lips and begins to play the first chorus of "Midnight Symphony." The film gradually increases in intensity, in terms of both music and picture sequences, finishing with drum solo, dance, and Illinois Jacquet's eloquently screaming tenor sax soaring over the ensemble's final chorus of "Jammin' the Blues."

6

Private 39729502 Young (1944–1945)

During the takes for *Jammin' the Blues* Lester received a written summons to report to the army immediately. This came close to knocking him out, but it was not the first time Lester had had such a summons. During the previous year both he and Jo Jones had received several, including urgent telegrams, but they had ignored them, something quite normal for traveling musicians to do, since they could always claim that they had not been around when the post arrived. The army, however, had other means that could be employed when conscripts were reluctant to report to the draft board.

Toward the end of September 1944, during Basie's last week at the Plantation Club, the FBI sent an agent to the club. "This young guy came out one night—zoot suit on, big chain down to the knees like Cab Calloway," Buddy Tate recalls. "He introduced himself, and we thought he was a fan. He stayed all night, and he said, 'I'd like for you and Lester and Sweets and Jo to be my guests—and he bought drinks and drinks and drinks all night."

"At the end," Tate continues, "he pulls his badge and shows it to Lester and Jo Jones. 'Be at this address at 9 o'clock in the morning, or we'll come and get you and you'll go to jail for five years.' It upset Lester. He said, 'Goddam it! Ain't that a bitch! The little guy—I liked him. He gained my confidence. I started to turn him on!' I said not to worry, because by this time Lester's drinking a quart of 100 per cent proof a day, and they won't want Jo either because he's crazy. But man—the next day, they put them in."[1] Lester went straight from the Plantation Club to the Down Beat Club, where Lee was playing, and told him what had happened. The next morning Lee drove him down to the draft board building on 8th Street.

The conversations Lester had with the officers there were to prove disastrous since, against his will, he managed to make a false and negative impression. He was honest and forthright in what he told them; among other things, he revealed that he had smoked marijuana for the past eleven years. This, coupled with a different skin color and different conditions, would on its own have been enough to be rejected. The officers, however, could see from the papers in front of them that both Lester and Jo Jones had draft-dodged for over a year, and they probably wanted to make use of the occasion to an example. Over and above this, Lester, without realizing it, gave them the impression that he was play-acting so as to be rejected. Buddy Tate recalls, for example, that Lester "went down there talking his hip talk, 'Well, voodaroony, I see you got Von Hangman's eyes. So I'm going to have to play my role.' Prez cracked them up. They thought he might be putting on an act, so they passed him."[2]

The medical examination revealed that Lester had contracted syphilis and that he occasionally suffered from epileptic fits. He was told that he was to have a lumbar puncture. Since he was terrified of being jabbed and also knew that it was extremely painful, he used liquor as an anesthetic. This led, however, to him being obliged to spend the night in a padded cell, not the best start to his life as a soldier. On September 30 Lester was inducted and sent to Fort MacArthur in southern Los Angeles for five weeks' basic training.

On the very same evening he turned up at the Down Beat Club, to Lee's great consternation. "What are you doing here?" Lee exclaimed. "And he said, 'I jumped the wall.' You know, and so he came over the wall and I took him back, and he went back over the wall and got back in camp, but it's a thing that he could not adjust to, you know? He did not adjust very well to being ordered around, you know; he had a resentment for that, and personally, I don't think they should have put him in the army in the manner which they did."[3]

Lee wasn't the only one who thought so. Both Lester's manager Milt Ebbins and Norman Granz tried to persuade the authorities to send Lester back home again, referring to the fact that they considered him ill-fitted both mentally and physically to be a soldier; but all such pleas were in vain. There is no doubt that Lester's call-up was on false premises and that the U.S. Army made an unfortunate mistake on this occasion.

First and foremost, Lester was an extremely original character, not only as a musician, but also in his manner, as was abundantly clear if one shared his company. The piano player John Lewis thinks that he heard a way of speaking similar to Lester's in Albuquerque, and variations of it in Oklahoma City, Kansas City, and Chicago at the end of the twenties and the beginning of the thirties. He can also recall that these people, like Lester, were well dressed, with porkpie hats and all. "So his speech and dress were natural things he picked up," says Lewis. "They weren't a disguise—a way of hiding. They were a way to be hip— to express an awareness of everything swinging that was going on."[4] This desire to be himself and to be hip was further underlined by Lester being the first musician to wear dark sunglasses, as can be seen on photographs of him as far back as 1939. This fashion was later adopted by a host of bop musicians and persisted far into the 1950s.

Lester also wanted to be his own boss as far as possible, and therefore, as Lee has explained, he could not stand being pushed around. He was also of a lazy disposition physically; he wanted to do things at his own speed, without hurrying. This relaxed nature of his, which so clearly can be felt in his playing, was simply part of his personality. "He's been a strange guy as long as I've known him," Norman Granz narrates. "I remember watching Lester walk to a rehearsal. It was a block down the street. They were waiting for him. Lee yelled, 'Hurry up, Lester.' But Lester dragged his horn on the sidewalk and took his time. You never could rush him. We've been with him with planes to make, curtains going up. I've never seen him make a hurried move. Coleman Hawkins once told me: 'I think *I* can get relaxed, but I don't know anyone who can get as relaxed as *he* can.' "[5]

The individuality of the common soldier was, of course, stifled in the army, since everyone was to be standardized, dressing and thinking alike. It takes a robust personality to withstand the incessant shouting and ordering around by one's superiors, and it must have been virtually intolerable for Lester, who hated violence and unpleasant people—and who was sure to be on the receiving end of racist remarks if he didn't jump to it quickly enough.

His sense of justice was highly developed; added to this was the fact that he was pretty thin-skinned. So he experienced the first few weeks of basic training as a protracted nightmare. At the time he was more than thirty-five years old and in fairly poor physical shape. For nearly twenty years he had lived at night and slept in the daytime; now he was being asked to change on the spot to a completely different cycle. The restrictive conditions of the first five weeks, which meant that he had to do without both marijuana and liquor, must also have been a trial for his body to adapt to. In spite of the fact that he had landed in an environment as different from his own as is conceivable, Lester tried to cope and make the best of a bad job. His hope was that he would be sent to a military band. This was no idle fancy, since many of the jazz musicians from the Los Angeles area did their military service not as private soldiers but in military bands, either at the Great Lakes Naval Training Center in Illinois, or at the air base at Santa Ana in southeast Los Angeles. This was the case for such musicians as Snooky Young, Gerald Wilson, Dudley Brooks, Willie Smith, and Jimmy Nottingham. Unfortunately, the chance for an easier type of military service slipped through Lester's fingers.

After completing basic training at the beginning of November, Lester and Jo Jones went through a couple of camps, including Fort Ord just outside Los Angeles, where a photographer took a picture of them playing on their instruments. It was an idyllic propaganda shot, completely devoid of any link with reality, since neither of them had any time to play just then. On December 1 they were transferred to Fort McClellan in Alabama, where they joined the Infantry Replacement Training Center. Despite his willingness to cooperate, Lester had by this time already clashed on several occasions with those in command, finding it difficult to adapt to strict military discipline. This in turn led to his becoming unpopular with his superiors, who punished him by refusing to allow him to become an army musician.

The officer who had the final say in this case was the conductor of the regimental band. He had had a classical education and belonged to the black upper middle class, which meant that he did not count jazz players as being worth anything, since they lacked a proper musical education on a par with classical musicians. The trombone player Jimmy Cheatham was in the regimental band at the time, and he recalls that Jo Jones sometimes played and that Chico Hamilton was a regular member of the band, the 173rd Army Ground Forces Band. This was one of the top regimental bands in the United States, and for this reason the conductor wanted the very best musicians available. Even so, despite Lester's reputation as a musician, he was refused permission to join the band.

"This warrant officer was from Atlanta—can't remember his name now—but he had taught at Atlanta University and Morehouse and all the different colleges around there," Cheatham recalls. "He would not really sanction, believe it or not, Lester Young coming into the band. Here was this snobbery, this social thing that existed. . . . Lester Young was just another soldier being trained."

"We would get him in sometimes, like for a rehearsal," he continues. "And the guys in his company—a lot of them knew about him, they were trying to protect him—they would sneak him in. When they'd go out on their different training problems, they'd pass right by the band building and they'd just walk Lester right in there. And when they'd come back, he'd be ready and they'd walk him right back out. But no, he was never formally approved for the band."[6]

Lester felt that this disposition was grossly unfair, and he was very cut up about being refused permission, especially since two of his colleagues, Jo Jones and Chico Hamilton, had been allowed to participate. Lester was proud of being a musician and knew his worth as one. Maybe he felt the injustice that much more since it was a black, one of his own, who had turned him down.

Instead of being enrolled as a musician, he was made mess orderly in E Company, Second Training Battalion in the first training regiment, which was under the command of Captain William Stevenson, a white officer from Louisiana, who had thus grown up with a special attitude toward blacks, one that was to prove fateful for the unfortunate Lester.

On New Year's Day there were exercises on the obstacle course. Lester was injured when he fell backwards and wounded himself. The wound was so bad that he was hospitalized and had to have a minor rectal operation, after which he had so much pain that he was obliged to take pain-killing pills for a long time afterwards. During his three weeks in the hospital he was examined by Fort McClellan's leading neuropsychologist, Luis Perelman, who described Lester's state on being discharged in the following way: "His diagnosis on discharge is Constitutional Psychopathic State, manifested by drug addiction (marijuana, barbiturates), chronic alcoholism and nomadism. . . . It is felt he is purely a disciplinary problem and that disposition should be effected through administrative channels."[7]

Stevenson received Perelman's report, but he did not help Lester in any way, apart from keeping an eye on him. As soon as he was discharged from the hospital on January 24, Lester was back on duty. He himself felt that he was in need of some time for convalescence, since he was still suffering considerable pain. To lighten the pain he got hold of some painkillers without medical prescription.

On January 30 he was sent to the battalion headquarters for special service. Here Captain Stevenson noticed him and, as he didn't feel Lester was having too good a time of it, asked him what was wrong. Lester replied that he was "high" and when pressed by Stevenson showed him some pills. Stevenson then got hold of the company commander, Lieutenant Hutton, and both of them went with Lester and searched his locker. There they found more pills, some marijuana, and a couple of bottles containing a pink liquid which smelled of alcohol. They confiscated what they had found and handed it over to First Lieutenant Joe B. Humphreys at regimental headquarters, who sent it to be analyzed by Scott Holman, a chemist at the United States Narcotics Division in Atlanta. Holman wrote back on February 3, describing the confiscated goods in the following words: "One and one half cigarettes which were marijuana. Three capsules which contained barbiturates. Eleven tablets which were barbiturates. Barbiturates are habit forming drugs but do not come under the Harrison Narcotic Drug Law. They are not permitted to be sold in numerous states without a doctor's prescription. I believe Alabama is one of the states having such law."[8]

In the meantime Lester had been arrested, and on February 1 he was charged according to the 96th Article of War with "on or about 30 January 1945, wrongfully having in his possession habit-forming drugs, to wit, about one ounce of marijuana and about one ounce of barbiturates, said drugs not having been ordered by a medical officer of the camp."[9]

This resulted in a court case where Humphreys was the investigating officer. As early as February 5 he had a conversation with Lester, who informed him

that he had been using dope for eleven years and had been smoking marijuana for ten years. That in civilian life he was a musician and played tenor saxophone in Count Basie's band, for the past ten years. That prior to coming into the Army he used dope and drank whiskey continuously, and usually smoked five or six "sticks" a night. That he told his draft board and every Army doctor that has looked at him that he has the habit. That he was just careless or the captain would never have found the barbiturates or marijuana on him. That he intended to hide them but was feeling so good that he put it off too long. That he had no prescription from an Army doctor, although other doctors had at times given him the pills. That he is 35 years of age and has never harmed anyone. He says that if it hadn't been for dope he would not have been in the hospital and guesses they were trying to break him of the habit. That in civilian life his habit kept him broke but he felt good all the time. That he got the stuff which Captain Stevenson took from him by buying it here at Fort McClellan. That it is hard to get but if you got the money you can get it. That he registered with the draft board in New York and later had his papers transferred to Los Angeles, where Count Basie was playing at "The Plantation" club when he was inducted.[10]

Lester had been given another mental examination two days previously. The report written by the military psychiatrist, Lawrence J. Radice, came to the same conclusion as Perelman's. "This man is a constitutional psychopath," he concluded. "During his early life his school and family adjustment were poor. He has been arrested several times and at present has a common law wife. For years he has drunk excessively and used drugs such as marijuana and barbiturates. In view of his undesirable traits and inadequate personality, he is unlikely to become a satisfactory soldier."[11]

The court finally met on February 16, at 8.10 A.M. Lester's appointed attorney was Major Glen Grimke, who asked for the accused to be acquitted. After this Captain Stevenson was called as a witness. First, he told how he had discovered that Lester was under the influence of drugs. During Grimke's cross-examination he admitted that he had suspected from the start that Lester used stimulants, but that he had not said anything to him, since he appeared to have control of himself. Grimke then asked Stevenson what it was that made him suspect drug abuse, upon which Stevenson answered, "Well, his color, sir, and the fact that his eyes seemed bloodshot and he didn't react to his training as he should."[12]

Humphreys was then called to the stand as a witness. Among other things, he revealed that Lester had readily told everything about his abuse, how he procured the drugs, and that he on no occasion had withheld information about his use of them while in the army. Scott Holman's report was laid before the court, after which it was Lester's turn, as the only witness for the defense, to come forward.

He was first cross-examined by Grimke, who asked him the following:

Q. How old are you Young?

A. I am 35, sir.

Q. You are a musician by profession?

A. Yes, sir.

Q. Had you played in a band or orchestra in California?

A. Count Basie, I played with him for ten years.

Q. Had you been taking narcotics for some time?

A. Yes, sir.

Q. How long?

A. For ten years, this is my eleventh year.

Q. Why did you start taking them?

A. Well, sir, playing in the band we would play a lot of one-nighters. I would stay up and play another dance and leave and that is the only way I could keep up.

Q. Any other members of the band, I mean, any other musicians take them?

A. Yes, all that I know.

Q. When you first appeared before the draft board, when you were drafted into the service, do you remember that occasion?

A. Yes, sir.

Q. Did they know you had this habit of taking habit forming drugs?

A. Well, I'm pretty sure they did, sir, because before I went to join the army I had to take a spinal and I didn't want to take it and when I went down I was very high and they put me in jail and I was so high they took the whiskey away from me and put me in a padded cell and they searched my clothes while I was in the cell. I was in that day and the second day they took me upstairs and this is the fifth camp I have been on and so. . . .

Q. You say you were pretty high. What do you mean by that? Do you mean because of the whiskey?

A. The whiskey and the marihuana and the barbiturates.

Q. When they took the whiskey did they say anything to you to indicate that they believed you were taking habit forming drugs?

A. Well, all they did was just take the whiskey and lock me up for these days.

Q. What I want to know is, the board that inducted you; have you reason to believe that they knew you took habit forming drugs? Did you tell them you took it?

A. Yes, sir.

Q. Now since you have been at Fort McClellan, Alabama, have you been in the hospital?

A. Yes, sir, I was there for about three weeks.

Q. Did you go on sick call?

A. Yes, sir, I went on sick call and they gave me some kind of a slip.

Q. Why?

A. Well, in training, on the obstacle course I hurt myself and I went to the dispensary and they ordered me to go to the hospital and while there they found out about it. I was first in Ward 32 and they changed it to Ward 36 and the doctor was giving me the same pills you have there. He gave me one at nine o'clock in the morning and one in the afternoon and five at night and nine o'clock at night.

Q. The doctors in the hospital did this?

A. I think it was Captain LeBell.

Q. Did they state to you why they did?

A. No, sir, because I was in another hospital and they gave me some pills.

Q. They didn't state why?

A. No, sir.

Q. How long were you in this hospital there?

A. From the 1st of January to about the 22nd or 23rd.

Q. Then what happened to you?

A. Then we came out and they sent us back to duty.

Q. Were you marked duty in the sick-book?

A. That is not what they told me but when I got there I found out.

Q. When you returned to the company from the hospital, what were your duties; what did you do?

A. Well, this is what the Captain Stevenson was telling. I was sitting in the dayroom. I had the understanding when I left the hospital.

Q. What did you do when you came out of the hospital; go to bed?

A. Sent me out on the field.

Q. Carry a full pack?

A. I don't know.

Q. Carry a light pack?

A. It was a pack and a rifle.

Q. Did you have a cartridge belt?

A. Yes, sir.

Q. And that is when you immediately returned from the hospital?

A. Yes, sir.

Q. Immediately after you returned from the hospital?

A. Yes, sir.

Q. You remember this captain who was sitting here as a witness?

A. Yes, sir, I do.

Q. Was he the captain of your company when you first reported?

A. Yes, sir.

Q. When you first reported to his company that he commands now, was he the commanding officer of it?

A. Yes, sir.

Q. Did you ever have any conversation with him about narcotics?

A. Yes, sir, one morning when I was sitting in the dayroom.

Q. Did you tell him that you used it?

A. Well, he asked me about it and said that he knew that I was very high.

Q. When you refer to being very high, would you explain that?

A. Well, that is the only way I know how to explain myself.

Q. When you mean you have taken these narcotics you are not referring to just taking liquor or whiskey?

A. Yes, sir.

Q. It is not whiskey alone that makes you high when you refer to being high?

A. No, sir.

Q. Now if you do not take these drugs, smoke these things, does it affect you in any way physically?

A. Yes, sir, it does. I don't want to do anything; I don't care to blow my horn and I don't care to be around anybody.

Q. Affects you badly?

A. Just nervous.

Q. Could you do this training here if you left them alone?

A. No, sir.

Q. Why?

A. Because I tried it, sir, I tried it truthfully.

Q. Have you had any of these drugs recently in the last few days?

A. Haven't, not since I have been in the stockade now.

Q. Feel pretty nervous now?

A. I think about it all the time.[13]

After that it was the prosecutor's turn to examine Lester. This took only a short time, since he was only interested in finding out how Lester

obtained the pills. Lester replied that he had gotten them without a prescription.

This concluded the examination and, since the counsel for the defense
did not wish any more witnesses called, they proceeded to the verdict,
which was reached by secret written ballot. Three of the four judges
returned a verdict of guilty, and he was condemned "to be dishonorably
discharged the service, to forfeit all pay and allowances due or to become due, and to be confined at hard labor, at such place as the reviewing authority may direct, for one (1) year."[14]

The entire trial had lasted only one hour and thirty-five minutes. Lester was given the maximum sentence for his offense, without any miti-
gating circumstances being taken into account. In a summing-up of the
case, written on February 27, the following remarks are made:

The record is legally sufficient to support the findings and the sentence. Possession of habit forming drugs which were not prescribed by an army doctor is
clearly proved by uncontradicted evidence. Testimony of the accused indicates
he used drugs during the past ten years, that the draft board knew it at the time
of his induction, and further he cannot get along without them. . . . The record
of accused both civilian and military shows that he is not a good soldier. His
age as well as the nature and duration of his undesirable traits indicate he can
be of no value to the service without proper treatment and severe disciplinary
training.

The sentence of dishonorable discharge, total forfeitures, and confinement at
hard labor for a period of one (1) year imposed by the court is both legal and
appropriate. It is noted that accused has never been subjected to disciplinary
training and evidence of his continued use of drugs is based largely on his own
statements. In view of these facts together with the possibility that his undesirable traits may be corrected by proper treatment and disciplinary training it is
recommended that the sentence be approved, but execution of the dishonorable
discharge be suspended until his release from confinement. The United States
Military Barracks, Fort Leavenworth, Kansas, is the appropriate place of confinement.[15]

And so Grimke's convincing handling of the case, which presented
Lester in the best light possible and at the same time showed that he
never ought to have been inducted, or at any rate should have been sent
home after the psychologists' reports, was in vain. The U.S. Army would
not admit that it had made a mistake and retained him in its ranks despite the blatant irrationality of the whole situation. The human aspects
of Lester's case were completely ignored, and the old number was trotted out that everything could be righted simply by using disciplinary
measures. One would have thought that those officers responsible for
judging the suitability of conscripts to be soldiers would, after so much
contact with people, have gained enough psychological insight into their

work to know what they were doing. It can scarcely be a matter of pride for the U.S. Army that it committed so many errors in succession in Lester's case.

However, he was not sent to Fort Leavenworth. Once more he was unlucky, for on March 12 the verdict was altered and he was sent to Fort Gordon in Georgia, one of the worst states as regards racial discrimination. What he had to go through there must remain a matter of conjecture, but he became so desperate at one point that he tried to escape. "A soldier at Camp Gordon, who was a bass player and knew Prez, managed to send him out on a detail to build a bridge," Jo Jones narrates. "By this time he was so terrified that he actually tried to run away. I don't think he ever told a soul about this except me. 'But then I got into the bushes and I saw those people with the guns,' he said, 'and I came back.' " [16]

His stay at Fort Gordon was, however, alleviated by the fact that he was able to start playing once more. There was a dance for the noncommissioned officers every Sunday. Lester played on these occasions in a small ensemble consisting of the guitar player Fred Lacey, who became a regular member of Lester's own group in 1946, the drummer Paul Metz, the bass player Billy Goodall, and the piano player Gil Evans. Evans knew Lester from the latter's stay in Los Angeles in 1941–42, and he himself was stationed at Oliver General Hospital, about ten miles from Fort Gordon. Every Sunday he brought along a couple of bottles of whiskey and some marijuana cigarettes, which were discreetly passed on to Lester for his private consumption. Lester had been stripped of his military wages, so he was unable to get hold of any stimulants for himself.

The military authorities took no chances with Lester; when he was to go to the officers' mess to play he was accompanied by two armed privates. The privates were not allowed to mix with the officers, so they waited on the bandstand next to the band until after the dance was over, when they accompanied Lester back to the prison barracks.

There was also a fifteen-man big band at Fort Gordon, which Lester obviously was keen on playing in, but the military authorities refused permission. The musicians themselves were eager to have Lester play with them, and a white trumpet player who was in the military police agreed to take Lester from the black part of the camp across to the Recreation Hall where the band used to practice, without any of the officers noticing anything. "All day long he was playing his horn," Jo Jones—who had gotten permission to visit Lester—relates, "and then at the end of the day they put him back on the other side of the tracks like he'd been digging ditches, but he wasn't. Somebody would always stand at the window and watch for somebody to come into the Recreation Hall to see if any officers came over." [17]

Jo Jones played too during his visit, and he also relates that the trumpet player, so as not to lose face before the other black players, was forced to humiliate Lester by saying, "Come on, nigger" to him when he was going to be fetched, whereupon Lester would answer, "Yessir, boss." The situation was so bizarre that this playacting was necessary on both sides, even though they were friends. Lester never dared tell his black prison-mates the truth; otherwise he risked being killed for working with the whites.

The military authorities gradually realized that there was no point in retaining Lester in their ranks, and on December 15, 1945, two months early, he was released.[18] He was given back his civilian clothes and a sum of money. His journey to Los Angeles was also paid for. "I'm out, I'm out. That's all that matters," he exclaimed in relief, overjoyed to be a free man once more.[19]

His traumatic stay in the army had an important impact on Lester, leaving an indelible mark on his whole personality. Being so thin-skinned meant that he was defenseless in the face of the conflicts he as a black man was forced to meet. Without a doubt, the rough, brutal tone typical of an army barracks was especially injurious to a man like him. He felt himself at the mercy of the military authorities, who never tried to help him when he got into difficulties but simply sought to grind his face in the dirt even more. Six months after returning home he was asked about his stay in the army. He answered: "A nightmare, man, one mad nightmare. They sent me down South, Georgia. That was enough to make me blow my top. It was a drag."[20]

The drummer Willie Jones was close to Lester during the last couple of years of his life. He relates that "one of the things that hurt Lester when he was in the army was, that he did a lot of work in the United States Army for the band, but he was never allowed to play in it. But Lester didn't talk about that, he just talked about 'D.B. Blues'—Disciplinary Barracks—like, you know: 'I served my country, and look what I'd get!' "[21]

Lester expected to be treated in the same friendly and polite way he always treated others, and he never said a bad word about anyone. He never understood why people could be so mean to each other. "Sensitivity? There he was, Lester Young," Jo Jones said. "Very sensitive. Lester loved human beings. He did not understand how a human being could mistreat another human being. He would never tell you that a guy was no good, but if he came in Lester was upset. Just to see this guy threw him out, but fluffed the evening off. I'd say 'People basically do things wrong because they don't know any better and when people do things right it's because they know better.' I used to sit with Pres and tell him that and he'd say 'Yes, but why? Why are they like that?' I'd say, 'I don't know.' He never did much talking, he talked on his horn, left everybody alone. But he just didn't understand how you could mistreat another person.''[22]

His time as a soldier matured Lester, socially speaking. It was only then that he first became fully aware of the unreasonable and discriminating behavior blacks could be exposed to in a country like the United States, which was so strongly dominated by whites. He had, of course, met with isolated instances of racial discrimination over the years, but isolated instances were not the same as fifteen months of daily humiliation in the army. "Those who knew Pres before the war felt deep changes in him when he returned from the army," relates the journalist Alan Morrison, who knew Lester for almost twenty years. "His experiences in the Southern army camps embittered, soured, changed him profoundly. . . .

His army service was marked by tragedy, tension, appalling indignities, spiritual and physical torture. When he came out of it, his spirit was twisted and sore and he hated with an intensity he had never before known. He deeply mistrusted practically any whites and realized as never before the injustice and inhumanity under which Negroes in the South lived. And not only the South. A feeling of revenge lingered in him for years.''[23]

Harry Edison, who also knew Lester for more than twenty years, has the following comments on Lester's time as a soldier:

The army just took all his spirit, you know, and I think it was the worst thing that could happen to a musician to be put in the army. After he had played an instrument all his life you can't give him a gun and tell him to be a soldier. You can't, because they weren't born to be disciplined like the army does. Prez hadn't the mind of being disciplined, no musician had. None of them came out any good, and most of them couldn't play their horns like they could before they went into the army. Some of them were fortunate enough to come in the bands, and some of them were stationed around New York. But Prez was unfortunate enough to be sent South, and that was the worst thing that could happen to him. Well, I don't have to tell you how the South was, because everybody can read about it all over the world. It is like South Africa. We have apartheid going in the South of the United States, too, but we try to keep it a little more quiet than in South Africa. I have played camps with Basie's band. We used to play a lot of the camps on the U.S.O. shows, and sometimes when we played a camp we had to play one show for the white soldiers first, and after the hall was empty then we'd do a concert for the black soldiers. So there was apartheid in the army, and it was the worst that could happen to Lester Young to be sent to a Southern camp. Not only didn't he want to be a soldier, but he wanted to be in a place where he could feel like he was free, you know, where he could go play his horn if he wanted to. The army made him conscious about discipline, but he wasn't born to take orders like that, you know.[24]

Lester was a gentle person who looked for beauty in life, just as he sought it in music. Therefore his ideals were constantly coming into conflict with the realities of life in a harsh society. He rarely talked about the knocks he had to take; but in his own way, he managed to express some of the frustrations that built up in him, in that he said what really mattered to him through the medium of his music. For this reason it was a good thing that, in spite of everything, he managed to do some playing during the last part of his stay at Fort Gordon; even so, the military and Lester were worlds apart—they never came to understand each other or each other's problems.

7
Busy Years as Bandleader and Soloist (1946–1955)

After being discharged, Lester flew directly to Los Angeles, where Norman Granz had spent some time and energy trying to arrange for his return to the job of being a musician. One of the most important things he had done was to secure a three-year record contract between Lester and Eddie Mesner from the local company Philo (which had changed its name to Aladdin in the summer of 1946), a contract Lester signed in late October 1945.[1] Only a few days after his return to civilian life he was busy fulfilling his contract, both as a player and as a bandleader.

On arrival in Los Angeles Lester moved into a house just round the corner from Central Avenue, where the club The Bird in the Basket was situated. "Contrary to stories you've heard about Prez, Prez was a pretty smart man, an individual," the singer Earl Coleman recalls. "Prez had a beautiful home, but he built his home with the idea in mind for cats who didn't have much money, who couldn't afford to pay much rent—maybe couldn't pay any at all, but if they had something on the ball Prez would not leave them outdoors. That's what the house was built for."[2]

Such helpfulness on Lester's part was nothing unusual, since he was always incredibly considerate and attentive toward others and always shared any form of surplus income with other people; just like Louis Armstrong, he lent money to anyone who came along and asked. Neither was he niggardly in sharing his knowledge of saxophone technique; as previously mentioned, he had helped Ben Webster and Budd Johnson, as well as Buddy Tate. The saxophone player Paul Quinichette had similar experiences with him and is also able to give an example of how loyal Lester was to those he really liked: "One time when I was playing at the Village Vanguard in New York, Mary Lou Williams and Ben

Webster came down and tried to insult me. They were going to carve me. So Lester heard about it, and he had actually taught Ben how to play. 'You leave my man alone,' he told him, 'or I'll go up there and tear you up!' See, Ben was all bark and no bite. He wanted to show off, but he'd give you the shirt off his back."[3]

About the time Lester came to Los Angeles, the first bop band arrived on the West Coast. It was the alto saxophonist Charlie Parker's group, which, apart from Parker, consisted of the trumpet player Dizzy Gillespie, the piano player Al Haig, the vibraphone player Milt Jackson, the bass player Ray Brown, and the drummer Stan Levey. The arrival of the group was eagerly awaited, and the opening evening at Billy Berg's Trouville Club was a great attraction. The two-month engagement was a success, even though there were contrary rumors circulating at the time. "If you want to think of it as being a total flop you would be mistaken," recalls the alto sax player Sonny Criss, who visited the club on several occasions during that period. "I don't recall it that way because the club was packed every night. Naturally there were a lot of people in the audience who didn't know or understand what was going on, but at the same time there were many who enjoyed the music. Contrary to the reports Bird and Dizzy did not play to audiences of 10 or 12 people. Billy Berg's was a unique club, in the sense that it was in the center of Hollywood and it was the first really cosmopolitan club with a great deal of publicity behind it where Negro and white people mixed without any pressure."[4]

Lester was of course down there too, to listen to the young musicians and at the same time to hear the latest from New York. He also took part in a number of jam sessions in the many spots along Central Avenue, for there were still no permanent jobs to be had. On the other hand, Granz had Lester included in his plans for a large concert he had been trying to arrange for some time. After a modest start in 1942, when he got the idea of holding jam sessions where the audience paid to come in, he had taken the leap on July 2, 1944, from a jazz club to the Philharmonic Auditorium—the largest concert hall in Los Angeles, capable of seating more than 2,800. The concert was a success, and he was therefore eager to hold another of the same type. The date had to be postponed time after time, however, because of problems with the concert hall's management, especially C. H. Brainard, who was not prepared to agree to some of the racially enlightened conditions Granz wanted to introduce for both players and public. Granz insisted on white and black musicians being allowed to perform together on the bandstand and also that the audience be mixed, without any form of discrimination. Brainard maintained that there must not be more than 50 percent black musicians taking part, that advertising for the concert was to be only in the daily press, and that the concert not be given the title "Jazz at the Philharmonic." Together with Mesner, Granz eventually came to an agreement with the management, so that the concert was able to take place on January 28, 1946, about two months later than originally planned, starting at 8.15 P.M. The magazine *Down Beat* was also involved in the arrangements and on that occasion presented a couple of the winners of its annual vote on the best musicians of the year. This meant that the concert could be called "Down Beat Magazine Award Winners Concert."[5] Apart from the musicians of the year, the alto sax player Willie Smith and the tenor sax player Charlie Ventura, the following musicians took part: Lester, Charlie Parker, Dizzy Gillespie, the trumpet players Al Killian and Howard McGhee, the piano players Mel Powell and Arnold Ross, the bass player Billy Hadnot and Lester's brother Lee on drums, plus Anita O'Day and the Gene Krupa Trio. The concert was a sellout and was such a great success that the enthusiastic audience took to dancing in the aisles. An unfortunate consequence of this was that Brainard forbade Granz to hold any further concerts in the Philharmonic Auditorium.

In the following months Lester also took part in other concerts, including some arranged by the Armed Forces Radio Service (AFRS), whose weekly radio programs were recorded with an audience fetched from several military camps.

After Charlie Parker's group had completed their engagement for Billy Berg, shortly after Granz's concert, they all returned to New York, with the exception of Charlie Parker himself, who stayed in Los Angeles. One of the places he got work was The Bird in the Basket, and he often used to look up Lester. At the beginning of February Parker was offered the chance to make a recording for Ross Russell's company, Dial. The rehearsals for the recording, to be made on February 17, took place in Lester's rooms.[6] Lester was on his own in the apartment, since he and Mary in the course of the fall of 1945 had decided to go their separate ways. Their marriage had not been a success, apart from which Lester preferred to avoid any further painful episodes resulting from their different color and Mary's temperament.

The success Granz had reaped from the concert at the Philharmonic Auditorium made him eager to arrange another, with an ensuing tour to the East Coast. He collected some of the best musicians of the time, including Lester, Buck Clayton, Coleman Hawkins, the piano player Kenny Kersey, the guitar player Irving Ashby, the bass player Billy Hadnot, and the drummer Buddy Rich. The tour started with a concert held in Los Angeles on April 22, 1946, at the Embassy Theatre, which seated 1,000 less than the Philharmonic Auditorium. Apart from the tour's regular musicians, Granz had invited Charlie Parker and Willie Smith along as guest soloists. This concert was also a success, and Lester— maybe inspired by Coleman Hawkins's presence—played some of the best jazz he ever achieved at a concert.

Before leaving with Granz and the troupe, which he continued to call Jazz at the Philharmonic (JATP), Lester managed to take part in a charity concert in the Royce Hall Auditorium at the University of California, together with such musicians as Nat King Cole's Trio, Benny Carter's Orchestra, Bumps Myers, Red Callender, and many more. Herb Jeffries was master of ceremonies, and the arrangement, whose profits were to go to a university grant, was a success, with an audience of more than 1,500. "The Carver Club, U.C.L.A. student organization, presented a jazz concert at the University's campus auditorium recently that not only pointed up the role of music in aiding race relations but also supplied a very satisfactory afternoon of entertainment," *Down Beat* reported.[7]

After touring the West Coast, with concerts in San Diego and San Francisco, Granz took the group east; the JATP troupe gave a concert in Chicago's Civic Opera House on May 14. It was a huge box-office success for Granz, with every seat sold—3,600 in the audience—whereas the musical returns were only reasonably satisfactory. *Down Beat* called it "a dismal flop musically. Lack of good production was the main failure."[8] Things went a lot better when the musicians reached New York. Here Granz had booked the troupe for four of the pop concerts that were held on every Monday throughout the summer in Carnegie Hall. The JATP troupe gave concerts on May 27, June 3, and June 17; Granz had booked members of the band from Café Society Uptown and Downtown for his concert on June 10.

The music at these concerts was of varying quality, but Lester seems to have been in fine form here too. Apart from the musicians he had with him from the West Coast, Granz also hired various New York musicians for these concerts, such as the sax players Georgie Auld and Illinois Jacquet, the trumpet players Roy Eldridge, Joe Guy, and Dizzy Gillespie, and the singers Sarah Vaughan and Billie Holiday. The first two concerts were reviewed by Leonard Feather, who wrote that "the first concert opened with 'Philharmonic Blues,' followed with 'Lady Be Good,' 'I Can't Get Started,' and 'Sweet Georgia Brown.' The jam-packed hall was in a jumpin' groove not seen since the early Benny Goodman days of 1936."[9] He wrote of the next concert that "Billie Holiday, always tremendously popular with Carnegie Hall audiences, sang 'She's Funny That Way' (her new Commodore recording), 'All of Me,' 'Billie's Blues,' and 'Them There Eyes,' accompanied by her friend and greatest admirer Lester Young with Joe Guy on trumpet."[10]

For the final concert on June 17 Granz had collected together an all-star gathering, featuring such names as the trombone players J. J. Johnson and Trummie [sic] Young, the trumpet players Roy Eldridge and

Dizzy Gillespie, and the tenor sax players Allen Eager, Illinois Jacquet, and Lester. "Musical high-spots of the evening," wrote *Down Beat,* "were on 'Just You Just Me' with Buck Clayton, Trummie Young, and Lester Young playing superbly. . . . All three came on later in the show to huge hands on individual solos." [11]

Granz's first tour with the JATP troupe finished with an extra concert on June 22 at the Chicago Civic Opera House, after which Lester traveled back to New York to play at the Spotlite Club for a week in July. After this he went back to Los Angeles for a month, among other things to do some recordings, and by late summer he was back in New York, this time to assemble his own band.

Lester seems quickly to have recovered his self confidence after the humiliating months in the army. His playing was full of joie de vivre, optimism, and drive. "When Lester came out of the army I thought he was playing better than at any time in his life," Buck Clayton says. "He was really happy to be out, and all that talk about him being a broken man is quite wrong. He had a rough time in the army—I was always glad that my army service kept me near New York, as opposed to Lester and Jo Jones who were sent to Alabama. But when we joined JATP Lester was so happy to be playing with Hawk. I completed the front line, and I got so much fun listening to those two that often I'd forget to take my own solo." [12]

When Lester settled in New York in the late summer of 1946, he was very eager to form his own band again. Wiser now as a result of earlier bitter experiences, he tried to get a contract with a music agent. He was already bound by a recording contract and, since he had also been a success as a soloist in Jazz at the Philharmonic, it wasn't difficult for him to agree terms with Moe Gale, New York's largest agent in the field, who booked bands and entertainers for the Savoy Ballroom and the Golden Gate. In joining the Gale Agency, Lester acquired as companions such well-known names as Sarah Vaughan, Erroll Garner, Dinah Washington, Jimmy Lunceford, and Ella Fitzgerald. He found musicians for his own band by combing the small clubs along 52nd Street and by frequenting such favorite old jam session haunts as Minton's Playhouse. When Lester was last in town, swing had been the thing at these places, but in the intervening years bop music had gradually gotten the upper hand. In the wake of this new jazz a frenzied debate had sprung up, dividing jazz into two fanatical camps, one for and one against bop. Swing music was almost ignored during this debate, since it was on its way out. The larger swing big bands had trouble surviving, and many older musicians were hard put to find work unless they chose to play New Orleans jazz, which was enjoying a revival as a contrast to bop, or tried to learn how to play bop music.

The first few months must have been somewhat confusing for Lester

on account of the often violent dimensions a meeting between supporters of one faction or the other could have; his own position was, however, never in doubt. He was open to new ideas and could not understand why it was so hard for older musicians to accept them. "We all
love to be young and new," he said in an interview a couple of years
later. "These guys love to come in, but they hate to go out. They'll ring
the bell on me for talking like that, but it's the truth. Sure, bop can be
pretty—but my music is swing!" [13]

Lester's liking for the new jazz is not difficult to understand. Many of
the young bop musicians were rebels and used music as a means of
attracting attention to injustices in society. They also wanted to be given
recognition for their own and for their music's sake and refused to be
included among the large group of black musicians who curried favor
with a white audience by resorting to "Uncle Tomming." Lester had
had such thoughts himself for years, so it was natural for him to find
suitable material for his band among such young kindred spirits.

To begin with he chose musicians from both the swing and the bop
camps. Among the moderates were such players as Rodney Richardson,
whom Lester knew from his days with Count Basie, the guitar player
and singer Fred Lacey, who had played together with Lester at Fort
Gordon, and the drummer Lyndell Marshall. Blowing with him was the
trumpet player Maurice "Shorts" or "Shorty" McConnell, who had
previously played in Earl Hines's and Billy Eckstine's big bands and
who played in a style not unlike that of bop. Lester would dearly liked
to have had the piano player Bud Powell, the greatest exponent of bop
on his instrument, but attempts fell through at the last moment, as Bill
Triglia, who played with Lester in 1956, can recall:

Lester was drunk and went into Minton's one night, which was like a second
home, and they're all up there jamming, so he went in and started playing. All
of a sudden he heard this gorgeous pianist, looked round, and somebody had
taken the piano over, and it was Bud Powell. He didn't know his name yet, it
was the first time he heard him. During the trumpet solo, Fats Navarro was
playing the trumpet, he heard this beautiful piano playing, so light and so beautiful. Then Lester played, and the pianist played behind him so beautiful, and
then he played a piano solo after that, and it was beautiful. When the set was
finished Lester Young ran right over to him and said: "Son, what's your name?
You play so beautiful!" So he told him: "My name is Bud Powell," so Lester
said to him: "I'm going to Chicago next week. Are you working? I'd love to
hire you." So Bud Powell said: "I ain't doing anything, baby, I'm available."
So Lester hired him and he was stoned at the time, he was drunk, so he invited
Bud over to the bar and bought him a drink, and they decided what he's gonna
get paid, you know, 150 or 200, whatever. He was very fair, Lester, he certainly
wouldn't try to cheat him. He didn't do that to anybody, never. So, they had a
drink at the bar together and then Lester left and he made a date, he told Bud

Powell the arrangements would be made: "Be at the airport, because we don't have to get tickets, we'll get the tickets right, because it's a weekday, so it's not crowded." And he made up with him to be there two days later at 10 o'clock in the morning, and he wrote it on a piece of paper to make sure that Bud Powell wouldn't forget.

Two days later Lester gets at the airport, and he's got his band, and these fellows walk up, and he knows three of the fellows and the one he doesn't know he figures is Bud Powell, so he says: "Hey, how're doing, man!" and asks him his name. The guy says: "Hey, Prez!" so they get their tickets and fly up to Chicago and check in at the hotel and go to the gig. When they go to their job, at the very first tune they play Lester turns round and say: "That's not Bud Powell!" He only heard eight bars and knew it wasn't Bud Powell, so he walked up to the fellow and said: "Hey, you sound nice, what's your name?" and the guy said: "My name is Dense Thornton." Bud had sent him because he'd got a job with Charlie Parker in the meantime, so he couldn't do it, so he sent Dense Thornton. Lester Young said to me: "He's good, but it wasn't Bud Powell. Bud Powell is a genius!"

He heard him and loved him when he heard him, but he was so drunk that he forgot what he looked like, but he didn't forget what he sounded like![14]

Argonne Dense Thornton also used the new style of playing and came to Lester, whom he stayed with for almost two years, after a year with Ben Webster.

The engagement in Chicago took place at the Hurricane Lounge in Garfield and was originally planned to last a month, starting on Thursday, October 3, 1946. The band's success was such, however, that the engagement was prolonged for another four weeks, until December 1. "Lester Young's opening at the Hurricane Lounge was the biggest in local history," was the verdict of the *Chicago Defender*.[15]

Lester's stay in Chicago was very important for him personally, as it was here that he met his next wife, a black woman whose name was also Mary. She traveled with Lester to New York when the job at the Hurricane Lounge expired, and they both moved into the Mark Hotel on 43rd Street. With his new Mary, Lester had a more balanced and stable relationship than with his previous wife. They soon agreed to get married, and the bass player Gene Ramey was best man at the wedding. Mary had a good influence on Lester and managed to get his drinking down to a reasonable level during the first years of their marriage. She gave him support and helped him as much as she could, as well as trying to understand him to the best of her ability. They were inseparable, and she sometimes went with the band when they had an engagement away from home. In 1947 they had a son, christened Lester Jr., and on New Year's Eve 1956 a daughter, who was called Yvette.

Lester was very fond of animals, and when they lived at the Mark Hotel they kept a cat. "He always talked about his cat," Gene Ramey recalls. "He called her Philharmonic. And he said something to the cat one day, and the cat didn't like it and jumped out the window. From the eighth floor! He insulted the cat. The cat jumped. So he said it hurt him so badly."[16]

For the next ten years Lester and his band were kept very busy, and up to 1950 most of the jobs to be found were outside New York. The incessant traveling didn't give much time for a normal family life, but this certainly suited Lester down to the ground. He wasn't much of a family man, even though he was very fond of Mary and his children. Nor did he ever forget Beverly, who had become a strapping teenager by now. Whenever his travels took him past Minneapolis, he always paid her a visit; sometimes she even went with the band when they were on tour.[17]

The practical side of leading a band was still anathema to Lester; fortunately, he was soon handed over by Gale to Charlie Carpenter, a singer formerly connected to Earl Hines's band, who became his personal manager. This came about in the following way: Carpenter was rung up on Christmas Day, 1946, and asked if he would be Lester's manager for a single job, on New Year's Eve, in Newark. Carpenter reluctantly accepted; he went to Gale's office, where Frank Sands put him in the picture, and on New Year's Eve he went with Lester's band to the job in Newark. Everything went fine. Lester liked him and his way of managing things, so he invited Carpenter to be his manager on a tour to Chicago just after the beginning of the new year. This tour also went off satisfactorily for all involved and led to the signing of a contract making Carpenter Lester's manager.[18]

Carpenter and Lester got on well with each other for many years, and Carpenter always went along on the band's tours. "Charlie Carpenter was a good influence on Lester," Junior Mance, Lester's piano player throughout 1949, recalls.

He was a business man and he would keep things together, because Lester was very loose and informal and we were young, so we needed somebody out there to keep things in order.

Carpenter didn't have that much to say about the music. Carpenter was a manager and he took care of all the business. He would make suggestions, but he wasn't that big influence on what Lester or the rest of the band played. If Lester didn't like the musicians Carpenter got to the group, he wouldn't keep them. No, Lester had the last word to say on that.

Carpenter had good ideas about the musicians too, pretty much like Lester's, you know. I don't even remember, if any time, Lester being made to do something he didn't want to do, or to play with somebody he didn't want to play with. He always had complete freedom as far as that was concerned.[19]

The drummer Roy Haynes supports this statement in that he remembers that when the band was increased to include three men in the front line, this was the result of a mutual agreement between Carpenter and Lester.[20]

Haynes became Lester's drummer on October 25, 1947, when Lyndell Marshall fell ill and returned home to Washington. Haynes can vividly recall that evening, because he was to play first for Billie Holiday at a Town Hall concert before going to the Savoy Ballroom to be Marshall's stand-in. Lester liked his playing so much, however, that he told him he could stay as long as he wanted. Haynes stayed with the group for almost two years, until midsummer 1949.[21] He became one of the best drummers Lester ever had, and the power, imagination, and resilience he exuded helped Lester's ideas to blossom even further, as can clearly be heard on the live takes from that period.

And so it must presumably have been an exception when Lester was given a scathing review, such as after his Town Hall concert with Sarah Vaughan on November 8, 1947. Vaughan was praised to the skies, whereas Lester "wallowed around the stand," according to *Down Beat*. "He played out of tune and without ideas and in general justified every idea the lay public has about jazz musicians. He was consistently cut by his own trumpet player, Shorts McConnell, who got off some good jazz in stern competition with the iron foundry drumming of Roy Haynes, the wrong-noted bassing of Tex Briscoe and the lack-lustre support accorded by pianist Dence Thornton."

"Young's performance would have been pitiful done by any musician," the review continues. "Displayed by one of the greatest names in jazz, who can still play as much as any other reed man in the business, Lester's playing was not only inadequate, but a flat proof of the fact that you have to be in perfect physical condition to play good jazz."[22]

After such savage criticism Lester got the opportunity of giving the reviewer a reply: "I think that was the greatest concert I ever played in my life. Other people criticized the band. The only people that didn't like my playing were you, my manager Charlie Carpenter and Shorts McConnell—and this I just can't understand, because the rest of my friends told me it was real mad."[23]

Maybe the reviewer focused so much on Lester's behavior on the bandstand, that he was unable to evaluate the concert properly. A tape of the concert reveals namely, that the band was not at all bad, and that Lester was cheerful, joking with the audience in between numbers and creating an inspired performance.

Lester had now become the father of a son, so it was no longer easy for the little family to live at the Mark Hotel. His earnings were good at this point, so he and Mary decided to move into a nice apartment on 140th Street in Harlem. "He got an apartment up in a place where other rich, black people were," Bill Triglia narrates. "A nice hotel with a doorman downstairs, a sitting room where you waited before you went upstairs. It was up in Harlem some place, and he was so proud of it, because he could now bring in his wife and little son. It was a three room apartment, but it was a classic place.''

"The morning after the first night he stayed there he went down to go out for breakfast," Triglia continues, "because he didn't have the stuff to cook food yet, and as he was going out, there's Charlie Parker sitting downstairs, so he walked over to him and said: 'Bird, what're you doing here?' Charlie Parker said: 'I found out you've moved in, so I'm moving in here too!' And Lester was so happy, he told me: 'I was so thrilled, you know, having Charlie Parker living right next to me!' ''[24] The Young family lived in this apartment until around 1949, when Lester bought his own house in St. Albans, Queens, at 116-12 168th Street.

The music played by Lester's band changed, from the fall of 1948 onward, to a more modern style. This was partly because all the musicians who were swing-minded were soon replaced; Lester's style also reflects the distinct influence of the younger musicians. This can most clearly be heard in the up-tempo numbers, where many of the solos are disfigured by many superficial and vapid—though technically often brilliant—runs. The new members of the band were the piano player Freddy Jefferson, the trumpet player Jesse Drakes, and the trombone player Ted Kelly, who replaced the guitar player Fred Lacey. Jesse Drakes was a member of the band up to 1955, interrupted only by short periods when he had to take jobs in other bands because Lester was out touring as a soloist with JATP.

As with so many of the changes in the band, it was something of a coincidence that Lester noticed Drakes. It happened when Drakes was playing with Deke Watson at the Savoy Ballroom. "Pres was playing opposite us," Drake recalls, "and that's when I got the invitation to play with Pres. The manager came over and said, 'Would you like to play with Pres?' I gave the manager my address and forgot about it. One night Charlie Carpenter came in and rang my bell at two in the morning. He says, 'You're the trumpet player from the Savoy Ballroom, do you remember me?' 'Yeah.' He says, 'Well, Shorty McConnell has finally packed it in and Pres likes you, I like you and you seem to be a clean-cut guy, that's what we want.' I said all right, so I packed my stuff, got in his car and he drove me to Washington that morning. This was in the latter part of '48.''[25] Drakes also relates how difficult it was to play with Lester, since he rarely played the shared passages the same way twice. "Well, it was an education," he says. "An education I never really seemed to learn. Pres always had something that puzzled me and once I thought I had figured it out, he'd come and play it another way. And I'd go home and think about it again.''[26]

Once in a while Carpenter was unable to accompany the band when it was on tour. It was then Drakes's extra job to keep an eye on Lester.

"He never went into a restaurant to eat,' he recalls. "I used to bring food to his room. He thought people were looking at him. But when you see a gentleman in a big black pork pie hat, long black coat, down to his ankles, hair hanging down almost to his shoulders—people are going to look at you. But it was his choice to dress like he felt. And to make sure he ate, it was my job, and my thought, to make sure to bring food into his room before he went to work."[27]

Although Lester's band had three men in the front line at this point, there weren't many rehearsals. Roy Haynes, during his entire stay with Lester, can only recall two, and these took place only when new members were included for the first time and were restricted to the actual passages where the new member was to play.[28]

The main feature of the group's music was solos. Presentation of the individual numbers was less important, since so few of the passages were arranged in advance—somewhat surprising, since Lester otherwise took his music so seriously. On the other hand, he was loth to put music into a straitjacket, wanting as much freedom and room for imagination as possible. This meant that it was relatively easy for a new musician to take part at short notice. As leader of the band and its foremost soloist, Lester was of course the main attraction, the person people came to hear; even so, he was generous in awarding as much solo space to the others in the band as they desired. The reason was that he knew that the only place one could develop as a perfomer was on stage—he himself experimented all the time. Harry Edison, for instance, can recall that Lester never stopped trying out new ideas on the bandstand, for where else were they to be tried out? If the ideas didn't work out to begin with, he kept on until they did.[29]

Music was the main thing in his life, and he wanted his fellow musicians to take it as seriously as he himself did. This could lead to complications, since there was such a large age difference between him and the other musicians—fifteen to twenty years on average. Once, after an especially bad rehearsal, it all got a bit too much for him and he exclaimed, "It takes pretty people to make the music pretty, and ain't a single pretty bastard in my band!"[30]

What he demanded first and foremost of himself and his musicians was originality, but this was a demand he felt only a few people were able to live up to. "The trouble with most musicians today is that they are copycats. Of course you have to start out playing like someone else. You have a model, or a teacher, and you learn all that he can show you. But then you start playing for yourself. Show them that you're an individual. And I can count those who are doing that today on the finger of one hand," was his verdict in 1949.[31]

He never changed his opinion about this. "Every musician should be a stylist," he said on a subsequent occasion. "I played like Trumbauer when I was starting out. But then there's a time when you have to go out for yourself and tell your story."[32] "You've got to have style that's all your own," he elaborated. "A man can only be a stylist if he makes up his mind not to copy anybody. Originality is the thing. You can have tone and technique and a lot of other things but without originality you ain't really nowhere. Gotta be original."[33] Down through the years there were, however, some musicians among the talented youngsters in the band who were in possession of the originality Lester was looking for. This was, for example, true of the piano players Junior Mance, Kenny Drew, Wynton Kelly, Horace Silver, John Lewis, and Gildo Mahones, of the drummer Roy Haynes, and of the trumpet players Tony Fruscella and Art Farmer. The reason for the frequent changes in the lineup after 1949 was that Lester took part in the annual JATP tours, which lasted for some two months in the fall, or in other, even longer tours. This meant that many of his musicians had to find other employment during the periods Lester was on the move.

One of the longest tours he made with his own band took them right across the country to San Francisco in February 1948. A review of the band's performance differs widely from that of the Town Hall concert. "The outfit is a versatile one," Ralph Gleason wrote, "more so than you might expect, with both Briscoe and Lacey singing fine ballads and Lester knockin' off lots of good tunes in fine, danceable tempos. Most impressive when heard were a nice version of 'Just You, Just Me,' 'How High the Moon' which the boys managed to brighten up considerably by giving it a little Caribbean touch a la 'Early in the Morning,' Lacey's and Briscoe's vocals and the wonderful, wonderful Lester Young solos. The rhythm section is solid now, Haynes is a very impressive drummer and, given a chance, this band might click in a rather big way."[34]

On a two-month tour of one-nighters starting in December 1948, the band played in Canada for the first time. This took place in Toronto, from which the following story was reported to the *Chicago Defender:*

Because Canadian mailboxes look like the fire-boxes that dot street corners in America, Lester Young and his band returned to the states with a batch of picture postcards that they had intended to mail.

Playing a dance here at the Eaton auditorium, the tenor sax star and his six-piece combo on their first visit across the border wanted to send their friends in the states greetings from Canada. But when they left their hotels on the way to the dance halls, intended to mail them, they failed to find the familiar mail-boxes they all knew. It wasn't until they had returned to the states that they learned that all Canadian postal drops are painted a firebox red.[35]

Shortly after the band arrived home after this long tour, Junior Mance

He came to Chicago to play a concert, a dance or something, and I was playing in a small club with Gene Ammons. He stopped by the club to see Gene and heard me and offered me the job, and two weeks later I joined the group. I stayed with him for about a year, and then he went back on a long tour with Norman Granz and I rejoined Gene Ammon's band.

When I was with Lester we were all young. I think I was the youngest at that time, 18 or 19, and the bass player was about a year older than myself, Leroy Jackson. Roy Haynes was in his early twenties, and Jerry Elliott, the trombone player, was around 21–22 or something like that. Jesse Drakes was the oldest, he was about 23 or 24.

But I think that may have been a coincidence, because I was in the band part of the time with Jo Jones, "Old Man" Jo Jones. After Roy filled in he was in the band for two or three months. It didn't really change the music, because at that time Roy was a different drummer from what he is now. Roy was a straight ahead swing drummer. He truly played modern, but Jo played modern, too. At that time you couldn't call Jo an old time drummer, no. For me it was equally satisfying playing with both of them. Roy you could consider a little more modern, but he approached the music the same as Jo Jones. It also depended on how the rest of the group was. When I was with the group and Jo filled in, much of the players were younger players, and Jo swung us, he really did. It didn't change anything when Jo came in after Roy played.

We had three men in the frontline, trumpet, trombone and tenor. Sometimes it was just tenor and trumpet, and then there were times, when we were just four, quartet, Lester and the rhythm section; it varied. It was a very, very free thing, you know. The only time we had rehearsals maybe were at the record sessions. Most of the time it was a very free thing with the three horns, you know. He'd call a tune and we played the melody. Sometimes the horns would maybe on the spot improvise something. He always let everybody play solos, you know. Lester liked variety, even when he played the same tunes he was playing different most of the time. On the bandstand he would call the tunes and play the melody line, and he usually played the first chorus. Sometimes he told somebody else: "Play the first chorus!" if there was a trumpet player or a trombone player, you know, very informal. The only time he probably directed who'd play the solos was at the recording sessions. Back then when I played with Lester LP's were just coming in, and I think the first record date I did with Lester everything was 78's. You had to keep it to a certain amount of minutes, the record couldn't go over three minutes. With Lester it was: "Junior, you play solo on this one, and Jesse, you play solo on the next one." It was the only time there was any formality as far as that concerns.

You know, Lester was probably the only man I've played with, where you didn't think of him as being a bandleader. He was always one of the guys. He was a leader, but he wasn't, he didn't insist on anything of what we wanted to play, you know. He was more like one of us, one of the sidemen. It was like a band with all sidemen and no leader, I just mean the closeness and the friendliness in the group.

We travelled most of the time by train, because Lester didn't drive, I didn't drive, so most of the time we travelled by trains, but occasionally we flew. Lester's wife didn't go with us too often, she'd stay behind him.

Playing with Lester was a great experience to me and I learned a lot of songs. He knew every tune in the book. He was always coming up with tunes that were not really jazz tunes, but if he played them they were jazz tunes! Lester listened a lot to ballads, and he always listened to the lyrics. In fact he told me once: "If you want to play ballads you should know the lyrics too, because you can then get more out of them, you know, more than the composers had in mind."

I remember most of Lester's record collection was either Billie Holiday or Frank Sinatra, and he was listening to the lyrics of all the tunes. And I know he was right. He was closer to the melody than most jazz players who were following the chord changes. He was following the chord changes too, but he was playing more of what the lyrics were saying. That way he could play fewer notes but get more out of it than people who were playing around the chord changes, every tone in the chord or something. I think it was one of the biggest lessons I've learned from him about playing ballads. I know some of the musicians used to say that the only person Billie Holiday really liked to play behind her was Lester Young, because he never got in the way. "Sweets" Edison used to do the same thing behind Billie, he was probably the only other one outside Lester that could do that."[36]

When Lester had an engagement, he was always in good time. "He's of the old school," Charlie Carpenter recalls. "He felt obligated professionally to be on time. In fact, Al Cooper, who used to promote concerts around New York, once said: 'The one thing you have to worry about Lester is he gets to town *too* early.' "[37] On one occasion, however, things went terribly wrong. "It was in 1949," Carpenter recalls. "Lester had missed a train in Washington because he'd fallen asleep in the station. He was due in New Bedford, Massachusetts, for a one-nighter. Instead of waiting for the next train, he became panicky. He hired a taxi to Newark, chartered a plane to Providence, and then took another taxi to New Bedford. I think it cost him at least $250. He was an hour late and worked three hours overtime for nothing."[38]

Lester had not signed a new recording contract when his contract with Aladdin expired after the recordings of December 1947, but in the fall of 1949 he signed a double contract with Norman Granz. Granz, who had had an arrangement with Mercury to distribute his records was now starting to build his own record company, which down through the years changed its name from Clef to Norgran to Verve to Pablo. On this occasion Lester signed up for the 1949 JATP concert tour and also signed a long-term contract, which later was renewed several times.

The music Granz released consisted partly of studio recordings and partly of concert recordings, since he had had the bright idea that if so many people were interested in coming to his Jazz at the Philharmonic concerts, then there must also be a potential record market to be tapped. So the music from the preceding year's concert was released just before the next tour was to begin in September. This meant that it could serve both as an advertisement for the coming concert and also as an apéritif for the next JATP release. Most of the recordings were taken from the start of the tour on the East Coast, since Granz could make use of the Carnegie Hall recording equipment, using technicians who were familiar with the acoustics of the hall. Later there were also recordings from Chicago's Civic Opera House and from the Shrine Auditorium in Los Angeles.

By means of his concerts Granz wanted both to bring jazz to a wider audience and to help to break down racial barriers. The musicians he selected for his concerts had to fulfill his demands as to consistently high quality of performance. At the same time, they were all musicians whom Granz valued highly, no matter the color of their skin. "I don't hire people because I think they're going to draw people," he once said. "I hire them on one standard only and that's if I like the way they play— but I pay them according to how well they draw. If they draw well, people infer that's the primary reason for being on the show. That's not true, because I can defend anyone's being on my show. His reason for being on it is very simple: I like him."

"First and foremost I like consistency in a jazz artist," he continued. "I can't give blind adulation to these peak-and-depth men."[39]

At the same time, Granz expected his musicians to be exemplary in their JATP role during the tours, which gradually grew from covering most of the states in the United States to include Europe, North Africa, Asia, and Australia. This was not normally a problem. Even though Granz wanted jazz to reach as wide an audience as possible, he maintained a somewhat formal atmosphere at the concerts, which were, for example, always introduced by playing the American national anthem. During a long tour tensions between certain musicians or between musicians and the arrangers of the concerts were bound to crop up, and such frustrations could manifest themselves in different ways, including humor—at which Lester was an expert—practical jokes, or, more naturally, through the music itself.

During the 1955 tour the solemnity of JATP concerts at one point became just too much for the tenor sax player Illinois Jacquet. Shortly before the curtain went up in Seattle and the "Star and Stripes" was about to be played, Illinois, more than a little drunk, stepped forward and began a long, ironic, circus-like solo which had the jam-packed audience in the Civic Auditorium roaring with laughter. The only person who couldn't see the funny side of things was, of course, Norman Granz, who literally dragged Jacquet behind the curtain to give him a talking to.[40]

While on tour the musicians were always housed in the most expensive hotels. They traveled first class and sometimes used a plane hired by Granz especially for that purpose. This sometimes led to racial confrontations when the troupe was touring the southern states, where the best hotels were normally reserved for whites. If he was unable to house all his musicians at one hotel, Granz used to fly out of the town the same evening. Once, in Miami, a different solution was found—Granz booked them all at the town's best hotel for blacks. To avoid any unpleasantness Lester refused to live with the others at expensive hotels and always checked in at a hotel for blacks.

The national tours were always on the same lines, starting in New York—or, once in a while, in Hartford, Connecticut—on a Saturday evening in mid-September and finishing six to seven weeks later in Los Angeles, having toured about forty-five towns, in some of which two concerts were given on the same evening. Even though several changes in the programs were made over the years, they too were, broadly speaking, on the same lines, always starting with a jam session. After this, most of the concert was devoted to single groups and soloists, with a jam session finale in which most of the reeds and brass used to take part.

Lester took part in the tours from 1949 to 1957, except for the years 1954 and 1956. His reasons were not simply economic. It was true that he was excellently paid, usually earning $750 a week—which meant that he could earn about $5,000 on the tour, a sum which was net profit. This should be compared with wages at Birdland in New York, which were $125 a week for a musician. But Lester's yearning for recognition and fame was the prime reason for his touring with JATP. The tours were well publicized, and each year saw sold-out concert halls throughout the country. In the mid-fifties Granz could also reckon on 25,000 copies of JATP LPs being ordered in advance.

Even if the plans for the tour were pretty strict, everything about JATP was well organized, so all the musicians had to do was move from town to town and play each evening. From a musical point of view, the tours were a bit of a rest cure for Lester, since the time he actually played during a concert rarely exceeded an hour all told. At the same time, he enjoyed being with the many musicians he knew and respected. To find an outlet for his love of playing, he sometimes went on the town after a concert—if there was enough, which wasn't often—to see if he could find a place where he would be allowed to join in the music.

Even though the conditions were fine, Lester's relationship to Granz and JATP gradually became more ambivalent, since he felt cooped up, unable to play the way he wanted to deep down. Lester had become known as "the original honker," and he felt that it was a strain to live up to the name. On one occasion Granz tried to make Lester play a bit more like the audience wanted, to put in a few more "honks" on his saxophone, but Lester refused with the words "I blow the onlyest way I know!"[41]

He wanted to meet the audience's expectations, but at the same time he tried to play as he felt at the moment. This conflict in turn led to an large increase in his liquor consumption during the tours, especially during the trips to Europe which he made in 1952, 1953, 1956, and 1959. He often disappointed his audience, since most of his solos didn't attain the level they would have under normal circumstances. And so it is not at all surprising that he was at his best in ballads or slow-tempo blues numbers, where he felt himself freer and untrammeled by the "honker" role.

Lester managed to find release for some of the emotional tension that built up inside him during these tours by sitting in at various places after the concerts. During his European tours he was a frequent guest at all sorts of clubs, something noticed and commented on by the French critic Frank Tenot: "Lester and Barney Kessel were the two musicians of the JATP troupe that year who played as much as they could. . . . One night Lester said: 'There are too many people at the concerts and I don't think my music interests them; they've come for something else. I bore them. I prefer to play before those who like my music.' "[42]

In 1949 Lester took part in the jam-session section, together with the trumpet player Roy Eldridge, the trombone player Tommy Turk, the tenor sax player Flip Phillips, and a rhythm section consisting of the piano player Hank Jones, the bass player Ray Brown, and the drummer Buddy Rich. For the concert in New York, Granz had also invited Charlie Parker along as a guest soloist. A young Canadian piano player, Oscar Peterson, was also invited up onto the bandstand to join in. From 1950 on he was to become one of the mainstays of Granz's concert tours.

Reviews in *Down Beat* of the New York concert were reasonably good; about Lester they wrote that he "for the most part, seemed to be playing in good Lesterian fashion, although in one concession to ego he included a few honks, with the audience astutely taking up the cue."[43]

Flip Phillips was another steadfast musician in the JATP troupe during the 1950s. He was also good at repairing saxophones. He took care of Lester's on several occasions when something was wrong with it. "To tell you about Prez," Buddy Tate recalls, "if you once do him a favor, he never stop paying you back. Flip told me he got nine cigarette lighters that Prez had given him because he'd fixed his horn for him all the time. He'd come to Flip and say, 'Lady Flip? My baby ain't acting right. You'd better do something for her.' And Flip said he was standing over him watching him and Flip said, 'Look now, Prez, if I'm going to fix it, take your ass on in the other room somewhere. I know what the fuck I'm gonna do. Leave me alone!' "[44]

On arriving back home in New York after the JATP tour at the beginning of November 1949, Lester had to find a couple new musicians for the group, since Mance, Haynes, and Elliott had found other work in the meantime. They decided to do without a trombone player; Carpenter suggested Connie Kay as the new drummer. Kay played with Lester during the month of November 1949, once again during the summer of 1952, and finally in a long period stretching from July 1953 to February 1955.

"I was with Young off and on for five or six years," Kay relates. "Lester and I were like buddies. When I joined him, I already knew him, but he didn't know *I* was joining him. I met him down in Penn Station and asked him what he was doing, and he said, 'I'm waiting for the drummer, Lady Kay,' which is what he always called me. 'Well, I'm the drummer,' I said. 'What! You're the drummer?' and he fell out." [45] Kay also relates that Lester was shy and felt uneasy in a crowd of people, or with someone he didn't know. He also recalls that Lester brought a fifth of scotch along with him to the job each evening and that the entire band used to drink some of it to stop Lester from getting too drunk. He also thinks that Lester felt he was not getting the recognition he deserved and that eventually he did not care much whether he lived or not. Kay also used to try to get him to play the clarinet again, but Lester always replied, "Lady Kay, I'm saving that for my old age."

Some of the other musical expressions Lester used were the following: "Have another helping," which meant that the soloist in question should take another chorus; "Have a trio," which meant a three-chorus solo; "the bridgework" was the B-piece in a standard melody, sometimes also referred to as "George Washington," the bridge over the Hudson River. If he used the phrase "Justus, please" to others in the band, it meant that they were to play "Just You, Just Me"; "Afternoon of a Basie-ite" he rechristened humorously "An Afternoon of a Baseball Player."

During the fall of 1949 the Royal Roost, a jazz club on Broadway where Lester's group had played a few times, was forced to close. Its former owners, however, wanted to open a club which was mainly to support modern jazz on the other side of the street, at 1678 Broadway. For this reason they wanted to call the place Birdland, after Charlie Parker. Another jazz club called the Clique had previously existed at the same address, but there was trouble with the license for some reason, so the opening evening kept on having to be postponed. When the license eventually was granted, the first show started, on December 15. It lasted three weeks and was called "A Journey Through Jazz," since it depicted the development of jazz from the Dixieland of the twenties to the Swing of the thirties, the bop of the forties, and the cool jazz of the fifties.

Lester was invited to participate as a representative for swing music, succeeding Max Kaminsky's group. "Next stop on the journey is swing," *Down Beat* wrote about him, "and, with appropriate remarks from interlocutor Williams about the emergence of Benny Goodman and Count

Basie, on comes Lester Young, than whom could be swingier. Lester proceeds to give a good cross-section of himself, with some basic Basie blowing here, some JATP hullabaloo there, and just plain ol' Prez to fill in the intervals. It's a good, representative performance."[46]

On this occasion Lester was accompanied by, among others, the piano player Dick Hyman, who recalls:

I was there primarily to play with Max Kaminsky's Dixielanders, which was a band that included Munn Ware on trombone, Sol Yaged on clarinet, Max, of course, on trumpet, Irv Lang on bass, and George Wettling on drums. But they also asked Irv and me to play with Lester. We both stayed on after Max's engagement was finished. In fact, I was the house pianist at Birdland for several months, and I played with Lester in other engagements at Birdland. I worked with him, and I worked with Flip Phillips and Bill Harris, and one night I played with Charlie Parker when Bud Powell didn't show up. During the opening show I also played with Hot Lips Page and Stan Getz and someone they billed as "that new young singer": Harry Belafonte! We played with Lester during that winter of 1950 on and off for several engagements, it seems to me. There might have been one in 1951 as well, but I don't really remember. We never rehearsed. Lester would count off and say something like "three C's and two F's," which meant that we'd do the blues for three choruses in C and then go to F. We played some odd tunes. The first time he called for "Lavender Blue," I thought he was kidding, it was such an unlikely song. We just played, whatever it was, and there were no problems. Lester repeated his numbers a lot, however.

He played wonderfully in that last style of his, not his youthful style. I don't know really how to describe it. It was kind of a weary-but-still-trying way of playing, it seems to me. Weary, but still somehow with bursts of energy, if that's not an impossibility. Not the straight-ahead way he played on the early Basie records, but a lot looser, and, I guess, not as tight and inventive as his early days.

I never spoke with him much, because he always talked in a coded way, and I found him hard to understand. He'd say, "Ding-dong," by the way of a greeting, but I don't recall any conversations at all off the stand.

I also played one job with him at a black dance-affair at the Laurel Hall in Newark, which Joe Shulman, his bass player at the time, got me on to. Joe was his contractor then, and he asked me to go with them to Chicago also, but the money was very low, and I couldn't do it for that reason and probably because I had some other commitments. That leads into one of the famous Lester stories that I heard later: The sideman says to Lester, "I'm sorry, Prez, but I can't go on the road for $45.00 a week! How can I live?" To which Lester replies in that funny, high-pitched voice, "You got to save your pennies if you want to play with Prez!"

I'm not sure Lester was as well-paid as people might think. He was one of the most important musicians, but I doubt that he was making all that much money anywhere. Remember, this was before jazz was a big concert attraction. The only concerts around were the Norman Granz Jazz at the Philharmonic series, and Lester did play for Granz. I'd be surprised if he made a great deal in nightclubs. At that time at Birdland the ordinary non-stars like me were making something like $125 a week. Of course, that doesn't indicate what Lester's salary might have been, but in retrospect, the whole operation seemed a bit sleazy.

On the bandstand Lester would get into his peculiar stance. At that time he no longer held the saxophone at right angles to his body, as he had when he was younger. He just held it straight in front of him, one leg in front of the other, not moving much, sort of clutching the horn. His eyes were heavy-lidded and appeared partially closed, sort of like a flag at half-mast. He had very little interplay with the audience, although they were enthusiastic, and not much with the musicians in the group, either. But I never felt as if he was ignoring us. It was a group that worked without much direction from him; everyone knew what to do. And Jo Jones, with his smile and personality, made up for any lack of personality on Lester's part.

Jo used to play a break that baffled me every time. I tried to get him to explain it to me, because I could never find four beats. He demonstrated it in slow motion for me one time, but at normal tempo, I couldn't understand it. It always seemed to have five beats somehow. Maybe Jo was putting me on.

The Birdland jobs were not at all the same personnel, whenever they were. Jo Jones may not have been the drummer every time, and Irv Lang and Joe Shulman both played bass at different times that I was with the group. It's a long time back. I was thrilled to play with Lester, and his playing was still impressive, but it was an entirely different way from his youthful playing. I was 23 then, and I thought of Lester as an old man. Looking back, I'm glad I had the time to do it then. And the energy! The hours were 9:00 to 3:00 A.M. or 10:00 to 4:00 A.M., alternate sets for a six-hour stretch.

There was a funky atmosphere in the club. I mean they really had a sinister kind of people hanging out at the bar. There was actually a murder at Birdland one night, but not while I was playing there. The piano was next to the edge of the bandstand, right in front of the bleachers, the rows of chairs where people sat who didn't want to be at the more expensive tables, and when I got into a solo, they'd holler, "Work! Work!"[47]

This special atmosphere was not lessened by the fact that the club's emcee was an unusual personality by the name of Pee Wee Marquette, whose characteristic nasal falsetto can be heard on numerous live broadcasts from Birdland. He was a midget from Puerto Rico and became very unpopular because he used to buck everybody for money all the time. If a musician refused to pay he wouldn't announce him at all, or he would mispronounce his name; for example, "Ladies and gentlemen. Here comes Mr. Fip Phillips!" The musicians thought he was a drag, and one evening when he again asked Lester for some money, Lester turned him down, saying, "Get away from me, you half a motherfucker!"[48]

Birdland was to be Lester's most permanent place of work during the ensuing years, with numerous engagements each year. He got his first long engagement as early as January 1950, and *Down Beat* gave him a good review: "Lester Young, the only ingredient held over from the opening show, was blowing in better form than these ears have heard him in a long time. Undoubtedly some measure of credit for this can be taken by Jo Jones, whose drumming was providing Pres with the relaxed drive that he knew of yore. Relaxing in turn, Lester was drawing on and bringing up to date a good deal of the old Basie material with an imagination and lyrical turn of phrase which was really worthy of the man who has been such an enormous influence on saxophonists in recent years. He was getting good support from Dick Hyman on piano and Irv Lang on bass."[49]

The repertoire Lester played with his group consisted of blues—almost invariably his own compositions—standard numbers plus several popular themes that he heard on the radio, like "Lavender Blue," which so surprised Dick Hyman. "He's often a year or a year and a half ahead of everybody else," Jo Jones recalls. "He catches something on the radio he likes, and he starts playing it—like 'How High the Moon.' He and Marlowe Morris were playing it at Minton's before it became widely popular in jazz. He was the one who first started playing 'Polka Dots and Moonbeams' and 'Foggy Day' again. He finds things that have meaning to them, and soon other people are playing or singing them again."[50] When Lester was at home he used to listen to music on the radio, and his tastes were wide. Leonard Feather once gave him a blindfold test, and Lester confessed that the only type of music he didn't go for all that much was classical music, though he liked some of that too.

His interest in singers in particular sometimes resulted in his beginning to sing when he was out on a job, and he was not without talent. "Lester Young startled some of the newcomers to Birdland by bursting into song occasionally during his recent stay," *Down Beat* once wrote. "He's no Sammy Davis Jr., but he sure swings."[51]

"On a date, I play a variety of tempos," Lester adds. "I set my own tempos and I take my time. I wish jazz were played more for dancing. I have a lot of fun playing for dances because I like to dance, too. The rhythm of the dancers comes back to you when you're playing. When you're playing for dancing, it all adds up to playing the right tempo. After three or four tempos, you find the tempo they like. What they like changes from dance date to dance date."[52]

Dick Hyman could not play in Lester's group all the time, since he was house pianist at Birdland, but Jesse Drakes recommended a friend he had grown up with in Harlem, Kenny Drew. His first job with Lester was at the Savoy Ballroom in the week starting February 20, 1950.

"When I played with Lester Young we only practiced once," Drew relates.

Lester asked Jesse Drakes, Jo Jones, myself and Joe Shulman, who was going to replace Aaron Bell, to come to Nola Studios on 52nd Street and Broadway to practice a little, as we were going to Chicago the next day. It only lasted for three to three and a half hours, but we didn't play all that much music. We had some of Lester's gin—he drank gin all the time—so we got plenty of drinks. But it was really good, since we got to know each other. Lester was a nice person and we often talked together when we traveled by plane or by train on a tour. We also went to Canada, to Toronto, for a week, where we played at the Town Tavern in October or November.

When Lester came on the stand his movements were a little bit feminine, so that people looking at him might think he was a homosexual. Then Jesse Drakes would come in and he always had make-up on, so the front line—the trumpet player and the sax player—looked a little strange. I actually felt a bit stifled, maybe the people down there thought I was one too! It was actually strange to see Lester Young, that beautiful musician, tiptoe over the stand.

Even though I played a bit more modern than the others and would have preferred a different bass player and drummer, it was great fun and pretty good. I had many nice evenings with the group and it was one of the great experiences of my life to play together with Lester Young.

As I said we only had the one practice, but gradually certain arrangements emerged even so. For example, Lester might say one evening: "Blues in F," but after a week or maybe a fortnight, when we played it again, we had an idea of how we should play it, because we had gotten an impression the previous time we had played it. It found a form that got better and better after a few months, because we had actually made an arrangement.

Lester nearly always played the themes on his own and that was because he wanted to have as much freedom as possible to interpret in his own way. He preferred to be alone with the melody, but at the end of the numbers Jesse sometimes joined him, but not always.[53]

Aaron Bell played bass in the group in February–March 1950 and once more in 1952. He recalls: "I learned an awful lot about playing with him, because he gave me more freedom. I hadn't done too much soloing on bass before, so this was good for me. Because he knew I was still at the university, he called me 'Professor.' 'Take it, Professor,' he'd say. Prez and Teddy Wilson were great guys to work with. They never bugged you, never argued, never put you down, but made you feel they appreciated what you were doing. Sometimes, because of where I was living in the Bronx, I'd be late, and I'd charge in, taking off my coat, running to the bass. 'Hi, there!' Teddy would say. 'I'm sorry,' I'd reply. 'Oh, that's all right. Have a taste?' And he wouldn't go on the stand until I got there. Prez was the same way if I was late. 'Well, Professor, you gonna make it tomorrow?' he'd ask. 'I'm gonna *be* here tomorrow, on time,' I'd answer. They were both good for me, because they took inhibitions about playing away, and sort of bolstered my ego."[54]

This attitude was typical of Lester, who had himself suffered from other musicians and critics criticizing his style of playing. He never forgot that, as a young man, he had more detractors than supporters of his style of playing during jam sessions, so he didn't want others to feel insecure or inferior as he had. "The critics used to call me the honk man. Mike Levin said I had cardboard sound and that I couldn't play my horn. You dig? That made it harder to play my horn. That's why I don't put the kids down. They're all playing. It depends on whether *You* dig them." [55]

"That's why I always let me little kiddies play solos," he explained on another occasion. "That way they don't bother me when I solo. In fact, sometimes I get bawled out by people who want to hear me play more, but I believe if you're paying a man to play, and if that man is on the bandstand and can play, he should get a chance to tell his story." [56]

That fall, 1950, Lester took part in JATP's jam session section, where the brass and reeds were reduced to Lester, the trombone player Bill Harris, Harry Edison, and Flip Phillips—the smallest group in JATP's history. Coleman Hawkins had a section to himself, and that year the reviews were only moderately enthusiastic. *Variety,* for example, said about the premiere that an "interesting aspect of the program was the different styles by the trio of tenor saxmen. Hawkins showing refinement, Phillips excitement and Young indifference," [57] while *Down Beat* after a concert in Chicago gave only the following words to Lester's playing: "Pres displayed his only initiative of the night on 'Ghost of a Chance.' " [58]

About New Year's 1951 another couple of changes to the group took place; Kenny Drew was replaced by John Lewis, and Joe Shulman by Gene Ramey. At that time Jesse Drakes was with another band, and so Lester played alongside Tony Fruscella, then only twenty-three, for a short time. Unfortunately, Tony didn't stay as long as he himself wanted to, since he was maneuvered out. Bill Triglia relates:

When Bill Clark and Joe Shulman was in Lester's rhythm section around 1950, Tony Fruscella was with him, a beautiful trumpet player, he's dead now. I've heard that somebody came in and recorded them at that time, but I've never heard the record of it. Fruscella was a white fellow and very friendly with Miles Davis and used to jam with him. He played with myself and Red Mitchell a lot. He had a beautiful sound. He didn't play high, he didn't play flashy, but he played beautiful low register, very modern.

When Kenny Drew left and some jobs came up, John Lewis was playing with Lester. According to what I heard, and Tony Fruscella was a good friend of mine, Tony used to get drunk with Lester. Lester loved him. He didn't play the same style as Lester, but it fit nicely, it was a beautiful contrast, but John Lewis didn't like Tony. Tony said he didn't like him because he was properly white, I don't know, but John Lewis tried to get somebody else on. The next job they had Lester's manager didn't call Tony Fruscella and he was so hurt, because he

Lester Young with Flip Phillips (ts) and Bill Harris (tb) on the Jazz At The Philharmonic tour, September-October 1950. From the collection of Don Schlitten.

loved Lester, you know. He wanted to stay with him, he was a young fellow and very tender. As a fact his career went down after that. He worked with Gerry Mulligan and Stan Getz and then disappeared. Tony loved Lester Young and he thought John Lewis was the reason he was fired.

There was a lot of politics in it. Lester Young was glad to get John Lewis, because he was playing with Dizzy Gillespie at the time and a lot of modern guys. John Lewis had a lot of power in his own way. He was a quiet man, but he knew how to manipulate, and he got somebody else on, I don't know if it was Jesse Drakes. I can't believe it, because Jesse Drakes couldn't play close to Tony Fruscella.[59]

Whoever John Lewis got hold of, he did not stay in the group for long, since the recordings made with Lester in January 1951 are without a trumpet player, and Drakes did not return to the group until May.

John Lewis was with Lester for about eight months, from December 1950 to August 1951. "Jo Jones was generally on drums, and either Tony Fruscella or Jesse Drakes on trumpet," he relates. "We worked at places like Bop City, in New York, and we travelled to Chicago. He would play the same songs in each set on a given night, but he would often repeat the sequence the following week this way: if he had played 'Sometimes I'm Happy' on Tuesday of the preceding week, he would open 'Sometimes I'm Happy' this Tuesday with a variation on the solo he had played on the tune the week before; then he would play variations on the variations the week after, so that his playing formed a kind of gigantic organic whole. While I was with him, I never heard anything of the coarseness that people have said began creeping into his playing. I did notice a change in him in his last few years. There was nothing obvious or offensive about it. Just an air of depression about him."

"If Lester was wronged, the wound never healed," he continues. "Once at Bop City, he mentioned how people had always bugged him about the supposed thinness of his tone. We were in his dressing room, and he picked up his tenor and played a solo using this great big butter sound. Not a Coleman Hawkins sound but a thick, smooth, concentrated sound. It was as beautiful as anything I've ever heard."[60]

There is an explanation as to why Lester was able to produce this round, soft tone. During his early career he was constantly criticized for his light alto sax-like tone, but at that time he used to play with a metal mouthpiece, probably made by Otto Link, whose products usually produce a light, pleasant tone. Lester had used ordinary bamboo reeds with such mouthpieces, with a hardness that never exceeded medium, since he always played with relatively soft reeds. From about 1942–43 on he changed to an ebony mouthpiece made by Brilhart, which he used for the rest of his career. This mouthpiece has a white plastic inlay on the upper side, which is clearly visible on several of the photos taken after 1943. He used plastic reeds with this mouthpiece, reeds which began to be produced in the early 1940s and which gave a fuller, rounder sound. Advertisements for these reeds appeared in *Down Beat* from January 1943 on. There are two types. One, introduced by Rico, is called Plasti-cover and consists of a bamboo reed coated with a thin layer of plastic. This was to retain the flexible quality of the bamboo, giving it at the same time the life span of a plastic reed. The other type was made entirely of plastic; two brands, Betcha and Luellen Plasticane, were among the first to come on the market. In an interview in 1950 Lester said, "I always have a plastic reed on my tenor,"[61] but he didn't mention which type, nor did he say how long he had been using them. Knowing Lester's lazy disposition, it is highly probable that he changed over soon after they came out, since they got rid of the eternal switching and checking of reeds which plagues the lives of reed players.

The change to the Brilhart mouthpiece can clearly be heard on recordings, where there is a great difference between the light, airy tone of 1940 and the darker, coarser tone after 1943. Added to this is the fact that Lester, thanks to his blowing technique, was able to make his sound fuller and more beautiful and so impress John Lewis.

Lewis supplements his thoughts about Lester's playing with these remarks about Lester the man: "Lester is an extremely gentle, kind, considerate person. He's always concerned about the underdog. He always wants to help somebody. It is true that he doesn't like unpleasantness and that he'll avoid it if he can, but isn't that true of most of us?"

"The basic mark of Lester," he goes on, "is that he's always young; he stays young in his playing and in his person. Some people are always crying for love and kindness; but Lester doesn't cry. The way he seems to see *being* is: 'Here we are. Let's have a nice time.' "[62]

John Lewis is not alone in thinking this, since Bill Triglia has also remarked: "Lester was a showman, but he didn't do it for the showmanship, he did it for the music. If the music excited him enough he would dance on the bandstand. When he was happy he had a funny little dance, beautiful and smooth, he looked like a dancer. If I was playing good or somebody else was playing good and he liked it he said funny things. He had many, many remarks—I forgot his words—in his own language. He was happy with the music and he was a happy fellow on the bandstand. It would seem like showmanship when he did it, but it was just the way he was, you know. He came from the old school where you entertained people. When you played for people you had to make them enjoy it, you know."[63]

Unfortunately, there are not many reviews of Lester's own groups, but in September 1951, shortly before he took off with Norman Granz and his JATP once more, he shared the bill at Birdland with Dizzy Gillespie's Quintet. At the time Lester's group had been completely reorganized, and *Metronome*'s reviewer wrote:

Lester showed up well, playing with more controlled vibrato and closer to the beat than I have heard him do for some time. His quintet of Earl Knight on piano, bassist Aaron Bell, drummer Al Jones and trumpeter Jesse Drakes swung well, producing a well-ordered sound pleasant to the ear after the sometimes haphazard Gillespie presentation.

Lester sounded like the man who made those tremendous Keynote sides with Slam Stewart and Johnny Guarnieri on "Tea for Two" and "The Bells," each of which he ended with the "Perdido" riff, swinging easily with an almost complete absence of the honking which he has been associated with lately.

Jesse Drakes cut Dizzy to my mind if only in the consistency of his solos. There was more emphasis on melody and thought than on technique and the audience seemed to appreciate it. The other three members of the combo played well although none was outstanding. If this was any example, Lester without Granz is a good combination.[64]

The reviewer was partially right in his last comment. Lester's contributions to JATP were somewhat uneven, but those recordings we have from the concerts are never indifferent. From the JATP concerts in 1951 there are no recordings available, and this is certainly because the quality was not good enough. The Carnegie Hall audience was partly to blame that year, since it was completely uncritical and encouraged the musicians to show off their worst side, which resulted in many of them playing to the gallery. *Down Beat* wrote after the concert that "the worse the guys blow the better the audience will like it, and the musicians themselves are cynically aware of this."[65] According to the reviewer, only three artists maintained a certain standard—Ella Fitzgerald, Oscar Peterson, and Lester, who was reviewed with these words: "Lester, surprisingly, made few concessions to the mean IQ level confronting him. Though his sound was inconsistent, he blew more cohesively than at his previous Carnegie appearance."[66]

During March and April 1952 Lester took part in JATP's first European tour, which visited Sweden, Denmark, France, Belgium, Holland, Switzerland, and Germany. Granz had also invited along Oscar Peterson and Hank Jones, Flip Phillips, the guitar player Irving Ashby, the trumpet players Roy Eldridge and Charlie Shavers, the drummers Gene Krupa and Max Roach, the bass player Ray Brown, and Ella Fitzgerald. They were all to be vaccinated before leaving, but since Lester was afraid of being stuck he first tried to persuade the doctor to pretend that he had vaccinated him. The doctor refused to agree to this; only after much convincing and assurances that it wouldn't hurt was the vaccination able to take place. Just as Lester almost always avoided signing contracts, he also refused to fill out the immigration forms. "He won't write," Norman Granz relates. "At least, he was the only guy on any of my tours for whom I had to make out his own immigration slip with his name and passport number."[67]

Lester didn't have the opportunity of playing with Max Roach very often, but they had known each other from the early 1940s, when both of them played at Monroe's Uptown House. Roach has been one of those who shaped modern drumming techniques, and one of the reasons he went his own way was on account of Lester. Roach can clearly recall the following episode from Uptown House: "When I was old enough to play with Young, I tried to sound like Jo Jones all the time. One evening, when I thought I had really played as well as Jones, Prez said to me: 'You know what, Lady Roach, you can't be in the choir until you've learned to sing your own song.' "[68]

On the whole, the concerts were well received; Oscar Peterson and Ella Fitzgerald were often singled out for praise. Lester's performances were somewhat uneven, according to how he felt at the time, so his reviews were pretty mixed. Sometimes he felt unable to live up to the high expectations people had of him; often they unrealistically expected something other than what they got.

The first concerts on the tour went well as far as Lester was concerned. After the concert in Stockholm, *Melody Maker* wrote that the "hit of the show was Ella Fitzgerald. Her half-dozen numbers received terrific applause. Oscar Peterson, too, rated high with the critics. From the remainder of the unit it was impossible to pick any one as better than the rest. Flip Phillips, Lester Young and Roy Eldridge all played well, and there was good work from Hank Jones, Irving Ashby, Ray Brown and Max Roach in the rhythm department."

"Each of the horn men obviously had his own particular following," the reviewer added, "and therefore appealed to a definite section of the audience."[69]

After the last Stockholm concert *Orkester Journalen* wrote: "His interpretation of the slow 'I Cover the Waterfront' and 'These Foolish Things' was great art and a wonderful piece of news to all those who had feared that Lester's inspiration and creativity were on the wane. Especially 'Things' at the second Friday concert was dazzlingly beautiful. His latest records have given the impression that his tone has been only so-so during recent years, but now he produced a clear, carrying 'sound' which was both beautiful and passionate. In the up-tempo numbers he was a model of relaxedness—he was a striking example of the hypothesis that great art can be created with modest means. Things really swung around him—his playing was broad, majestic and poised."[70]

The Copenhagen press were divided in their opinion of Lester's playing after the concerts in Denmark, but this is mainly due to the fact that the reviewer of the conservative paper *Berlingske Tidende* hadn't realized that Lester had developed since 1940, for he wrote that "Lester Young has completely changed his style since his time with Basie. He has become modernist and yesterday fell a lot short of his best performances."[71] The reviewer for *Information,* on the other hand, had experienced more and, after having praised Oscar Peterson's Trio, he wrote the following about Lester: "But the JATP ensemble also had its moments, especially when Lester Young played slow tempo solos and in the drumming of Max Roach. In Lester Young we are experiencing one of the most original jazz personalities ever, both in musical and human terms. His solos in 'I Cover the Waterfront' and 'These Foolish Things' were among the most captivating moments of the concerts."[72]

In Paris the concerts in the Salle Pleyel formed the conclusion of a week's jazz festival—"Salon du Jazz"—where Dizzy Gillespie and Sidney Bechet had been among the highlights. Unfortunately, the same cannot be said about Lester's playing, which took a dive in Paris. "The big disappointment was Lester Young, whose playing was a letdown to everybody," *Down Beat* wrote.[73] *Melody Maker*'s Mike Nevard didn't disagree. "Then Lester moved forward," he wrote.

The crowd spotted the move and roared in anticipation. He was their idol before he blew a note.

Whether he remained so afterwards it is difficult to judge. His playing was, in fact, extremely indifferent. . . .

Lester, tall and dignified—dressed in a dark suit—stands with head slightly inclined, eyes closed and blows. . . .

In the second number—"Undecided"—his playing was saturated with tricks. . . . Lester ended the set with "I Cover the Waterfront," probably his best solo of the evening.[74]

Music recorded from this Paris concert confirms Nevard's review. At this time Lester was certainly fed up with the concerts and all the adulation that went with them. That he was not tired of playing in spite of all this is revealed in the following anecdote of the French critic Charles Delauney: "The first time he came over with JATP, his short, mediocre stage appearance disappointed nearly every one of his fans. But pianist Henri Renaud and a few other musicians managed after the concert to take him to the Tabou where he sat in with the local band and really *blew*. There we discovered that Lester could still blow when he wanted to, when he was in the proper environment or mood."[75]

Lester enjoyed being in Paris on the three days off the JATP had while there. He wasn't exactly a museum addict, but he made up for this by holding parties every day in his room at Claridge's Hotel, together with colleagues and fans. He made a pair of true friends in the couple Maurice and Yvonne Cullaz, and, being a gentleman, he called Yvonne "Lady Queen," a nickname he always used on subsequent visits to Paris. Maurice Cullaz has given us his impressions of Lester and recalls that during this stay he was both convivial and entertaining. Suddenly, though, he would get a distant look in his eyes and seem far away for a long time, until, with a painful expression, he would pull himself together and take part in the festivities once more.[76]

Leaving the hotel room, they would carry on until the early hours of the morning in the various clubs found everywhere in the lively jazz scene on the left bank of the Seine. Rue de la Huchette was dotted with small dives like Le Chat Qui Pêche, Caveau de la Huchette, and Riverside. Not far from there on the Rue Galande lay Les Trois Mailletz, an old, well-known club, where vintage swing music was played. On the Rue Dauphine, Le Tabou was to be found, where musicians used to meet after work and where a jam session was nearly always in the offing, and close by—on the Rue St-André-des-Arts—lay Le Caméléon, which often had more modern jazz on its program. Lester played several times in small swing bands, and on one occasion he was in such a good mood that he danced for several hours.

From Paris JATP traveled to Brussels, where Lester got a better reception after the concert than he had in France. "Lester plays like he has for the past 15 years," one critic wrote, "and he is still a leading light among tenor players. His interpretation of 'I Cover the Waterfront' is a masterpiece,"[77] a view shared by a Swiss colleague after the concert in Zurich, where Lester also played solo in this number.[78]

Slightly less than a fortnight later he returned with the other musicians to New York. They were all tired and sated with the many things they had experienced, yet in possession of a surprised and pleased impression of their European audiences. "The reaction of the audience in Stockholm, and, as it turned out later, throughout Europe, was completely different from the reaction of a U.S. audience," Norman Granz said after arriving home. "They listen to you, applaud, and stamp their feet indicating that they'd like more; but there is no shouting or whistling during the solo, nor any of the outcries that mar a pretty tune."[79]

"I wish Americans *listened* to jazz as Europeans do," Oscar Peterson later commented. "They regard it as part of American culture, as an art form. Even at the JATP concerts, the crowds were largely attentive and receptive, and the shouting and whistling came when a man finished his solo, not during it. Over here, too many of the club owners and the people who come to hear jazz regard it as just entertainment, a background for drinking and conversation."[80]

Within a few days of returning home, Lester began a long engagement at Birdland. Once more there were changes in the rhythm section, which Carpenter had reconstructed while Lester was away. It now consisted of the talented twenty-year-old piano player Wynton Kelly, the bass player Aaron Bell, and the drummer Lee Abrams, who, with a single exception, was Lester's permanent drummer for the next eighteen months. Unfortunately, Kelly was unable to stay with the group after early July, when he was called upon to do military service, but his replacement was

Gil Coggins, who had his first job with Lester at Pep's Musical Bar in Philadelphia. After that there was a six-week job at Birdland, starting on July 13, which was something of an event, since Lester was reunited with Count Basie's band for the first time since 1944.

Basie's band alternated with Lester's quintet for a fortnight, starting on July 24, and since this was the first time in four years that Basie was to play on Broadway with a big band, expectations were at a high pitch, both regarding his band and his reunion with Lester. Most of New York's jazz nobilities were present at the premiere, and Basie's band lived fully up to expectations. *Down Beat* wrote, "Count Basie today has the most exciting band in the business; and, as always, the most danceably exciting too."[81]

After Basie had played the evening's first series, "it was announced over the loudspeakers that Lester was to play together with Basie's band," *Orkester Journalen* reported,

and Lester received a welcome ovation which was mainly motivated by nostalgia. The audience had come so to be reunited with the Count's and Lester's shared era of greatness—just the sight of both of them together on the stand brought a tear from many a jazz enthusiast's eye. But there was to be more than the visual to bring tears to the eye. They began with "Ev'ry Tub" and as soon as Lester took the first break on his tenor sax the audience was in ecstasy. After that they were treated to fabulous jazz. Lester was apparently not in great form during his visit to Sweden last spring, but his slanderers should have heard him that evening—it was the old Lester at the peak of his powers. When the first number was over it wasn't only the audience who went wild—the entire Count Basie band stood up and applauded Lester, even though the band deserved its share of the applause. Then came "Swingin' the Blues," "Jumpin' at the Woodside," "Topsy" and all the others—all you had to do was to let yourself be borne along by the band's spark and Lester's relaxed solo flights.

Then Lester played with his own small band—himself, plus trumpet and a three-piece rhythm section—but, even though he could maintain his form, there wasn't as much to be had as when he played together with Basie. It was one of those unforgettable jazz evenings."[82]

Unfortunately, there are no recordings from the premiere itself, but there are some tracks from a week later in the engagement that justify *Orkester Journalen*'s and *Down Beat*'s eulogies. Basie's fantastic, efficient rhythm section spurred Lester to better performances than with his own rhythm section, which gave the impression of being anemic in comparison, although it was by no means bad. The combination of Lester and Basie's big band was such a success that Lester was invited on several occasions during the next five years to appear as a guest soloist with the band. That he was happy about this is clear from his last interview, where he said about Basie's band: "Nice eyes. I'll always bust my nuts when I play with them."[83]

One of the new members of that fall's JATP troupe was the guitar player Barney Kessel, who has written about his impressions of Lester in a couple of articles. He records that "when we were on the Jazz at the Philharmonic tour in 1952, we had to fly to an engagement in a plane with two propellers. Lester exclaimed upon seeing the plane, 'You've got to give me four lungs before I can do some skywriting' "[84] Kessel also discusses the qualities in Lester's playing, especially emphasizing his "tone (sound), time (playing in synchronization with the rhythmic pulse), the most melodious and lyrical lines, and swing. Lester always got a groove, always came in on a solo, and he could unmeddle the rhythm section if it had worked its way out of a groove."[85]

Oscar Peterson, as well as Barney Kessel, played quite a lot with Lester, both with and independently of JATP. He contributes the following description of Lester: "To play in a rhythm section with Lester Young had to be one of the most joyful experiences for any member of that fortunate section because, when he decided to really get into a tune, he would start playing some of those beautiful, long marvelous-shaped lines that would stretch from one part of the tune to the other. And, when he played like this, there was no way possible for you to escape playing well for him."

"Lester, in short, had this remarkable ability to transmit beauty from within himself to the rhythm section," he concludes. "Whenever we played up tunes, he'd step to the microphone, raise that horn to that peculiar angle at which he always held it, and play some lines that were so relaxed that, even at a swift tempo, the rhythm section would relax."[86]

Peterson too has a couple of examples of Lester's special way of talking. "Whenever a rhythm section got a little busy behind him—especially the drummer—he would turn around and say to them: 'May I have my tinkey-boom, please?' and turn away from the rhythm section and continue to play as if nothing had happened."

"Although very slow to anger, Pres did have a temper," Peterson continues. "On various occasions, I can remember him sitting quietly among some people who persisted in annoying him. As a last resort, he would lean over and say: 'Pres, if you don't leave Lester alone, we're going to have a waltz.' And when he said this, he was totally serious. Moreover, the person to whom he was saying it took it seriously. Lester Young was not a small man; he was well over six feet and was one of the strongest musicians that I ever knew."[87]

Sometimes Oscar Peterson shared a room with Lester during the JATP tours and took care of him, in the sense that he made sure Lester got reasonably regular meals. After 1951 Lester's drinking had increased and his interest in eating lessened. Peterson can also recall that Lester's day only really got going after the evening's concert and that he rarely ate before nearly 3 A.M. The meals he ate were, like his drinking habits, strange. He often mixed the most unlikely things together, following a can of sardines with ice cream, for example.

Lester was always extremely popular with his colleagues. When he met some of his old buddies on the JATP tours, they sometimes couldn't resist a bit of friendly teasing. The piano player Hank Jones recalls an episode that took place during the JATP tour of 1952: "Once Lester had to leave the bus. Charlie Shavers and Roy Eldridge knew that Lester loved whiskey and always kept a bottle of it, and they decided to play a trick on him. Before Lester came back on the bus they took his liquor and hid it. When Lester came back on the bus he looked for it and kept looking for it, and finally he found it and went to the front of the bus and said: 'Whoever has taken my whiskey I'm their mother's very best man!' "[88]

In mid-February 1953 Lester traveled once more with JATP to Europe, this time on a five-week tour to Sweden, Norway, Finland, Denmark, Germany, France, England, Switzerland, North Africa, Italy, and Ireland. On that occasion Norman Granz had assembled almost exactly the same musicians that had been on the JATP tour the previous fall, that is, the trumpet player Charlie Shavers, the sax players Flip Phillips, Willie Smith, and Lester, the piano player Oscar Peterson, the guitar player Barney Kessel, the bass player Ray Brown, the drummers J. C. Heard and Gene Krupa, and the singer Ella Fitzgerald.

Lester's performances on this tour, on which Mary accompanied him, form a descending curve. The reviews from Scandinavia are fine, but he disappointed his audiences toward the end of the tour. "But Lester was there," *Orkester Journalen* wrote, after first having criticized Shaver's playing.

Admittedly he played unevenly last year, but this year! All those who were disappointed at his performances during his last visit must surely have changed their minds now. Apart from that, he is being given greater prominence this year and, if the truth be told, I stuck it out through five concerts for his sake. You never quite know what's going to happen when he gets going. . . .

In the slow parade of soloists Lester was several notches above the others, especially during the two last concerts on Thursday, where he gave "I Can't Get Started" his special and inimitable care and attention. He seemed just as thrilled with the melodies "I Cover the Waterfront" and "She's Funny That Way." And the result was always warm, wonderful jazz.

After a too hasty rendition of "Cotton Tail," which J. C. Heard dominated with an adroit drum solo, the general jam session was rounded off with "Lester Leaps In," where Lester was given seven or eight choruses to let himself go on. In the auditorium it was rather difficult to hear what he was playing, but I heard some of the concerts from the lighting booth . . . where the acoustics were perfect and good old Pres blew almost as in the good old days.[89]

The last two towns visited in Scandinavia were Copenhagen and Malmö, where Lester fulfilled the audiences' expectations as well as he had in Stockholm. "Lester Young produced the best music in the JATP band, with a slow number as a special highlight,"[90] the Copenhagen newspaper *Information* wrote, while after the concert in Malmö one could read that "J.A.T.P. played as expected, i.e. predominantly fresh, brash stomping music aimed at pleasing the audience. But there was also some more refined stuff. This came from Ray Brown, for example, with his unique bass playing and from Lester Young, who in some marvelous bars played roughly twice as well as on his visit here last year."[91]

On arriving at Kastrup airport in Copenhagen, Lester was met by the trombone player John Darville, who had been chosen to accompany the musicians into town. "Young walked very slowly," Darville relates, "and at one point I asked him: 'How is your good friend Vic Dickenson?' Young stopped in his tracks and stared emptily in front of him, after which he spun round, looked me straight in the eyes and said: 'My very, *very* good friend!' "[92]

The visit to England was quite an event, since the English musicians' union had been very restrictive regarding foreign musicians and bands up to that point; but Granz managed to get his band to London—the first American band in eighteen years to achieve this feat. He got two concerts booked at the Gaumont State Theatre by offering the Ministry of Labour to fly his troupe in and out on the same day and also to play for free. The money from the ticket sales was to be distributed to victims of a flood which shortly before had ravaged large parts of the east coast.

On the way from the airport to the hotel the taxis stopped at various famous places, including Buckingham Palace. All the musicians got out to take photographs, but Lester stayed where he was to drink the bottle of whiskey Mary had just fetched him. When the others came back with their cameras over their shoulders, Lester made the following witty comment when he saw Granz's Contax: "That little eye can't see far, can it?"[93]

By this time Lester was fed up with all the hullabaloo that surrounded him. He was definitely much more at ease in more intimate surroundings than Granz could provide, without being surrounded by numerous members of the press, photographers, and back-slappers. In a short interview after the London concerts he complained to Derek Young about all the uproar he had to go through, both physically and mentally. "I'm tired of all this noise. I like to play cool," he said. "I've nothing against this country, but all this rushing around . . . I'm losing my weight. . . . Man, I'm so tired!"[94]

That he was tired is borne out by the reviews—he got a very mixed reception. "When Lester finally walked on the stand the crowd gave him their biggest ovation," *Melody Makers* reports. "He stood there, gnawing his lip. And when he sidled up to the mike, head cocked to one side like a fondled spaniel, we hoped the Lester of old had returned. He hadn't. Lester had finally handed his Jazz At The Phil supremacy to Flip Phillips, the hard-blowing Herdman from Long Island."[95]

But there were some good moments, as John McKellen recalls. "He walked almost hunched up and looked incredibly shy," he later wrote. "On one up tempo tune, I remember him standing at the microphone, his eyes staring into the spotlight and just one finger moving up and down, producing just one of many trick fingerings that produced that 'OOH WAA' sound, which apparently has so much commercial value, whilst the rest of the troupe performed behind him. You could tell his love for playing in the ballad medley, and his 'These Foolish Things' and 'I Cover the Waterfront' were very moving and seemed so personal and out of place in such a businesslike situation."[96]

The feeling of unease Lester experienced at these large concerts is also revealed in the description Cullaz has given of that year's Paris concert: "In the evening at the first concert I'm standing in the wings with 'Lady Queen.' We're all ears. After several choruses Lester, whose features are showing even more fear and trembling than usual, turns his back on the audience, walks towards the back of the stand and approaches the wings, hesitant and sombre. We call out: 'Lester . . . Pres.' He looks towards us. His face lights up and takes on an expression which is both teasing and full of delight. But, we think, he surely can't see us in the half-dark of the wings. 'Lester . . . Pres . . . can you recognize us?' He answers, somewhat indignantly: 'Lester never forgets his nice eyes.' "[97]

After the concerts Lester went back to the hotel with Maurice Cullaz, 'Lady Queen,' and some of the other musicians, including the trumpet player Bill Coleman, who had settled in Paris. In his room he freshened up some old memories with Coleman and underlined the stories with some of his typical expressions, such as "You see . . . Lester was right . . . ding dong bell . . . Pussy's in the well."[98]

The stay in Paris lasted five days and was planned as a sort of break in the tour. Lester, though, was so tired of the whole thing that he asked Granz for money to return to New York. Granz managed to persuade him to continue the tour, but his eagerness to play did not return, despite the break, as this review from Milan shows: "Lester Young was a shadow of his former self; a living drama of personal weakness, a victim—it seems—of drugs; he was hardly there at all. He only played a little and only a glimpse of his personality was caught in his fragmentary, incomplete phrasing. He left us feeling utterly miserable: we thought of the artist he once was and of the place he rightfully has in the history of jazz and find it hard to understand that it should all end like this."[99]

Fortunately, this trough only lasted for a short while, for Lester was still able to play some superb solos. The recordings from that year are of varying quality, from the very bad to the most inspired he ever made, solos of real class, no matter how affected by stimulants he was. Ernie Wilkins has said that when Lester was to appear as a guest with Basie's band at Birdland during this period, they tried to arrange it so that he played early, before he had had too much to drink.[100]

Certain things suggest that Lester was going through a personal crisis during the first half of 1953, a depression that made him unable really to believe in himself and to feel he was accepted and liked. His own piano player at this time was Horace Silver, who relates:

Prez'd feel like nobody liked him. But I could understand that because he went through hell being an innovator. He had the nerve to be daringly different, so everybody was putting him down—critics criticizing his tone, criticizing his playing—some musicians too. It scarred him inside.

I was riding home from a gig one night in the car and I don't know how we got into this conversation, but somehow I felt he felt dejected or something and he told me—he called everybody "Prez"—he said, "Well, Prez, I really don't think nobody really likes old Prez." I said, "Well, Prez, how can you say that? You've got all of those tenor players idolizing you and trying to play like you— from Stan Getz to Zoot Sims to Al Cohn to Dexter Gordon and Gene Ammons." He said, "Yeah, but I don't know, Prez. I just don't feel like nobody really likes old Prez." That's the way he felt. He was a very sociable person if you could get next to him, but he'd come off the bandstand and go right in the dressing room. He wouldn't go out till it was time to go on the bandstand again. If we were on the road he'd stay in his hotel room all day, and he'd either send out for food or get his food in a paper bag and come back and eat it in his room.[101]

There are several possible reasons for Lester's mental down trip, some connected with the personality of the man himself. He preferred to keep away from strangers and avoid them as far as possible; if he couldn't do so, he would keep them at a distance by means of his eccentric way of behaving and talking. He was only open and natural with people he trusted, such as his family, musicians in his own band, and other people he felt secure with and did not suspect of trying to make use of him economically.

Another reason may have been his relationship with Carpenter. According to Kenny Drew, Carpenter was a strict taskmaster and something of a perfectionist who always insisted that things should be well organized and on time.[102] Lester's more relaxed lifestyle couldn't harmonize with Carpenter's in the long run, and Lester's increasing addiction to drink was a source of irritation to his manager, who certainly spoke to him about it. "I always knew I was in for trouble when I went to the back door at Birdland, and he'd be sitting right on the edge of his chair, rubbing his hands," Carpenter relates.

"Lady Carpenter," he'd say, "how are your feelings?"

"I'm fine, Lester."

"I want you to know I'm not high tonight!"

He was so high he was blind. He hadn't worked yet, hadn't perspired, hadn't started to show it. He had built up an immunity, but the heat would get to him. Contrary to what anybody thought, Lester was not a drug addict. He had musicians that used heroin and cocaine. The minute they drew that stuff out, Pres would say, "Out! When you get past a stick or a glass, you have passed Pres." He never did anything but smoke pot or drink. Never. When he said, "Out!" he meant for them to go to their room, because he didn't want them around him.[103]

That Carpenter gradually got on Lester's nerves is confirmed by Bill Triglia, who says that "the only time Lester was mad was about his agent, Charlie Carpenter. He used to cheat him all the time. He couldn't do anything he wanted, Carpenter predicted everything. Carpenter even got him the men at that time."[104]

A third reason for Lester's depression was the fact that none of the musicians of the younger generation, who were in Lester's debt for their own musical development, ever came up to him and said how much he had meant for them. Lester was a person who always repaid with interest anyone to whom he was indebted, and he therefore expected the same from others. He fully realized his own importance for the development of jazz and therefore reckoned on gleaning some recognition from the right people. That he went unrewarded was a great disappointment to him and made him feel that they didn't care about him.

In 1953, however, he received prestigious recognition—he topped the list in *Metronome*'s annual vote of the year's best musicians on respective instruments. Several magazines—*Down Beat* and *Orkester Journalen* among them—used to have such votes, so that it was possible to read both the critics' and the readers' opinions. Even so it was extremely rare for Lester to top these lists. This had happened only three times previously, namely, when he won *Down Beat*'s poll in 1944, and in 1945 and 1947 when he won *Esquire*'s Silver Award. *Metronome*'s prize also included cutting a record, on which Lester, as a member of the Metronome All Stars, gives an inspired performance in "How High the Moon" and "St. Louis Blues," with a beautiful, delicate obbligato accompaniment to Billy Eckstine's singing.

Lester took his music very seriously, and this sometimes meant that the audience disappointed him and made him feel frustrated. He often felt they didn't care about what he was doing on stage, especially during the slower numbers. "That singing that everybody talks about," he said to an interviewer in 1955. "I'm just being funny. But I sing lyrics with my horn, and I'd like to play those slow ballads—but the people make so much noise, by the time you play a chorus and a half you wish it was long over. Not like that everywhere. Funny, they come in to hear, but I guess they get goin' on the drinks." [105]

Apart from his depression Lester also experienced an identity crisis, which made it difficult for him to express himself on his saxophone. This had to do with the fact that the tenor sax player Paul Quinichette had formed a small group patterned on Lester's which came to alternate with Lester's at Birdland in the spring and fall of 1953. Lester felt that this had been badly organized by the management, since Quinichette's style of playing was so close to his own at that point that it was virtually impossible to hear the difference between them. After the first evening Lester went up to Carpenter and said, "I don't know whether to play like me or Lady Q, because he's playing so much like me." "He wasn't putting Paul down," Carpenter continues. "Why, Paul is the only man I've ever known him lend a tenor to. But that night Paul sounded so much like Lester that Lester was at loose ends as to what to do." [106]

In a review of their last joint appearance in *Down Beat,* Nat Hentoff writes about Lester's group: "Pres retains his honored title more in the echo of past greatness than present achievement. He still has his superb sense of rhythmic subtleties and his conception is never banal. But Lester's tone has greyed, and he just doesn't seem to care very much any more in performance. This may well be true only of the sets I heard during this engagement and at other times recently. Reports from France are that in informal jamming during his last visit there, Lester was as exciting as ever."

"In his present quintet," he continues, "Lester has Jesse Drakes, trumpet; Connie Kay, drums; Cecil Wilson, bass; and Gildo Mahones, piano. They're all adequate but, like Pres, rarely seem lofted beyond the requirements of a night's competency." [107] Hentoff got the bass player's name wrong, however; his name was not Wilson but Winston. Kay and Mahones had joined the group a couple of months earlier, after Lester had finished his fall tour with JATP. They stayed until February and December 1955, respectively, whereas Winston was standing in for Gene Ramey for that November engagement.

In the spring of 1954 Lester's group was on tour again, right across the country to San Francisco and Hollywood. Lester normally traveled with his regular group on longer tours, but gradually it became more and more usual for him to be sent out by the Gale Agency as a soloist to be accompanied by a local rhythm section in, for example, Philadelphia or Washington, D.C., for a weekend or for a job that lasted a week at the most.

One of the most important jazz events of 1954 was the first Newport Festival in Rhode Island, organized by George Wein, who also owned the jazz club Storyville in Boston. The festival was a huge success, with about 13,000 fans attending on July 17 and 18. Lester was there both days and used the first day to be with Billie Holiday, who had just returned home after a successful tour in Europe. In Newport, Billie was reunited after a space of fifteen years with Teddy Wilson, Jo Jones, and Buck Clayton, who, together with the bass players Milt Hinton and the baritone sax player Gerry Mulligan, made up the quintet which was to accompany her. Lester stood waiting in the wings listening. Finally he couldn't hold himself back, and during the end of the first number he wormed his way—in a move that was completely unscheduled—over to the others on the stand with the words, "Well, I'd better go out and help the Lady," after which he accompanied the rest of her numbers with the most beautiful of obbligatos.[108]

On the following evening he performed in a successful tribute to Count Basie, together with Oscar Peterson, Ray Brown, Buck Clayton, Vic Dickenson, and Herb Ellis. "Vic Dickenson was easily the stand-out and Prez was fine," *Metronome* wrote. "His comparatively new style of playing with his horn perpendicular to the floor had some of the wags in the press box holding their heads sideways so as to see the old Prez. It was an elaborate joke but it caught on."[109]

The reunion with Billie Holiday was subsequently blown up in *Down Beat* with the headline "The feud is over,"[110] but the truth is that there had not been any serious rift between them, rather—for Lester at any rate—an involuntary pause since their last performance together during a week in February 1951 in Philadelphia. The reason for this pause is to be found with Billie, who got annoyed with Lester on that occasion; she felt he was interfering in her business affairs and told him to mind his own business. Lester, who always tried to avoid unpleasantness of any sort, didn't take the initiative after that for any kind of musical collaboration, even though he still was very fond of her. "Lady Day? Many moons no see. Still nice," was his reply to Derek Young in London in 1953.[111]

Billie was sometimes highly undiplomatic in her remarks, and she often hurt Lester without intending to. For example, on several occasions one could read in interviews with her that "he *was* my favorite tenor player." It also hurt him that she had not used him on any of her innumerable gramophone recordings since 1941—which indeed was a strange thing. However, Lester's spontaneous behavior at this Newport Festival revived their old feelings for each other, and they later appeared together on several occasions.

In the fall of 1954 they both took part in the two all-star concerts Patricia Music publishers held in Carnegie Hall and in Boston, although they did not appear on the stand simultaneously. Also on the program were Count Basie's band, Sara Vaughan, Charlie Parker, the Modern Jazz Quartet, and Bill Davis's Trio. The concert in New York got a mixed reception, though Lester's contribution—like Sarah Vaughan's and

Count Basie's—was well received. "The Basie Aggregation joined Young in an invigorating rendition of 'Stomping at the Savoy.' Pres blew with particular fullness and warmth, and left the audience cheering for more," was how *Down Beat* described the concert.[112]

That same fall another reunion took place, when the Waldorf Astoria held a twentieth anniversary party for Count Basie as a bandleader. There were 450 invited guests, and the whole arrangement was organized by the Friends of Count Basie Committee, under the leadership of John Hammond and Willard Alexander, the two people who had been foremost in paving Basie's way to success. At the time—Sunday, November 2—Lester was playing in Chicago, but he was flown to New York as a special surprise for Basie.

After the speeches were over, the curtain was drawn aside and, to Basie's astonishment, the band on the stand consisted of as many members as possible of the original group that set out from Kansas City in 1936. Only Hot Lips Page, who lay critically ill in the hospital, Carl "Tatti" Smith, who had emigrated to South America, and Buster Smith had been unable to come. It was an emotional reunion. After the opening number Basie himself took over the piano from Erroll Garner, and the band played a string of the old classics, including "One O'clock Jump," "Sent for You Yesterday," and "Every Tub." The evening finished with Basie's current band taking over the stand and playing several numbers from their latest repertoire.

Shortly before Christmas Lester was on the stand with Basie once more. Birdland celebrated its fifth birthday with a concert on December 16, in which Sarah Vaughan, Jimmy Rushing, Stan Getz, the Erroll Garner Trio, and the George Shearing Quintet also took part, besides the Lester Young Quintet and Count Basie and His Orchestra. The event was broadcast on both television and radio, and Lester played an excellent solo in "Jumpin' at the Woodside" with the Basie band. The concert was to be a sort of prelude to the tour that Birdland's manager, Morris Levy, had arranged to take place from February 11 to March 7, 1955, under the title "Birdland Stars '55." The tour was less of a hassle than JATP's, since it restricted itself to the eastern United States and was scaled down to a level Lester could cope with.

The tour was a success for Levy and for all those taking part. After the concert in Topeka, Kansas, for example, it was reported that "a crowd of 3,000 foot-stomping, hand-clapping Topekans had themselves a ball at Municipal Auditorium Friday night as the Birdland Stars of 1955 blew what cats described as 'a real swinging gig'. . . . The performers played with an intricacy and delicacy that often left the crowd of jazz-starved Topekans gasping."[113]

Less than a week after the tour was over Charlie Parker died. A concert was held in Carnegie Hall on April 2 in his memory, which was also to raise money for a fund for his two children, Kim and Laird. The hall was sold out; the packed audience of 2,800 listened to a three-hour concert which started at 12:15 A.M.

Leonard Feather covered the event for *Melody Maker:*

The most memorable moments came at the start of the show. Hazel Scott, who had been one of the most effective workers on the committee that organised the fund and the concert, appeared on-stage (looking exceptionally beautiful), and asked for—and received—complete silence while she read an appropriate poem by the Negro writer Countee Cullen, in memory of Bird.

She then asked the entire audience to stand, and announced: "Charlie Parker will now play 'Now's the Time,' " And so Charlie himself started the concert, as his immortal record of that name was relayed through the Carnegie Hall loudspeakers.

To sustain the mood achieved by this idea, Lester Young came on and played the first live performance of the evening, a slow and subdued solo that showed him at his greatest.[114]

All the other reviewers agreed with Feather about Lester's performance. *Orkester Journalen* wrote that "Lester Young played, accompanied by among others Horace Silver on piano and Art Blakey on drums. Lester's heartfelt interpretation of 'I Can't Get Started' was among the absolute highlights of the concert."[115] Barry Ulanov wrote the following warm words in *Down Beat:*

It was most fitting that the recent memorial concert for Charlie Parker should have opened with Lester Young's tribute. It was right for so many reasons. Right, because the line from Lester to Charlie is as direct as it is distinguished. Right, because these two musicians more than any other two made modern jazz what it is. Right, because their incomparable contributions to our music stand side by side for all of us to hear and admire and applaud.

Sure, it was sad hearing Lester right after Bird, listening to him play "I Can't Get Started" a few minutes after all of us in Carnegie Hall had listened to Bird's "Now Is the Time" on the P.A. system.

But it was heartwarming too. The sounds went so well together, one set of long lines after another, one striking personality after another, one persuasive modernist after another.

And it reminded some of us that there were still giants in our midst and that jazz was not entirely for the history books and the nostalgic anecdotes. Here was a master of his horn whose place was assured alongside Louis Armstrong and Bix Beiderbecke and Duke Ellington and Charlie Christian, one of the men who made our music, still blowing, blowing beautifully.[116]

After this, all different styles of jazz musicians paid their tribute to Parker, including Stan Getz, Oscar Pettiford, Dizzy Gillespie, Al Cohn, Henry "Red" Allen, Thelonious Monk, Buster Bailey, Billie Holiday,

Lee Konitz, Kai Winding, Lennie Tristano, J. J. Johnson, Tony Scott, and Gerry Mulligan.

A month later Lester took part in a charity concert in Carnegie Hall, which held a "Jazz and Variety Concert" on May 6, 1955, for the Lighthouse, the New York Association for the Blind. The concert was presented by John Hammond, who had assembled in the first set—"Spirituals to Jazz Hour"—a program consisting of Sister Rosetta Tharpe and Marie Knight, Alex Kallao, Buddy Rich, Billie Holiday, Count Basie's band, Lester, and Clifford Brown and the Max Roach Quintet. Lester played first as a soloist with the Count Basie band plus Buck Clayton in "Lady Be Good," after which he, Clayton, and Basie—now on a Hammond organ—Eddie Jones, Buddy Rich, Billie Holiday, and her regular accompanist, the piano player Carl Drinkard, gave a rendition of "Stormy Weather." Among the best known in the ensuing "Variety Hour" were Les Paul and Mary Ford, as well as Bill Haley and his Comets.

That summer Lester participated in the second Newport Festival, which had been extended to three days. He took part on the final evening, Sunday, July 17, after the Modern Jazz Quartet's successful appearance. "Next was some rollicking, happy jazz from Count Basie, piano; Lester Young, tenor; Ruby Braff, trumpet; Ed Jones, bass; and Jo Jones, drums," *Down Beat* reported. "First up was 'Lester Leaps In,' and he did. Then Jimmy Rushing came up to sing 'Little Girl' and two encores, and it was evident to everyone that this group was having fun."

The review continues: "Basie was positively beaming, Pres was striding around helping Braff and Rushing with his backgrounds, and it all captured wonderfully the essence of Kansas City jazz. Or any jazz."[117]

The *New York Times* also had words of praise for the group's performance: "Then along comes a small combination consisting of Count Basie, Lester Young, Jo Jones and Ruby Braff with an uproarious example of controlled chaos. With Jimmy Rushing doing the vocal solos, the music was earthy and lowdown. Anti-intellectual no doubt, but a real emotional experience backed by a solid rhythm, delivered by superb instrumentalists who were turning their techniques to something else besides abstractions in jazz."[118]

This year Lester had told Norman Granz in advance that he did not want to take part in the JATP tour. Stan Getz, who got the chance to take over Lester's spot, fell seriously ill in Sweden, however; as a result Lester took part at short notice. He played in the first half of the concert, which Granz this year had divided into a jam session, a modern jazz section, a swing section, and a ballad medley. Oscar Peterson, Ray Brown, Herb Ellis, and Buddy Rich made up an excellent, well-knit rhythm section, which accompanied the musicians in the first set of the evening's program, in which Lester took part in all but the swing section.

The brass and reeds in the jam session's blues numbers consisted of Dizzy Gillespie and Roy Eldridge on trumpet, with Flip Phillips, Illinois Jacquet, and Lester on saxophone. After the premiere at Carnegie Hall on September 16, Nat Hentoff wrote in *Down Beat:* "Opening a medium tempo blues with swinging piano, Oscar was followed by Flip, who was professional and kept his exhibitionism to a minimum. But when Pres came on immediately afterwards, the contrast was startling. Pres' chorus wasn't a great one, but the phrasing was so much more tasty and swung so much more easily than Flip's that it presented a striking lesson in the difference between jazz greatness and just proficiency."[119]

Immediately afterwards came the modern section, which Hentoff described thus: "The rhythm section remained the same and the modern representatives were Dizzy and Pres (who has been modern since the day he started blowing, probably). The two combined in an attractive middle tempo blues in minor that featured excellent Gillespie; absorbing Pres (the man's conception continues to be one of the marvels of jazz), and vigorous Oscar."[120]

Concluding the first set was a ballad medley, introduced by Lester's interpretation of "I Didn't Know What Time It Was," which received the following review: "Pres, it should be noted, played very well all through the evening and his ballad especially underlined how expressive he can be through a markedly economical use of notes that are flowingly combined in a phrasing and tone that keeps him president when he wants to be."[121]

During the tour two unpleasant incidents took place, both resulting from racial prejudice. "Norman insisted that tickets be sold without regard to race, first come, first served," Dizzy Gillespie relates, "and the authorities didn't like it in Charleston, South Carolina. We had a special chartered plane. Something happened with the promoter's license because it was a mixed audience. The local officials didn't like that, and Ella Fitzgerald's maid had to take all the money and put it down her bosom and go to the plane. We had to sneak outta there because they didn't like it."[122]

Things in Houston were worse. "In those days, it was a very tough city and very, very prejudiced, in many ways more so than Dallas, which wasn't too far away," Granz recalls.

Well, the show began. We had a double-header. There were some cats standing backstage, and one of my rules was never to let anybody backstage when my show was on. These were two or three white cats, and I asked them who they were. They just showed me their badges. They were like plainclothesmen, and they said, "We like jazz. We just wanna watch the jazz concert."

So I said, "O.K., if you stand back, that'll be all right." And I think Krupa was playing at that time. Well, Prez, Illinois Jacquet and Birks started to play dice in Ella's dressing room. . . . And all of a sudden, these cats break the door down. They didn't even . . . they coulda turned the handle. These three cats who were standing there. . . . They came in with flashlights and guns drawn and all that bullshit. The same guys that said to me, "Well, we're jazz fans." They were police, of course, and they said, "You're all under arrest for gambling." [123]

The police arrested Dizzy Gillespie, Illinois Jacquet, Ella Fitzgerald, and her dresser Georgianna Henry, together with Granz and took them all down to the station. How Lester avoided being taken too is a mystery. After a brief interrogation, during which Gillespie maintained he was Louis Armstrong (!), Granz managed to get them all released on bail, so that the show could go on. Afterwards he put one of his best lawyers, Abe Herman from Fort Worth, on the case, and his efforts were not in vain, because the court in Houston finally had to retract their accusation of illegal gambling.

During the tour a warm friendship sprang up between Lester and the piano player Bobby Scott, who was scarcely eighteen at the time and whom Lester used to call Bobby Socks on that account, a name later shortened to Socks. They traveled by coach and plane together, and they probably sought each other's company because they were both considered to be outsiders by the others on the tour, Scott on account of his age and Lester on account of his personality. Later Scott was to write a long, warm article about their relationship and the impression the famous Lester made on a young, immature musician.

"For a reason I have never been able to isolate, he shouldered the burden of being resident jester on that 1955 tour," Scott recalls.

And he was good at it. His brand of storytelling was unique. It was littered with so many "motherfuckers" that it was shushed down, and out, when we found ourselves in the company of the general public. But when we traveled in quarantine, he was allowed to stretch out, and never since then have my sides ached so much.

He would have mock fights with Roy Eldridge and other "shorter" fellows who would grab his arms as if to do him up. "Midget motherfuckers!" he would cry in pretended desperation. "Lawyer Brown, Lady Pete!" he would call to Ray Brown and Oscar Peterson. "Socks! You gotta help me with these midget motherfuckers!" Only Prez could carry it off. For minutes afterwards, he'd mumble to himself, still in his fiction and dramatic mockery, "Those . . . *midget* . . . *motherfuckers!*" And he would say, "Socks, I could take 'em—one at a time! But the midget motherfuckers gang up on me! They gang up on ol' Prez!"

Nobody ever made so much fun so consistently, so hard, so freely. Sometimes, when he was on a roll, it went on for days. Not jokes, or one-liners, although he had a few of those. No, it was always situational and personal. As I'm writing this, I can *hear* him again, hear the fake dramatic pauses, the ham acting, the truncated exclamations he was known for and, most of all, the disarming sweetness. The bastard!

It takes a considerable amount of confidence to laugh at one's self. "Dr. Willis Wiggins," as he referred to himself, had it. He knew all about what Rodney Dangerfield has turned into a science. Prez tripped that thin line between self-depreciation and wholesome abandon. To my eye, unseasoned at the time, there was a truth I couldn't see.

He had the courage that makes for *self*. The quality of bravery that never asks dumb questions or looks for conspiracy in honest words. The great danger of *becoming* your musical expression was one to which Lester never succumbed. It set him apart from other musicians, made less by their inability to be something other than their music. No one who knew him would call him a "regular guy." Not ever. But he *could* be, if he so chose. That in itself broadens his humanity. . . .

You could call him superstitious, though not to the degree that it froze him. Willie Smith, he once told me, was a "number" person. Prez said that if Willie came up with the wrong numerical position on boarding a plane, he was apt to get off it. Lester felt a huge surge of anxiety if a very ill person—or worse, one in a wheelchair—got onto our flight.

"God damn it, Socks," he'd groan, "it's a Johnny Deathbed!" His eyes would remain fixed on the plane's entrance—until he saw a child, or an infant, board. If it was an infant, he eased immediately, noticeably. Though he never talked about religion, Prez let me know that the Deity was to be taken for granted. He obviously believed in the fair mercy of God, for the presence of the infant on our flight ruled out any chance that God would take out the entire flight to collect the Johnny Deathbed. The implications that vibrated outward from this view amused, and stimulated, me greatly. It was Lester's conviction that people about to take the Big Journey ought to be in their "cribs" waiting, not out here where innocents might have to share their fate. He felt we shared responsibility with the Deity, and had to "get our shit together."

I always felt that I must have said something or done something that *signaled* Prez. He was a believer in such things, always open to the unspoken, the unexpected, even to the unwelcome sign. It is told he had two weeks left of a gig in Europe in 1959 when he upped and flew back home to his almost immediate death. A sign, no doubt, danced before his eyes in Paris.

There was a brilliance to Lester's other-worldliness that made me weigh what is called *educated*. Lincoln defined learning as telling ourselves what we knew all along to be the truth, but were afraid to tell ourselves. Prez *sensed* everything. He was somehow aware that the gray matter in the cranium is a first-class deceiver, and relied on intuition. Once, when we were looking for a restaurant in a city new to both of us, he said too comfortably, "One more block, Socks, and we'll eat." He was right! I've since credited a good deal of his obliqueness to a preoccupation with inner voices he let lead him. Often people thought they had run up against an alcoholic mist too thick to penetrate. But that was rarely the case. He just wasn't listening, for there were moments when his lucidity was remarkable, though his intake of grass and booze had been his usual.[124]

Lester liked simplicity, not only in his own playing, but also in his accompanists. Once Scott came into a nightclub where Lester was playing with a local rhythm section. Lester came over to him and complained about the piano player. "Oh Socks, baby, I'm glad to see you here! This boy playin' piano plays *very well*. But he puts eight changes where there oughta be two! You know me, Socks. Somethin' like 'These Foolish Things,' I mean, I like the E-flat chord, the C-minor, the F-minor seventh, the B-flat nine. You know. Shit. I can't play when there are eighty-nine motherfuckin' changes in a bar!"[125]

"Lester was very aware of how people broke hearts with their tongues," Scott continues. "A man misjudged as often as Prez was, and offended so easily, would know about that. Accordingly, his own observations were couched in 'unknown' terms, that he might not give offense. I saw it as a very responsible behavior. In any case, Prez wasn't a presumptuous man and considered his judgments no more important than anyone else's. He was sensitive but not touchy. He took the ribbings of his colleagues well. For instance, every few nights, with much aplomb and mock assurance, Oscar Peterson would lay in those 'extra' chord changes during Lester's solo in the Ballad Medley. During a concert in the Montreal Forum, Prez sidled back to the nine-foot grand piano, unaware that just below him and inside the instrument was an open microphone. Turning to Oscar his puzzled, pleading face, he said, 'Where are you motherfuckers at?' The audience's laughter sounded like Niagara Falls."[126]

Scott and Lester used to talk about everything under the sun on the tours. Among other things, Lester told about this episode from his family life:

Two "sanctified" old ladies lived behind Prez on Long Island, their yards abutting his. They had never conversed with him, indeed did not know him or anyone else who didn't belong to their church congregation. As Lester dressed rather zoot-suit, drank, and played jazz, they had reached their own opinion of him.

One summer afternoon, while the ladies were back-porching and gossiping, Mr. Young and his son, Little Lester, sauntered into the yard and commenced to toss a ball around. The ladies couldn't but start revising their opinion of their neighbor. "Isn't that nice?" they chirped, watching father and son.

They were still watching when Prez decided he'd had enough ball-tossing. He and Little Lester walked to the back door. Prez tried the knob. He turned his face down toward Little Lester and said, *"There,* you dumb motherfucker, you done locked us both out the house!"

The ladies never recovered.

Prez used profanity—and *all* language—creatively. And he had the oddest gentle way of saying *motherfucker*.[127]

"As a vehicle for his high humor, he conjured up a conspiracy against the two of us," Scott continues.

Often, if we boarded a flight at the last minute, the seats we got were served dinner last. Too often we were just digging into our food when the plane began its descent. Lester trotted out his paranoia, blaming everyone from the Midget Motherfuckers to the White House. I couldn't eat for laughing. He'd squinch up his face in a deviltry that could bring me near to wetting myself, and mumble, "You see this shit, Socks? You see *this?*" He would shake his head, glancing furtively toward the back of the plane where "the enemy" sat. His voice, still softly clandestine, would push out, "They're tryin' to *get* us, Socks." And of course I had to go along with him or let the splendid humor of it die.

The quiet that surrounded and covered Lester was of a contemplative nature and origin. If he allowed me to "divert" him, he did it out of an interest in, and love for, me. He didn't need diversion. Small things could and would draw his interest and attention.

Whatever he was in his totality, and no one is privy to such knowledge of another, the one observation I could make about him was that the peace that emanated from him was a glowing proof of a *balanced* personality.

Happiness depends, it has always seemed to me, on the health of one's moral condition. Lester was a happy person, no more besieged than the rest of us. But he had the conviction that gives a fighter staying power. He never gave up what was consistent with his values. He skirmished frequently, as sensitive people do, with becoming a number instead of a name, a figure rather than a living person, a reputation instead of a producer of beautiful music.

He knew what made him happy and what he would have to tolerate, and his baleful puss told you how hard it was sometimes to keep apart the rights and the wrongs in the affray. At the time, I found his complaints nothing but griping. Now that I am a man and have, as the Indians say, walked a mile in his moccasins, I have become an echo of those gripes. He experienced doubts of tremendous size, and often converted them before my eyes into something else.

When I arrived at the airport apron one morning, I made my way through the small group of passengers and found Prez with a perplexed and doom-filled face, eyeing our aircraft. It was a DC-3, slightly worn-looking but otherwise apparently fit.

"Socks, baby, it's a *two-lunger!*" Prez felt much safer in a four-engine aircraft. "We gotta have a *four*-lunger, Socks. Shit! You lose one, you still got *three!* One of *these* motherfuckers goes, an' we only got *one* lung left!"

Moments later, having accepted the inevitable, he was sitting next to me, back in his groove, snapping his fingers at the engines outside the window, and hollering (to the chagrin and embarrassment of the tour members): "Get it! Get . . . *it!* God . . . damn . . . IT!" He talked to the engines, shouting his encouragement as we barrelled down the runway. He was still hollering, to the shushing sounds of Ella Fitzgerald and Norman Granz, when the creaking weight of metal lifted up out of the uncloroxed clouds into the sunshine.

He smiled then. He had fortified himself with Dewars. He whispered, "It's only gettin' here that bothers me, Socks." I told him I had no inclination to be a bird, either. And yet he trusted the pilots implicitly. "They got their shit together," he said. I have never enjoyed travelling as much since then.[128]

Lester's health gradually deteriorated on the tour, and shortly after his return to New York everything that had been accumulating in his mind during the past years culminated in a nervous breakdown. Mary got him admitted to Bellevue Hospital on the East Side of Manhattan. Here he got psychiatric help, and this, together with good, nourishing food and no liquor, made a new man of him.

He went home shortly before Christmas 1955 with his self-confidence boosted and eager to play again. He received money to pay the hospital from Norman Granz, who was generous enough go keep him and his family during the next few weeks, while Lester was recuperating. Granz came to visit him from Los Angeles during the first days of 1956 and, when he saw how well Lester felt, quickly got him in the recording studio together with swing musicians like Teddy Wilson, Roy Eldridge, and Jo Jones. The result was tremendous and shows Lester at the peak of his capacity, demonstrating an unusual expressiveness. Everything looked good, but Lester was faced with a fairly harsh dose of reality, because he began to recognize the fact that he was no longer the leader of a band on a permanent basis.

8

The Last Years
(1956–1959)

When Lester was admitted to the hospital, his band broke up and all future jobs were cancelled, since nobody knew when he would be well enough to stand on a stage again. From that time on, until he stopped being Lester's manager at the end of 1957, Carpenter chose to let Lester be without a regular rhythm section. On engagements outside New York he used to appear mainly with local rhythm sections, while Carpenter hired musicians for each of the less and less frequent jobs that came up in New York itself.

The plan was that Lester should tour with the Birdland Stars in the spring of 1956, and he did in fact manage to recover sufficiently to join them on the tour, which lasted for most of February. As it had a year before, the tour began in New York, where there were three concerts spread over two evenings and where it was obvious that Lester was happy to be performing in front of an audience again. The reviews were favorable; *Down Beat* wrote that "Lester Young, in warm, flowing form, contributed an eloquent 'Confessin' and a swinging 'Jumping at the Woodside' in front of the Basie band."[1] *Variety* said the following: "After a swinging Basie start with 'Ble-blop Blues' and 'Red Top,' the show falls into a modern groove with the Bud Powell Trio and East-West Jazz Septet. There's too much of a sameness in their attacks and each would be more effective if spotted farther apart. All the others come off solidly and Lester Young's torrid tenor-saxing had the aud jumping."[2]

Lester was in the best of spirits. He was in fine fettle throughout the tour, and his cheerfulness had an infectious effect on the other musicians. The trumpet player Thad Jones from Basie's band recalls that it was during this Birdland tour that Lester began the infamous water pistol battles and not, as is popularly believed, at Birdland itself. "It was during the period when we did the Birdland tour," he recalls, "because I think Sonny Payne was involved in it and several other members of the orchestra, you know."

They used to sneak up to each other and squirt each other with waterpistols. It was a good way to let off steam and have a little fun at the same time. It was quite harmless and everyone enjoyed it and nobody got hurt, but everyone had fun, you know, so in that respect it was a necessary part of the existence on that bus at that time. We had to have something to relieve that monotony, you know, travelling. Some of the jumps we were making were distances of 500 miles and we were doing one-nighters out there, so, you know, everybody got a little uptight, because there's a lot of tension involved in travelling and preparing yourself to go up stage and perform at your peak. So everybody looked forward to the time where we could work in one city for maybe three or four days and check into a hotel and sort of relax and catch some of your sleep. The little waterpistol fight broke the monotony of the very hard and difficult travel period.[3]

Jones continues:

We all travelled in this very large Greyhound bus, they called it the Sceny-cruiser. It was an extra large bus Greyhound was making at that time. I got a chance to talk with Lester and I found him to be an exceptionally warm and human person and very thoughtful, extremely thoughtful and considerate of everyone, a very gentle man. When you talked to him the things he would say always seemed to have strong roots and seemed to be very human. They were simple things, but very powerful and sometimes quite funny. You found yourself being amused by him until the impact of what was said sort of reached in and grabbed you, and then you realized that it was a very deep and moving thing that had been said. And it was something to be listened to and to be thought about and possibly to be used as a word of advice or guidance. And he was quite humorous, very humorous.

But his humor was like true humor. He didn't say things that struck you as humor just to be funny. It was a statement of life that's been made and he said it in such a wonderful way that it turned out to be a form of humor, but it was his own special brand of humor, and he used special phrases to describe everything that nobody else used, nobody. They were all of Lester Young. It was oblique language, you know. It could be referred to as double-talk in a way. It was coded, but in his own special form, but if you listened to it for a while you got the meaning of it. . . .

On this bus I was very fortunate to be sitting in the same areas as Lester Young. The most of us sort of—I guess you could call us more or less free-spirited—used to migrate to the back of the bus where we could carry on our conversation, because the people who sat up near the front of the bus wanted to relax and sleep and have a little more peace and quiet. The ones who wanted to talk and to sort of relive the evening's high moments and low moments or whatever the moments were or to enjoy the foolishness of all the adventures we encountered on the road, we all went to the back of the bus, and Lester was there. I was sitting on the back seat and between us was a gentleman who was Bud Powell's personal attendant on the road, a guy with the name of Weaver. He was quite a large fellow.

I was drinking quite a bit in those days myself, so Lester and I were more or less companions in that respect. Perhaps it was one of the things that made us compatible with one another, plus the fact that we both liked to talk, and that's when I found out how much a profound philosopher Lester was. In a ten minute conversation with Lester you could get enough philosophy, wisdom and truth to keep you busy and thinking about it for two weeks. He was a very deep man, and I think he was totally committed and dedicated to his art.[4]

After the Birdland tour Lester played in clubs in the eastern states for most of the spring of 1956, spending one week in Toronto. Bill Triglia was engaged to play in the group that summer, has some lively memories of his time with Lester:

I had played with him a couple of nights before for Red Garland, before he went with Miles. He couldn't make it a couple of nights so he gave it to me, and the nights I worked I remember Hot Lips Page was playing with Lester Young. It wasn't in New York, it was in Pennsylvania, Philadelphia or something like that. I played two weekends, Friday to Sunday nights, like that. It was a good band, for I remember Curly Russell was playing bass.

With Lester we had no rehearsals. We went on the bandstand and got a couple of drinks or something like that to feel good before we went to play. Lester always had a bottle of cognac and said: "Come on, have a taste!" He tried to make you feel good, you know, so you could play. Louis Armstrong was like that too. He always had liquor in the backroom before the job.

Lester said little things now and then, gave you a hint about how the music should be. He was nice all the time with how he wanted things. He didn't like drummers to drop too many bombs. He liked bassplayers that would play pretty low notes, nice low notes at the right time. He used to call them "deep sea divers." When the bassman was playing high he wouldn't say anything, but when he hit a few low notes Lester would turn around all smiles and say something nice to let him know he liked that: "You deep sea diver, that's beautiful!" Just to give him that idea to play more like that, you know. And he gave everybody a chance to solo. If you soloed something and played good, it would please him and he played better, you know, he got more interested. He wasn't the person who got jealous when you played good. He was generous as can be, very honest, you know, beautiful man.

I played with him, I guess, on and off for about a year or a year and a half, on different little jobs. He didn't only use me as a pianist. Sometimes when he called me I couldn't do the job because I had something else. I was trying to make a living, so he had to use other fellows, you know. He didn't have a group at that time. In fact, the last permanent group he had that I know of, was the one with Gildo Mahones. From that point on he wasn't getting much work. He called once in a while when he had parties. He'd do a dance up in Pennsylvania with five pieces, sometimes six pieces, sometimes he would get a trombone player, a fellow from Philadelphia. He would get two–three days out of town, you know, Baltimore, Boston. He'd get something out on Long Island and he'd get a place up on Hammond once in a while. He'd get a good crowd too, but usually it was two bands, Lester Young's and somebody else. I remember one job when Charlie Mingus played with him too, just a couple of nights. He subbed for somebody who couldn't make it and he came down and played. He was crazy about Lester and he liked to talk, and Lester used to let him do all the talking. He just played the songs, and Mingus sort of took over the band. He played two or three nights with us and I think it was in Baltimore or Philadelphia. It was a lot of fun, and Mingus had a strong personality, you know.

At Birdland a lot of musicians sat in. The first time I worked Birdland with Lester was opposite Stan Kenton's band. One night Philly Joe Jones walked in, and we were playing very good that night. Lester was in [a] good mood and he was playing very good. There was a little mirror back of the bandstand, and I was facing that way, I could see in the mirror and I saw Philly Joe Jones coming down the steps into Birdland. He stopped and looked up at the bandstand, and Lester was playing a solo that sounded so good. Philly Joe walked right through the middle of the club to the bandstand to the drums, and Gus Johnson got off the drums. He just moved over and Philly Joe started playing and Lester didn't see him. When he played at that particular time he faced the other way and he was playing very passionately, you know. He played something like "Indiana," something bright, and Philly Joe just sat down and there was hardly a beat missing. He sounded way better as soon as he started playing, but Lester never looked around. He got better, he heard the sound of the drummer was even more modern, so he really took off.

And then, maybe two choruses passed by, all of a sudden—I was really concentrating because the drummer was so beautiful, I didn't look at the mirror—all of a sudden I see this guy passes me. He grabs the bass and Gene Ramey gets off the bass, and it was Oscar Pettiford! Now, Lester didn't see him either. By that time he was playing at the side of the bandstand. When he was happy he sometimes walked around. And when Oscar Pettiford got up and grabbed the bass he even got better! We played that song for 45 minutes, the whole set!

I remember vividly that particular night. The air-conditioning had broken down at Birdland and it was during August 1956, and it was so hot and we were all like sweat. When we got finished Pee Wee Marquette came up and said: "Come on, man, get off!" He tried to interrupt because we were playing right over time. Stan Kenton's band were sitting around waiting to get on. Lester Young wasn't the big star at this show, it was Kenton who drew all the people, but the musicians in Stan Kenton's band loved Lester. They knew he was a genius, Conte Candoli, Bill Perkins, Zoot Sims, Stan Levey, all the good players.

When we finished that tune the place erupted. They gave us a big hand. It was the best Lester had played during his two weeks. When he turned around—he didn't even hear the people applaud—he turned around to see who he was playing with. He probably knew, he knew everybody's playing, but anyway, he turned around and he had a happy look on his face and said: "Would you care for another taste?" And Philly Joe Jones just came over and gave him a big hug and said hello.

When we walked off the bandstand all the fellows from Stan Kenton's band said. "Oh, boy, we don't want to get on the bandstand, we don't want to follow that!" It sounded so beautiful.

He was marvelous, that particular man. When he got in the mood he could play so beautiful. Some young musicians thought he was old and dated, that he was losing it. I don't think [so]. He was just depressed because he couldn't get good work. I used to drive him home from Birdland and he said: "Miss Carpenter, she don't treat me no good." He was afraid to say anything to Carpenter. I had the feeling he was afraid of him, you know. Carpenter had something on him, some grip over him. He was unhappy because he couldn't get a steady band. The clubs were not paying him the money he deserved. He had to get young kids, you know. He wanted young musicians, he was looking ahead, but he wanted to get the best ones. He couldn't get the best ones, because the money wasn't good enough, you know, so Carpenter got him the older guys out of work. When Gus Johnson couldn't get anything else he got him. The time when Gildo Mahones played with Lester I remember seeing Connie Kay, and Percy Heath on bass sometimes. Maybe he was substituting, because Percy Heath was clubdating and beginning to play with Miles.

One time when we were working at Café Bohemia Count Basie's band came down. They were working up at Birdland, and the whole band came down to wish Lester a happy birthday. A few of them sat in, Frank Foster, and Richie Powell sat in on piano. I sat down listening because there were a lot of musicians who would make a tribute to Lester and jam with the band, and Sonny Rollins came down to see him too, and I was sitting with Sonny. They took a break and Lester came over to Sonny and gave him a big hug and said: "So nice of you to come down. Come on up, won't you come up and play with me?" But Sonny Rollins said: "I just want to listen. It's so nice to listen to you, I don't want to play." Afterwards when Lester got off to play Sonny told me how much he loved him, he was crazy about Lester Young. Charlie Parker and Lester Young were his two favorites.

Lester didn't like concerts, he preferred to play for dancing. He loved dances better than concerts, where people just sit there and listen to you, because he said: "Half the time there'll be some shit put out, and the people look up and they don't know whether it's good or not. Sometimes you'll put on an act, and they'll clap when you're playing bad." That's what a lot of musicians used to do, but Lester never did that, he just played what he really felt, you know. He preferred they'd dance and I agree with him too, because if the people are dancing you see them moving, and the excitement from the rhythm of the music is gonna make them feel good. If you play a nice ballad they'll hug and they'll be warm and close together and they'll enjoy it, you know. With the audience he made little announcements now and then, but not like Charlie Mingus. He knew what was going on, he was a brilliant man. He didn't speak God's English, but he was well-spoken and knew how to explain.

He told me a story once. He was playing up in Chicago with a quartet a couple of years before I was with him. He used to call me "B." It was the nickname Billy Eckstine had, so I was feeling pretty proud when he called me B too. He said: "B, one time I was playing up in Chicago, and I had a nice band up there. I had just finished my chorus and I hear that beautiful trumpet. I looked around and it's Miles, Miles Davis! Can you imagine, that's a little genius. And when he'd finished the tune I asked him, 'Miles, what're you doin' up here, where are you working?' And Miles said: 'I'm not working. I fooled up, I felt like playing.' I said: 'What do you mean, you fooled?' And he said: 'I'm in New York, and I felt like playing.' Can you imagine that, B? He hops a plane in New York just to have a little jam with me! You know, that made me feel so good!'' It thrilled him to know that Miles took a plane 900 miles to play with him. It must have cost him $60 or more, and $60 was a lot of money in the 1950's. Miles was already a star.

Lester was such a beautiful man. He always talked a lot about Louis Armstrong. At the time the black people were calling Louis Armstrong names because they say he went commercial. Lester used to tell me his people—meaning the black people—they were all wrong. They shouldn't put Louis down. Louis Armstrong didn't get commercial. He was so grown up, so advanced musically, he didn't have to just play the horn and play jazz. He could sing and he could sing beautiful. Lester was on Louis Armstrong's side. He thought it was bad that the black people would make remarks behind Louis's back, you know, saying that he was getting commercial and going after the money, because Louis Armstrong cared less about money than anybody. He gave it all away, gave all the money away, just like Lester. Lester used to give all his money away too. He was easy to borrow money from.

Don Ferrara played two, three or four days with us, and I remember Art Farmer sent him in. He was working the job, but he didn't show up. He was beginning to get a lot of work. When I played with Lester Young, Art Farmer only played a couple of the nights. He was always getting something else that paid better, and then he sent another trumpet player, you know.[5]

Lester appreciated Art Farmer greatly and really wanted to have him as a regular member of his group after the Birdland tour. It was a pity he didn't succeed, for Farmer's lyrical and melodic style of playing fitted nicely with Lester's own conception.

In 1956 Lester was not invited to take part in the Newport Festival: instead he appeared as soloist with the Count Basie band at the New York Jazz Festival, which took place on August 24 and 25 at a huge stadium on Randall's Island. Basie appeared as the finale on both evenings, but Lester only took part on the first evening, where Basie followed a marvelous section with Sarah Vaughan.

"After Sarah we fastened our seat belts and took off with Basie," Leonard Feather wrote in his review. "Pres was in there for a couple of numbers with the band, but from this seat it didn't quite jell."[6] Maybe Feather had a seat where it was difficult to hear what came from the bandstand, for the reviewer for *Orkester Journalen* had a more positive experience. "The good Count led his troops in great waves of swing," he wrote, "which swelled out into the night, thanks to the first-class loudspeaker installations. Pleasure was not lessened by Lester Young joining the band for the last two numbers. The Basie band and Lester seemed to inspire each other and both of them reached superb jazz heights.''[7]

That fall Lester received an offer to take part in Granz's Jazz at the Philharmonic and in the European tour Morris Levy from Birdland had arranged with a Birdland show, which was to include the Modern Jazz Quartet, Bud Powell, Miles Davis, and Lester. With two offers at the same time, Lester tried to play one off against the other to get as much money as possible. He usually earned $750 a week from Granz with JATP, but Carpenter managed without difficulty to fix an extra $100 a week for Lester. Lester was still not satisfied and rang up Granz several times to try to get him to agree to $1,000. Granz declined, so when Carpenter managed to get Levy to pay $1,250 a week, Lester accepted the offer for the European tour.

The tour was to start with a couple of concerts in Paris on November 2 and finish three weeks later, but Levy arranged for Lester to come to Paris at the beginning of October to appear as guest player at the distinguished Club St. Germain on the Rue St. Benoit, close to the Place St-Germain-des-Prés. Here he was accompanied by some of the best French jazz musicians—the piano player René Urtreger, the bass player Pierre Michelot, and the drummer Christian Garros, a rhythm section which was later to follow the Birdland show around Europe as accompanists for Miles Davis and Lester. The week before the rest of the musicians arrived from America Lester's quartet made a brief tour of some of the larger French towns that were not on the Birdland show's itinerary.

The American musicians' arrival in Paris was celebrated by a reception at the American Embassy on the Champs Elysées. The journalist Alun Morgan, who came to the French capital to cover the start of the tour for *Jazz Monthly,* was also present at the Embassy and wrote this about Lester:

My first sight of Lester Young in Paris was in an unusual but apt setting. It was at the American Embassy reception given to welcome the stars of Morris Levey's [sic] "Birdland" tour before their Salle Pleyel concert on November 2nd. Faultlessly attired in evening dress, glass in hand, Lester moved regally from one group to the next, nodding [to] acquaintances, amiably answering questions and posing with Miles Davis for the photographers. In the lofty-ceilinged, panelled rooms of the Embassy with their full-length mirrors and uniformed attendants at the doors, the jazz President held office with dry humor and great charm. Less than two hours later he was walking on stage at the Pleyel in his nervous, almost apologetic manner, glancing apprehensively at the audience which had just given a tremendous ovation to Miles Davis's set.

I sat through both concerts that night and heard Lester play the same four numbers at each, commencing with his own *Jumping with Symphony Sid,* continuing with *Polka Dots and Moonbeams* and *Three Little Words* and closing with *Lester Leaps In,* a tune he must have played [as] often as Hawkins has done *Body and Soul.*

To say that he played brilliantly is the truth, but it can give no real indication of his wealth of ideas and superb execution. The bell of his instrument remained in the same position relative to the microphone during the performance and his volume of sound was consistent throughout his range. Technically then he was without peer, but a musician needs more than technique to become a jazzman. Lester Young has the necessary extra qualifications and proved that timeless jazz can be created without resorting to trick effects or complicated improvisations whose only connection with the thematic choruses lies in the use of the same harmonic progression. In a word, melody was the keynote of Lester's success. . . .

To close Lester's set at the Pleyel concerts Miles Davis came on to join forces on a themeless *Lady Be Good.* The pairing was a productive one despite some raised eyebrows amongst the pigeon-hole purist brigade. The shared closing choruses were split in an unusual manner; Lester played four bars, Miles took eight, Lester sixteen, Miles four, etc., but there were no awkward moments. The contrast between the long, serpentine tenor phrases and Miles' beautifully clean double-tempo passages was stimulating.

Our last sight of Lester came at the end of the concert when he walked on to play *How High The Moon* with Miles Davis and the Modern Jazz Quartet, a not entirely successful performance but an inevitable climax to the show.

It was a wholly satisfying experience to see and to hear Lester Young in such good form; earlier this year he suffered a severe illness but now he looks and sounds fit and well.[8]

French reviews of Lester were also positive. *Jazz Hot* wrote: "Lester Young was a delightful surprise for those who had previously heard him at Jazz at the Philharmonic. Of course, it wasn't the Lester of the Count Basie records: the illusions and the enthusiasm were gone. But the Lester of 56 seems to have pulled himself together: he plays with more swing and nonchalance a pithy music, slightly decadent, but extremely pleasant to listen to! Lester is always a personality: he is not one of those musicians produced on a conveyor belt."[9]

On the other hand, *Orkester Journalen*'s review was more subdued: "Lester Young was something of an anti-climax after Miles Davis' fascinating and committed trumpet playing. Moreover Pres was tired after his touring in France and his lazy, swingy solos had little of the fresh musical wealth of ideas which characterized Miles' improvisations. A beautiful 'Polka Dots and Moonbeams' and a swinging 'Lester Leaps In' were what the two concerts yielded of Lester. When he finished the first set, together with Miles, with 'Lady Be Good,' the contrast between these two musicians was even more apparent. Lester is certainly not finished as a creative artist, but the right place for him is definitely not the concert stage after a grueling tour. His routine and even temperament made him able, even so, to demonstrate the presidency."[10]

The Swedish magazine is on its own, however, in its view of Lester's playing at this concert, for the French *Jazz Magazine* also praises Lester's playing with Miles Davis: "In the Pleyel, one of the star turns was the amazing meeting between Lester Young and Miles Davis, who played with visible enjoyment. Their interpretation of 'How High the Moon' was definitely a jazz-highlight and seldom has one seen the President so gay. Paradoxically enough, he, of all the musicians present, was the greatest 'showman.' "[11]

It is quite clear that Lester had a good time and enjoyed being on stage with Miles Davis; some of the photographs from the tour show him with an almost happy smile on his face. His performances at the later concerts on the tour, however, were of varying quality. This may well have had something to do with his liquor consumption, which, while reasonable during the first months of the year, had swiftly risen to the level it had been at before Lester was admitted to the hospital.

All four Paris concerts were a success and played to full houses, and so a couple of extra concerts were planned for what originally was to have been a day of rest halfway through the tour. From Paris the tour proceeded to Holland. From there *Melody Maker*'s man on the spot wrote home enthusiastically about the Modern Jazz Quartet and Miles Davis, but felt that Lester's performance had not lived up to expectations. "Next we heard Lester Young—my first big disappointment," he wrote. "He played well below his own (admittedly high) standard at both concerts, although he was better at Amsterdam than at Haarlem. At times we heard a few bars of greatness; at others, rather tasteless burbling and phrases restricted to one note."

He continued, "Joined by Miles for 'Lady Be Good,' Lester improved, but the trumpet was the instrument which held my attention and the spells when Miles was not blowing were, for me, at any rate, an anticlimax."[12]

A local reviewer did not disagree all that much but gave Lester a few kinder words to take with him: "Lester sounded better than when I saw him with Jazz at the Philharmonic a few years ago, but I am afraid that he will never again be the outstanding soloist of the late 'thirties and early 'forties. Nevertheless, his rendering of 'Polka Dots and Moonbeams' was beautiful."[13]

From Holland the tour moved on to Belgium, after which the Birdland show visited no less than six towns in Germany before traveling to Scandinavia. From the concert in Freiberg, which was broadcast over the radio, several recordings have been made which show Lester at his most uninspired. *Jazz-Podium* was also, generally speaking, disappointed with his concerts in Germany. "Young is a wonderful musician with a masterly technique," they wrote, "who has given a lasting contribution to jazz. His performance gave no clue as to whether he can continue this development. What he showed us was a presentable contribution to the program, but no music which could be described as an experience. The applause was for the Lester Young who has given jazz something significant, not the man who had just played."[14]

On the other hand, music has been released from the tour that reveals how relaxed and eager to play Lester could be if he was in the right surroundings. The concert hall was obviously not the right place for him, for, on "Lester Young in Europe," recorded at a jazz club in Frankfurt, he really extends himself, in, among other numbers, a blues where he plays a solo for more than ten minutes. He also sat in on other occasions; after a concert in Berlin he played, for example, with the guitar player Johannes Rediske's quintet at the club Badewanne.

In Stockholm Lester came to the concert obviously drunk, so his performance was a disappointment. *Orkester Journalen*'s reviewer reported:

The minutes he spent on stage were among the most embarrassing I have experienced in large public gatherings, and a man in the condition Lester was in then ought never to be allowed out in front of an audience. But he could still play! To a certain extent during the first concert at any rate, really well even at times, though for the most part he played nothing except long, loose notes. In general he seemed to be a pitiful parody of himself. He was at his most successful during the slow *Polka Dots and Moonbeams* and, if one hadn't seen him yawn, it might have been a number to be approved of without reservation. . . .

As the next thing on the program we "witnessed" a duet, as it's nicely called, between Lester and Miles. They played a version of *Lady Be Good* which was completely improvised throughout and which demonstrated pro primo how badly they were in tune and pro secundo how badly they sounded together. Even so, it must be admitted that there were a few pleasant solos.[15]

After Sweden the troupe traveled to Denmark. The concert in Copenhagen got reviews similar to that in Stockholm: "Young's tenor playing is admittedly absent-minded and incoherent in the fast numbers," a journalist wrote, "but in the slow ones one can still sense the great soloist with the anguished, almost whispering tone, which is so rich in its knowledge of life."[16] "Lester Young was a great disappointment," another reviewer wrote. "A single chorus in 'Polka Dots' shows a glimpse of former days. The rest was routine and at times completely incoherent. He was a shadow of himself."[17] *Politiken*'s reviewer agreed and also felt that "only in the ballad *Polka Dots and Moonbeams* did he live up to those heights we know he can reach—or could at any rate. Yesterday it was *routine* and nothing more."[18]

Lester Young and Miles Davis with the Birdland Show in KB-Hallen, Copenhagen, November 14, 1956. Courtesy of Politikens Pressefoto.

The tour then proceeded to France, with concerts in Lille, Paris, and Strasbourg, then on to the three largest towns in Switzerland, Zurich, Geneva, and Basle, before finishing with concerts in Milan and Turin in northern Italy and Marseilles and Lyons in southern France. In this final phase of the tour Lester was once again in fine form and got splendid reviews in Italy. One newspaper wrote, "On this unusually fortunate day Lester Young was also present, the leading man among modern saxophone players, and he showed his great melodic inspiration and his strong 'drive.' "[19] Enthusiasm was no less great in the Italian magazine *Musica Jazz,* which wrote the following: "This time 'Birdland's' formula was unmistakable: a Miles Davis who was more intractable and introvert than usual (his best number was, in my opinion, 'What's New'), a Lester Young in scintillating form and brilliantly himself, very modern and versatile (his tonal inventiveness was manifold in numbers like 'Polka Dots and Moonbeams,' 'Three Little Words; and 'Lester Leaps In'), a Bud Powell, alas, more neurotic than usual, and finally the Modern Jazz Quartet."[20] Thus the tour ended as it had begun as far as Lester was concerned, with a couple of concerts where he was in top form.

After returning to New York he could relax for only a few days before being sent down to Washington by Carpenter to play at Olivia Davis's Patio Lounge on 13th Street for a week, accompanied by the piano player Bill Potts's trio. Fortunately, Potts hit on the idea of having the last two days' music recorded; it was later released on four LPs with the title "Lester Young in Washington." The informal and relaxed atmosphere of this job allowed Lester to produce some of the best music from his late years in both slow and fast numbers, and it is obvious that he was having a good time with the rhythm section. Although Lester also had a recording contract with Granz, Potts somehow got round that, as he narrates here:

My old friend Norman Williams—we were friends since we were teenagers—had contracted the job at Olivia Davis' Patio Lounge in Washington, and we were to back up the name attractions that came in. We worked two or three acts, I think, before we found out that Lester Young was going to be with us. A dream come true.

As the days went by we tried to figure out how we could get some of this on tape. At the time I was working at U.S. Recording Company, and Willie—Norman Williams—said he would hire me to record the thing. There was a little portable machine in the dressing room, and we used to hang out and talk with Lester Young, a lovely man. If the world was full of men like him there would be no wars, there would be all love. He saw the portable machine Willie had, and we asked him if we might set it up one night and record a couple of tunes just for posterity. He said: "That's all right."

Then we started thinking more and more about the accessibility of the equipment of the U.S. Recording Company. We bought three microphones, two Magnecorders and 1,200 foot reels of tape.

He came in that night to work and looked up at the stand and saw three microphones, and on the piano I had two Magnecord taperecorders and a set of earphones. I remember he looked up at me and said: "No, no Billy! Norman will kill me!"

Then we decided to figure out a way. We did know that he loved Hennessy Cognac, so we bought the biggest bottle we could, had it gift wrapped and gave him a card and thanked him so much for the pleasure of working with him. He opened the package, looked at the nectar of the Gods and said: "I don't think that Norman will really kill me!" So we went downstairs and taped it with the agreement that nobody'd get any copies.

I never realized they were as good Lester Young as I found out they were. We had just one week with him, but I got to know him. I was working late one night at the U.S. Recording Company, and I didn't even know Lester was in town, and there's a knock on the door. There's no business at night there and I just opened the door and out there stands Lester Young. "Pres, what on earth are you doing!" He said: "I just wanted to be here with you!" He was that kind of guy. He was unique. He changed the world for a whole lot of saxophone players.

We had no rehearsal, we just agreed on tunes that we all knew. He was getting better and better and we were getting more like one. We were three scared kids. I was 28 then, I was a scared kid, but he made it all so lovely. He was a kind man, and there was so much love in his gorgeous solos.[21]

It was an unforgettable week for the trio to play with such a famous musician as Lester. "We had our own band room upstairs," Potts continues, "and during intermissions, the four of us would just hang out. Willie, Jim, and I would spend most of the time picking Lester's brains as well as listening to some great stories of the old days. He was such a nice man with a great sense of humor and never said anything unkind about anyone. On the bandstand he was a gas! He would lean over to me and say softly and sweetly, 'Billy . . . G's, if you please,' then snap his fingers on two and four until I kicked off the tempo."[22]

During the last weeks of that year Lester had gotten a job at Jimmy Garofolo's Café Bohemia at 15 Barrow Street in Greenwich Village with a quintet consisting of the trumpet player Idrees Sulieman, the piano player Sinclair Raney, the bass player Gene Ramey, and the drummer Willie Jones. On December 22 Lester got the recognition from musicians he had been longing for for such a long time. Leonard Feather handed over to him on that evening a copy of his *Encyclopedia Yearbook of Jazz,* where there was the following special dedication: "Presented to Lester Young, awarded greatest ever tenor saxophone by a jury of one hundred fellow artists in Leonard Feather's *Encyclopedia Yearbook of Jazz,* Musicians Musician Poll 1956."

The ceremony was transmitted over the radio, and Lester only just managed to say thank you before he was interrupted by a nervous speaker, who insisted on announcing the next number before Lester had finished speaking. Lester received fifty-two votes in all, against Hawkins's thirty-four and Stan Getz's seventeen. He himself had voted for Coleman Hawkins, Ben Webster, Paul Gonsalves, and Stan Getz as the tenor sax players he liked most. The prize didn't mean any change to his day-to-day existence, but it gave him a certain redress and took away some of the bitterness he had felt up to that point toward the younger musicians.

At the same time something happy and exciting took place on the home front. On New Year's Eve Mary gave birth to a daughter, who was christened Yvette. Lester often went out with her in the pram. One day he met Jo Jones, who teasingly asked him what he felt about babies in diapers. "Well," Lester answered, "I don't mind the waterfall, but I can't stand the mustard!"[23]

After the job at the Café Bohemia, Lester left New York once more to play at the Town Tavern in Toronto and, after that, at the Loop in Cleveland. Sulieman was his trumpet player for the next few months in jobs in New York, while Willie Jones became Lester's regular drummer—also in the New York area—right up to his death. Jones recalls:

The first time I met Lester Young, I'm not exactly sure of the date, but I believe it was in the early part of 1956, and I was working with Charlie Mingus at the time. We were playing in a club in Philadelphia, Pep's Musical Bar, and Charlie Mingus's band was going on first, and then Bud Powell's Trio would go on, and then Lester Young would come on and play with Bud Powell and close the show.

I had seen him before with Count Basie's band, but I have never had the opportunity to sit down and talk with him. Philadelphia gave me that opportunity, because what happened was that we played in the middle of the bar. The people used to sit around this bar and we would be in the middle, up high, so they could see us from all different sides. It was a big, large bar and they had chairs and tables away from the bar, where people could look down on the bar, and we were in the middle of this big circle bar. So, when I would come off the bandstand after we got finished playing one day he would sit at the end of the bar where you could walk out, so he told me, he said: "You know, you play a lot of drums to be takin' a lot of that abuse from Charlie Mingus!" When he said that to me I thought: "Wow!" and said: "Can I come by your hotel and sit down and talk with you?" So he said: "Yeah."

The hotel is now torn down and it was called John Bartram Hotel. I went by his hotel room and we sat down and he started talking, and then, that day, I got a concept of Lester Young that I never knew as a kid for listening to the records, seeing him with the Count Basie Band and seeing him play with the Jazz at the Philharmonic and the things like that, you know, playing at Birdland and all that. I had one image of the man, but when I went to the hotel room it was like another man, an even greater man in his ideals, because it was comparable with mine. That was when I met him, it was in the early part of 1956. When I went to the hotel and we started talking he complimented me with everything, you know, my style, you know, and that made me feel very, very good, and I told him, that if the opportunity would ever arise I would love to play with him. I even went so far as to say that he didn't have to worry about the money, I'd just love to play with him. So he said: "Write your number down!" And then I opened up in 1956 in December at the Café Bohemia.

That was my first job with Lester, and opposite the band was Max Roach's Quintet with Max on drums, Kenny Dorham, Sonny Rollins, George Barrow and Joe Knight on piano. Max would open it up and then we would go on next. Max lived in Brooklyn at the time, so I would go to work every night with him. Max would drive by my house, pick me up and then we would go on the way, because we were old friends. That was the beginning of my career with Lester Young.

I remember one evening Lester was downstairs in the basement at Café Bohemia when I came downstairs. He was standing up with his hands behind him and a cigarette looking like a professor, and his saxophone was in the chair. When I came downstairs he said: "Oh, let's have a conference!"

"OK."

"Do you see the instrument there?"

"Yes!"

"That is a woodwind."

"Yes."

"Now, behind me all you do is tinkety-boom, tinkety-boom! Now, when the trumpet player comes in you can do whatever you wanna. Boom! Bam! But behind me, tinkety-boom, tinkety-boom, and we got it made."

So that's all I did.

When I first went with Lester at Café Bohemia he fascinated me. First of all he was to me something that I wanted to reach as a kid. That just captured me, the mere fact that I was playing with Lester Young, you know. He would hold court, he was a philosopher, and when he would be in the dressing room downstairs he would start discussing a lot of the current events of the day, and he would also talk about his life. He would have this language in which he would discuss those things and how he felt about them. One thing he taught me, he used to say: "You have a good technique, Lady Jones, but what's your story?" I said: "What do you mean?" "I mean, a musician is a philosopher and a scientist, and he uses the science of music to project the particular philosophy he subscribes to, so you have a good technique, but what's your story?" That's when I discovered that he was a philosopher.

He was a highly intelligent man, a great man, one of our real great giants. I mean, he had his own language, you know, the way he would depict things, but he was extremely intelligent. One thing that used to behove me is, that when he would hold court he was always getting to a point, and he wanted to make sure that he had the undivided attention of all those that were in his presence before he reached the next level. It would never fail that someone would say: "Oh, what time is it? Say, man, are you going to see so-and-so?" So they would get off philosophically, but it never really hurt him.[24]

In February and March 1957 he once again took part in Morris Levy's Birdland Stars tour, and once more he was guest soloist with the Count Basie band. "Lester Young flashed on and off in a too short appearance to open the second half," *Down Beat* wrote after the concert in Carnegie Hall. "He blew *Polka Dots and Moonbeams* and *Lester Leaps In* with the Basie band, a reminder of how great he can sound with a full band blowing behind him. *Moonbeams* was handsomely done, with a series of beautiful choruses built in the best Young tradition. On *Lester,* he booted the band from the opening note." [25]

Lester was in the same good form throughout the tour, for the trombone player Benny Powell can remember that he seemed to get better and stronger every time he stood on stage with a big band behind him.[26] Thad Jones recalls: "To me it was like a magic moment in the tour that repeated itself every night, when Lester began to play. When we arrived in Kansas City I was very fortunate to share a suite of rooms with Lester and we got a chance to talk. He never really talked about his person, but he was just making observations and comments upon the things that we talked about. And as he spoke you came to realize that what he said was right and very clear."

"He was drinking quite heavily and I knew he wasn't eating," he continues, "so I used to try and get him some food. I was asking what he wanted and he would tell me to bring him something back, but when I'd bring it back—he didn't want to leave the room—the next day it would still be there untouched. So I knew he wasn't eating, and I used to talk to him and say he'd have to eat something. He'd say: 'Yeah!' and he'd put me off in such a nice way." [27]

A fortnight after the tour was over Lester was soloist at the Blue Note in Philadelphia for a week, where things also went well for him. "Lester Young, in good form, had some bright backing the week of April 1 at the Blue Note," *Down Beat* reported. "Specs Wright, drummer of Carmen McCrae, sat in all week with pianist Red Garland and bassist Slam Stewart. On opening day, Al Haig and Ray Bryant filled in for Red." [28]

Just a few weeks later Lester traveled once more to the Town Tavern in Toronto, where he was accompanied by the piano player Norm Amadio's trio. Once more he was very successful, according to the account Pete Schmidt has written of that engagement:

Indolently, almost a little nervously—Lester stood on the stand of the "Town Tavern" and he already had good contact with the audience. This could be judged from the applause which spontaneously came his way after a few choruses. We had managed to get a good seat close to the stand and Lester soon had us bewitched by the wealth of ideas of his tenor playing. There was nothing indifferent or accidental about his playing; with no nonsense, but with a self-willed phrasing and brilliantly constructed choruses, one evergreen after the other tripped off his tongue: Three Little Words, Just You—Just Me, Lady Be Good, Tea for Two. These alternated with such ballads as These Foolish Things, Talk of the

Town, I Can't Get Started, in which the velvety, almost melancholic tone of his instrument created a unique atmosphere of deep emotion. And then he laced his performances with humorous, small details, as in such numbers as A Spanish Town, played in beguine tempo, or Blues for Norm. This enticed our house pianist to relinquish his usual well-mannered reserve and goaded him on to some choruses, for which his closest friends and patrons gave him a convivial and benevolent pat on his well-upholstered shoulders.

Whatever Lester played was just as impressive. The "Prez" of the "Town Tavern" was a musician who took pride in his work and enlightened his audience, an audience which he knows understands him, sympathizes with him and appreciates the intimate nature of his style of playing. For me the highlight was Lester's improvisations on Indiana. He played the first chorus straight—without any flourishes or variations on the theme—but, even so, his version was immediately different as regards tonal treatment from the hundred or so other versions of Indiana. Then Lester changed key, and then it took off; chorus upon chorus followed with Prez developing his ideas with brilliant logic; sometimes he seasoned his interpretation with witty phrases, at other times he held a note for two beats, and then nonchalantly "caught up" by means of nimble quavers. . . .

Norm was hard put to it to keep pace and got into a real sweat during those ten minutes, but swung as well as sweated. This was to Lester's credit, a Lester who seemed to be just as fresh and unused in the last chorus as he had been at the outset. All in all there were many highlights in this rendition of Indiana, though no wild abandon at any point. This was more than compensated for by an abundance of drive and the overall impression of one of the foremost jazz musicians of today."[29]

Although things were looking up for Lester on the musical side, he was well on the way to ruining himself physically. He drank to excess and rarely ate. It was as if he was possessed by a subconscious urge to self-destruction, which by degrees was ruining his constitution. His drinking can be explained partially by a desire to allay a constant toothache. His teeth were in a pitiable state, because his aversion to doctors had kept him from seeking professional help for many years.

Thad Jones also points to another possible cause. "There were so many people who copied his style and his attitude and his approach to the saxophone that never fully extended credit to him for being the originator," is his opinion. "This casual disregard by a lot of musicians and a lot of critics and so-called historians, I think, did a lot to cause a lot of the unhappiness he must have felt, the pain and the inner despair of the man that maybe created the need to overdrink. One never knows about those things, but just based on the effect that the same type of attitude had on other musicians, you know, I would have to say it probably affected him the same way."

He adds: "You could feel pain in the man, I could, but he was still one of the most humorous, and he had the greatest sense of humor you'd ever seen in a man in your life. It was a beautiful sense of humor. He was able to laugh at life. In the midst of all of the pain of it he was able to laugh at it. That's probably the greatest tribute I can pay the man. He lived it. He lived in it, and I think he understood it much better than we. Life was cruel to him, cruel in a way it denied him the rewards of it. He was denied that and it still didn't make him lose his sense of humor."[30]

Lester also used the alcohol to deaden his headaches and other pains caused by his untreated syphilis. The consequences of this disease became more pronounced in his forties and brought on other symptoms such as sporadic epileptic attacks, a slow way of walking, insomnia, fits of depression, and an emotional instability which sometimes made him weep. More serious, however, was a progressive paresis which gradually forced him to slow down his phrasing in numbers at fast tempos.

At about this time it became difficult for him to find jobs in New York, since the clubowners would not tolerate his drinking and because an unfortunate episode at Small's Paradise on 135th Street and 7th Avenue in New York soured his already bad reputation. That evening Lester had an epileptic attack and fell down from the stand. This was unfortunately interpreted as drunkenness by the club owner. The entire band was fired the same evening, without Lester being given a chance to explain. He felt that this was very unjust, especially since he could do nothing to counteract the rumors that spread as a result of this episode. Willie Jones can remember that evening and what it came to mean for Lester:

When I had passed the excitement of being a young musician being privileged to play with one of the masters and then got into the reality of the situation, that's when I realized that in his last days he was a hurt man, and he died with a broken heart. As a matter of fact, if you listen to the last interview he had in Paris, that's him. You know, a lot of times he would use words that some people would turn as curse words, because he wanted to be emphatic of what he had to say, like in his music he would use an accent. So when he'd use those words he was really accenting it, you know.

One of the things that he said on the interview was his attitude about the way he had been treated as an American citizen who loved his country, loved his people and loved his profession. And I'll tell you that he was a man that was so hurt he was like trying to dry on his own tears. That's when he used to play a song that Frank Sinatra used to sing, "I Guess I'll Hang My Tears Out to Dry." I remember he used to play that over and over. So there was never bitterness, he wasn't what you'd call a bitter man, and he wasn't a hateful man, he was a hurt man. When you listen to the tape from Paris and listen to it carefully you will hear a man that's deeply hurt. It's like: "Can't you see what's happening? Does life really have to be this way?" you know.

The reason why I say that is because he felt that what happened to him he allowed it, whether it was knowingly or unknowingly, it happened to him. In his last days people a lot of times were talking about how much drinking he used to do and would do, and he would do that to keep from being evil. He was a hurt man, you know, and at one point they completely characterized the man as a drug ad, characterized the man as somebody that you could not depend on, that he might show up one day and might not show up the next. That wasn't true. Lester Young was an epileptic, and he would have a fit, and that's what he once had at Small's Paradise. I was there and Gene Ramey was there and Sinclair Raney was the pianoplayer. We were all in the band at the time when this happened. He got sick on the opening night. He wasn't drunk, but they labeled it as that and they used that. The man got a seizure and got the reputation as being drunk, so that's what happened up there. When he had that seizure there was a big hullabaloo when he got fired because he was drunk, but he wasn't, you know, but he had to live with it.

The reputation they'd built up on him that he was not dependable, that kind of lip-service gets out on you,, and then they were exploiting his condition. He was hurt, because he had said certain things to certain promoters that he didn't like, so they didn't like him, and they wanted to punish him. So in his punishment, you know, it just affected him the way he was being treated and what he gave. He told me that when he first met Norman Granz, Granz just had one suit when he came out there and put the concerts together. Norman Granz talks about that he was the first one to integrate the audience out there, but who helped him to do that? He didn't play no music, but who did the people come to see?—Him, Lester!

Monte Kay is a guy who is a bigtime producer, he's the guy that started jazz in Central Park. He became the producer for United Artists, and he wanted to produce Lester with strings and all that. Monte even gave him an advance. I know, because I was there and we sat and talked about it. The only reason why it didn't happen was because Norman Granz set an option on them, picked up the option, and it never happened. There was something very deep between Norman Granz and Lester. Norman Granz, the way he is today, is because of Lester Young. I don't know if he would say that if he would be that honest. But it was Lester Young who made Norman Granz, and that was why the bitterness was so severe. Love can turn into hate.

Lester didn't have many jobs at that time. We had a job in Brooklyn, it was a club, and Dizzy was there. The guy who had brought Dizzy in hadn't paid Dizzy his money or something like that, and somebody called us up and said that the guy would like to have Lester Young come to the club, and we didn't know that Dizzy was there and that they had a big rub because of the money.

So we said OK, and it was two days before the gig so we tried to find a bassplayer. The only bassplayer we could find that was available was Wilbur Little, a bassplayer from Washington. He was not in Local 802 at the time, he had just come in from Washington, but we got him because he could play. They used to have a union man, Mr. Kenneth Roven, so he came around and said to us outside: "Pluck out your union cards!" And then: "What are you doing with this man here? He's from Washington D.C. and he's not in the Local!" We told Mr. Roven that it was a quick game in the last minute and that we couldn't get another one, we've tried every bass player and that we should have one that could play, because this was with Lester Young, and after we got past that hurdle: "What are you doing working in here? You have no business working here. Dizzy Gillespie's got this man in court!" Nobody had told us the guy was in court, and we had no knowledge of this. There was no sign up that there were no work in there.[31]

In the summer of 1957 Lester had a couple of successful engagements outside New York, however. First, he took part once more in the Newport Jazz Festival, and a week later he visited Chicago to play in one of Joe Segal's Modern Jazz Concerts at the Casino Moderne, at 913 East 63rd Street.

In Newport Lester appeared once more with the Count Basie band, which formed the finale of the four-day-long festival on Sunday evening, July 7. Lester was in three of the sets, first as a solo feature, then in a program together with Jimmie Rushing, and finally in the grand finale— "One O'clock Jump"—which was to be the climax of the festival, since the Basie band was given another powerful solo injection in the form of Illinois Jacquet and Roy Eldridge.

Lester played quite outstandingly, as can be heard on the record of the concert which was subsequently issued. According to *Down Beat,* there was no doubt which set was the best: "Highlight of the evening was a reunion of Basie and drummer Jo Jones, Lester Young, and singer Jimmie Rushing. With Jo on drums and Prez wailing on tenor, Rushing and the Basie band built a set which was easily the most exciting and swinging of the entire evening."[32]

From Newport Lester went to Chicago and traveled from there to Los Angeles to record for Norman Granz, including a single number on a new metal clarinet he had received from a fan shortly before. While he was on the West Coast Granz invited him to take part in the third annual "Jazz Night" at the Hollywood Bowl, which took place on August 22. Lester played in the first group, which consisted of Harry Edison (tp), Ben Webster (ts), Oscar Peterson (p), Herb Ellis (g), Ray Brown (b), and Louis Bellson (dr); as a special surprise, Jimmy Rushing came on stage and sang a couple of numbers.

The group opened with a typically JATP-style quick blues improvised on the spot, followed by a ballad medley, where Lester played "Polka Dots and Moonbeams." "Overall, Young's playing was a sickly disappointment, only shadowly suggesting his greatness," *Down Beat* wrote. "With the emergence of Rushing, however, Prez came alive. When the portly singer rocked into his second tune with the jam group, 'Goin' to Chicago,' Lester played the blues as though he meant it, as if he were swinging for Jimmy alone."[33] After this Gerry Mulligan performed, then the Bob Brookmeyer Quartet, the Oscar Peterson Trio, the Stan Getz Quartet, and June Christy, accompanied by the piano player Benny Aronoff. During Getz's set an unheard of thing happened. Knowingly or unknowingly, he chose to play the same ballad that Lester had just played. "If comparison here is in order," *Down Beat*'s reviewer noted, "let it be noted that Getz's rendition, in conception and execution, was vastly superior to Young's. But it was a little saddening, and not quite fair, for the pupil so publicly to humiliate the onetime master." Finally, the whole front line stepped forward, together with June Christy and the entire rhythm section, to finish this emotional evening with "How High the Moon."

The first week of September saw Lester at the Town Tavern in Toronto, and a week later he set off on what proved to be his last tour with Jazz at the Philharmonic. Right from the start at Carnegie Hall he was weak, and he had just enough strength to complete the tour. This accounts for the tone of the reviews. The *New York Times,* for example, wrote that "Mr. Young, whose light, floating style was considered for many years to be the ultimate in tenor saxophone expression, was surprisingly inarticulate at fast tempos although he built a very well constructed solo on a slow ballad."[34]

There was nothing amiss with his eagerness to play, for after the concert in Cleveland on September 18 he went into town with some of the other musicians and sat in at a club. "Anita O'Day, appearing at the Modern Jazz Room that night, stepped aside to listen to Lester Young and Sonny Stitt, who each sat in for a set, much to everyone's enjoyment," *Down Beat* later wrote.[35]

During this tour a small incident took place that shows Lester in a nutshell. While the bus was on its way to Detroit from Willow Run airport, most of the musicians tried to take a nap during the hour's journey. Lester was catnapping in an aisle seat when Sonny Stitt took out his saxophone and began walking up and down the aisle playing all his licks. "Nobody paid any attention to him," Stan Getz recalls "so finally he went over to Lester and said, 'Hey, Prez, whadda you think of that?' Prez, his eyes half closed, said, 'Yes, Lady Stitt, but can you sing me a song?' "[36]

After the tour, in November, Lester traveled to Detroit to appear at the Rouge Lounge. From here he went to Chicago, where he played partly at the Stage Door and partly at the Crown Propellor Lounge, both situated on East 63rd Street. He lived during these two weeks at the Pershing Hotel, not far from the clubs, at the corner of 64th Street and Cottage Grove, but he was so weak that he had to be helped out of the hotel into a car so as to be able to perform. The tenor sax player Johnny Griffin played with him at the Crown Propellor Lounge and remembers this engagement especially, since it was the last time he saw Lester alive.

"I left Art Blakey's Jazz Messengers then went Chicago and played with Prez immediately after he played with Gene Ammons in a club called the Stage Show Lounge," Griffin relates.

It was in the winter 1957–58, I think it was around Thanksgiving. I can't remember what rhythm section it was. It was Chicago musicians, maybe Wilbur Cameron on drums, I'm really not sure.

We did only four–five concerts at this time. Prez wasn't in good shape. He was in a very bad condition actually. I couldn't get him out of the hotel to come to my house. I couldn't get him out of his hotel room. He was living at the Pershing Hotel and was lying in the bed listening to his old records that he'd made with Basie and his quartets afterwards, which hurt me very much, because I loved him very much, very much. The next time I saw him was at his funeral.

When we played together he wasn't in good shape, he wasn't feeling too well, and we didn't play anything fast. Actually I had to help him to the microphone to play. I mean, he really was that weak, and I couldn't get him to eat. He was drinking some concoction he was making of . . . it was not his normal drink, he used to drink gin, you know. He was drinking bourbon and wine mixed up, something really weird, maybe cognac and wine, I can't remember. Actually it was sad. It was a sad experience to see him in a shape like that. It was not a happy experience to see a master deteriorating.

I used to hang out with him quite a bit, drinking together, talking and joking, always since I was a baby in the Forties. He accepted me for some reason, as did most of the older musicians, like Ben Webster, all the Basie men, the Duke Ellington men. I was playing with Lionel Hampton's band in 1945, and when we came to New York everybody like Coleman Hawkins would embrace me, the little kid! It's fantastic to have grown up and to have idolized these people, including Prez, and they accepted you and were so warm and encouraging.

He was the most beautiful man, the trunk of the swing tree, I would like to say. No Prez—no Bird, no Dexter, no Coltrane, no Miles either. Prez was truly the master of time and space, nuances and understatements.

He liked young musicians if they were creative, really. Prez was so soft. For instance, when talking about being hip: There are only two musicians I really consider at that level, and the one is Lester Young, the original hipster, and the other is Thelonious Monk.[37]

A few days after returning home from Chicago Lester was invited to participate in a television broadcast—his first—for CBS. The jazz critics Nat Hentoff and Whitney Balliett, plus the producer Robert Herridge, had put together an ambitious program with the title "The Sound of Jazz," which was so great a success that, just like *Jammin' the Blues,* it has become a classic of which one never grows tired. Among those taking part were Henry Red Allen's Allstars, with such players as Coleman Hawkins, Rex Stewart, Vic Dickenson, and Jo Jones, Jimmy Giuffre's Trio, with Jim Hall and Jim Atlas, as well as Count Basie's Allstars and Mal Waldron's Allstars with Billie Holiday.

The idea was that Lester should play with both Basie and Waldron, but during the rehearsals it turned out that he was so weak that he was persuaded to drop Basie—where his solos were divided equally between Ben Webster and Coleman Hawkins—so that he could save his strength for the takes with Mal Waldron and Billie.

The trumpet player Doc Cheatham can remember from the rehearsals that "Billie was in fine spirits, and everybody was kidding and laughing, talking a mile a minute with each other. She invited us to have greens and ribs and stuff at her place after the session, and a lot of 'em went. There was a great feeling—all except Lester, who just kept to himself, sat apart. Lester was very quiet and sad that day. He didn't have much to say to anybody. Even during the session he was very solemn."[38]

During the take Billie sat on a stool, with the other musicians standing around her, except for Lester, who had been allowed to sit in a chair. When it was his turn to play solo, "he blew the sparest, purest blues I have ever heard," Hentoff recalls. "Billie, smiling, nodding to the beat, looked into Prez's eyes and he into hers. She was looking back, with the gentlest of regrets at their past. Prez was remembering too. Whatever had blighted their relationship was forgotten in the communion of the music. Sitting in the control room I felt tears, and saw tears on the faces of most of the others there. The rest of the program was all right, but this had been its climax—the empirical soul of jazz."[39] Hentoff's remarks are no exaggeration whatsoever. Listening to just the music on record is a moving experience; not only Lester's playing, but also Billie's singing gets hold of you really deep down, plucking at the heart-strings.

Very shortly after the television broadcast Mary at last managed to get Lester admitted to Kings County Hospital on Clarkson Avenue in Brooklyn. He was treated for a number of complaints, of which malnutrition, alcoholism, and cirrhosis of the liver were the most serious. Carpenter can recall that Lester's condition was so serious that he could die at any time. "The doctor called it within two months," he relates. "He said he'd live two years at most."[40]

Lester returned home in January 1958 to be confronted with a hopeless situation. Carpenter did not want to be his personal manager any more, and Gale & Gale Agency refused to have him in their fold, so from then on he had no professional manager, although Willie Jones took it upon himself to try to find Lester work.

Lester had been told by the doctors that his life was in immediate danger if he did not stop drinking. He ignored the warning, and after being discharged from the hospital, he continued to live as before, despite Mary's pleas for him to stop, or at least cut down on, his consumption of spirits. Norman Granz came to New York in both February and March to make records with him, but things went badly; from the final session—where Lester used only his metal clarinet—nothing was good enough to be released. "Lester was juiced and totally out of it," Granz relates. "Nothing worked."[41]

There were several reasons for Lester's drinking. One of them might have been his inability to settle down to a quiet suburban life in St. Albans. Already as a soldier he had been labeled a "nomad," and the following years' vagabond existence on tour can scarcely have improved the situation, even though he loved his family. Another reason for his alcoholism had to do with the situation he himself had more or less brought about: he was out of work, without a professional employer, and unwanted on stage in New York. Willie Jones narrates:

He kept drinking because of the reputation and the attitude that they had towards him and the promoters had towards him, that it was difficult for him to get work because of this particular characterization. He became so hurt, and like I said, he kept drinking. He had so much to give and was so great an artist, so his wife—you know, notably to see one's husband just destroying himself and be upset of what's going on—she couldn't take it, and she tried to tell him.

One day in the spring of 1958 I received a telephone call from a lawyer, who was Miles Davis' lawyer by the name of Harold Lavette. Harold called me up and said: "Lester Young wants to move into the Alvin Hotel," and Lester wanted him to get in touch with me. The reason for this is, because we used to get jobs around Brooklyn and New York for Lester so he could work and play, because, you know, those guys had put that reputation on him. I said to myself, well, I didn't have that kind of money, so we'd bring him back and we'll do something.

Like I said earlier, Max was living in Brooklyn at the time, on Willoughby Avenue, and I called up Max and told him that Lester wanted to move into the Alvin Hotel, and that he should bring him by my house. Max said: "As soon as we'd get to your house, you come over here," so we went from my house to Max's house, and from Max's house we checked Prez into the Alvin Hotel, because he said he wanted to look down on Broadway and look at Birdland, so when we got there we tried to figure out what to do.

See, the people that really helped Lester Young up at the Alvin Hotel when he moved in there were Max Roach, Sonny Rollins, Miles Davis, "Papa" Jo Jones, and I was assigned to be there to watch him and to do things, but these were the people that took care of the rent up there. Max never talks about it, but when we moved Lester in at the Alvin Hotel Max Roach put in the first money to pay the bill.

There was a funny thing that Lester was doing at the time. See, Lester Young was very, I'll only say, he used the word, very religious, because that could almost be contradictory to someone who would say: "How can you be religious and drinking?" But he was a man that had deep belief in a supreme power that he used to term "The Old Master." When we first moved him into the Alvin Hotel, until I got a room there on the same floor, the first couple of days I stayed in the room with him. It was about a week or something. One of the things he would do before he'd take a drink in the morning was to go to the bathroom. I mean, that was a ritual, and what he was doing in there I can't tell you, if he was on his knees or standing up or whatever he was doing. But he would go in there and close the door and had what he had to say to "The Old Master," and then come out and start his day, you know, take a drink or what he had to do. That's one of the things that I noticed about him.[42]

Even though Lester now lived separately from Mary, there was at no point any talk of a divorce, for he kept in regular contact with his family, even after Elaine Swain—a friend he had known for several years and who had previously lived with other musicians—moved in with him. Elaine was kind to him. But even though she managed to get him to eat a little, she couldn't reduce his liquor consumption, and so things got steadily worse.

Rumors concerning Lester's miserable condition spread like wildfire in jazz circles, and even though some people thought he had brought it upon himself, there were others—apart from those already named by Willie Jones—who tried to help as well as they could. One of them was the trombone and vibraphone player Tyree Glenn, who was generous enough to offer Lester a job playing with his quintet as long as he wanted to, which Lester gratefully accepted.

The piano player Hank Jones, by some quirk of fate, happened to meet Lester at this point, and he can recall how much of a shock it was for him to see Lester so weakened and wasted that he could hardly get out of bed. "Lester was working with Tyree Glenn in a club," Jones relates. "I wasn't a member of the band, but was working around in the night-clubs of New York City. During the last two weeks of the engagement or so Lester didn't show up for work. Tyree Glenn wanted to give him the salary he didn't get for the weeks before, so when Lester didn't come he gave me the money to pay him."

"Lester was staying at a hotel called Alvin on the corner of Broadway and 52nd Street," he continues. "It was a very bad hotel, but a lot of musicians stayed there because the rent was cheap. I went up to his room and knocked on the door, and after the third or fourth knock I heard somebody say, 'Come in.' I opened the door—the door was open—and I looked around, but didn't see anybody. I saw the covers of the bed rubbed up as if somebody had just come out of bed, but—believe me or not—Lester was *in* bed."[43]

One day Marshall Stearns came on a visit. Stearns was a professor of English but took a keen interest in jazz and had shortly before established the Institute of Jazz Studies. He could see how bad Lester was and understood at the same time that what he needed most of all was a doctor who also could give him psychiatric help. One of Stearns's friends, the psychiatrist Dr. Luther Cloud, met these requirements. The two of them paid a visit to Lester but did not mention Cloud's profession, since Stearns knew of Lester's phobia about doctors. Cloud managed quickly to gain Lester's confidence, however, and after a couple of weeks he was able to confide that he was a doctor, to question Lester more openly, and to begin treatment.

"Soon I happened in on him," Cloud recalls, "while he was sitting at the window, fingering the sax, and watching Birdland. What a sad kind of voyeurism, I thought. Then I found that a part of his interest was in what sax players would be arriving to perform."[44]

When they talked about the young tenor sax players coming to play at Birdland, Cloud discovered that Lester had an ambivalent attitude toward them, since he was both proud of the fact that they used a style he had invented, but was also uneasy about it, since he now felt unsure as to what style he himself should use. "They're picking the bones while the body is still warm," Lester once said. "When they come off and I go on, what can I play? Must I copy *them?*"[45]

"I saw that he was definitely schizophrenic," Cloud continues.

Yet, in a kind of partly arrested, semicontrolled way. Alcohol, for example, dissociated him yet gave him the minimum comfort he needed to survive at all.

And, of course, pot and alky together are A-1 schizo triggers. One quickens time and one slows it. One widens space and one narrows it.

I didn't say, "Stop drinking," of course. Or, "Eat more." But I got him on heavy concentrated vitamins. Wanted to inject them but found him scared to death of the needle and of hard dope.[46]

Lester was also preoccupied with thoughts of death at this time, and Luther Cloud had the idea of getting him to talk with a minister. In 1956 Reverend John Gensel had come to New York and had begun to build up a congregation around St. Peter's Church on the corner of 54th Street and Lexington Avenue, one that tried to attract jazz musicians. "Lester lived at the Alvin Hotel, which was on 52nd Street and Broadway, directly across from Birdland," Gensel recalls.

I think it was on the fourth floor as I remember, and I called him and asked if I could stop by to see him. I did stop by to see him, and we got acquainted and I used to visit him a number of times in his apartment where he lived. That's where I got to know him a little bit.

I do remember one time he looked out the window at Birdland, and he said: "When many of my friends come in and out of there I'll see them. I have a home out on Long Island, and when the grass is green it's pretty. But I'll much rather be here where I can see my friends." Rather than be out there where the grass is nice and green, not in the country exactly, but away from the hustle and bustle of life, he evidently wanted to be there in the midst of activity and where he could see his friends that he knew coming in and out of the club where he had played himself.

We talked not too much about his family background. He had his own way of talking, you know, and I recall that one time he told me, that in between sets this one woman coming up and talking and talking to him, and finally he said to her: "I know what your name is." And she said: "You do?" And he said: "Yeah," and she said: "What's my name?," and he said: "Your name is Mary, but I don't know which one." I don't know if he meant Mary Magdalene or Mary, the mother of Jesus, or—you know.

He also used to fantasize a bit. He said: "I know what they are waiting for!" I said: "Who? What do you mean?" "Well," he said, "these persons want to make money out of me. As soon as I die there'll be some memorial albums out on me." And he spoke in that sense in a kind of, I'll not say bitterly, but at least with the idea that he was gonna be used. Rather than giving him work while he was alive, when he could enjoy it, they'd wait until he died, and then of course, being the famous person that he was, they would capitalize. And, of course, that was exactly what happened.

And he said: "When I die they'll dedicate to me a casket. I'll be lying there and people will come by and they'll think I'm dead. But I'll not be dead at all. I'll know that they are there!"

He did speak in a strange sort of way. One time I called him, and I said: "How are you, Prez?" And he said: "I'm okay, I don't feel a draft.' Of course what he meant was "I'm all right." If he did feel a draft it would mean that he wasn't accepting me, you know.

He was very congenial, and I enjoyed talking with him. I don't know if Lester was religious. We were talking about church one time, and I only have one real religious story about him. He said: "Well, one time I was playing I came to church, and I went in quiet and sat in the back, and as soon as the minister saw me, he started to talk about the Devil Music and the sin and so forth." And he knew that Lester knew that he was talking that way because he saw him coming in and knew he was a jazz musician. And then Lester indicated to me that he hadn't used the church ever since, because he felt somewhat alienated from the church. I guess it was part of his alienation with the society to a certain extent. The very fact that the way the preacher preached that day indicated that what Lester was doing was wrong and sinful. According to his viewpoint it was only indicative of what happened to him in society in some respect. It doesn't mean that he wasn't accepted by many and loved and so forth. Of course he was, but we remember the hurts more than we remember the good things, you know.[47]

The critic Ross Russell also visited Lester at his hotel once and recalls that "my most vivid impressions were the bottles of Gordon's gin, a dozen or more, standing in front of the mirror on his dresser, waiting to be opened, and Lester's desire to talk, not about music, but about Western movies, which he attended almost every afternoon in the triple-bill, twenty-five cent fleabag houses on Forty-second Street. Plots of these pictures were described in detail."[48]

With Dr. Cloud's help Lester gradually regained his strength and put on weight. One afternoon at the end of May, while he was sitting in his hotel room talking to Willie Jones, Marshall Stearns arrived on a visit. He had had the idea of creating some sort of publicity about Lester so that he would get another chance to get out to the clubs and play. Jones recalls:

Marshall Stearns said: "Lester, I'm going over to Birdland and tell them to celebrate your birthday in show business."

So Lester said: "Well, that's fine."

"So you will know the world has not forgotten the great Lester Young."

"That's great."

"How much money do you want, Lester?"

"A hundred dollars."

"Okay. Come on Willie, let's go down."

We went across the street and went downstairs to Birdland, and Marshall Stearns said to Oscar Goodstein, the manager of Birdland: "Lester Young is across the street. He feels like the world has forgotten about him."

"Oh, yeah?"

"Yeah, I think we shall celebrate a night for him down here."

"That's great. I didn't know Lester was over there. Yeah, we can do that. How much money does Lester want?"

"Lester Young wants a hundred dollars."

"When Lester Young is coming here we have a scale of 50 dollars."

"No, we don't want to do that. We have given Lester Young a word."

If anything, Marshall Stearns was a great man, so he said: "It's up to you. You give the 50 and I give the other 50, then he's got 100."

"God bless you. When Lester is coming in here he is coming in here for 50. So you can do whatever you want with your 50, so it's okay."

So we went back across the street to the hotel room to tell Lester, and Stearns said to me: "Don't tell Lester what he said. Don't tell Lester. I'll make sure he gets the hundred dollars."

I said: "Okay," but told Lester anyway.

We went in on a Monday night with Doug Watkins, Nat Pierce, Curtis Fuller, myself and Lester Young. Dan Morgenstern wrote about it, so that's what came about because of Marshall Stearns.[49]

The celebration, called "Thirty Years in Showbusiness," was held on June 2,[50] a Monday, which was normally the musicians' evening off, when the stand was available for anyone who felt like playing or for an improvised jam session.

The place was packed, and Lester's quintet was on in the first set. "The downbeat is soft, the tempo medium," Morgenstern wrote.

"Pennies from Heaven" is a haunted song. Not a mild summer rain this but a gray November drizzle. The pennies are few and worn, thin and smooth. The tone is choked, the phrasing halting . . . not from inability but from pain. The last note dies and Lester looks up from a troubled sleep. Silence. The faces of the musicians who have backed him, so gently, so sympathetically, are intent and serious. Then the applause, warm and strong and friendly—not the applause of a concert audience. "Mean to Me" is not a lament but a quest; climbing in uncertain terrain, gaining a foothold and finally reaching solid ground where one can walk once more. And Prez smiles and the young band, having helped to cause the smile, are in turn infected. From then on it is walkin' and talkin'. Prez, having prayed, is now ready to preach. "Up 'n Adam" jumps. The master begins softly, gaining in volume and heat with each consecutive chorus (can one speak of choruses where there is unbroken continuity?), coming up shouting like the old Prez (did they say he was no more?) and suddenly there is a new astonishing Prez as well!

Back of him, cool Doug Watkins, elegant in his double-breasted Ivy League suit, new in approach as well as clothes, is coming on like Slam Stewart's little brother, singing, bowing and having a quiet ball. Shy Willie Jones, knowing how to drum softly yet hotly, knowing how to join the party without slamming the door and grabbing all the whisky, uncorks a drum solo that has a message and which is to be merely the first in a triad of uniquely original excursions into time and timbre. With humor, whimsey and a strong, good foot he is the first new drummer to bring Zutty, the old master to mind. Nat Pierce, laying down the right chords in the right places as if he's there to help; striding out on his own having listened to Erroll and James P. And Prez . . . Prez walking over to whoever is speaking his piece, saying "yes," "ahm," "yeah"; digging everybody, before taking it out with a "Catch me somewhere along the way." The audience shouts "Yeah Prezerini" . . . some handclapping—and then it's over and everybody's happy—Sid beaming from inside for a change and Prez hugging his horn as he retires to his corner.[51]

After this, "Symphony" Sid announced the other band of the evening, consisting of three trombones, an alto sax, and a rhythm section. After their set, it was Lester's turn once again; he set off with "Lester Leaps In."

Horn up high, tempo solid, rhythm gentle but firm behind him. Then the stop-time things: Stop time, suspend time—go around it, behind it, in front of it—always on time and on to time. Lester leaping in and bouncing back, spiralling up like a diver in reverse, joining time and space in sound. Can Prez still blow? Oh, baby! "Waterfront." "Prez Baby" somebody calls out when the last leap has returned to earth with four bars of half-speed for landing gently, the plea in the voice is implicit. *"Right* now," says Prez who has just made Curtis Fuller blow like he never blew before—and didn't even know he could. He forgets, not too much later, but undoubtedly will never forget. Prez covers the Waterfront, all of them. He covers them with a tenor saxophone sound that vibrates right through everything and everybody; giving us the message from so deep within himself that it is beyond word-meaning, merging all, as he and his instrument have merged. This is what jazz can be, what jazz can do. Only the greatest arts can do this, and how rarely it is done in our century!

Almost without pause Lester glides into "Tea for Two," fast, fast, but unhurried." Surging like a river, like blood through the veins . . . runs and cascades of notes and tones whole and sustained—that good old tension-relaxation riff. Tea for two, me an' you . . . tea for we.[52]

After another set with the other band it was time for the official ceremony. A large cake with candles and champagne were brought in. And so Lester, who had just gone up onto the stage to start playing, had to come down again and blow the candles out, greet people, and receive their congratulations. He still had his saxophone round his neck and, while he cut the cake with one hand, he played—very suitably—some bars of "I Didn't Know What Time It Was" with the other. After this he went onto the stage once more and began playing "There'll Never Be Another You," finishing off with "Jeepers Creepers," with both Roy Haynes and Bud Powell sitting in.

After this festive occasion things went better for Lester in terms of his strength, his state of mind, and his ability to get jobs. The first job he had was three weeks at Birdland, from the beginning of July. "It was Curtis Fuller on trombone, Junior Mance playing piano, Paul West on bass, myself and Lester," Willie Jones recalls.

Then Lester went to do Newport, and we had Jimmy Forrest the night Lester went there, to take Lester's place. We did three weeks there, our group, Dinah Washington and Mitchell/Ruff Duo, that was the bill. Dwike Mitchell played the piano and Willie Ruff played the bass and doubled on French horn. It was a chamberlike thing where they changed the time and all that.

Let me tell a humorous story from that Birdland engagement. The reputation got around that Prez was sick, that he folded. Prez was sitting in a chair, quiet, and it was like on a Wednesday night. He was playing like "I Cover the Waterfront," "I Didn't Know What Time It Was," you know, real melancholy songs, and Sonny Stitt came in that night. Sonny asked if he could play, and Prez said: "Yeah," so he took out his alto and he would play. Later that night when we got back to the hotel Prez said: "They don't think I know when they are out for a kill, but who were out for a kill, Lady Stitt!" I said: "No, not really. Sonny Stitt loves you. He digs you, you are the baddest cat." Then comes Saturday night, and, you know, musicians always have that competitive spirit, just like boxers and fighters. Sonny Stitt came to the bandstand again, and this time he had his tenor and he said: "Can I play something with you, Prez?" Saturday night Prez wasn't sitting down in his chair, he was standing up, so Prez said: "Come on!" so he came on the stage, and that was mistake number one. "What do you wanna play, Prez?" And Lester said: "Let's play 'Lester Leaps In.' " That was mistake number two. Mistake number three: he let Prez play first—and that was a different Lester Young! When Prez got finished playing, man, Sonny stood up there and looked with amazement! Lester could never get straight, he played with Dinah and he played with the Mitchell/Ruff Duo. That was when all the guys recognized that Prez was not what they thought he was. When the time called for it he was there to deliver.[53]

The 1958 Newport Jazz Festival was a tremendous comedown as far as Lester was concerned. The arrangers had malplaced him in a Dixieland group which was to appear on the evening of Saturday, July 5. To make matters worse, the gods had laid on inclement weather. "Rain began to fall during a Dixieland set by pianist Don Ewell, Tom Bryant, Jo Jones, Clayton, Teagarden, Pee Wee Russell and Lester Young," *Down Beat* reported. "Pres was horribly out of place in the group, and blew to suit his discomfort. He played with a noticeable lack of enthusiasm, and with none of the technique or inspiration that made him president.''

"As the rain pelted down,'' the reviewer continues, "more than half of the huge audience streamed out of the park. The set fell apart, with a ballad medley dropped after Pres played a lustreless *I Cover the Waterfront*. The group struggled through *Muskrat Ramble* and a blues, and Young laid out through the most of it. It was a dreadful waste of a jazzman to have included him in this context.''[54]

This review hits the nail on the head; the music issued from this concert demonstrates only too clearly how much Lester felt out of it. He was pretty down anyway at that point. Before the concert he had met Buddy Tate, who was there to rehearse a set with Billie Holiday. The two of them traveled back to New York together. Tate recalls:

Prez was sick then. It was getting to him, you know, he was really failing. He was short-winded, he didn't have any stamina, couldn't hardly fill his horn, you know what I mean? Couldn't control his sound.

That day we had a rehearsal with Billie, and Prez couldn't find the place. The hall was really hard to find, and Prez is sincere about everything. I mean, like he didn't even want to be late, you know. We'd been playing about an hour, rehearsing about an hour and a half, just going over some things to play for her and little riffs and things we was going to play behind Billie, you know. So man, when he came in, when he found the place, he came in and walked to the door, like he'd come in from that foyer there and he stops and he spies us and he got this big wide hat on and the crown's about that high. He really looked comical, you know. And man, everybody broke down and started laughing. And man, it hurt his feelings, you know, because everybody was laughing at him. He says: "I don't see what's so fucking funny with you ladies. I've been looking for this fucker for two hours and a half and there ain't a damn thing funny. Now, I don't see nothing for you all to laugh about.''

So we says: "Oh, Prez, we didn't mean anything like that, we just . . . ,'' you know. He told me later on: "Hey, Tate. You know, I was really surprised that you laughed at me.'' I said: "No, we weren't laughing at you. I had a hard time finding the damn place myself. No, we didn't mean it like that.'' So he was all right after that. Just give you some idea of how sensitive he was, you know.

It was hard to get back to New York. You had to go to Providence and wait a long time. You had to take a bus to Providence and maybe miss a train, then catch a train from Providence to New York. So he was up there, he and his lady. He had his lady and a friend that had driven him there in a Cadillac. He's sitting in the back in the middle of the seat like the way those big engines ride down in Oklahoma, you know, big hat on. So he says: "You ride with me.'' I said: "Well, I'd love to, Prez.'' He said: "You've got to. You don't go back over there. You ride with me.'' So I says: "Okay.'' He says: "And as a matter of fact, I want you to be my manager today, to take care of my business for me, pick up my money.'' He was playing at the Birdland. He says: "They docked me, you know. They're not going to pay me for the night. But that's all right.''

He heard me play a set, so he said: "Gee, you sound good. I've been back there listening. You've got it together. You really sound good. I haven't done too well, you know. I've been down right to rock bottom. I started to call on you because I've been reading about you." I used to let him have money, you know, a lot of times. He used to like to gamble, you know, and lose his money and I'd loan him money, a hundred or something like that because I didn't have any of those habits, see.

I said: "Well, what the hell. You know if I got anything, you're part of it." He says: "I know that, but a man's got his pride. You know, a man must have his pride."

So, you know, I tell you, when I got in the car that night with him, first thing he did, he opened his wallet like this and turned me on, you know. He lit up. He said: "Now, let's review the books. I haven't done so well, you know." I says: "What do you mean?" He says: "I never really made it on my own." I said: "What do you mean, you haven't made it? Man, you're a legend. You and Hawk." He says: "Yeah, but all the other ladies that they say play like me make all the money." So I says: "Well, I don't think you're a good businessman, I'll tell you that now. But you could have made it. I can even book you. All the world knows you and nobody have trouble. . . . But maybe you just don't take care of business." He says: "Well, I think the ladies come to hear me, but I don't get the money." I said: "Well, you're not a good businessman, as I said. I told you that."

So we talked all about that and he told me. We got lost and it took us nine hours to get from Newport. I'm glad, because those last nine hours was the last time I spent with him and we talked all night. So I picked up his money for him and took care of his business and everything. He told me: "Just send my wife a hundred dollars. Just dont' say nothing."

I sent her a yard and he wanted to give the guy some money that brought him up and he wouldn't take nothing. He got insulted. He said: "No, you're my friend, man. I don't want any money."

He carried me to my apartment uptown and everything. So he says: "I'll tell you what I would like for you to do. If you know any place where I can get me a bottle. I'd appreciate it because there's not going to be anything, tomorrow's Sunday and I won't be able to get me a bottle until late, you know? And I'll pay some dues."

And really, that's the first thing. . . . There's a guy walked all night right on my corner with bottles in his pocket and he's selling them. And she [Elaine Swain] said to me: "If you do, the doctor done said any drink, he might start hemorrhaging to death. And I know he would die if you bought him a bottle and he did start hemorrhaging." So I wouldn't do it.

I could have went right to the bootlegger and got it. But you know, when she told me that, I would have felt badly all my life had I bought him a bottle of whiskey and it killed him right then and there. But that's why I didn't. That's all he wanted me to do for him and I didn't. And you know, sometimes that bugs me. So my wife said: "I think you did the right thing."[55]

After the engagement at Birdland Lester did not have much to do in the month that followed, just one evening at the Black Pearl in New

York and a weekend in Philadelphia at Pep's Musical Bar. In Philadelphia he met Chris Albertson, who at the time was making a series of broadcasts for radio station WCAU. Albertson had a musician in the studio for each broadcast who gave his opinion of the records being played. Afterwards Albertson cut his own voice, so that the finished broadcast gave the impression of being music plus commentary. Things did not go quite as planned with Lester, however, since he was more in the mood to talk about himself than about the records. And so the final result was an interview, where the two of them talk about Lester's life and career.[56]

Lester's desire to start afresh was so strong that he did not renew his contract with Norman Granz in September 1958, but instead signed up with Monte Kay from United Artists. The same month he took part in a charity concert in Carnegie Hall to benefit Mary Lou Williams's new project, the Bel Canto Foundation, a home for elderly or weak musicians. A wealth of famous names, plus the Xavier Symphony Orchestra, took part, including Roy Eldridge, Dave Lambert, Jon Hendricks, Les Jazz Modes, Roy Haynes, Thelonious Monk, Eddie "Lockjaw" Davis, Charlie Persip, Allen Eager, and Chuck Wayne.

Less than a week after this gathering, on September 25, Lester appeared for the last time before a television camera to take part in Art Ford's "Jazz Party" for WNTA. It was a mixed bag of musicians he came to play with, stylistically speaking. Even so, the music swings fabulously, and everybody, including Lester, seems to be enjoying themselves, with laughing and joking going on all the time. He played in two numbers—"Mean to Me" and "Jumpin' with Symphony Sid"—with Coleman Hawkins, the trumpet players Henry "Red" Allen and Charlie Shavers, the trombone player J. C. Higginbotham, and the clarinet player Pee Wee Russell in the front line. They were backed up by a five-man-strong rhythm section with Willie "The Lion" Smith leading, plus the vibraphone player Henry Shepherd, the guitar player Dick Thompson, and the bass player Vinnie Burke, while Sonny Greer took care of the drums. The sound of the transmission has fortunately been recorded on tape, but the visual part has been lost; otherwise one could certainly have seen an extra guest in the studio looking out of Lester's saxophone case with large eyes—for on his way to the studio he had picked up a stray kitten which he found irresistible.

November and December were a busy time for him, with bookings every day. He had a two-week engagement at the Five Spot in New York starting on November 14, followed by a fortnight at the Showboat in Philadelphia and then three more weeks at the Five Spot. The last week of the year was spent at various clubs and hotels in Chicago, before starting the new year playing yet again at the Five Spot.

"The last job we had was at the Five Spot," Willie Jones recalls.

That was a funny job. It wasn't work for me, it was the greatest thing in my life to play with Lester. I liked all the musicians, you know, but that level of playing, that concept, you know. Valdo Williams played piano and Gene Ramey played bass.

At that time he started thinking about renewing his life, and he started to let his hair grow long, like the Duke did in his later years. And then, when we were out at the Bowery, you know, the Five Spot was down at the Bowery downtown where you'd see all the bums in that neighborhood. Well, what happened was that a lot of these guys that you'd characterize as street people would walk by the window and look in. So when they looked in they could look directly to the bandstand, so Lester would look to the window and he would raise his hand like to say: "Come in!" So they started coming in! Joe Termini, the owner, would stop them in the door: "Hold it, you can't come in!" But they said: "He called us in!" But Termini would never go to Lester and say: "Lester, will you kindly stop doing that." He would come to me and ask me. The reason for that was the way we used to work. According to the Union, Lester would work as a single, and then I had the responsibility of paying the men. So that's why he would come to me and say: "Hey, Willie, would you kindly tell Lester to stop calling these guys in?" So I said: "You tell him!" That was a great experience, and Lester enjoyed it.

See, one of the things I learned from Lester was that his father, you know, was at Tuskegee, and that was a kind of philosophy. That was a real industrious type of philosophy, so Lester was very industrious in his thinking. But he was also an American that believed in the principles of democracy, the principles of equality, and he recognized that there were people who opposed those concepts, you know. That's what his thinking was and the way he felt, and like I said, he would refer to what happened to the music, to the inventiveness of the music and about the greediness of the promoters. They didn't take any considerations to the audience or the performers. The music that we have today, a lot of the inventiveness of it has left.

The greed of the few people that wanted to play God and control everything, they deprived the world of such great beauty, and that's one of the reasons why he died. He said to me that he wanted to split and go to Paris, but it was just the way around—he went to Paris and came back and split!

The last time I saw him alive was at the Alvin Hotel just before he went to Paris, and he said: "There's three things I want you to remember. Number one: Take your time. Because if you do not take your time you might stumble, and if you stumble you might not get up. Secondly: Don't have a faint heart. Don't be nervous, don't be scared. Stand up for whatever you believe in. And thirdly: Don't give up!"

The other principles that he taught me are: the philosophy of the spirituals, the musician as a philosopher and a scientist, that we have made a major contribution to this country and we are Americans. Prez opened my eyes. Once he told me: "Go down to the audience, see what the plumber is thinking, what the carpenter is thinking, so when you go to the stage you can help tell their story."

It took me years to grasp a lot of things he was saying, especially his concept of philosophy and the spirituals. The philosophy is a philosophy of equality, and our music must be melodious and melodic.

When you think of those big songs, "You Got Shoes, He Got Shoes," it's equality. "Lay Down Your Sword and Shield," "Were You There When They Crucified My Lord," "Nobody Knows the Trouble I've Seen," it's equality. So his playing is just an extension of that concept. It's universal and people can feel it all over.

He used to have a saying: "All the physicians come to hear the musicians!" We should bring some beauty into the world. When you play for the people you can call yourself great all you want. You are not great until the people say you are. And when the people say you're great, you don't argue about that. You say: "Thank you!" That's what I was taught.[57]

At the start of Lester's first engagement at the Five Spot, the photographer Herb Snitzer and the journalist Robert A. Perlongo came to take a series of pictures of him.[58] Perlongo remembers especially from that visit Lester's careful treatment of his saxophone, which he had given the pet name "Baby." "He was not comfortable away from it, and tried at all times to keep it in sight," he recalls.

When he was on the stand and not playing, he held the horn cradled in his arms, with both hands curved around it. . . .

Working with a photographer who was doing a picture story on Lester, I found that it would be necessary, for a particular shot, to move Lester's horn from the piano-stool he had set it down on. I asked him for permission to do so.

"Sure, Pres," he said. "But hold it carefully; you dig? That's my life."[59]

Things were really beginning to work out for Lester once more. He had some new posters made, and offers began to pour in. He received one from Paris to be guest soloist at Le Blue Note, but declined first time round. A better offer came shortly afterwards which he couldn't resist, and he decided to leave. When this engagement was over in March 1959, he was to have joined Norman Granz's JATP troupe, which was to start its European tour at that point.

Shortly before he left Lee came to New York and visited him at the Alvin Hotel. It was to be their last meeting, and in a commemorative article on Lester, Leonard Feather wrote that Lee on that occasion upbraided him for his way of life.[60] Lee later commented that this was scarcely the right word. "Well, you know," he said, "you got to remember that he was my older brother, and as far as the word—I think that's a bad word, 'upbraiding' him, because I would not do that with him, because I had an awful lot of respect for him. Because it was our teaching, you know . . . no, I couldn't do it. It was done, but it was not done in that manner. It's a bad choice of words. But it's just—well, he was not a good business man, you know; he was just a true artist. And they could take advantage of him from every angle that you could think of, you know."[61]

Before Lester left New York in mid-January he went to St. Albans to say goodbye to Mary, Lester Jr., and little Yvette. Elaine went with him to the airport. In Paris he booked in on the second floor of the Hôtel de la Louisiane—for nostalgic reasons, perhaps—which is situated on the Rue de Seine and which forms the western boundary of the old Latin quarter.

On his first evening he went over to Le Blue Note, which was on the Rue d'Artois, a tiny street between the Champs Elysées and the Rue de Fauburg Saint Honoré and running parallel to them, not far from the Arc de Triomphe. This was also Stan Getz's last evening as guest soloist, and when they met in the bar Lester greeted him with a huge smile and said: "You're my singer!" [62]

At Le Blue Note, Lester then played for eight weeks. To begin with, the rhythm section consisted of such fine musicians as the piano player René Urtreger, the bass player Pierre Michelot, the guitar player Jimmy Gourley, and the drummer Kenny Clarke, the last two being American musicians who had settled in Paris. Lester had great respect for these players, especially for Urtreger, who was able to accompany him the way he really liked. Unfortunately, neither Urtreger nor Michelot was able to play at Le Blue Note for more than the first month. The bass player's place was then taken by Jean-Marie Ingrand and the piano player's by Jackie Knudde and subsequently Harold Kauffman—both proficient piano players, but not reaching Urtreger's high standard or his sensitivity as an accompanist.

Michelot used to drive Lester home at around four or five in the morning when the job was over. He can recall the following episode: "Imagine an endless corridor at a hotel at four o'clock in the morning. Right at the far end, clad in striped pajamas, with a broad-brimmed hat on his head and holding a saxophone, turning around and talking to himself—Lester Young, ghostlike, as he seemed to me. That's how Prez was throughout his life: eccentricity in person." [63]

The Cullazes were also with him several times during those months. This time Maurice relates that "on certain evenings, with Klook on drums, there were moments of the great Lester, but apart from that there seemed to be a lack of resilience, a world-weariness, a half-voluntary resignation about him. He tells us that he's been very ill and that he will die within a few months."

"He's back home," Cullaz continues. "He orders wine, or cognac—anything we want—he drinks while he listens to *Lester Young-Count Basie,* which has been issued on the Savoy label. He seems to be measuring the time that has passed since he made those recordings, with pain. As if all that is a thing of the past. 'He really could play, that fella,' he seems to be saying to himself. He is listening as if to another musician. A superb musician, who surprises and transports him . . . a young imitator, whom he'd like to be jealous of, but is also proud of!"[64]

Another welcome guest who often visited Le Blue Note during the first month Lester was playing there was Billie Holiday. She was in Paris until February 22, 1959, and gave several well-attended concerts at L'Olympia. Otherwise she was engaged to sing at the Mars Club, and once in a while she would get up on the stage at Le Blue Note with Lester and sing a set with him. The author James Jones, who was also in Paris that winter, met Billie and Lester on several occasions. He can recall that Lester always had to haggle with Ben Benjamin—the owner of Le Blue Note—over prices for drinks.

"The Pres" still wore his celebrated porkpie hats, and when he dressed, slowly and carefully, to go out into the streets after his last set, it was always something of a major performance. Framed by the big fur collar of the long coat he loved to wear, his long gaunt face with the deep, purple, sick-looking hollows under the eyes would look out at you with a sort of princely helplessness.

I found his music as great as ever, though there were some who said it was not. But they never said it in his presence. He was a scrappy individual, who liked to carry a straight razor in his pocket which he loved to pull out and display, wide open. When he had his girlfriend Lady Razor with him, he said, nobody messed with him. I never heard of him using the razor. And scrappy or not, he had a marvelous sense of humor, and he loved females. He loved to sit at the bar between sets, trading quips with my good-looking wife. More than half the time she had him roaring with laughter.[65]

The Danish graphic artist Thomas Winding also visited Le Blue Note and recalls that Kenny Clarke, who wasn't feeling too good that evening because of influenza, had gotten Kansas Fields to sub for him. "Lester Young had more air in his tone than ever before," Winding relates. "From the moment he began playing to the point when the sound came more than 20 seconds passed—no exaggerating!—but after that it just poured out of him, one ballad after the other: There'll never be another you, I can't get started, Polka dots and moonbeams, Almost like being in love, etc. Many of them he played several times, but without repeating himself. His playing was so full of gusto, yet during the breaks he looked pretty tired and leaned up against the grand piano with his forehead pressed against the open lid."[66]

Lester didn't like to live alone and, since he lacked female company at the hotel, which he never left unless he was to appear on stage, he managed to get a woman called Erika to move in with him. She was the rich daughter of a German managing director who owned several factories in Frankfurt, and Lester referred affectionately to her as "Miss Wiggins."[67]

Lester had a hot-plate installed in his room so that from time to time he could prepare some of the spiced dishes from New Orleans he was so fond of,[68] but he gradually lost his appetite and eventually stopped eating altogether. This was catastrophic for him, since his liquor consumtion became larger and larger. Finally he had lost so much strength that he had to be helped down the stairs to a taxi so that he could get to the jazz club. Eventually he moved to the Hôtel d'Angleterre, at 91 Rue le Boetie, close to Le Blue Note. He felt so low at one point that he contacted Dr. Luther Cloud. "He didn't write," Cloud informs us, "but 'phoned one afternoon after several weeks. He was brought-down, not happy, he said, with the combo he had to play with. He leveled with me: he had gone on brandy. Heavily, I judged."[69] Having learned a bitter lesson from New York, where rumors about his abuse of alcohol had almost ruined his career, he only drank a little before the job and consumed the rest up in his hotel room .

Some of Lester's music from these months in Paris has fortunately been preserved and is witness to the fact that his creative talent, despite shortness of breath and failing strength, was still intact. The radio was there on several occasions to record him at Le Blue Note—the last time was only two days before he left Paris—and Norman Granz even managed to have a last finger in the pie, since he contacted Eddie Barclay from the record company Compagnie Phonographique Française and asked him to make some studio recordings with Lester, for a possible later record. Barclay got Lester into the studio, together with Urtreger, Gourley, Jamil Nasser, and Kenny Clarke, but Lester was not completely satisfied with the result, for he said about a couple of the ballads, "I can make them better."[70]

Apart from this, Jean-Louis Ginebre and Michel Netter got Lester into a radio studio, where he took part in a broadcast with the trumpet player Idrees Sulieman, Urtreger, Michelot, Gourley, and Clarke. This recording session also took place just two days before Lester returned to New York, and it was the only time Sulieman got the opportunity of playing with Lester in Paris. He himself had a fine quartet at that time, consisting of the legendary piano player Oscar Dennard, Jamil Nasser, and the drummer Buster Smith. They played for a long period of time at Le Chat Qui Pêche in the Rue de la Huchette in the middle of the Latin quarter.[71]

Lester's stay in Paris was also noteworthy for posterity, since it was here that he gave his best and longest interview. Throughout his career he was interviewed on only a few occasions, but in this interview Lester deals very thoroughly with what he is and stands for, apart from talking about his childhood and his career to the journalist François Postif. "I made a lot of interviews, and among them I made one with Lester Young," Postif recalls.

I used to meet him at the club, and we had some nice discussions and talking, and one day I asked him: "Can I make an interview wtih you for *Jazz Hot?*" And he said: "Okay, no problems. Come tomorrow at 6 p.m. at my hotel."

I remember it was a very cold day, and when I came to his hotel the window was open and it was very cold. Lester was lying in bed. He was drinking port and listening to the record player. I remember it was Count Basie at Newport with "Lester Leaps In."

I had a very big tape recorder. It was not like the K7 tape recorders we're working with now. They are tiny, but this was a big one, very heavy (I think it was a Ferrograph), so I plugged the Ferrograph in the AC and Lester began to talk. I remember he told me: "Can I speak nasty?" And I said: "Okay, no problem." He was very relaxed and very pleased to talk.[72]

The August 1958 interview with Chris Albertson reveals quite clearly that it was recorded with a radio broadcast in view, for Lester uses acceptable language only. In the Postif interview, on the other hand, he pulls no punches and laces his sentences and remarks in a way that is 100 percent his own. One of the things he had not expected to encounter in Europe—and Postif had difficulty in understanding this—was racial discrimination. Lester had clearly been shaken by his experience:

"I'd have left here the other night if I had five hundred dollars. I just can't take that bullshit, you dig? It's all bullshit, and they want everybody who is a Negro to be a Uncle Tom or Uncle Remus or Uncle Sam and I can't make it."

"Not here, you know, not in France," Postif insisted.

"Sh-i-i-t! Shit! Are you kidding? I've been here two weeks, I've been taking up on that. Well, I won't tell you what I know jumped off right here. Seeing is believing and hearing is a bitch. That's a sound—right here in gay Paris. Maybe it wouldn't happen to you, you dig? You're not a black person like I am, you dig? They're gonna take advantage of me. But all I can do is tell you what happened, and I'm not gonna tell you that part of it. But it did happen. By somebody you wouldn't believe, too, a great person. But it's the same all over, you dig? You just fight for your life, that's all. Until death do we part, you got it made. But it's the same way."[73]

Certain things that people said about him bugged him, especially rumors that were circulating that he was a homosexual or a drug addict:

But people do mind—it's so obvious, you know. If you want to speak like that, what the fuck I give a fuck of what you do, what he do, what he does, what nobody do? It's nobody's business!

So why are you going to get into it and say: "Oh, he's an old junky"—Goddam! I go crazy thinking of that! He's an old junky, he's an old funky, he's old funking, and all that shit! That's not nice, you know. Whatever they do, let them do that, enjoy themselves, and get your kicks yourself. Why you envy them because they enjoy themselves? Fuck it, you dig? All I do is smoke some New Orleans cigarettes, that's perfect. No sniff, no shit in my nose and nothing, no, I'll drink and I'll smoke.

But a lot of people think I'm on this. I don't like that. I resent that like a bitch. If I ever find the motherfucker . . . would . . . ivy-divy. . . . Shit, I'd go crazy! Don't put that weight on me, I know what I'm doing.[74]

Lester also talked about his music, about his hopes of coming home to New York once more and recording with strings, and about his ideal band:

I developed my saxophone to play a sound like an alto, make a sound like a tenor, make a sound like a bass and everything, and I'm not through with it all yet. That's why they get all trapped up. They say: "Goddam, I never heard Prez play like this!" That's the way I want them. That's modern, dig? Fuck what you played back in '49. It's what you play today, you dig? So that's why they get lost and walked out. Do you play the same thing every day?

I got a man in New York now, writing some music for me when I get back. I got bass-violin, two cellos and a viola and a French horn. See what I mean? And the three rhythm, you know, goes through that. Umm! I'm gonna take my time, and I'm gonna just try this. Say, if it don't come out right, fuck it. I'll say no. But it's my first time and I always wanted to do that. Norman Granz never did let me make a record with no strings, you know. Yardbird made millions of records with strings. . . .

In my mind, the way I play, I try not to be a repeater pencil, you dig? I'm always loosening spaces, laying out, or something like that. I don't think you'll catch me like that, playing like "Lester Leaps In," or something like that. That's my crip, you know, that type of shit.

I can play a bass clarinet. Wouldn't that upset everything? I'd say that would kind of upset everything, wouldn't it, if I'll bring up a bass clarinet? I can play all those instruments.

Give me my little three rhythm and me—happiness. That's four, the four Mills Brothers. That's for me. I can relax better, you dig? I don't like a whole lotta noise no goddam way. Take them trumpets and trombones and all that shit, fuck it!

I'm looking for something soft right now. Like a little puff that the lady put on her pussy when she cleans up, and shit like that. Soft eyes for me. I can't stand no loud shit, you dig? And the bitches come in a place in New York, and them trumpets would be screaming and shit. The bitches put their fingers in their ears, you know? It's got to be sweetness, man, you dig? Sweetness can be funky, filthy, or anything—but which part do you want?[75]

Postif's ability to make Lester feel secure—combined, surely, with Lester's premonition that he was soon going to die—helped Lester to let it all out in this interview, making it something special among all the interviews he ever gave.

Gradually his strength began to ebb away. Since he was now in considerable pain, but did not want to go to a doctor, he told Benjamin that March 13 would be his last appearance at Le Blue Note, a week earlier than planned. He had to give up plans to join JATP and, on the afternoon of March 13, he telephoned Elaine and asked her to fetch him from the airport the following day. His leaving Paris was celebrated with all due style, and it was visibly a relief for Lester that he was on his way home. "The night before he returned to America the Blue Note gave him a farewell party," James Jones recalls. "He had been saying for some time that he was homesick and anxious to get home, and that night he was happy. When he put on the porkpie hat and long coat, he shook hands all around, even with Ben Benjamin."[76]

"Lester was very ill when he was playing for me. It was almost pathetic," Benjamin himself recalls. "He wanted to go home because he said he couldn't talk to a French doctor. He had ulcers and I'm afraid he drank a little too much."[77]

The flight to New York was one long nightmare for Lester, who was in such pain by this time that he bit his lips until they bled. He also began to bleed internally and to vomit up blood. On his arrival at Idlewild Airport (now called John F. Kennedy Airport), he was so ill and weak that Elaine immediately suggested that he be taken to a hospital. Lester would under no circumstances agree to this and asked instead to be driven home to the Alvin Hotel. Once back in his room, he sat in his usual armchair by the window and looked for the last time at 52nd Street, Broadway and Birdland, while he listened to his indispensable records and chased one drink with the next one. From that afternoon till midnight he drank a bottle of vodka and most of a bottle of bourbon, without eating anything whatsoever.

An hour after midnight Elaine finally rang for help, as Lester, dozing in his bed, began to move his mouth as if he were playing the saxophone. The doctor got there twenty minutes later. Lester died at around 3 A.M. on Sunday, March 15.

The police also arrived. They confiscated Lester's saxophone, a ring, a wallet, and $500 in traveler's checks, as surety for the $76 Lester still owed the hotel, since it was at first feared that Lester had died as the result of violence. The cause of death was quickly ascertained, however, and the confiscated property returned to Mary. "He had technically a condition called oesophagial varicoses," Dr. Cloud explains, "which means varicose veins attached to the oesophagus . . . when they rupture they bleed, they bleed internally. The only way to save somebody is to have them in a hospital where you can put tampons and squeeze it and stop the bleeding. Of course Lester bled all the way across the Atlantic and died in a few hours."[78]

The funeral took place at Universal Chapel on the corner of 52nd Street and Lexington Avenue on March 19. Many people turned up to pay Lester their last respects, including Henry "Red" Allen, Rudi Blesh, Bill Coss, Sonny Greer, Leonard Feather, John Hammond, George Hoefer, Billie Holiday, Jo Jones, Alan Morrison, Timme Rosenkrantz, Jimmy Rushing, Tony Scott, and Billy Taylor. Count Basie's wife, Catherine, came on behalf of the band, since none of them could be present, as they were on tour in California. As for the family, Lee came from Los Angeles, together with their mother, Lizetta. Beverly arrived from Minneapolis, and Mary brought Lester Jr. with her.

"No platitudes came from the Rev. O. D. Dempsey, who gave the eulogy," *Down Beat* wrote. "Dempsey—an assistant to Representative Adam Clayton Powell, and a close friend of Young's—showed a keen insight into the creative drive of the musician, and an appreciation of his significance to younger musicians. Lester, he said, was always seeking the best he could offer."[79]

Billie Holiday had been looking forward to singing at the ceremony, but Mary prevented this, since she was afraid that Billie—who was ashen and obviously in a bad way—would cause a scene. Instead, the blind Al Hibbler sang a piece he had composed for the occasion, "In the Garden," and the trombone player Tyree Glenn, who had played briefly with Lester the previous year, played a beautiful muted "Just A-Wearyin' for You." After this J. C. Higginbotham, Milt Hinton, Illinois Jacquet, Budd Johnson, Jimmy Jones, Ed Lewis, Jimmy Rushing, Buddy Tate, Earle Warren, and Dicky Wells bore out the coffin, which was then laid to rest in Evergreen Cemetery in Queens.

In the days that followed the announcement of Lester's death, many people, both in writing and orally, expressed their deep grief at losing him. Thad Jones can suitably, on their behalf, round off by giving a short description of the man and some of his own thoughts on the conditions under which black musicians, Lester included, have always had to live:

The black musicians seem to be the ones who suffer the most for their art. They suffer with it and they suffer because of it. It seems that every time one of them will become an artist in a musical sense, then he has to take on that extra burden. Maybe that's why the music comes out the way it does. Without that the music will be ordinary. Maybe without the pain and the humiliation, the rejection, the fighting for recognition, the constant struggle, the music itself will be without vitality. Who knows? I would hate to think that that would be it. I would like to feel that it was because of the love that the person has in him that creates this very unusual, this very vital, this very beautiful expression.

Where Lester is now he must know that the path he carved out is being walked on by many people of every instrument. Lester was a very majestic player. He didn't have to write a long dissertation to make a monumental speech, because everything he said had the stamp of royalty on it. No matter how spare he was, it was stamped with royalty and it was stamped with dignity. He was one of the first people that utilized space in his music. He felt that there was beauty in space and flurried it with ideas and flurried it with design.

I can only say that he is truly missed, really. Not only for his musicianship, but also because of him as a person. The world is much sadder without him.[80]

APPENDIX A
List of Jobs and Engagements

Information listed here is derived from several sources. Some comes from interviews, but most of the jobs in the 1934–56 period were listed in every issue of journals such as *Down Beat, New York Amsterdam News,* and *Chicago Defender;* other facts can be found in various concert reviews in such magazines as *Melody Maker, Metronome, Variety,* or local newspapers. To complete the list for Lester Young's stay with Count Basie I have borrowed some data from the band itinerary in Chris Sheridan's *Count Basie: A Bio-Discography* (Greenwood Press, 1986) as well as Count Basie and Albert Murray's *Good Morning Blues* (Random House, 1985), both of which proved very helpful.

Nov. 1919–Oct. 1926	*Billy Young Band*
Nov. 1919–Nov. 1921	On tour with Hagenbeck & Wallace Circus
Nov. 1921–Apr. 1922	On tour via TOBA circuit
Apr.–Nov. 1922	On tour with Hagenbeck & Wallace Circus
Nov. 1922–Apr. 1923	On tour via TOBA circuit
Apr.–Nov. 1923	On tour with Hagenbeck & Wallace Circus
Nov. 1923–Apr. 1924	Warren, Ark.

Apr.–Nov. 1924	On tour with Billy Clark's Carnival Show to Indianapolis, Ind., Seattle, Wash., Sandgap, Ky., Lexington, Ky., Bowling Green, Ky., Knoxville, Tenn., Harlem, Ky., Chattanooga, Tenn., Tiptonville, Tenn., Flomaton, Ala., Greenville, Miss., Palatka, Fla., Roanoke, Virginia
Nov. 1924–Apr. 1925	On tour via TOBA circuit to Atlanta, Ga., Greenville, S.C., Pensacola, Fla., Columbus, Ga., Tampa, Fla., Lakeland, Fla., Mobile, Ala.
Apr.–Nov. 1925	On tour with a carnival show
Nov. 1925–Apr. 1926	Minneapolis, Minn.
Apr.–Oct. 1926	On tour with Lackman & Carson Show to Carbondale, Ill., El Reno, Okla., a.o.
Nov. 1926–Nov. 1927	*New Orleans Strutters* Radison Hotel, Minneapolis, Minn. St. Paul Hotel, Minneapolis, Minn. Tour to the Dakotas
Nov. 1927–Jan. 1928	*Young Family Band* Tour to Salina, Kans.
Jan. 1928–Jan. 1929	*Art Bronson's Bostonians* Tours to the Dakotas, Nebraska, Colorado, Kansas
Jan.–Autumn 1929	*Young Family Band* Albuquerque, N.Mex. Tour through New Mexico and Arizona and to Aldrich Theater, Oklahoma City, Okla., Phoenix, Ariz.
Winter 1929–1930	*Eddie Barefield-Lester Young Duo* Minneapolis, Minn.
c. Mar.–May 1930	*Walter Page's Blue Devils* Ritz Ballroom, Oklahoma City, Okla.
May–Nov. 1930	*Art Bronson's Bostonians* Tour to Denver, Colo., Scotts Bluff, Nebr., a.o.
Nov. 1930–June 1931	*Eddie Barefield's Orchestra* Nest Club, Minneapolis, Minn.
June–c. Sept. 1931	*Eugene Schuck's Cotton Club Orchestra* Tour through Minnesota

c. Sept. 1931–Spring 1932	*Frank Hines's Orchestra* Nest Club, Minneapolis, Minn. *Paul Cepha's Orchestra* South Side Club, Minneapolis, Minn. *Gene Coy and His Happy Black Aces*
c. Mar. 1932–May 1933	*The Thirteen Original Blue Devils*
Mar.–Apr.	Ritz Ballroom, Oklahoma City, Okla.
May–June	Tour to Oklahoma, Texas, Missouri, Iowa, Kansas, Nebraska, a.o.
June–Sept.	Dreamland Ballroom, Little Rock, Ark.
Oct. 1932–Apr. 1933	Ritz Ballroom, Oklahoma City, Okla.
May	Tour to Kentucky and West Virginia
May–Nov. 1933	*King Oliver and His Orchestra* Tour to Kansas City, Mo., Tulsa, Okla., Kansas, a.o.
Nov. 1933	*Clarence Love's Orchestra* El Torreon Ballroom, Kansas City, Mo.
Dec. 1933–Feb. 1934	*Bennie Moten-George E. Lee Band* Club Harlem, Kansas City, Mo.
Feb.–c. Mar. 25, 1934	*Count Basie and His Cherry Blossoms*
Feb. 1934	Cherry Blossom, Kansas City, Mo.
Mar. 1–c. 25	Terrace Gardens, Little Rock, Ark.
c. Mar. 25–July 15, 1934	*Fletcher Henderson and His Orchestra*
Mar. 31	Detroit, Mich.
Apr. 4	Columbus, Ohio
Apr. 6	Toledo, Ohio
Apr. 8	Savoy Ballroom, Chicago, Ill.
Apr. 9	Davenport, Iowa
Apr. 10	Des Moines, Iowa
Apr. 11	Omaha, Nebr.
Apr. 12	St. Joseph, Mo.
Apr. 13	University of Kansas, Kansas City, Mo.
Apr. 14–May 30	Tour to St. Louis, Mo., Evansville, Ind., Louisville, Ky., Lexington, Ky., Huntington, W.Va., Bluefield, W.Va., Philadelphia, Pa., Charleston, Ind., Wheeling, W.Va.
June 1–7	Apollo Theater, N.Y.C.
June 8–c. 15	On tour

c. July 15–Sept. 1934	*Andy Kirk and His Clouds of Joy* Vanity Fair Club, Kansas City, Mo. Pla-Mor Ballroom, Kansas City, Mo.
Sept.–Nov. 1934	*Rook Ganz's Orchestra* Nest Club, Minneapolis, Minn.
Nov. 1934–c. Feb. 1935	*Boyd Atkins's Orchestra* Cotton Club, Minneapolis, Minn.
c. Mar.–Apr. 1935	Freelance in Kansas City, Mo., at the Sunset Club and the Subway
Apr.–May 1935	Yellow Front Saloon, Kansas City, Mo.
June 1935–Feb. 1936	*Rook Ganz's Orchestra* Cotton Club, Minneapolis, Minn.
Feb.–Sept. 1936	*Count Basie and His Barons of Rhythm* Reno Club, Kansas City, Mo.
Aug. 1936	Tour to Tulsa, Okla., Muskogee, Okla., Okmulgee, Okla., Oklahoma City, Okla., Wichita, Kans., Omaha, Nebr.
Sept. 9, 1936	Labor Temple, Kansas City, Mo.
Oct. 1936	*Louie Metcalf and His Orchestra* Bedford Ballroom, Brooklyn, N.Y.
Oct. 31, 1936–Dec. 12, 1940	*Count Basie and His Orchestra*
Oct. 31	Paseo Hall, Kansas City, Mo.
Nov. 2	Paseo Hall, Kansas City, Mo.
Nov. 6–Dec. 3	Grand Terrace, Chicago, Ill.
Dec. 7	Vendome Hotel, Buffalo, N.Y.
Dec. 8–23	Tour to Detroit, Mich., New London, Conn., a.o.
Dec. 24, 1936–Jan. 20, 1937	Roseland Ballroom, N.Y.C.
Jan. 22–29	Paramount Theater, N.Y.C.
Feb. 1–12	William Penn Hotel, Pittsburgh, Pa.
Feb. 15–28	Ritz Carlton Hotel, Boston, Mass.
Mar. 1–12	Howard Theater, Washington, D.C., Gettysburg, Pa., Cotton Club, Cincinnati, Ohio
Mar. 13	Energetic Park, Scranton, Pa.
Mar. 14	New York Hot Club, N.Y.C., and Emma Jettick Park, Binghamton, N.Y.
Mar. 15–20	Apollo Theater, N.Y.C.
Mar. 23	Howard Theater, Baltimore, Md.

Mar. 24–31	On tour to Cincinnati Cotton Club, Ohio, Adams Theater, Newark, N.J., Hartford, Conn.
Apr. 1	Savoy Ballroom, N.Y.C.
Apr. 15–12	Nixon Grand Theater, Philadelphia, Pa.
Apr. 23–29	Howard Theater, Washington, D.C.
June 4–10	Apollo Theater, N.Y.C.
June 25–30	Savoy Ballroom, N.Y.C.
July 7	Hartford, Conn.
July 8	Hotel Ritz-Carlton, Boston, Mass.
Aug. 10	Hotel Ritz-Carlton, Boston, Mass.
c. Oct. 21–Nov. 3	Hotel Meadowbrook, Cedar Grove, N.J.
Nov. 5–11	Apollo Theater, N.Y.C.
Nov. 12–18	Howard Theater, Washington, D.C.
Nov. 19	Princeton University, Princeton, N.J.
Nov. 20–30	On tour one-nighters
Dec.	Fox Theater, Detroit, Mich., and Nixon Grand Theater, Philadelphia, Pa.
Jan. 1, 1938	Roseland, Boston, Mass.
Jan. 2	Hamilton Park, Waterbury, Conn.
Jan. 7–8	Astor Theater, N.Y.C.
Jan. 14	Johnson City, N.Y.
Jan. 15	Scranton, Pa.
Jan. 16	Carnegie Hall, N.Y.C., and Savoy Ballroom, N.Y.C.
Jan. 17	The Ritz, Pottsville, Pa.
Jan. 20–26	Loew's State Theater, N.Y.C.
Jan. 28	The Casino, Washington, D.C.
Jan. 30	Harrisburg, Pa.
Feb. 2	The Armory, Baltimore, Md.
Feb. 3	Red Bank, N.J.
Feb. 4	Williams College, Williamstown, Mass.
Feb. 5	Portland, Maine
Feb. 10	Cornell University, Ithaca, N.Y.
Feb. 11	Rochester, N.Y.
Feb. 12	Cornell University, Ithaca, N.Y.
Feb. 17	Wilmington, Del.
Feb. 18	The Strand, Philadelphia, Pa.

Feb. 20	Club Fordham, Bronx, N.Y.C.
Feb. 22	Roseland Ballroom, N.Y.C.
Feb. 25–Mar. 3	Apollo Theater, N.Y.C.
Mar. 4	Wellesley College, Wellesley, Mass.
Mar. 5	Bronx, N.Y.C.
Mar. 7	Washington, D.C.
Mar. 9	Garden City, N.Y.
Mar. 11	Yale University, New Haven, Conn.
Mar. 12	Hartford, Conn.
Mar. 13–19	Savoy Ballroom, N.Y.C.
Mar. 20	Madrid Club, Harrisburg, Pa.
Mar. 22	The Market, Wheeling, W.Va.
Mar. 23	East Market, Akron, Ohio
Mar. 24	Lexington, Ky.
Mar. 25	Cotton Club, Dayton, Ohio
Mar. 26	Vanity Fair, Huntington, W.Va.
Mar. 28	Mount Hope, W.Va.
Mar. 29	Genoa High School, Bluefield, W.Va.
Mar. 30	Charleston, W.Va.
Mar. 31	The Armory, Louisville, Ky.
Apr. 1	Memphis, Tenn.
Apr. 2–4	Masonic Temple, Birmingham, Ala.
Apr. 5	Chattanooga, Tenn.
Apr. 6	Sunset Casino, Atlanta, Ga.
Apr. 7	Bowling Green, Ky.
Apr. 8	St. Louis, Mo.
Apr. 9	Kansas City, Mo.
Apr. 10	Omaha, Nebr.
Apr. 11	New Municipal Auditorium, Kansas City, Mo.
Apr. 12	Topeka, Kans.
Apr. 13	Wichita, Kans.
Apr. 14	Tulsa, Okla.
Apr. 15	Muskogee, Okla.
Apr. 16	Oklahoma City, Okla.
Apr. 17	Forth Worth, Tex.
Apr. 18	Shreveport, La.
Apr. 19	Waco, Tex.

Apr. 20	San Antonio, Tex.
Apr. 21	Houston, Tex.
Apr. 22	Port Arthur, Tex.
Apr. 23	Houston, Tex.
Apr. 25	Galveston, Tex.
Apr. 26	Beaumont, Tex
Apr. 27	Houston, Tex.
Apr. 28	Dallas, Tex.
Apr. 29–May 1	The Casino, Fort Worth, Tex.
May 2	Little Rock, Ark.
May 3	St. Louis, Mo.
May 4	Evansville, Ind.
May 5	Louisville, Ky.
May 6	Lexington, Ky.
May 7	Charleston, W.Va.
May 9	Durham, N.C.
May 13–19	Apollo Theater, N.Y.C.
May 20	Atlantic City, N.J.
May 21	Philadelphia, Pa.
May 22–28	Savoy Ballroom, N.Y.C.
May 29	Asbury Park, N.J., Randall's Island, N.Y.
May 30	Trenton, N.J.
June 1	Washington, D.C.
June 2	Baltimore, Md.
June 3	Brooklyn, N.Y.C.
June 4	Swing Festival, Randall's Island, N.Y.
June 9	Allentown, Pa.
June 11	Lakewood, Pa.
June 12	Swing Festival, Madison Square Garden, N.Y.C.
June 13	Rochester, N.Y.
June 14	Syracuse, N.Y.
June 15	Worcester, Mass.
June 16	Brunswick, Maine
June 17	Cambridge, Mass.
June 18	Narrangansett, R.I.
June 19	Shady Rest, Plainfield, N.J.

June 23	Millsboro, Del.
July 1	Pittsburgh, Pa.
July 2	Jamestown, N.Y.
July 3	Greystone Ballroom, Detroit, Mich.
July 4	Jamestown, N.Y.
July 11–Nov. 12	Famous Door, N.Y.C. Sept. 1, afternoon; also Swing Festival, Randall's Island, N.Y.
Nov. 13	Savoy Ballroom, N.Y.C.
Nov. 17–22	Tour to Cotton Club, Nashville, Tenn., St. Louis, Mo., Howard Theater, Washington, D.C.
Nov. 23–29	Paramount Theater, Newark, N.J.
Nov. 30–Dec. 6	Paramount Theater, N.Y.
Dec. 7	Earle, Philadelphia, Pa.
Dec. 8	Trenton, N.J.
Dec. 9–15	Hippodrome, Baltimore, Md.
Dec. 16	Cleveland, Ohio
Dec. 17	Huntington, W.Va.
Dec. 18	Cleveland, Ohio
Dec. 19	Dayton, Ohio
Dec. 20	Cincinnati, Ohio
Dec. 21	Cleveland, Ohio
Dec. 22	Geneva, N.Y.
Dec. 23	"From Spirituals to Swing" concert, Carnegie Hall, N.Y.C.
Dec. 24–29	The Strand, N.Y.C.
Dec. 30	Reading, Pa.
Dec. 31	Geneva Armory, N.Y.C.
Jan. 2, 1939	White Plains, N.Y.
Jan. 6–12	Nixon Grand Theater, Philadelphia, Pa.
Jan. 13–20	Howard Theater, Washington, D.C.
Jan. 21	Crystal Ballroom, Hartford, Conn.
Jan. 22	Savoy Ballroom, N.Y.C.
Jan. 23	Norfolk, Va.
Jan. 24	Richmond, Va.
Jan. 25	Baltimore, Md.
Jan. 27–Feb. 4	Apollo Theater, N.Y.C.
Feb. 5	Manhattan Club, N.Y.C.

Feb. 7	Pittsburgh, Pa.
Feb. 8	Youngstown, Ohio
Feb. 9	Toledo, Ohio
Feb. 10	Ann Arbor, Mich.
Feb. 11	Flint, Mich.
Feb. 12	Savoy Ballroom, Chicago, Ill.
Feb. 13	Milwaukee, Wis.
Feb. 14	Indianapolis, Ind.
Feb. 15	Akron, Ohio
Feb. 16	Toronto, Canada
Feb. 17	Queen's Union, Ont., Canada
Feb. 18	Paradise Theater, Detroit, Mich.
Feb. 21	Oxford, Ohio
Feb. 23–26	Orpheum, Memphis, Tenn.
Feb. 27–28	Nashville, Tenn.
Mar. 2	Kansas City, Mo.
Mar. 3	Campus Dance, Lawrence, Kans.
Mar. 4	Topeka, Kans.
Mar. 5	St. Louis, Mo.
Mar. 6	Queensboro, Ky.
Mar. 7–8	Chicago, Ill.
Mar. 9	Paradise Theater, Detroit, Mich.
Mar. 10–11	Cleveland, Ohio
Mar. 13–31	Southland Restaurant, Boston, Mass.
Apr. 3	Portland, Maine
Apr. 4	Roseland Ballroom, Boston, Mass.
Apr. 7–13	Apollo Theater, N.Y.C.
Apr. 14–20	Royal Theater, Baltimore, Md.
Apr. 21–27	Howard Theater, Washington, D.C.
Apr. 28	Durham, N.C.
Apr. 30	Danville, Va.
May 1	Civic Auditorium, Raleigh, N.C.
May 2	Petersburg, Va.
May 3	Roanoke, Va.
May 4	Asheville, N.C.
May 5	Columbia Auditorium, Columbia, S.C.
May 8	Savannah, Ga.

May 9	Macon, Ga.
May 10	Charlotte, N.C.
May 12	Columbus, Ga.
May 15	Augusta, Ga.
May 16	Atlanta, Ga.
May 17	Chattanooga, Tenn.
May 20–June 30	Sherman Hotel, Chicago, Ill.
July 1	Lake Shore Club, Chicago, Ill.
July 2	Gary, Ind.
July 3	South Bend, Ind.
July 4	Youngstown, Ohio
July 5	Columbus, Ohio
July 8	Brooklyn, N.Y.
July 10	Atlantic City, N.J.
July 11–Sept. 3	Famous Door, N.Y.C.
Sept. 4	Youngstown, Ohio
Sept. 7–20	Roseland Ballroom, N.Y.C. Sept. 19, afternoon, Manhattan Center, N.Y.C.
Sept. 21	Stamford, Conn.
Sept. 22	Newark, N.J.
Sept. 23	Savoy Ballroom, N.Y.C.
Sept. 24	Buffalo, N.Y.
Sept. 25	Cleveland, Ohio
Sept. 26	Indianapolis, Ind.
Sept. 27	St. Louis, Mo.
Sept. 28	Municipal Auditorium, Kansas City, Mo.
Sept. 29	Omaha, Nebr.
Sept. 30	Denver, Colo.
Oct. 2	Sweets Ballroom, Oakland, Calif.
Oct. 5–11	Paramount Ballroom, Los Angeles, Calif.
Oct. 12	Vogue Ballroom, Los Angeles, Calif.
Oct. 14	San Diego, Calif.
Oct. 16–29	World's Fair, Treasure Island, San Francisco, Calif.
Oct. 31	Sacramento, Calif.
Nov. 1	Stockton, Calif.

Nov. 2	Los Angeles, Calif.
Nov. 3	Glendale, Calif.
Nov. 4	San Bernardino, Calif.
Nov. 9	El Paso, Tex.
Nov. 11–12	Fort Worth, Tex.
Nov. 13	San Antonio, Tex.
Nov. 14	Galveston, Tex.
Nov. 15	Houston, Tex.
Nov. 16	Henderson, Tex.
Nov. 17	Port Arthur, Tex.
Nov. 18	Baton Rouge, La.
Nov. 19	New Orleans, La.
Nov. 20	Monroe, La.
Nov. 21	Little Rock, Ark.
Nov. 22	Birmingham, Ala.
Nov. 23	Atlanta, Ga.
Nov. 24–25	Jacksonville, Fla.
Nov. 27	Macon, Ga.
Nov. 28	Knoxville, Tenn.
Nov. 29	Louisville, Ky.
Nov. 30	Bowling Green, Ky.
Dec. 1	Evansville, Ind.
Dec. 2	Casa Loma Ballroom, St. Louis, Mo.
Dec. 3	Chicago, Ill.
Dec. 4	Detroit, Mich.
Dec. 5	Columbus, Ohio
Dec. 6	Huntington, W.Va.
Dec. 7	Pittsburgh, Pa.
Dec. 8	Baltimore, Md.
Dec. 9	N.Y.C.
Dec. 10	Bridgeport, Conn.
Dec. 14	Trenton, N.J.
Dec. 15	Wilmington, Del.
Dec. 17	N.Y.C.
Dec. 22	Newark, N.J.
Dec. 24	"From Spirituals to Swing" concert, Carnegie Hall, N.Y.C.
Dec. 25	Sunnybrook Ballroom, Pittsburgh, Pa.

Dec. 27	Charleston, W.Va.
Dec. 28	Strassburg, Va.
Dec. 29	Richmond, Va.
Dec. 31	Worcester, Mass.
Jan. 1, 1940	Philadelphia, Pa.
Jan. 6	Brooklyn, N.Y.C.
Jan. 12–18	Apollo Theater, N.Y.C.
Jan. 19–25	Howard Theater, Washington, D.C.
Jan. 26–Feb. 9	Golden Gate Ballroom, N.Y.C.
Feb. 10	Manhattan Center, N.Y.C.
Feb. 11	Baltimore, Md.
Feb. 12	Orange, N.J.
Feb. 13	Roseland Ballroom, Boston, Mass.
Feb. 16	Hamilton, N.Y.
Feb. 17	Rochester, N.Y.
Feb. 18	Waterbury, Conn.
Feb. 19–Mar. 18	Southland Restaurant, Boston, Mass.
Mar. 23	Springfield, Mass.
Mar. 24	Harrisburg, Pa.
Mar. 25	Philadelphia, Pa.
Mar. 26	Milford, Del.
Mar. 27	Newark, N.J.
Mar. 28	Wrentham, Mass.
Mar. 29	Portland, Maine
Mar. 30	Lawrence, Mass.
Mar. 31	Waterbury, Conn.
Apr. 1	Albany, N.Y.
Apr. 2	Roseland Ballroom, Boston, Mass.
Apr. 4–10	Loew's State Theater, N.Y.C.
Apr. 11–17	Flatbush Theater, Brooklyn, N.Y.
Apr. 18–24	Windsor Theater, Bronx, N.Y.
Apr. 25–28	Carlton Theater, Jamaica, Queens, N.Y.
Apr. 30	Abingdon, Va.
May 1	Bluefield, W.Va.
May 2	Beekley, W.Va.
May 3	Charleston, W.Va.
May 4–5	Cincinnati, Ohio

May 6	Lexington, Ky.
May 7	Wheeling, W.Va.
May 8	Morgantown, W.Va.
May 9	Logan, W.Va.
May 10	Dayton, Ohio
May 11	Cleveland, Ohio
May 12	Buffalo, N.Y.
May 13	Pittsburgh, Pa.
May 14	Akron, Ohio
May 15	Bradford, Pa.
May 16	Baltimore, Md.
May 17	Philadelphia, Pa.
May 18	Paterson, N.J.
May 20	Lancaster, Pa.
May 21	Atlantic City, N.J.
May 24–30	Apollo Theater, N.Y.C.
June 15	Newark, N.J.
June 17	Rocky Mountain, N.C.
June 18	Charleston, N.C.
June 19	Charlotte, N.C.
June 20	Roanoke, Va.
June 21	Winston-Salem, N.C.
June 22–23	Washington, D.C.
June 24	Buckaroo Beach, Va.
June 25	Petersburg, Va.
June 26	Asheville, N.C.
June 27	Johnson City, Tenn.
June 28	Moonlite Gardens, and Cotton Club, Cincinnati, Ohio
June 29	Jamestown, N.Y.
June 30	Vermillion, Ohio
July 1	Yankee Lake, Ohio
July 3	Evansville, Ind.
July 5–11	Regal Theater, Chicago, Ill.
July 12–19	Coney Island, N.Y.
July 20	Dayton, Ohio
July 22	Greystone Ballroom, Detroit, Mich.
July 23	South Bend, Ind.

July 24	Richmond, Ind.
July 25	Paducah, Ky.
July 26	Memphis, Tenn.
July 27	St. Louis, Mo.
July 28	Tulsa, Okla.
July 29	Municipal Auditorium, Kansas City, Mo.
July 30	Tulsa, Okla.
July 31	Little Rock, Ark.
Aug. 1–7	Chicago, Ill.
Aug. 9	State Lake Theater, Chicago, Ill.
Aug. 10–11	Savoy Ballroom, Chicago, Ill.
Aug. 13	State Lake Theater, Chicago, Ill.
Aug. 16	Gary, Ind.
Aug. 17	Kansas City, Mo.
Aug. 18	Topeka, Kans.
Aug. 19	Denver, Colo.
Aug. 22–Sept. 8	Paramount Theater, Los Angeles, Calif.
Sept. 9	Oakland, Calif.
Sept. 10	Hollywood, Calif.
Sept. 13	Oklahoma City, Okla.
Sept. 14	Wichita Falls, Tex.
Sept. 15	Dallas, Tex.
Sept. 16	Houston, Tex.
Sept. 17	Henderson, Tex.
Sept. 18	Galveston, Tex.
Sept. 19	Shreveport, La.
Sept. 20	Port Arthur, Tex.
Sept. 22	New Orleans, La.
Sept. 23	Monroe, La.
Sept. 24	Greenville, Miss.
Sept. 25	Birmingham, Ala.
Sept. 26	Atlanta, Ga.
Sept. 29	Auburn, Ala.
Sept. 30	Savannah, Ga.
Oct. 1	Columbus, Ga.
Oct. 2	Greenville, S.C.
Oct. 3	Florence, S.C.

Oct. 4	Washington, D.C.
Oct. 5	Rochester, N.Y.
Oct. 6	Canton, Ohio
Oct. 7	Detroit, Mich.
Oct. 8	Cleveland, Ohio
Oct. 9	Cincinnati, Ohio
Oct. 10	Bluefield, W.Va.
Oct. 11	Beekley, W.Va,
Oct. 12	Charleston, W.Va.
Oct. 14	Raleigh, N.C.
Oct. 15	Richmond, Va.
Oct. 18–24	Apollo Theater, N.Y.C.
Oct. 25	Baltimore, Md.
Oct. 27	Lyric Theater, Bridgeport, Conn.
Oct. 29	Lake Champagne, Conn.
Nov. 8	Manchester, N.H.
Nov. 9	Portland, Mass.
Nov. 10	Taunton, Mass.
Nov. 11	Boston, Mass.
Nov. 12	Gardner, Mass.
Nov. 13	Claremont, Mass.
Nov. 23	New Haven, Conn.
Nov. 25	Salisbury, Md.
Nov. 28	Philadelphia, Pa.
Nov. 30–Dec. 12	Savoy Ballroom, N.Y.C.
Dec. 19	Make Believe Ballroom, broadcast over WNEW, N.Y.C.
Dec. 22, 1940	*Hot Lips Page and His Orchestra,* broadcast over WNEW, N.Y.C.
Dec. 29, 1940–Mar. 17, 1941	*Freelance Sessions in N.Y.C.*
Dec. 29	Matinee Jam Session, Village Vanguard, N.Y.C.
Jan. 12, 1941	Matinee Jam Session, Village Vanguard, N.Y.C.
Jan. 26	Jimmy Ryan's, N.Y.C.
Feb 27–Mar. 17	Kelly's Stable, N.Y.C.
May–Nov., 1941	*Lee Young's Esquires of Rhythm* Club Capri, Los Angeles, Calif.
Dec. 1, 1941–Feb. 8, 1943	*Lee and Lester Young's Band*

Dec. 1, 1941–c. Apr. 20, 1942	Club Capri, Los Angeles, Calif.
May 1–c. Aug. 25	Trouville Club, Hollywood, Calif.
Sept. 1, 1942–Feb. 6, 1943	Café Society, Downtown, N.Y.C.
Feb. 8	Press Club Auditorium, Washington, D.C.
Mar.–Sept. 30, 1943	*Al Sears Bigband*
Mar.–Apr. 10	Renaissance Casino, N.Y.C.
Apr. 13–Sept. 30	On tour for USO to military bases all over the United States
Oct. 8–14, 1943	*Count Basie and His Orchestra* Apollo Theater, N.Y.C.
c. Oct. 20–Dec. 1, 1943	*Dizzy Gillespie Quintet* Onyx Club, N.Y.C.
c. Dec. 1, 1943–Sept. 24, 1944	*Count Basie and His Orchestra*
c. Dec. 1, 1943–Jan. 1, 1944	Lincoln Hotel, N.Y.C.
Jan. 13–19	Adams Theater, Newark, N.J.
Jan. 21–27	Stanley Hotel, Pittsburgh, Pa.
Jan. 28–Feb. 2	Club Paradise, Detroit, Mich.
Feb. 4–10	Riverside Club, Milwaukee, Wis.
Feb. 12–13	Castle Farms, Cincinnati, Ohio
Feb. 25–Mar. 2	Fay's Club, Philaelphia, Pa.
Mar. 8–Apr. 1	Roxy Theater, N.Y.C.
Apr. 2	Fats Waller Memorial Concert, Carnegie Hall, N.Y.C.
Apr. 6–May 31	Lincoln Hotel, N.Y.C.
June 2–4	Metropolitan Theater, Providence, R.I.
June 5–7	Plymouth Theater, Worcester, Mass.
June 9–11	State Theater, Hartford, Conn.
June 12–22	Regal Theater, Chicago, Ill.
July 4–6	Palace Theater, Columbus, Ohio
July 7–13	Palace Theater, Cleveland, Ohio
July 14–17	Palace Theater, Youngstown, Ohio
July 21–27	Tower Theater, Kansas City, Mo.
Aug. 1–14	Orpheum Theater, Los Angeles, Calif.
Aug. 16–22	Golden Gate Ballroom, San Francisco, Calif.
Aug. 24–30	Orpheum Theater, Oakland, Calif.
Sept. 3–4	Sweet's, Oakland, Calif.
Sept. 7–24	Plantation Club, Los Angeles, Calif.

Jan. 28–June 22, 1946	*Jazz at the Philharmonic*
Jan. 28	Philharmonic Auditorium, Los Angeles, Calif.
c. Mar. 15	AFRS radio broadcast, Los Angeles, Calif.
c. Apr. 22, afternoon	AFRS radio broadcast, Los Angeles, Calif.
Apr. 22	Embassy Auditorium, Los Angeles, Calif.
Apr. 23	Royce Hall Auditorium, Los Angeles, Calif.
Apr. 24–May 13	On tour through California to San Diego, San Francisco, a.o.
May 14	Civic Opera House, Chicago, Ill.
May 27	Carnegie Hall, N.Y.C.
June 3	Carnegie Hall, N.Y.C.
June 17	Carnegie Hall, N.Y.C.
June 22	Civic Opera House, Chicago, Ill.
July 17–25	Spotlite Club, N.Y.C.
Oct. 1946–June 1949	*Lester Young Band*
Oct. 3–Dec. 1	Hurricane Lounge, Chicago, Ill.
Oct. 24	Also JATP concert at Chicago's Civic Opera House
Dec. 3–24	Three Deuces, N.Y.C.
Dec. 25, 1946–Feb. 1947	On tour
Dec. 25	Huntington, W.Va.
Dec. 26	Richmond, Ky.
Dec. 27	Cincinnati, Ohio
Dec. 29	Buffalo, N.Y.
Dec. 30	Trenton, N.J.
Dec. 31	Newark, N.J.
Jan. 3, 1947	Youngstown, Ohio
Jan. 5	Savoy Ballroom, N.Y.C.
Feb. 5	Tulsa, Okla.
Feb. 6	Dallas, Tex.
Feb. 7	Fort Worth, Tex.
Feb. 10	Fresno, Calif.
Feb. 11	San Francisco, Calif.
Feb. 12	Vallejo, Calif.

Feb. 13	Richmond, Calif.
Feb. 14	Bakersfield, Calif.
Feb. 15	El Cintro, Calif.
Feb. 21–Mar. 3	Club Riviera, St. Louis, Mo.
Mar. 7–13	Club Paradise, Detroit, Mich.
Mar. 14–31	On tour
Apr. 11–24	Club Bali, Washington, D.C.
May 11–17	Savoy Ballroom, N.Y.C.
May 18–25	Superior Club, Newark, N.J.
May 26–June 8	Savoy Club, Boston, Mass.
June 12–25	Baby Grand, N.Y.C.
June 26–July 17	On tour
July 18–26	Zanzibar, Philadelphia, Pa.
July 27–Aug. 15	On tour
Aug. 16–Sept. 1	Stage Door, Milwaukee, Wis.
Sept. 5–18	Club Bali, Washington, D.C.
Sept. 19–Oct. 8	Famous Door, N.Y.C.
Oct. 9–15	Downbeat Club, N.Y.C.
Oct. 17–23	Hotel Astoria, Baltimore, Md.
Oct. 25–30	Savoy Ballroom, N.Y.C.
Nov. 8	Town Hall, N.Y.C.
Nov. 13–30	Downbeat Club, N.Y.C.
Dec. 1–7	Argyle Club, Chicago, Ill.
Dec. 8–16	On tour
Dec. 25–26	Wintergarden, Bronx, N.Y.
Dec. 27	Elizabeth, N.J.
Jan. 7, 1947–Feb. 16, 1948	Washington Social Club, Seattle, Wash.
Feb. 17–Mar. 1	Blackshears Club, San Francisco, Calif.
Mar. 2–Apr. 1	On tour
Apr. 2–15	Club Bali, Washington, D.C.
Apr. 16–June 18	On tour
June 19–July 8	Emerson's Café, Philadelphia, Pa.
July 9–15	Apollo Theater, N.Y.C.
July 30–Aug. 5	Howard Theater, Washington, D.C.
Aug. 8–Sept. 19	On tour
Sept. 20–Oct. 2	Emerson's Café, Philadelphia, Pa.
Oct. 8–13	Club Bali, Washington, D.C.

Nov. 11–17	Café Tijuana, Cleveland, Ohio
Nov. 25–Dec. 8	Royal Roost, N.Y.C.
Dec. 9, 1948–Feb. 13, 1949	On tour
Jan. 9	Auditorium, Saginaw, Mich.
Jan. 10	Eaton Auditorium, Toronto, Canada
Feb. 14–Mar. 13	Blue Note, Chicago, Ill.
Mar. 17–Apr. 14	Royal Roost, N.Y.C.
Apr. 9	Also Carnegie Hall, N.Y.C.
June 6	Carnegie Hall, N.Y.C.
Sept. 17–Oct. 31, 1949	*Jazz at the Philharmonic*
Sept. 17	Carnegie Hall, N.Y.C.
Oct. 14	Civic Opera House, Chicago, Ill.
Oct. 25	Civic Auditorium, Pasadena, Calif.
Oct. 31	Shrine Auditorium, Los Angeles, Calif.
Dec. 15, 1949–May 12, 1950	*Lester Young Band*
Dec. 15, 1949–Jan. 25, 1950	Birdland, N.Y.C.
Feb. 12	Esquire Dance Hall, N.Y.C.
Feb. 18	Laurel Hall, Newark, N.J.
Feb. 20–25	Savoy Ballroom, N.Y.C.
Mar. 4–30	Birdland, N.Y.C.
Mar. 31	Audubon Ballroom, N.Y.C.
Apr. 2–15	Argyle Club, Chicago, Ill.
Apr. 17–24	421 Club, Philadelphia, Pa.
Apr. 28–May 12	Birdland, N.Y.C.
Sept. 15–Oct. 31, 1950	*Jazz at the Philharmonic*
Sept. 15	Bushnell Memorial Auditorium, Hartford, Conn.
Sept. 16	Carnegie Hall, N.Y.C.
Oct. 15	Civic Opera House, Chicago, Ill.
Oct. 31	Shrine Auditorium, Los Angeles, Calif.

Besides these cities the tour went to Atlanta, Ga., Baltimore, Md., Boston, Mass., Buffalo, N.Y., Cincinnati, Ohio, Cleveland, Ohio, Columbus, Ohio, Dallas, Tex., Dayton, Ohio, Denver, Colo., Des Moines, Iowa, Detroit, Mich., Flint, Mich., Houston, Tex., Indianapolis, Ind., Kansas City, Mo., Milwaukee, Wis., Minneapolis, Minn., Montreal, Canada, New Orleans, La., Newark, N.J., Norfolk, Va., Oakland, Calif., Omaha, Nebr., Philadelphia, Pa., Pittsburgh, Pa., Portland, Ore., Sacramento, Calif., St. Louis, Mo., Salt Lake City, Utah, San Antonio, Tex., San Francisco, Calif., Seattle, Wash., Syracuse, N.Y., Toronto, Canada, Vancouver, B.C., Washington, D.C., Winnipeg, Canada.

Nov. 16, 1950–Sept. 13, 1951	*Lester Young Band*
Nov. 16–22	Town Tavern, Toronto, Canada
Jan. 4–24, 1951	Birdland, N.Y.C.
Feb. 8–12	Philadelphia, Pa.
Feb. 21	Carnegie Hall, N.Y.C.
Feb. 24–Mar. 17	Birdland, N.Y.C.
May 10–23	Birdland, N.Y.C.
June 18–23	Showboat, Philadelphia, Pa.
June 24–30	Savoy Ballroom, N.Y.C.
Aug. 2–8	Birdland, N.Y.C.
Aug. 10–23	Blue Note, Chicago, Ill.
Aug. 25–Sept. 13	Birdland, N.Y.C.
Sept. 14–Nov. 22, 1951	*Jazz at the Philharmonic*
Sept. 14	Bushnell Memorial Auditorium, Hartford, Conn.
Sept. 15	Mosque Theater, Newark, N.J., and Carnegie Hall, N.Y.C.
Oct. 30	Music Hall, Houston, Tex.
Nov. 22	Russ Auditorium, San Diego, Calif.

Besides these cities the tour went to R.P.I. Field House, Albany, N.Y., Municipal Auditorium, Atlanta, Ga., Coliseum, Baltimore, Md., Symphony Hall, Boston, Mass., Academy of Music, Brooklyn, N.Y., Kleinhan's Music Hall, Buffalo, N.Y., Taft Theater, Cincinnati, Ohio, Music Hall, Cleveland, Ohio, University of Missouri, Field House, Columbus, Ohio, Fair Park Auditorium, Dallas, Tex., Memorial Auditorium, Dayton, Ohio, City Auditorium, Denver, Colo., RKO Downtown Theater, Detroit, Mich., Liberty Hall, El Paso, Tex., I.M.A. Auditorium, Flint, Mich., Murat Theater, Indianapolis, Ind., Music Hall, Kansas City, Mo., Municipal Auditorium, Long Beach, Calif., Shrine Auditorium, Los Angeles, Calif., Memorial Auditorium, Louisville, Ky., Dinner Key Auditorium, Miami, Fla., Milwaukee Auditorium, Milwaukee, Wis., Municipal Auditorium, Minneapolis, Minn., Municipal Auditorium, Norfolk, Va., Auditorium, Arena, Oakland, Calif., Academy of Music, Philadelphia, Pa., Syria Mosque, Pittsburgh, Pa., Municipal Auditorium, Portland, Ore., Mosque Theater, Richmond, Va., Municipal Auditorium, Sacramento, Calif., Keil Opera House, St. Louis, Mo., Municipal Auditorium, San Antonio, Tex., Civic Auditorium, San Francisco, Calif., Municipal Auditorium, Seattle, Wash., City Auditorium, Toledo, Ohio, National Guard Armory, Washington, D.C.

Dec. 3–8	421 Club, Philadelphia, Pa.
Jan. 1952	Birdland, N.Y.C.
Mar. 26–Apr. 21, 1952	*Jazz at the Philharmonic*

Mar. 27–30	Konserthuset, Stockholm, Sweden
Mar. 31	Göteborg, Sweden
Apr. 1–2	KB-Hallen, Copenhagen, Denmark
Apr. 3	Stadsteatern, Malmö, Sweden
Apr. 6–9	Salle Pleyel, Paris, France
Apr. 10	Brussels, Belgium
Apr. 11	The Hague, The Netherlands
Apr. 12–13	Amsterdam, The Netherlands
Apr. 14–15	Zurich, Switzerland
Apr. 16	Lausanne, Switzerland
Apr. 17	Geneva, Switzerland
Apr. 18–19	Frankfurt, Germany
Apr. 20	Hamburg, Germany
April 25, 1952–Aug. 25, 1952	*Lester Young Band*
Apr. 25–June 29	Birdland, N.Y.C.
June 30–July 5	Washington, D.C.
July 7–12	Pep's Musical Bar, Philadelphia, Pa.
July 13–Aug. 25	Birdland, N.Y.C.
Sept. 12–Oct. 31, 1952	*Jazz at the Philharmonic*
Sept. 12	Bushnell Memorial Auditorium, Hartford, Conn.
Sept. 13	Carnegie Hall, N.Y.C.
Sept. 14	National Guard Armory, Washington, D.C.
Sept. 15	Municipal Auditorium, Norfolk, Va.
Sept. 16	Mosque Theater, Richmond, Va.
Sept. 17	Coliseum, Baltimore, Md.
Sept. 20	Academy of Music, Philadelphia, Pa.
Oct. 11	Civic Opera House, Chicago, Ill.
Oct. 31	Shrine Auditorium, Los Angeles, Calif.

Besides these cities the tour went to Bloomington, Ill., Boston, Mass., Bridgeport, Conn., Brooklyn, N.Y., Buffalo, N.Y., Cincinnati, Ohio, Cleveland, Ohio, Columbus, Ohio, Dallas, Tex., Davenport, Iowa, Dayton, Ohio, Denver, Colo., Des Moines, Iowa, Detroit, Mich., El Paso, Tex., Flint, Mich., Fort Lauderdale, Fla., Grand Rapids, Mich., Harrisburg, Pa., Indianapolis, Ind., Joplin, Mo., Kansas City, Mo., Kingston, Ont., Long Beach, Calif., Louisville, Ky., Miami, Fla., Milwaukee, Wis., Minneapolis, Minn., Newark, N.J., Oakland, Calif., Omaha, Nebr., Peoria, Ariz., Pittsburgh, Pa., Portland, Ore., Richmond, Va., Sacramento, Calif., St. Louis, Mo., San Antonio, Tex., San Diego, Calif., San Francisco, Calif., San José, Calif., Seattle, Wash., Topeka, Kans., Toledo, Ohio, Toronto, Canada, Vancouver, B.C., Wichita, Kans.

Dec. 1952–Feb. 13, 1953	*Lester Young Band*
Dec. 1952–Jan 21, 1953	Birdland, N.Y.C
Jan. 26–Feb. 13	Hi-Hat, Boston, Mass.
Feb. 15–Mar. 23, 1953	*Jazz at the Philharmonic*
Feb. 16–17	Konserthuset, Stockholm, Sweden
Feb. 18	Uppsala, Sweden
Feb. 19	Konserthuset, Stockholm, Sweden
Feb. 20	Göteborg, Sweden
Feb. 21–22	Colosseum, Oslo, Norway
Feb. 23	Helsinki, Finland
Feb. 24	KB-Hallen, Copenhagen, Denmark
Feb. 25	M.F.F. Stadion, Malmö, Sweden
Feb. 26	Ernst-Merck-Halle, Hamburg, Germany
Feb. 27	Munich, Germany
Feb. 28	Frankfurt, Germany
Mar. 1	Berlin, Germany
Mar. 2	Frankfurt, Germany
Mar. 3	Theatre Alhambra, Paris, France
Mar. 7	Salle Pleyel, Paris, France
Mar. 8	Gaumont State Theater, Kilburn, London, England
Mar. 10	Basle, Switzerland
Mar. 16	Teatro Augustus, Genoa, Italy
Mar. 17	Teatro Reposi, Turin, Italy
Mar. 18–19	Teatro Manzini, Milan, Italy
Mar. 20	Teatro Duse, Bologna, Italy
Mar. 22	Dublin, Ireland
Apr.–Sept. 1953	*Lester Young Band*
Apr.	Birdland, N.Y.C.
May	Band Box, N.Y.C.
July 2–15	Birdland, N.Y.C.
Sept.	Birdland, N.Y.C.
Sept. 11–Oct. 22, 1953	*Jazz at the Philharmonic*
Sept. 11	Bushnell Memorial Auditorium, Hartford, Conn.
Sept. 19	Carnegie Hall, N.Y.C.

Oct. 22	Shrine Auditorium, Los Angeles, Calif.
Oct. 23, 1953–Sept. 6, 1954	*Lester Young Band*
Oct. 23–Nov. 21	Bee Hive Lounge, Chicago, Ill.
Nov. 26–Dec. 2	Birdland N.Y.C.
Dec. 7–13	Emerson's Café, Philadelphia, Pa.
Dec. 14–20	Hi-Hat, Boston, Mass.
Jan. 21–27, 1954	Birdland N.Y.C.
Feb. 19–27	Midtown Hotel, St. Louis, Mo.
Mar. 1–7	Oasis Club, Hollywood, Calif.
Mar. 9–29	Black Hawk, San Francisco, Calif.
Apr. 1–28	On tour
Apr. 29–May 13	Birdland N.Y.C.
May 14–23	Comedy Night Club, Baltimore, Md.
June 1–6	The Loop, Cleveland, Ohio
July 1–20	Birdland, N.Y.C.
July 17–18	*Newport Jazz Festival,* Newport, R.I.
Aug. 1–8	Vic's Lounge, Minneapolis, Minn.
Aug. 30–Sept. 6	The Loop, Cleveland, Ohio
Sept. 25–26, 1954	*Patricia Music* tour
Sept. 25	Carnegie Hall, N.Y.C.
Sept. 26	Boston, Mass.
Oct. 1954–Jan. 1955	*Lester Young Band and freelance sessions*
Oct. 1–Nov. 15	Blue Note, Chicago, Ill.
Nov. 18–Dec. 1	Birdland N.Y.C.
Dec. 15–29	Birdland N.Y.C.
Jan. 1–15, 1955	Pep's Musical Bar, Philadelphia, Pa.
Feb. 11–Mar. 7, 1955	*Birdland Stars '55*
Feb. 11	Carnegie Hall, N.Y.C.
Feb. 20	Civic Opera House, Chicago, Ill.
Feb. 25	Municipal Auditorium, Topeka, Kans.
Mar. 3	Paramount Theater, Brooklyn, N.Y.

Besides these cities the tour went to Mosque Theater, Newark, N.J., Boston, Mass., Richmond, Va., Norfolk, Va., Raleigh, N.C., Philadelphia, Pa., Rochester, N.Y.

Apr.–Aug. 1955	*Lester Young Band and freelance sessions*
Apr.	Birdland N.Y.C.
Apr. 2	Also Carnegie Hall, N.Y.C.
May 5–23	Birdland N.Y.C.
May 6	Also Carnegie Hall, N.Y.C.
May 31–June 6	Copa Casino, Buffalo, N.Y.
June 20–26	Pep's Musical Bar, Buffalo, N.Y.
July 17	*Newport Jazz Festival,* Newport, R.I.
July 22–Aug. 11	Bee Hive, Chicago, Ill.
Sept. 16–Oct. 31, 1955	*Jazz at the Philharmonic*
Sept. 16	Bushnell Memorial Auditorium, Hartford, Conn.
Sept. 17	Carnegie Hall, N.Y.C.
Sept. 18	Boston, Mass.
Sept. 19	Paramount Theater, Brooklyn. N.Y.
Oct. 2	Civic Opera House, Chicago, Ill.
Oct. 23	Civic Auditorium, Seattle, Wash.
Oct. 28	San Diego, Calif.
Oct. 31	Shrine Auditorium, Los Angeles, Calif.

Besides these cities the tour went to Buffalo, N.Y., Cincinnati, Ohio, Cleveland, Ohio, Columbus, Ohio, Dallas, Tex., Dayton, Ohio, Denver, Colo., Detroit, Mich., Houston, Tex., Indianapolis, Ind., Kansas City, Mo., Long Beach, Calif., Louisville, Ky., Milwaukee, Wis., Minneapolis, Minn., Montreal, Canada, Norfolk, Va., Oakland, Calif., Oklahoma City, Okla., Philadelphia, Pa., Pittsburgh, Pa., Portland, Ore., Sacramento, Calif., San Antonio, Tex., San Francisco, Calif., San José, Calif., St. Louis, Mo., Toledo, Ohio, Toronto, Canada, Vancouver, B.C., Washington, D.C.

Dec. 8–22	Birdland N.Y.C.
Feb. 3–27, 1956	*Birdland Stars '56*
Feb. 3	County Center, White Plains, N.Y., and Carnegie Hall, N.Y.C.
Feb. 4	Carnegie Hall, N.Y.C.
Feb. 18	Civic Opera House, Chicago, Ill.

Besides these cities the tour went to Mosque Theater, Newark, N.J., St. Louis, Mo., Kansas City, Mo., Washington, D.C., a.o.

Mar.–Nov. 1956	*Lester Young Band and freelance sessions*
Mar. 1–15	Club Basin Street, N.Y.C.
Mar.–Apr.	Pep's Musical Bar, Philadelphia, Pa.
Apr. 20–May 4	Bee Hive Lounge, Chicago, Ill.
May 5–10	Roosevelt Hotel, Detroit, Mich.
May 11–June 6	Birdland, N.Y.C.
June 11–18	Town Tavern, Toronto, Canada
Aug. 1–15	Birdland N.Y.C.
Aug. 22–Sept. 3	Café Bohemia, N.Y.C.
Aug. 24	Also *New York Jazz Festival,* Randall's Island, N.Y.
Sept. 5–19	Birdland, N.Y.C.
Oct. 12–25	Club St. Germain, Paris, France
Oct. 26–Nov. 1	On tour in France
Nov. 2–25, 1956	*Birdland Show*
Nov. 2–3	Salle Pleyel, Paris, France
Nov. 4	Haarlem and Amsterdam, The Netherlands
Nov. 5	Brussels, Belgium
Nov. 6	Düsseldorf, Germany
Nov. 7	Sportpalast, Berlin, Germany
Nov. 8	Mannheim, Germany
Nov. 9	Frankfurt, Germany
Nov. 10	Hamburg, Germany
Nov. 11	Munich, Germany
Nov. 12	Stadthalle, Freiburg, Germany
Nov. 13	Konserthuset, Stockholm, Sweden
Nov. 14	KB-Hallen, Copenhagen, Denmark
Nov. 16	Lille, France
Nov. 17	Salle Pleyel, Paris, France
Nov. 18	Strasbourg, France
Nov. 19	Kongreßhaus, Zurich, Switzerland
Nov. 20	Victoria Hall, Geneva, Switzerland
Nov. 21	Musiksaal, Basle, Switzerland
Nov. 22	Teatro di via Manzoni, Turin, Italy
Nov. 23	Teatro Nuovo, Turin, Italy
Nov. 24	Marseilles, France

Nov. 25	Lyons, France
Dec. 1956–Jan. 1957	*Freelance sessions*
Dec. 3–8	Olivia Davis's Patio Lounge, Washington, D.C.
Dec. 15, 1956–Jan. 4, 1957	Café Bohemia, N.Y.C.
Jan. 5–11	The Loop, Cleveland, Ohio
Jan. 12–18	Town Tavern, Toronto, Canada
Feb. 15–Mar. 17, 1957	*Birdland Stars '57*
Feb. 15	Carnegie Hall, N.Y.C.
Mar. 9	Civic Opera House, Chicago, Ill.
Mar. 10	Massey Hall, Toronto, Canada
Mar. 11	Forum, Montreal, Canada
Mar. 12	Taft Theater, Cincinnati, Ohio
Mar. 16	Paramount Theater, Brooklyn, N.Y.
Mar. 17	Washington, D.C.
Apr.–Sept. 1957	*Freelance sessions*
Apr. 1–7	Blue Note, Philadelphia, Pa.
Apr. 28	Opera House, San Francisco, Calif.
May 6–12	Small's Paradise, N.Y.C.
May	Town Tavern, Toronto, Canada
July 7	*Newport Jazz Festival,* Newport, R.I.
July 13	Casino Moderne, Chicago, Ill.
Aug. 22	Hollywood Bowl, Hollywood, Calif.
Sept. 1–7	Town Tavern, Toronto, Canada
Sept. 14–Oct. 7, 1957	*Jazz at the Philharmonic*
Sept. 14	Carnegie Hall, N.Y.C.
Sept. 15	Symphony Hall, Boston, Mass.
Sept. 16	Bushnell Memorial Auditorium, Hartford, Conn.
Sept. 17	Massey Hall, Toronto, Canada
Sept. 18	Music Hall, Cleveland, Ohio
Sept. 19	Syria Mosque, Pittsburgh, Pa.
Sept. 20	Ford Auditorium, Detroit, Mich.
Sept. 21	Academy of Music, Philadelphia, Pa.
Sept. 22	Keil Auditorium, St. Louis, Mo.
Sept. 23	Murat Theater, Indianapolis, Ind.
Sept, 24	Taft Theater, Cincinnati, Ohio
Sept. 26	Music Hall, Kansas City, Mo.

Sept. 27	Municipal Auditorium, Minneapolis, Minn.
Sept. 28	Milwaukee Auditorium, Milwaukee, Wis.
Sept. 29	Civic Opera House, Chicago, Ill.
Oct. 1	State Fair Auditorium, Dallas, Tex.
Oct. 2	Civic Auditorium, Seattle, Wash.
Oct. 3	Public Auditorium, Portland, Ore.
Oct. 5	Civic Auditorium, San Francisco, Calif.
Oct. 6	Memorial Auditorium, Sacramento, Calif., and Auditorium Arena, Oakland, Calif.
Oct. 7	Shrine Auditorium, Los Angeles, Calif.
Nov. 1957–Mar. 13, 1959	*Freelance sessions*
Nov.	Rouge Lounge, Detroit, Mich.
	Stage Door, Chicago, Ill.
	Crown Propellor Lounge, Chicago, Ill.
Dec. 5	CBS TV, rehearsal, N.Y.C.
Dec. 8	CBS TV show, "The Sound of Jazz," N.Y.C.
c. Feb. 14–16, 1958	Cork'n'Bib, Westbury, N.Y.
June 2	Birdland N.Y.C.
June 17–July 6	Birdland N.Y.C.
July 5	Also *Newport Jazz Festival,* Newport, R.I.
July 27	Black Pearl, N.Y.C.
Aug.	Small's Paradise, N.Y.C.
Aug. 19–25	Pep's Musical Bar, Philadelphia, Pa.
Sept.	Gem's Paradise, Brooklyn, N.Y.
Sept. 20	Carnegie Hall, N.Y.C.
Sept. 25	Art Ford's "Jazz Party," WNTA, N.J.
Oct.	Academy of Music, Brooklyn, N.Y.
	Mosque Theater, Newark, N.J.
Nov. 14–27	The Five Spot, N.Y.C.
Nov. 28–Dec. 3	Showboat, Philadelphia, Pa.
Dec. 5–24	The Five Spot, N.Y.C.
Dec. 26	Pershing Hotel, Chicago, Ill.
Dec. 27	Lockport-Joliet, Chicago, Ill.

Dec. 28	Evanston's Swedish Hall, Chicago, Ill.
Dec. 29	Robert's Show Lounge, Chicago, Ill.
Dec. 31, 1958–Jan. 5, 1959	The Five Spot, N.Y.C
Jan. 14–Mar. 13	Blue Note, Paris, France

APPENDIX B
Members of Lester Young's Permanent Groups, 1941–1955

This listing stops in December 1955, because Lester Young did not, after that time, have a band on a permanent basis, rather, musicians were hired from job to job.

Jan.–May 1941	Shad Collins (tp), Clyde Hart (p), John Collins (g), Nick Fenton (b), Harold "Doc" West (dr)
Dec. 1941–Jan. 1942	Guydner Paul Campbell (tp), Hubert Maxwell "Bumps" Myers (ts), Jimmy Rowles (p), Louis Gonzales (g), Red Callender (b), Lee Young (dr)
Feb.–July 1942	"Red" Mack Morris (tp), Hubert Maxwell "Bumps" Myers (ts), Jimmy Rowles (p), Louis Gonzales (g), Red Callender (b), Lee Young (dr)
July–Aug. 1942	"Red" Mack Morris (tp), Jimmy Rowles (p), Louis Gonzales (g), Red Callender (b), Lee Young (dr)
Sept.–Nov. 1942	Guydner Paul Campbell (tp), Hubert Maxwell "Bumps" Myers (ts), Charles Thompson (p), Louis Gonzales (g), Red Callender (b), Lee Young (dr)

Nov. 1942–Feb. 1943	Guydner Paul Campbell (tp), Hubert Maxwell "Bumps" Myers (ts), Clyde Hart (p), Louis Gonzales (g), Red Callender (b), Lee Young (dr)
Oct. 1946–Oct. 1947	Maurice "Shorty" McConnell (tp), Argonne Dense Thornton (p), Fred Lacey (g), Rodney Richardson (b), Lyndell Marshall (dr)
Oct. 1947–Autumn 1948	Maurice "Shorty" McConnell (tp), Argonne Dense Thornton (p), Fred Lacey (g), Dennis "Tex" Briscoe (b), Roy Haynes (dr)
Autumn 1948–Feb. 1949	Jesse Drakes (tp), Ted Kelly (tb), Freddy Jefferson (p), Dennis "Tex" Briscoe (b), Roy Haynes (dr)
Feb.–Mar. 1949	Jesse Drakes (tp), Ted Kelly (tb), Junior Mance (p), Dennis "Tex" Briscoe (b), Roy Haynes (dr)
Apr.–July 1949	Jesse Drakes (tp), Jerry Elliott (tb), Junior Mance (p), Leroy Jackson (b), Roy Haynes (dr)
Aug.–Sept. 1949	Jesse Drakes (tp), Jerry Elliott (tb), Junior Mance (p), Leroy Jackson (b), Jo Jones (dr)
Dec. 1949–Feb. 1950	Dick Hyman (p), Irv Lang (b), Jo Jones (dr)
Feb.–Mar. 1950	Jesse Drakes (tp), Kenny Drew (p), Aaron Bell (b), Jo Jones (dr)
Apr. 1950	Jesse Drakes (tp), Kenny Drew (p), Joe Shulman (b), Jo Jones (dr)
May–Sept. 1950	Jesse Drakes (tp), Kenny Drew (p), Joe Shulman (b), Bill Clark (dr)
Nov.–Dec. 1950	Kenny Drew (p), Joe Shulman (b), Bill Clark (dr)
Dec. 1950	Tony Fruscella (tp), John Lewis (p), Joe Shulman (b), Bill Clark (dr)
Jan.–April 1951	John Lewis (p), Gene Ramey (b), Jo Jones (dr)
May–July 1951	Jesse Brakes (tp), John Lewis (p), Gene Ramey (b), Jo Jones (dr)
Aug. 1951	Jesse Drakes (tp), Earl Knight (p), Gene Ramey (b), Jo Jones (dr)

Sept. 1951	Jesse Drakes (tp), Earl Knight (p), Aaron Bell (b), Al Jones (dr)
Dec. 1951–Feb. 1952	Jesse Drakes (tp), Earl Knight (p), Gene Ramey (b), Jo Jones (dr)
Apr.–June 1952	Jesse Drakes (tp), Wynton Kelly (p), Aaron Bell (b), Lee Abrams (dr)
July–Sept. 1952	Jesse Drakes (tp), Gil Coggins (p), Aaron Bell (b), Connie Kay (dr)
Nov. 1952–Feb. 1953	Jesse Drakes (tp), Horace Silver (p), Franklin Skeete (b), Lee Abrams (dr)
Apr.–June 1953	Jesse Drakes (tp), Horace Silver (p), Gene Ramey (b), Lee Abrams (dr)
July–Aug. 1953	Jesse Drakes (tp), Gildo Mahones (p), Leroy Jackson (b), Connie Kay (dr)
Sept.–Oct. 1953	Jesse Drakes (tp), Gildo Mahones (p), Gene Ramey (b), Connie Kay (dr)
Nov. 1953	Jesse Drakes (tp), Gildo Mahones (p), Cecil Winston (b), Connie Kay (dr)
Dec. 1953–Feb. 1954	Jesse Drakes (tp), Gildo Mahones (p), Gene Ramey (b), Connie Kay (dr)
Mar.–Sept. 1954	Jesse Drakes (tp), Gildo Mahones (p), Connie Henry (b), Connie Kay (dr)
Oct. 1954–Jan. 1955	Jesse Drakes (tp), Gildo Mahones (p), John Ore (b), Connie Kay (dr)
Feb.–Sept. 1955	Gildo Mahones (p), John Ore (b), (unknown) (dr)
Oct.–Dec. 1955	Jesse Drakes (tp), Gildo Mahones (p), John Ore (b), (unknown) (dr)

Notes

PREFACE

1. (Wetzler, Pegasus Verlag, 1959). 60 pp., including discography.
2. (Milan: Ricordi, 1961). 96 pp., including discography.
3. (Paris: Denoël, 1987). 264 pp., including discography.
4. (Tunbridge Wells: Spellmount, 1984). 94 pp., including discography.
5. (Boston: G. K. Hall, 1985). 22 + 190 pp.
6. Jazz Solography Series, 13, 2nd ed. (Oslo: Jan Evensmo, 1983). 76 pp.

CHAPTER ONE

1. On the conditions in New Orleans around 1900, see, inter al.: Siegel, Martin, ed. *New Orleans: A Documentary and Chronological History, 1539–1970* (Dobbs Ferry, N.Y.: Oceana, 1975); Frazier, E. Franklin. *The Negro in the United States* (New York: Macmillan, 1969); Foster, Pops. *The Autobiography of a New Orleans Jazzman, as told to Tom Stoddard* (Berkeley: University of California Press, 1971); Collier, James Lincoln. *Louis Armstrong* (London: Michael Joseph, 1984).

2. Henri, Florette. *Black Migration: Movement North 1900–20* (Garden City, N.Y.: Anchor Press, 1975).

3. Daniels, Douglas Henry. "History, Racism, and Jazz: The Case of Lester Young." *Jazzforschung* 16 (1984), pp. 87–103.

4. Lee Young, interviewed by Patricia Willard, November 8–15, 1977 (Jazz Oral History Project).

5. The precise time span is not known, since Tuskegee Institute records concerning students do not go back this far.

6. Charters, Samuel B. *Jazz: New Orleans, 1885–1963* (New York: Oak Publications, 1963), p. 56.

7. See note 4.

8. Interview with Irma Young, November 11, 1985.

9. Cross, Ralph D., ed. *Atlas of Mississippi* (Jackson: University Press of Mississippi, 1974).

10. Lester Young, interviewed by François Postif, Paris, February 6, 1959. All quotations from this interview are from the original tape. Transcriptions of it have been published in *Jazz Hot,* April 1959; *Jazz Review,* September 1959; *Jazz Hot,* June–Summer 1979; as well as in Martin Williams, ed., *Jazz Panorama* (New York: 1963). All editions, however, contain cuts and changes in Lester's language.

11. Ibid.

12. See note 4.

13. Ibid.

14. Leonard Phillips, interviewed by Bryant Dupré, January 26–28, 1983 (Jazz Oral History Project).

15. Ibid.

16. Balliett, Whitney. *Jelly Roll, Jabbo and Fats* (New York, Oxford University Press, 1983), p. 124.

17. See note 4.

18. See note 14.

19. Concerning the migration of and conditions for blacks in the northern industrial cities, see, inter al.: Henri, Florette. *Black Migration: Movement North 1900–20* (Garden City, N.Y.: Anchor Press, 1975); Jackson, Florence. *The Black Man in America 1905–32* (New York, Franklin Watts, 1974); Davis, George A., and O. Fred Donaldson. *Blacks in the United States* (Boston: Houghton Mifflin, 1975); Frazier, E. Franklin. *The Negro in the United States* (New York: Macmillan, 1969); Grant, Robert B. *The Black Man Comes to the City* (Chicago: Nelson-Hall, 1972); Weiss, Nancy J. *The National Urban League 1910–40* (New York: Oxford University Press, 1974).

20. See note 10.

21. Morrison, Alan. "You Got to Be Original, Man." *Jazz Record,* July 1946, p. 7.

22. See note 4.

23. See note 14.

24. Ibid.

25. Dance, Stanley. *The World of Duke Ellington* (New York: Scribner's, 1970), p. 103.

26. See note 14.

27. See note 14.

28. Ibid.

29. See note 4.

30. Wilmer, Valerie. "The Lee Young Story." *Jazz Journal,* January 1961, p. 4.

31. See note 10. "Kansas" wasn't Billy's pet name for Lester, but indicates that the drummer Kansas Fields was present at the interview.

32. See note 14.

33. Ibid.

34. Shapiro, Nat, and Nat Hentoff, eds. *The Jazz Makers* (New York: Rinehart, 1957), p. 246.

35. See note 10.

36. See note 21.

37. Hentoff, Nat. "Pres." *Down Beat,* March 7, 1956, p. 10.

38. See note 4.

39. Eddie Barefield, interviewed by Ira Gitler, November 20, 1978 (Jazz Oral History Project).

40. See note 14.

41. See note 4.

42. Feather, Leonard. "Here's Pres!" *Melody Maker,* July 15, 1950, p. 10.

43. McDonough, John. *Lester Young* (Alexandria, Va.: Time-Life, 1980), p. 11. Booklet included in Time-Life J-13, *Giants of Jazz: Lester Young.*

44. See note 14.

CHAPTER TWO

1. According to Military File, Private 39729502 Young, U.S. Army Reserve Personnel Center, St. Louis, Mo.

2. Leonard Phillips, interviewed by Bryant Dupré, January 26–28, 1983 (Jazz Oral History Project).

3. Ibid.

4. Lester Young, interviewed by François Postif, Paris, February 6, 1959.

5. Morrison, Alan. "You Got to Be Original, Man." *Jazz Record,* July 1946, p. 8.

6. See note 2.

7. Balliett, Whitney. *Jelly Roll, Jabbo and Fats* (New York: Oxford University Press, 1983), p. 122.

8. "Ben Webster Plays That BIG Tenor." *Down Beat,* October 5, 1955, p. 12.

9. Dance, Stanley. *The World of Duke Ellington* (New York, Scribner's, 1970), p. 131.

10. Wilmer, Valerie. "The Lee Young Story." *Jazz Journal,* January 1961, p. 4.

11. See note 9.

12. Zwicky, Theo. "Lloyd Hunter's Serenaders and the Territory Bands, Part 2." *Storyville,* no. 36 (August 1971), p. 207 suggests that Lester played with Eli Rice. Eddie Barefield has later declared that Lester never played in that band, but that he did himself play with Rice around this time.

13. Eddie Barefield, interviewed by Ira Gitler, November 20, 1978 (Jazz Oral History Project).

14. Gazzaway, Don. "Conversations with Buster Smith, Part 1." *Jazz Review* 2, no. 4 (1959), p. 20.

15. On territory bands, see, inter al.: McCarthy, Albert. *Big Band Jazz* (London: Barrie and Jenkins, 1974); Russell, Ross. *Jazz Style in Kansas City and the Southwest* (Berkeley: University of California Press, 1973).

16. The lineup of the band can be ascertained by consulting the sources cited in notes 12 and 15.

17. Ellison, Ralph. "The Charlie Christian Story." *Saturday Review,* May 17, 1958, pp. 42–43. Reprinted in his *Shadow and Act* (New York: Vintage Books, 1964), pp. 236–237. The year 1929 fits in with a tour with the Young Family Band, but at that time Christian was only thirteen years old, so maybe either 1930 or 1932–33 is more likely, when Lester visited the town with the Blue Devils and King Oliver.

18. See note 2. In Walter C. Allen and Brian Rust, *"King" Oliver,* 2nd ed., rev. by Laurie Wright (Chigwell, England: Storyville, 1987), it is claimed that Lester returned to Art Bronson as early as the fall of 1929 and stayed with him for eighteen months, whereas Phillips's reminiscences agree completely with the rest of Lester's engagements in this period.

19. *Down Beat,* November 19, 1947, p. 1. The names are listed under the photograph, but Sam Allen is wrongly called Sam Scott. The same photo is printed in *Storyville,* no. 46 (1973), p. 147, with the right names written directly onto the photograph, and in *"King" Oliver* by Allen, Rust, and Wright, mentioned above. However, in both places it is said that the musicians depicted made up King Oliver's reed section, and both 1930 and 1932 are given as the year when the picture was taken; but this does not fit in with Lester's own chronology.

20. Placksin, Sally. *American Women in Jazz* (New York: Wideview Books, 1982), p. 67.

21. See note 12, p. 209.

22. Letters to Frank Büchmann-Møller from Beverly Young, June 11 and September 14, 1986.

23. Jimmy Rushing. *Livin' the Blues.* Bluesway BLS-6017, liner notes.

24. Feather, Leonard. *From Satchmo to Miles* (New York: Stein and Day, 1972), p. 119.

25. Dance, Stanley. *The World of Earl Hines* (New York: Scribner's, 1977), p. 208.

26. "Blue Devils Hold Big Cabaret Fete." *Chicago Defender,* April 9, 1932, p. 5.

27. The film *The Last of the Blue Devils,* directed by Bruce Ricker, 1979.

28. Gazzaway, Don. "Conversations with Buster Smith, Part 2." *Jazz Review* 3, no. 1 (1960), p. 12.

29. Shapiro, Nat, and Nat Hentoff, eds. *The Jazz Makers* (New York: Rinehart, 1957), p. 248.

30. See note 2. After Bess's death Lester had taken up contact with Beatrice again; it is she Phillips refers to as Lester's wife, even though there was never mention of a proper marriage between them.

31. Feather, Leonard. "Here's Pres!" *Melody Maker,* July 15, 1950, p. 3.

32. See note 14, p. 22.

33. McDaniels, Jack. "Buster Smith." *Down Beat,* July 11, 1956, p. 13.

34. See note 14, p. 22.

35. See note 31.

36. See note 2.

37. Case, Brian. "Buddy Tate and the President." *Melody Maker,* December 1, 1979, p. 37.

38. Kaye, Harold S. "Francis 'Doc' Whitby." *Storyville,* no. 110 (1983/84), p. 53.

39. Interview with Adolphus Alsbrook, November 17, 1986.

40. See note 29.

41. Hentoff, Nat. "Pres." *Down Beat,* March 7, 1956, p. 9.

CHAPTER THREE

1. Concerning Pendergast's Kansas City and its musical life, see, inter al.: Dorsett, Lyle W. *The Pendergast Machine* (New York: Oxford University Press, 1968); Milligan, Maurice M. *The Inside Story of the Pendergast Machine* (New York: Scribner's, 1948); Redig, William M. *Tom's Town* (New York: Lippincott, 1947); Steinberg, Alfred. *The Bosses* (New York: Macmillan, 1972); Russell, Ross. *Jazz Style in Kansas City and the Southwest* (Berkeley: University of California Press, 1973).

2. Gene Ramey, interviewed by Stanley Dance, 1978 (Jazz Oral History Project).

3. Ibid.

4. Eddie Durham, interviewed by Stanley Dance, November 1978 (Jazz Oral History Project).

5. See note 2. "Bird" is Charlie Parker's nickname.

6. Shapiro, Nat, and Nat Hentoff, eds. *The Jazz Makers* (New York: Rinehart, 1957), p. 250.

7. Leonard Phillips, interviewed by Bryant Dupré, January 26–28, 1983 (Jazz Oral History Project).

8. Lester Young, interviewed by François Postif, Paris, February 6, 1959.

9. Allen, Walter C. *Hendersonia* (Highland Park, N.J.: Walter C. Allen, 1973), p. 306.

10. Jo Jones, interviewed by Milt Hinton, January 15, 1973 (Jazz Oral History Project).

11. See note 2.

12. Shapiro, Nat, and Nat Hentoff, eds. *Hear Me Talkin' to Ya* (New York: Rinehart, 1955), pp. 292–293.

13. See note 2.

14. *Chicago Defender,* May 5, 1934, p. 8.

15. Travis, Dempsey. *An Autobiography of Black Jazz* (Chicago: Urban Research Institute, 1984), p. 296.

16. See note 8.

17. Case, Brian. "Buddy Tate and the President." *Melody Maker,* December 1, 1979, p. 37.

18. See note 10.

19. *The Lester Young Story, Vol. 2.* Columbia, CBS JG 34837, liner notes.

20. See note 9, p. 292.

21. John Hammond later claimed to have been at the audition, but this does not tie in with his own statement in note 28.

22. See note 8.

23. See note 6.

24. See note 8.

25. Holiday, Billie, and William Dufty. *Lady Sings the Blues* (Garden City, N.Y.: Doubleday, 1956), p. 56.

26. "Henderson on Tour in the Middle West." *New York Amsterdam News,* April 14, 1934, p. 7; "New Musicians for Fletcher Henderson's Thirteen." *Chicago Defender,* April 14, 1934, p. 9.

27. "Going Backstage with the Scribe." *Chicago Defender,* June 16, 1934, p. 9.

28. Hammond, John. "John Hammond Discusses Franco-U.S. Attack on 'Mike.' " *Melody Maker,* June 2, 1934, p. 11.

29. "Chicago Hands All Its Music Honors to Lucius Millinder." *Chicago Defender,* April 14, 1934, p. 8.

30. *University Daily Kansan,* April 15, 1934, p. 1.

31. "Apollo This Week." *New York Age,* June 9, 1934, p. 4.

32. See note 10.

33. See note 8.

34. Fernet, Gene. "Clouds of Joy." *Sounds and Fury,* February 1966, pp. 24–25.

35. Hammond, John. "The New and Greater Cab." *Melody Maker,* July 28, 1934, p. 11.

36. Hammond, John. "Nouvelles d'Amerique." *Jazz-Tango-Dancing* (Paris), no. 48 (September 1934), p. 5.

37. McDonough, John. *Lester Young* (Alexandria, Va.: Time-Life, 1980), p. 14. Booklet included in Time-Life J-13, *Giants of Jazz: Lester Young.*

38. Lord, Tom. *Clarence Williams* (Chigwell, England: Storyville, 1976), pp. 360–361.

39. Mary Lou Williams, interviewed by John S. Wilson, June 16, 1973 (Jazz Oral History Project).

40. Morrison, Alan. "You Got to Be Original, Man." *Jazz Record,* July 1946, p. 8.

41. See note 7.

42. Dance, Stanley. *The World of Earl Hines* (New York: Scribner's, 1977), pp. 209–210.

43. See note 7.

44. See note 42, p. 157.

CHAPTER FOUR

1. *The Lester Young Story, Vol 1.* Columbia CBS CG 33502, liner notes.

2. Hentoff, Nat. "Pres." *Down Beat,* March 7, 1956, p. 9.

3. Interview with Adolphus Alsbrook, November 17, 1986. Alsbrook recalls this so precisely because he left Rook Ganz's band on the same day as Lester.

4. Basie, Count. *Good Morning Blues* (New York: Random House, 1985), p. 161.

5. Gene Ramey, interviewed by Stanley Dance, 1978. (Jazz Oral History Project).

6. McDaniels, Jack. "Buster Smith." *Down Beat,* July 11, 1956, p. 13.

7. Hammond, John. "Count Basie's Band and 'Boogie-Woogie' Pianist Tops." *Down Beat,* May 1936, p. 6.

8. Hammond, John. "Lester Young." *Jazz,* no. 3 (1959), p. 182.

9. Hammond, John. "Recollections." *Jazz and Blues,* August 1973, p. 8.

10. "Basie's Fine Music from One of the Town's Worst Dives." *Down Beat,* July 1936, p. 5.

11. Hammond, John. "N.Y. Swing Concert Proved Headache—Too Hard to Commercialize on Jam Music." *Down Beat,* June 1936, p. 6.

12. See note 4, p. 167.

13. See note 9, p. 9.

14. Hammond, John. "Kansas City a Hotbed for Fine Swing Musicians." *Down Beat,* September 1936, pp. 1, 9.

15. Buck Clayton, interviewed by Stanley Dance (Jazz Oral History Project).

16. Ibid.

17. Balliett, Whitney. *Jelly Roll, Jabbo and Fats* (New York: Oxford University Press, 1983), p. 122.

18. Lee Young, interviewed by Patricia Willard, November 8–15, 1977 (Jazz Oral History Project).

19. See note 5.

20. Postif, François. "Gene Ramey." *Jazz Hot,* March 1962, p. 23.

21. Kunstadt, Leonard. "The Story of Louie Metcalf." *Record Research,* October 1962, p. 9.

22. *New York Amsterdam News,* October 3, 1936, p. 10; October 24, 1936, p. 12; November 21, 1936, p. 14.

23. Driggs, Frank, and Harris Lewine. *Black Beauty, White Heat* (New York: William Morrow, 1982), p. 159.

24. See note 4, p. 176.

25. Jo Jones, interviewed by Milt Hinton, January 15, 1973 (Jazz Oral History Project).

26. Stewart, Rex. *Jazz Masters of the Thirties* (New York: Macmillan, 1972), p. 202.

27. See note 15.

28. Hammond, John. "Kirk, Basie and Norvo Knock Patrons for Loop—But Heidt Ruins Digestion." *Down Beat,* December 1936, pp. 3, 13.

29. See note 15.

30. Simon, George T. "Pick-up." *Metronome,* January 1937, p. 26.

31. Until now this date has been given as October 9, 1936, but this must be due to a printing error in Vocalion's catalog. The previous session took place on November 4 and the following on November 12.

32. Hammond, John. *John Hammond on Record* (New York: Summit Books, 1977), p. 379.

33. Evensmo, Jan. *The Tenor Saxophone and Clarinet of Lester Young 1936–1949* (Hosle, Norway, 1983), p. 2.

34. Interview with Roy Eldridge, New York, November 18, 1985.

35. Lester Young. *Laughin' to Keep from Cryin'.* Verve 2304 487, liner notes.

36. See note 32, p. 173.

37. Shapiro, Nat, and Nat Hentoff, eds. *Hear Me Talkin' to Ya* (New York: Rinehart, 1955), p. 310.

38. Simon, George T. "Dance Band Reviews." *Metronome,* February 1937, p. 24.

39. Hammond, John. "Goodman 'Killer' Arrangements Detracts from Band's Musicianship." *Down Beat,* February 1937, p. 7.

40. Chilton, John. *Billie's Blues* (London: Quartet Books, 1977), p. 2.

41. Interview with Harry Edison, Copenhagen, March 2, 1987.

42. Holiday, Billie, and William Dufty. *Lady Sings the Blues* (New York: Doubleday, 1956), pp. 56–57.

43. Berger, M., E. Berger and J. Patrick. *Benny Carter* (Metuchen, N.J.: Scarecrow Press, 1983), p. 313.

44. Hammond, John. "Lester Young (1909–1959)." *Saturday Review,* April 11, 1959, p. 53.

45. See note 39.

46. See note 25.

47. Dance, Stanley. "Of Count Basie and His Orchestra." *Jazz Hot,* May–June 1937, pp. 5–6.

48. Leonard Phillips, interviewed by Bryant Dupré, January 26–28, 1983 (Jazz Oral History Project). In fact Basie played in Washington at the end of April, not in March.

49. Interview with Freddie Green, Copenhagen, July 8, 1985.

50. See note 15.

51. See note 25.

52. See note 49.

53. Dance, Stanley. *The World of Count Basie* (New York: Scribner's, 1980), pp. 79–80.

54. See note 25.

55. See note 53, p. 79.

56. Ibid.

57. Downes, Olin. "Goodman Is Heard in 'Swing' Concert." *New York Times,* January 17, 1938, p. 11.

58. Simon, George T. "Benny and Cats Make Carnegie Debut Real Howling Success." *Metronome,* February 1938, p. 18.

59. Driggs, Frank. "Jimmy Rushing's Story." *Evergreen Review* 10, no. 40 (1966), p. 68.

60. Simon, George T. "Basie's Brilliant Band Conquers Chick's." *Metronome,* February 1938, pp. 1, 20.

61. "Chick, Basie Battle It Out in Swingtime." *New York Amsterdam News,* January 22, 1938.

62. "Webb 'Cuts' Basie in Swing Battle." *Down Beat,* February 1938, p. 2.

63. "Hammond Did Not Have Holiday Fired!" *Down Beat,* September 1938, p. 6.

64. Helen Humes, interviewed by Helen Oakley Dance, May 12, 1981 (Jazz Oral History Project).

65. See note 15.

66. Shaw, Arnold. *52nd Street: The Street of Jazz* (New York: Da Capo, 1977), pp. 127–128.

67. Ibid., p. 129.

68. Ibid., p. 346.

69. Collier, Mike. "Talking Trombone." *Jazz Journal International,* June 1985, p. 19.

70. Interview with Thad Jones, Knapstrup, Denmark, December 31, 1984.

71. See note 53, p. 105.

72. See note 49.

73. Ibid.

74. See note 25.

75. See note 41.

76. Buddy Tate, interviewed by Gary Giddins, March 1980 (Jazz Oral History Project).

77. *The Lester Young Story, Vol. 3.* Columbia CBS JG 34840, liner notes. The Basie band was on tour at that time, so Jones means the Savoy Ballroom in Chicago, where the band played on February 12. It was located on 47th Street and South Parkway and could easily accommodate 6,000 dancers.

78. Ibid.

79. See note 15.
80. Shapiro, Nat, and Nat Hentoff, eds. *The Jazz Makers* (New York: Rinehart, 1957), p. 254.
81. See note 77.
82. Lester Young, interviewed by François Postif, Paris, February 6, 1959.
83. Schaap, Phil. "Duels and Duets." *Oak Report* 1, no. 1 (1980), p. 19.
84. See note 76.
85. Ibid.
86. Interview with Willie Jones, New York, November 16, 1985.
87. See note 53, pp. 123–124.
88. See note 41.
89. Holiday, Billie. "Les Young Wasn't Carved." *Down Beat,* October 15, 1939, p. 4.
90. See note 66, p. 214. Bean was Hawkins' nickname.
91. Gitler, Ira. *Jazz Masters of the Forties* (New York: Collier, 1974), p. 205.
92. Gitler, Ira. *Swing to Bop* (New York: Oxford University Press, 1985), p. 38.
93. See note 15.
94. Smith, J. D. "From Spirituals to Swing." *Jazz Information* 4 (December 29, 1939), p. 4.
95. *The Lester Young Story, Vol.`5.* Columbia CBS JG 88268, liner notes.
96. Feather, Leonard. *From Satchmo to MIles* (New York: Stein and Day, 1972), p. 120.
97. "Lester Young, Count Basie Part Company." *Down Beat,* January 1, 1941, p. 14.
98. Flynn, Ed. "Basie Pays Ten Gs for His Release." *Down Beat,* January 15, 1941, p. 1.
99. "Chords and Discords." *Down Beat,* March 1, 1941, p. 10.
100. See note 80, p. 251.
101. See note 5.
102. Ibid.
103. See note 25.

CHAPTER FIVE

1. Interview with Max Gordon at the Village Vanguard, New York, November 11, 1985.
2. Gitler, Ira. *Swing to Bop* (New York: Oxford University Press, 1985), pp. 39–40.
3. McDonough, John. *Lester Young* (Alexandria, Va.: Time-Life, 1980), p. 45. Booklet included in Time-Life J-13, *Giants of Jazz: Lester Young.*
4. Feather, Leonard. "Here's Pres!" *Melody Maker,* July 15, 1950, p. 3.
5. Spellman, A. B. *Black Music: Four Lives* (New York: Schocken Books, 1970), p. 158.
6. See note 3.
7. Feather, Leonard. *From Satchmo to Miles* (New York: Stein and Day, 1972), p. 122.
8. Lee Young, interviewed by Patricia Willard, November 8–15, 1977 (Jazz Oral History Project).
9. Ibid.
10. Gitler, Ira. "Portrait of a Legend: Joe Albany." *Down Beat,* October 24, 1963, p. 20.
11. Callender, Red, and Elaine Cohen. *Unfinished Dream* (London: Quartet Books, 1985), p. 47.
12. See note 8.

13. Dexter, Dave. "Big Band Boom Has California on the Jump." *Down Beat,* August 15, 1941, p. 3.

14. Hoefer, G. "Early Prez." *Down Beat,* March 1, 1962, p. 18.

15. Simon, George T. *Simon Says* (New Rochelle, N.Y.: Arlington House, 1971), p. 268.

16. See note 8.

17. Ibid.

18. See note 11, p. 49.

19. Feather, Leonard. "Pres Digs Every Kind of Music." *Down Beat,* November 2, 1951, p. 12.

20. Holly, Hal. "Los Angeles Band Briefs." *Down Beat,* March 15, 1942, p. 13.

21. Holly, Hal. "Los Angeles Band Briefs." *Down Beat,* April 1, 1942, p. 13.

22. Balliett, Whitney. *Jelly Roll, Jabbo and Fats* (New York: Oxford University Press, 1983), p. 124.

23. See note 11, p. 48.

24. Jimmy Rowles, interviewed by Norman Saks, July 15, 1984. The trumpet player was in fact "Red" Mack Morris at that point.

25. Holiday, Billie, and William Dufty. *Lady Sings the Blues* (Garden City, N.Y.: Doubleday, 1956), p. 118.

26. Holly, Hal. "Los Angeles Band Briefs." *Down Beat,* July 15, 1942, p. 12.

27. See note 8.

28. Wilmer, Valerie. "The Lee Young Story." *Jazz Journal,* January 1961, p. 5.

29. See note 11, p. 54.

30. Sir Charles Thompson, interviewed by Helen Oakley Dance, May 1975 (Jazz Oral History Project).

31. Dance, Stanley. *The World of Earl Hines* (New York: Scribner's, 1977), p. 216.

32. Fisher, Al. "Temps Perdu." *Jazz Review* 2, no. 6 (1959), p. 42.

33. Dance, Stanley. *The World of Count Basie* (New York, Scribner's, 1980), p. 152.

34. Gardner, Mark. "Piano Peer." *Jazz Journal International,* May 1985, p. 6.

35. Jo Jones, interviewed by Milt Hinton, January 15, 1973 (Jazz Oral History Project).

36. Lester did not play with Basie in the radio broadcast of November 23, 1943, but did take part in an AFRS program thought to be recorded around December 1, 1943.

37. Wells, Dicky. *Night People* (London: Robert Hale, 1971), p. 62.

38. Gitler, Ira. *Jazz Masters of the Forties* (New York: Collier, 1974), p. 208. Ben is Ben Webster.

39. See note 37, p. 64.

40. Emge, Charles. "On the Beat in Hollywood." *Down Beat,* December 1, 1944, p. 6.

41. Interview with Harry Edison, Copenhagen, March 2, 1987.

CHAPTER SIX

1. Case, Brian. "Buddy Tate and the President." *Melody Maker,* December 1, 1979, p. 49. Neither Jo Jones nor Lester was in Basie's band on a radio broadcast on Monday, September 25. This suggests that it may well have been on Sunday, September 24 that the FBI agent visited the Plantation Club.

2. Buddy Tate, interviewed by Gary Giddins, March 1980 (Jazz Oral History Project).

3. Lee Young, interviewed by Patricia Willard, November 8–15, 1977 (Jazz Oral History Project).

4. Balliett, Whitney. *Jelly Roll, Jabbo and Fats* (New York: Oxford University Press, 1983), p. 125.

5. Shapiro, Nat, and Nat Hentoff, eds. *The Jazz Makers* (New York: Rinehart, 1957), p. 261.

6. Coyle, Owen D. "Moving On." *Mississippi Rag,* April 1977, p. 1.

7. Military File, Private 39729502 Young, U.S. Army Reserve Personnel Center, St. Louis, Mo.

8. Ibid.

9. Ibid.

10. Ibid.

11. Ibid.

12. Ibid.

13. Ibid.

14. Ibid.

15. Ibid.

16. Feather, Leonard. *From Satchmo to Miles* (New York: Stein and Day, 1972), pp. 123–124.

17. Jo Jones, interviewed by Milt Hinton, January 15, 1973 (Jazz Oral History Project).

18. See note 7.

19. See note 16, p. 124.

20. Morrison, Alan. "You Got to Be Original, Man." *Jazz Record,* July 1946, p. 9.

21. Interview with Willie Jones, New York, November 16, 1985.

22. Wilmer, Valerie. "Jo Jones Speaks Out." *Jazz Journal* 25, no. 12 (1972), p. 8.

23. See note 5, pp. 274–275.

24. Interview with Harry Edison, Copenhagen, March 2, 1987.

CHAPTER SEVEN

1. "Lester Young Signs with Philo." *Down Beat,* November 15, 1945, p. 3.

2. Gitler, Ira. *Swing to Bop* (New York: Oxford University Press, 1985), p. 181.

3. Dance, Stanley. *The World of Count Basie* (New York: Scribner's, 1980), p. 299.

4. Porter, Bob, and Mark Gardner. "The California Cats: An Interview with Sonny Criss." *Jazz Monthly,* April 1968, p. 8.

5. Advertisement, *Los Angeles Times,* January 27, 1946, sec. 3, p. 2.

6. See note 2, pp. 180–181.

7. "Jazz Goes to UCLA in Campus Concert." *Down Beat,* May 6, 1946, p. 16.

8. "Chicago Gives Granz Unit Biggest Gross." *Down Beat,* June 3, 1946, p. 4.

9. Feather, Leonard. "Duke Okays 'Be-Bop.' " *Melody Maker,* June 22, 1946, p. 3.

10. Ibid.

11. "Carnegie Bash Hits $4,400 Pot." *Down Beat,* July 1, 1946, p. 8.

12. Voce, Steve. "It Don't Mean a Thing." *Jazz Journal International* 28, no. 10 (1985), p. 18.

13. Feather, Leonard. "Here's Pres!" *Melody Maker,* June 15, 1950, p. 3.

14. Interview with Bill Triglia, New York, November 10, 1985.

15. Monroe, Al. "Swinging the News." *Chicago Defender,* October 5, 1946, p. 10.

16. Gene Ramey, interviewed by Stanley Dance, 1978 (Jazz Oral History Project).

17. Letter to Frank Büchmann-Møller from Beverly Young, June 11, 1986.

18. Dance, Stanley. *The World of Earl Hines* (New York: Scribner's, 1977), p. 158.

19. Interview with Junior Mance, New York, November 12, 1985.

20. Interview with Roy Haynes, New York, November 20, 1985.

21. Ibid.

22. "Vaughan Great, but Lester Slips." *Down Beat,* December 3, 1947, p. 3.

23. "Lester Young Replies." *Down Beat,* December 3, 1947, p. 3.

24. See note 14.

25. Rusch, Bob. "Jesse Drakes." *Cadence* 10, no. 3 (1984), p. 18.

26. Ibid., p. 19.

27. Ibid.

28. See note 20.

29. See note 3, p. 106.

30. Feather, Leonard. *From Satchmo to Miles* (New York: Stein and Day, 1972), p. 124.

31. Harris, Pat. "Pres Talks about Himself, Copycats." *Down Beat,* May 6, 1949, p. 15.

32. Hentoff, Nat. "Pres." *Down Beat,* March 7, 1956, p. 10.

33. Morrison, Alan. "You Got to Be Original, Man." *Jazz Record,* July 1946, pp. 8–9.

34. Gleason, Ralph J. "Swingin' the Golden Gate: Lester Leaps to Town as Twin City Ops Merge." *Down Beat,* March 10, 1948, p. 9.

35. "Lester Young Gets Kicks." *Chicago Defender,* February 5, 1949, p. 16.

36. See note 19.

37. Shapiro, Nat, and Nat Hentoff, eds. *The Jazz Makers* (New York: Rinehart, 1957), p. 259.

38. Ibid.

39. Millstein, Gilbert. "Hot Jazz Promoter." *New York Times,* September 20, 1953, sec. 2, p. 10.

40. "JATP-konserten i Seattle satte publikumsrekord." *Norsk Jazz* 2, no. 13 (1955), p. 1.

41. Kessel, Barney. "Lester Young, Part 2." *Guitar Journal,* January 1979, p. 22.

42. See note 37, p. 266.

43. Wilson, John S. " 'JATP' Kicks Off at Carnegie." *Down Beat,* October 21, 1949, p. 3.

44. Buddy Tate, interviewed by Gary Giddins, March 1980 (Jazz Oral History Project).

45. Balliett, Whitney. *Ecstasy at the Onion* (New York: Bobbs-Merrill, 1971), p. 173.

46. Wilson, John S. "Birdland Applies Imagination to Jazz." *Down Beat,* January 27, 1950, p. 3.

47. Interview with Dick Hyman, New York, November 8, 1985.

48. This episode was related by Mel Lewis, New York, November 8, 1985.

49. Wilson, John S. "Serge, Pres, Erroll Head Birdland Bill." *Down Beat,* February 24, 1950, p. 3.

50. See note 37, p. 269.

51. "Strictly ad Lib." *Down Beat,* June 15, 1955, p. 5.

52. See note 37, p. 269.

53. Interview with Kenny Drew, Odense, Denmark, November 13, 1984.

54. Dance, Stanley. *The World of Duke Ellington* (New York: Scribner's, 1970), pp. 205–206.

55. Coss, Bill. "JATP's Chief Executive: The President." *Metronome,* October 1955, p. 25.

56. See note 32.

57. "Jazz at the Philharmonic Packs Carnegie Hall, N.Y." *Variety,* September 20, 1955, p. 40.

58. " 'JATP' Racking Up Huge Grosses on Current Tour." *Down Beat,* November 17, 1950, p. 4.

59. See note 14.

60. Balliett, Whitney. *Jelly Roll, Jabbo and Fats* (New York: Oxford University Press, 1983), pp. 125–126.

61. See note 13.

62. See note 37, pp. 245.

63. See note 14.

64. Coss, Bill. "In Person, Lester Young, Birdland, New York." *Metronome*, October 1951, p. 21.

65. "Ella, Oscar Peterson Star as JATP Tour Begins." *Down Beat*, October 19, 1951, p. 1.

66. Ibid.

67. See note 37, p. 262.

68. Malone, Leonard. "Chancer med Max." *MM* (Copenhagen), no. 9 (1983), p. 10.

69. "Ella Steals the Show at JATP Debut." *Melody Maker*, April 5, 1952, pp. 1, 4.

70. Lindgren, Carl-Erik. "Organiserad jam i Konserthuset." *Orkester Journalen*, May 1952, p. 8.

71. "Ella og Oscar." *Berlingske Tidende* (Copenhagen), April 2, 1952, p. 5.

72. Wiedemann, Erik. "Ekstatisk jazz!" *Information* (Copenhagen), April 2, 1952, p. 6.

73. Fleiss, Marcel. "Flip Flips French Fans." *Down Beat*, May 21, 1952, p. 19.

74. Nevard, Mike. "JATP Brings Paris Fair to a Glorious End." *Melody Maker*, April 12, 1952, p. 4.

75. See note 37, p. 265.

76. Cullaz, Maurice. "Mon ami Lester." *Jazz Hot*, May 1959, pp. 13, 15.

77. Durselen, Roland. "Jazz at the Philharmonic." *Hot Club Magazine* (Brussels), May 1952, p. 35.

78. "Jazz at the Philharmonic." *Internationale Jazz-Podium*, June 1952, p. 8.

79. Granz, Norman. "Granz Tells Story of Tour; Lauds European Jazz Fans." *Down Beat*, June 4, 1952, p. 17.

80. Hentoff, Nat. "Europe Jazz Lags Well Behind Ours: Peterson." *Down Beat*, June 3, 1953, p. 4.

81. "Bill Basie Again Has Best Band for Beat, Excitement." *Down Beat*, August 27, 1952, p. 2.

82. Dahlgran, Claes. "Nytt från New York." *Orkester Journalen*, September 1952, p. 10.

83. Lester Young, interviewed by François Postif, Paris, February 6, 1959.

84. See note 41.

85. Ibid., p. 97.

86. Peterson, Oscar. "Reflections: Lester Young, President." *Sound* (Toronto), November 1975, p. 16.

87. Ibid.

88. Interview with Hank Jones, November 16, 1985.

89. Lindgren, Carl-Erik. "Ofrivillig jam med JATP." *Orkester Journalen*, March 1953, p. 6.

90. Wiedemann, Erik. "Mest for parterret." *Information* (Copenhagen), February 25, 1953, p. 6.

91. "JATP i Malmö." *Orkester Journalen*, March 1953, p. 17.

92. Interview with John Darville, Copenhagen, October 7, 1986.

93. Nevard, Mike. "Is Lester Still the President?" *Melody Maker*, March 21, 1953, p. 5.

94. Young, Derek. "He Holds His Office Graciously." *Melody Maker*, March 21, 1953, p. 4.

95. See note 93.

96. McKellen, John. Liner notes to *Lester Young "Pres,"* Esquire 32-158.

97. See note 76, p. 13.

98. Ibid.

99. Testoni, Giancarlo. "Jazz at the Philharmonic in tono minore." *Musica Jazz*, April, 1953, p. 1.

100. Interview with Ernie Wilkins, Odense, Denmark, November 13, 1984.

101. Ullman, Michael. *Jazz Lives* (Washington, D.C.: New Republic Books, 1980), p. 85.

102. See note 53.

103. See note 18, pp. 158–159.

104. See note 14.

105. See note 55.

106. See note 32, pp. 9–10.

107. Hentoff, Nat. "Caught in the Act." *Down Beat,* January 13, 1954, p. 6.

108. McDonough, John. *Lester Young* (Alexandria, Va.: Time-Life, 1980), p. 27. Booklet included in Time-Life J-13, *Giants of Jazz: Lester Young.*

109. Coss, Bill. "Jazz Festival—Tons of Swing and a Holiday Atmosphere." *Metronome,* September 1954, p. 16.

110. *Down Beat,* August 25, 1954, p. 1.

111. See note 94.

112. Altbush, Hannah. "Basie, Sarah Wail, but Some Others Suffer an Off Night." *Down Beat,* November 3, 1954, p. 20.

113. "Cats Who Know Had a Real Ball." *Topeka Daily Capital,* February 26, 1955, p. 6.

114. Feather, Leonard. "The Parker Memorial Concert." *Melody Maker,* May 7, 1955, p. 5.

115. Dahlgren, Claes. "Mäktigt Carnegie-uppbåd för Parker." *Orkester Journalen,* May 1955, p. 10.

116. Ulanov, Barry. *Down Beat,* May 18, 1955, p. 34.

117. Tracy, Jack. "Newport!" *Down Beat,* August 24, 1955, p. 24.

118. Schonberg, Harold C. "Music: Jazz Comes of Age in Newport." *New York Times,* July 18, 1955, p. 17.

119. Hentoff, Nat. "JATP Music Level Tops All Predecessors." *Down Beat,* October 19, 1955, p. 6.

120. Ibid.

121. Ibid.

122. Gillespie, Dizzy, and Al Fraser. *To Be, or Not . . . to Bop* (Garden City, N.Y.: Doubleday, 1979), p. 406.

123. Ibid., pp. 407–408.

124. Scott, Bobby. "The House in the Heart." *Gene Lees Jazzletter* 3, no. 2 (1983), p. 5.

125. Ibid.

126. Ibid., p. 7.

127. Ibid., pp. 6–7.

128. Ibid., p. 8.

CHAPTER EIGHT

1. "Birdland Tour in Fast Start." *Down Beat,* March 7, 1956, p. 24.

2. *Variety,* February 8, 1956, p. 44.

3. Interview with Thad Jones, Odense, Denmark, November 11, 1984.

4. Interview with Thad Jones, Knapstrup, Denmark, December 31, 1984.

5. Interview with Bill Triglia, New York, November 10, 1985.

6. Feather, Leonard. "Jazz at Randall's Island." *Down Beat,* October 3, 1956, p. 15.

7. Dahlgren, Claes. "Lyckad New York-Festival." *Orkester Journalen,* September 1956, p. 11.

8. Morgan, Alun. "Lester Young in Paris—1956." *Jazz Monthly* 2 (December 1956), p. 27.

9. "Le 'Birdland Show' à Pleyel." *Jazz Hot,* December 1956, p. 35.

10. Möllerstedt, Gunnar. "Lyckad Europapremiär för Birdland Show." *Orkester Journalen,,* November 1956, p. 14.

11. "Paris a acceuilli l'élite du jazz moderne." *Jazz Magazine* (Paris), December, 1956, p. 19.

12. Dawbarn, Bob. "The MJQ Are Marvellous." *Melody Maker,* November 10, 1956, p. 10.

13. Kop, Anton. *Melody Maker,* November 10, 1956, p. 10.

14. Zimmerle, Dieter. "Prominenz des modernen Jazz in Deutschland." *Jazz-Podium,* December 1956, p. 7.

15. Östberg, Lennart. "Underbar kammer-jazz." *Orkester Journalen,* December 1956, pp. 8–9.

16. "Møde med Miles Davis." *Information* (Copenhagen), November 15, 1956, p. 4.

17. "Blandet jazz-konfekt." *Berlingske Tidende* (Copenhagen), November 15, 1956, p. 10.

18. Ulrich, Torben. "Fin kammer-jazz—med skygger." *Politiken* (Copenhagen), November 15, 1956, p. 14.

19. "Il 'Modern Jazz Quartet' al teatro di via Manzoni." *Il Nuovo Corriere della Sera* (Milano), November 23, 1956, p. 4.

20. Testoni, Giancarlo. "Il Modern Jazz Quartet in Italia." *Musica Jazz,* December 1956, p. 35.

21. Radio interview with Bill Potts, around 1980.

22. Potts, Bill. Liner notes to *Lester Young in Washington DC 1956.* Pablo 2308 219.

23. Gelly, Dave. *Lester Young* (Tunbridge Wells: Spellmount, 1985), p. 65.

24. Interview with Willie Jones, New York, November 16, 1985.

25. "Birdland All-Stars Revue: Carnegie Hall, New York." *Down Beat,* March 21, 1957, p. 35.

26. Maher, Jack. "Down T' Bunny's." *Music U.S.A.* 76 (May 1959), p. 9.

27. See note 3.

28. "Philadelphia." *Down Beat,* May 16, 1957, p. 38.

29. Schmidt, Pete. "Lester kann auch anders . . ." *Jazz-Podium* 6, no. 7 (1957), p. 11.

30. See note 4.

31. See note 24.

32. Cerulli, Dom. "Newport Festival: Sunday Evening." *Down Beat,* August 8, 1957, p. 28.

33. "Jazz Night: Hollywood Bowl." *Down Beat,* September 19, 1957, pp. 39–40. The piano player's correct name is Aronov.

34. Wilson, John S. "Tenor Saxophone Stars at Concert." *New York Times,* September 16, 1957, p. 27.

35. Frost, Jan. "Cleveland." *Down Beat,* October 31, 1957, p. 41.

36. DeMicheal, Don. "A Long Look at Stan Getz." *Down Beat,* May 19, 1966, p. 19.

37. Interview with Johnny Griffin, New York, November 2, 1985. Thanksgiving Day is the fourth Thursday in November.

38. Sudhalter, Richard M. "Notes on the Music." In *Lester Young* (Alexandria, Va.: Time-Life, 1980), p. 51. Booklet included in Time-Life J-13, *Giants of Jazz: Lester Young.*

39. Hentoff, Nat. *Jazz Is* (New York: Limelight Editions, 1984), p. 50.

40. Dance, Stanley. *The World of Earl Hines* (New York, Scribner's, 1977), p. 159.

41. McDonough, John. *Lester Young* (Alexandria, Va.: Time-Life, 1980), p. 28. Booklet included in Time-Life J-13, *Giants of Jazz: Lester Young.*

42. See note 24.

43. Interview with Hank Jones, November 16, 1985.

44. Blesh, Rudi. *Combo: U.S.A.* (New York: Chilton Book, 1971), p. 105.

45. Ibid.

46. Ibid., pp. 106–107.

47. Interview with John Gensel, New York, November 12, 1985.

48. Russell, Ross. *Jazz Style in Kansas City and the Southwest* (Berkeley: University of California Press, 1971), p. 161.

49. See note 24.

50. "Le Retour du président." *Jazz Magazine* (Paris), no. 40 (August/September 1958), p. 13.

51. Morgenstern, Dan. "Lester Leaps In." *Jazz Journal,* August 1958, p. 1. This article was later published, with slight alterations, in *Jazz* 2, no. 3 (1963), pp. 12–13, 25, and in *Down Beat,* April 3, 1969, pp. 19–20.

52. Morgenstern, "Lester Leaps In," p. 3.

53. See note 24.

54. Cerulli, Dom. "Newport: Saturday Evening." *Down Beat,* August 7, 1958, p. 32.

55. Buddy Tate, interviewed by Gary Giddins, March 1980 (Jazz Oral History Project).

56. Interview with Chris Albertson, November 7, 1985. Albertson's interview with Lester is on tape at the Institute of Jazz Studies but has also been printed in Stanley Dance, *The World of Count Basie* (New York: Scribner's, 1980), pp. 28–33. Albertson cannot remember the actual date of the interview, only that it was a Sunday in August, which fits in with August 24, Lester's last evening at Pep's Musical Bar.

57. See note 24.

58. The pictures were subsequently published, with the title "Pres Plays a Date," in *Jazz: Metronome Yearbook* (1959), pp. 41–46.

59. Perlongo, Robert A. "A Portrait of Pres." *Music U.S.A.* 76 (May 1959), p. 43.

60. Feather, Leonard. *From Satchmo to Miles* (New York: Stein and Day, 1972), p. 126.

61. Lee Young, interviewed by Patricia Willard, November 8–15, 1977 (Jazz Oral History Project).

62. See note 36.

63. Malcon, Lucien. "Homage à Lester." *Jazz Magazine* (Paris), May 1959, p. 24.

64. Cullaz, Maurice. "Mon ami Lester." *Jazz Hot,* May 1959, p. 15. Klook was Kenny Clarke's nickname.

65. Jones, James. Introduction to Dan Morgenstern, *Jazz People* (New York: Harry N. Abrams, 1976), p. 16.

66. Winding. Thomas. "Også jeg fik sagt farvel." *Jazzbladet* (Copenhagen), May 1959, p. 10.

67. Luckey, Robert August. "A Study of Lester Young and His Influence upon His Contemporaries." Ph.D. Thesis, University of Pittsburgh, 1981, p. 74.

68. See note 63.

69. See note 44, p. 109.

70. See note 63, p. 23.

71. Interview with Idrees Sulieman, Copenhagen, March 26, 1985.

72. François Postif, interviewed by Norman Saks, Paris, Summer 1985.

73. Lester Young, interviewed by François Postif, Paris, February 6, 1959.

74. Ibid.

75. Ibid. The late Gil Evans was arranging the music for Lester's planned recording with strings. At this session Lester was supposed to double on bass clarinet as well.

76. See note 65, pp. 16–17.

77. "Lester Young Is Dead." *Melody Maker,* March 21, 1959, p. 1.

78. Davies, Russell. "You Just Fight for Your Life, till Death Do'ee Part." *The Listener,* August 13, 1981, p. 139.

79. "Lester Laid to Rest." *Down Beat,* April 30, 1959, p. 10.

80. See note 4.

Index

About the Author

FRANK BÜCHMANN-MØLLER, who is a Librarian at the Odense University Library in Denmark, has played jazz since the age of 15. A saxophonist, he appears regularly with a quartet and other groups at jazz clubs and in concert. An album of his compositions and arrangements was issued in 1975.